Machine Learning in Social Science

"Computational social science is reshaping sociology, and this book highlights the critical role Chinese sociologists play in that transformation. Written by an exceptional team based in China, it offers bold and original chapters that push the boundaries of theory, method, and empirical inquiry. Essential reading for anyone interested in the frontiers of contemporary sociology."

—Yu Xie, *Bert G. Kerstetter '66 University Professor of Sociology and Director of Center on Contemporary China, Princeton University*

"This book provides an excellent introduction to how machine-learning methods can be used for addressing important social-science questions. The authors have accomplished the difficult task of writing clearly and accessibly about a highly technical subject. The book covers a broad range of topics and includes numerous examples illustrating how machine-learning techniques can be fruitfully applied in social-science research. Its non-technical exposition makes it highly accessible and well suited as an introductory textbook across several social-science disciplines."

—Peter Hedström, *Professor of Analytical Sociology, Linköping University. Senior Research Fellow at Nuffield College, Oxford University*

Yunsong Chen · Zhuo Chen · Wen Ma ·
Guodong Ju

Machine Learning in Social Science

Applications and Advances

palgrave
macmillan

Yunsong Chen
School of Social and Behavioral Sciences
Nanjing University
Nanjing, China

Zhuo Chen
School of Social and Behavioral Sciences
Nanjing University
Nanjing, China

Wen Ma
School of Journalism and Communication
Nanjing University
Nanjing, China

Guodong Ju
School of Social and Behavioral Sciences
Nanjing University
Nanjing, China

ISBN 978-981-95-6464-4 ISBN 978-981-95-6465-1 (eBook)
https://doi.org/10.1007/978-981-95-6465-1

This work was supported by Nanjing University.

This Palgrave Macmillan imprint is published by the registered company Springer Nature Singapore Pte Ltd.
The registered company address is: 152 Beach Road, #21-01/04 Gateway East, Singapore 189721, Singapore

Preface

The origin of this book can be traced back to 2020, when my team and I were conducting a series of studies that used unsupervised machine learning to analyze cultural texts and supervised machine learning to model social dynamics. We noticed a clear shift in the intellectual landscape. The rapid growth of big data and artificial intelligence (AI) was changing the foundations of social research. The wider availability of multisource information opened new possibilities for understanding collective behavior and social change, while progress in computational modeling made it possible to uncover patterns once hidden in the complexity of social life. For social science, this transformation has particular meaning. The field has long tried to understand the connections between individual experience and social structure, yet the growing complexity of modern life now calls for new ways of observation and analysis.

Building on this awareness, our research gradually evolved into a reflection on how computation reshapes the production of knowledge. Algorithms are no longer merely technical instruments; they have become part of the ways knowledge is created, interpreted, and sustained across the social sciences. In the changing context, this interdisciplinary field is entering a new period of integration and renewal. Computational methods now open wider perspectives and provide more refined tools for examining social life across multiple scales. From this realization emerged the idea for this book. Machine learning has entered many areas of the social sciences, yet these endeavors remain scattered and without a shared foundation. We seek to weave a unified chain of them, to trace their common principles, and to offer a coherent account of how computation can deepen the study of society in the digital age.

Throughout the writing process, we found ourselves continually returning to a set of essential questions: as datafication becomes a defining condition of social life, and as algorithms become embedded in governance, culture, and everyday experience, how should social science reconceptualize prediction and explanation? How should it rethink the meanings of human action, structure, and significance within a new epistemic framework? These questions form the intellectual foundation of this book and guide its direction. Our purpose is to seek a renewed balance and dialogue between data and theory, between technology and the humanities.

Guided by this perspective, we focus on groups and communities that are often overlooked in grand narratives, as well as on cultural phenomena that traditional quantitative social science has struggled to capture in full. We seek to show how machine learning, especially supervised and unsupervised methods, can extend both the scope and depth of social research. Yet technology is not the ultimate concern of this book. It is, rather, a way of approaching a fuller understanding of society. Our hope is that this volume will serve as a practical guide for scholars, students, and readers interested in computational social science, helping to connect abstract algorithmic methods with the lived realities of human experience and to turn them into tools for interpreting people and their social worlds.

The completion of this book was made possible through the collaboration of my three co-authors, talented young scholars whom I have had the privilege to supervise. Their persistence, purpose, and passion have laid the foundation for this work. Together we have built one of the pioneering research teams in China dedicated to exploring the application of computational methods in interdisciplinary social science research, and we will continue to advance along this path.

With my co-authors, I would also like to express our sincere gratitude to the many colleagues whose generosity and expertise made this project possible. We owe special thanks to Xiaogang Wu, Anning Hu, Senhu Wang, Wansu Zhang, Wen Sun, Guangye He, and Ying Li, who assisted with data processing and offered thoughtful feedback that strengthened the manuscript. We are particularly grateful to Zhi Zhang,

Zhihui Fu, Xinyu Lu, Lifu Liu, and Tong Jiao, who assisted with the final proofreading and coordination of the book.

We have been fortunate to receive support from several distinguished institutions, including the Department of Sociology at Nanjing University, the School of Journalism and Communication at Nanjing University, the China Institute at the University of Alberta, the Hopkins–Nanjing Center (Nanjing University–Johns Hopkins University Center for Chinese and American Studies), and the Chinese Sociological Association. These institutions provided us with the time, resources, and an intellectually engaging environment in which this project could take shape. Portions of the research presented here have appeared in *Journal of Contemporary China*, *The Journal of Chinese Sociology*, and *Scientific Reports*, supported by grants from the National Social Science Fund of China.

Finally, we extend our deepest appreciation to Hua Bai and Ananda Kumar, the two editors at Palgrave Macmillan, whose patience, professionalism, and steady encouragement accompanied us throughout the preparation of this book.

Yunsong Chen
Nanjing University
Nanjing, China

Competing Interests The authors have no competing interests to declare that are relevant to the content of this manuscript.

Contents

Part IV Identifying Causality

List of Figures

Chapter 6

Chapter 7

Chapter 8

Chapter 9

Chapter 10

Chapter 11

Chapter 12

Chapter 13

List of Tables

CHAPTER 1

Introduction: The Rise of Machine Learning in Social Science

What is machine learning? Susan Athey of Stanford University, the first female economist to win the Clark Prize, defined machine learning in the context of social science, that is, to achieve tasks such as clustering, classification, and prediction by developing computer algorithms suitable for specific data (Athey 2018). To put it more precisely, machine learning tries to constantly optimize the performance standards of statistical calculation programs, enabling the program to achieve the task of "learning," discovering data characteristics and making a statistical prediction, based on a large number of data features.[1]

In the early days of computer data processing technology, social scientists were skeptical of it as a tool to help study social problems. On the one hand, the complexity of human society is much greater than that of nature; on the other hand, the available data and computing tools in traditional social sciences are relatively limited. However, the rapid expansion of information and data in the network era has brought unprecedented opportunities to social science. As early as 2009, Lazer and his colleagues predicted in *Science* that the era of computing social science would dawn (Lazer et al. 2009; Lazer and Jason 2017). In the past ten years, the

[1] Machine learning and data mining are often used as equivalent concepts in many disciplines and academic practice. Comparatively, whereas machine learning emphasizes that computer programs apply existing data information to new research objects, which is the so-called "learning," data mining emphasizes the extraction and simplification of data features.

Y. Chen et al., *Machine Learning in Social Science*,
https://doi.org/10.1007/978-981-95-6465-1_1

network has developed and research has accumulated rapidly. In addition to Lazer's original expectation, a new wave is surging. With the development of machine learning, the emergence of large-scale social survey data and big data, and the improvement of computer processing performance, the era of solving problems related to data, algorithms, and computing power, as well as realizing social understanding and prediction has dawned.

Another major impediment to the advancement of machine learning in social science has to do with the paradigm shift that is difficult to perform. Social scientists, whose main approach to the causal explanation of social processes is through description, explanation, and induction, are not accustomed to the social predictions that machine learning can achieve. Different from the generative modeling followed by classical statistical analysis, predictive modeling, as employed in machine learning, can account for model uncertainty and out-of-sample performance (Donoho 2017). Although social theory and data are rarely used to make predictions over a long period due to the complexity of social systems, the significance of prediction in the history of social science research cannot be ignored (Martin et al. 2016; Chen et al. 2021). Machine learning techniques can help interpolate potential indicators, generate new theories, and improve causal inference, which brings social prediction, once one of the most far-reaching topics, back to social science. In this book, Parts II, III, and IV illustrate cases of social prediction using machine learning.

In addition to social prediction, machine learning can help classify and cluster data to produce findings that differ from traditional methods. The ever-changing Internet has constructed datasets of unprecedented size and scope, recording all the footprints of people wandering, connecting, and aggregating in the social world. For social scientists, such a society built on data is a fertile ground that can provide new research resources and theoretical opportunities, where machine learning technology is the most effective discovery tool (Lazer and Jason 2017; Chen et al. 2021). It can reduce the dimensionality of data, thus helping social scientists process new kinds of data and theorize the relationships, structures, and topics within them. This technique of clustering can also be used to discover heterogeneity within populations, with insightful connections to the traditional inductive and deductive reasoning in social science (Bonikowski and DiMaggio 2016; Baumer et al. 2017). In this book,

Parts V and VI elaborate on the application of machine learning in text analysis.

Prediction and clustering tasks represent the two major categories of machine learning, supervised machine learning and unsupervised machine learning (Mitchell 1997; Li 2012). They are distinguished according to whether the target feature label is given in the dataset. This classification is based on the experience that the two tools are allowed to have in the learning process (Goodfellow et al. 2016). In supervised machine learning, the algorithm observes an output (Y) for each input (X). The output provides a target to predict. In unsupervised machine learning, the algorithm only observes the input and needs to make sense of the data without a prediction target or a correct answer (Molina and Garip 2019).

Supervised machine learning can provide the predicted label results by testing the fitting effect of the given training set model and applying the model to the test set in the data set with given features and labels. In the quantitative terminology of social science, when the covariate matrix (i.e., features X) and the explained variable (i.e., target Y) have been given, an appropriate algorithm would be adopted to fit the conditional expectation of the explained variable given the covariates, and the fitting effect would be evaluated against the real value of the explained variable. This process requires that the original label (Y) provided by the data set is objective and accurate, and the training set is consistent with the covariate standard of the test set, that is, the data set has to be independent identically distributed (IID).[2]

Take image recognition, a classic task in machine learning, as an example. To enable a computer to identify a "car" in an image, humans must first label a set of pictures manually. If there was a car in the picture, it would be marked as 1. Otherwise, it would be marked as 0 to generate a training set with a "standard answer." "Whether there is a car in the picture" is the explained variable Y, and the covariates X can be obtained by quantifying the image pixel information. By training the algorithm and adjusting the parameters, the properties of the explained variables can be

[2] The IID condition requires the training set and the test set to have the same probability distribution and to be independent of each other, so that the model obtained from the training set data can be applied to the whole dataset and the training effect can be guaranteed. To ensure the generalization capacity of the algorithm obtained from the training set, it is typical to use methods like random splits or cross-validation in practice.

predicted by using the covariate matrix information, and the prediction can be ideally accurate. Then, the algorithm obtained through training can be applied to the image library without manual marking, thereby realizing the real "automatic recognition." As for specific methods, supervised machine learning methods include regularized regression, decision trees, random forest, support vector machines, neural networks, Naïve Bayes, ensemble learning, etc.

Unsupervised machine learning is suitable for data sets without labels. When the covariate matrix is available and the explained variable is not, the algorithm will calculate the distance between different samples based on the given covariate information, and cluster the samples. This method is essentially a process of dimensionality reduction, which can be applied to unstructured data such as texts, pictures, audio, and video, and can expand the scale of empirical data available in the social sciences. For example, in image recognition, the algorithm directly processes the unlabeled image data set, calculates the similarity or difference degree of different pictures through the image pixel matrix data, and then makes the classification according to the principle of "minimum intragroup distance and maximum intergroup distance." The interpretation of category meaning is determined and defined manually. The common methods of unsupervised machine learning include cluster analysis, factor analysis, sequence analysis, principal components analysis, K-means clustering, topic modeling, community detection, etc. Among them, Latent Dirichlet Allocation (LDA) topic model and other topic modeling tools have been widely applied in cultural research within the social sciences (Blei et al. 2003). *Poetics*, a leading journal in the social sciences focusing on culture, communication, and the arts, published a series of studies based on topic modeling in a special issue in 2013 (Mohr and Bogdanov 2013).

The innovations in social prediction and clustering brought about by machine learning have undoubtedly opened the door to a new world of social science. These tools not only help improve existing methods such as counterfactual constructions in causal inference and supplementation of incomplete samples, but also provide new avenues for theory construction through data-driven discovery, as demonstrated in Part III. Furthermore, they enhance traditional approaches to causal inference via model optimization and high-dimensional data processing, as illustrated in Part IV. Together, these developments are reshaping the classical research paradigm, expanding the capacity of the social sciences to uncover the experiences of previously silent groups and their neglected cultural practices. They also extend social research across broader temporal and spatial horizons, allowing scholars to better understand the dynamics of diverse societies.

However, we must also be fully aware of the context in which machine learning techniques are applied. The exploratory results should be validated, especially in unsupervised machine learning, where the lack of explicit predictive targets makes robustness checks within the model or based on other external data necessary (Molina and Garip 2019). The ethical issues posed by machine learning also deserve special attention, as algorithms that define target variables based on specific category labels may reproduce existing social inequalities and discrimination (Barocas and Selbst 2016). Therefore, machine learning techniques can complement existing methods in social science, but they are not perfect, nor are they a substitute for traditional methods. It is exactly the vigilance rooted in the heart of social scientists that enables the leaders of disciplines, advocates of paradigms, reformers of thinking, and innovators of methods to consistently maintain the spirit of academic reflection, respect, and perseverance in the theoretical tradition at every critical historical juncture.

In this sense, excellent social science research must exemplify the rational use of advanced methods with humanistic feelings and theoretical concerns. Humanistic feelings, theoretical concerns, and methods of the times are indispensable to academic background, historical heritage, and the contemporary pulse of social science. Research without the above features, no matter how powerful its methods and data are, cannot obtain historical respect and academic depth. Meanwhile, research without scientific research methods, no matter how strong its theoretical consciousness and humanistic spirit are, cannot reach the real historical height.

Same as the introduction and emergence of every new thing and new field in the history of discipline development, the introduction and emergence of machine learning into the toolbox and thinking mode of social scientists will neither change the research merit of social science nor diminish the traditional social research paradigms and methods. Computational social science represented by machine learning is one of the frontier areas of quantitative social science research. Social scientists' constant inquiry into causal mechanisms, continuous pursuit of the breadth and depth of social information, and unremitting exploration of social processes and the certainty of social phenomena together constitute the historical drive and discipline's endogenous power in this frontier area.

If we approach methods such as machine learning in the right way, with both enthusiasm and caution, then we can make it work for us to explore social reality, which is what this book truly aims to convey. This book provides an exhaustive view of the principles of machine learning, its development, and its application in social science. Through diverse and rigorous studies, both social scientists and readers interested in social computing methods will be able to deepen their understanding of this new approach while drawing their insights into how to maximize the data's potential.

Part I of the book provides a literature review on the application of machine learning methods in social science. Chapter 2 focuses on supervised machine learning, which makes possible the paradigm of social prediction. Chapter 3 introduces unsupervised machine learning, highlighting its use in the field of cultural research.

Part II concerns vulnerable and minority groups, making predictions on immeasurable hidden data. Chapter 4 studies Chinese individuals who are victims of domestic violence and are reluctant to share their experiences in the questionnaire. Chapter 5 examines sexual minorities in China who are not comfortable being open about their sexual orientation. To understand the current situation of these groups, data supplementation using machine learning methods holds significant social value.

Part III reverses the traditional social research paradigm to develop novel theories. Based on the grounded theory, Chapter 6 demonstrates the computing grounded theory in producing theory from data through supervised machine learning algorithms, which can deepen the connection between causality and predictivity. Chapter 7 extends the work presented in Chapter 6 by conducting extensive testing on specific datasets to generate new theories of subjective well-being. It concludes with five major contributions of computing grounded theory.

Part IV focuses on causal inference and shows how machine learning can enhance the performance of traditional causal analysis methods. Chapter 8 examines the integration of supervised machine learning with classical causal tools such as Propensity Score Matching, Instrumental Variables, and quasi-experimental designs to improve covariate balancing, reduce bias, and optimize model fit. Chapter 9 introduces the framework of Double Machine Learning, which enables flexible causal estimation in high-dimensional settings and supports the identification of heterogeneous treatment effects, offering a robust solution for complex empirical questions.

Part V applies unsupervised machine learning methods to conduct large-scale text analysis, focusing on topic modeling to explore underlying themes and patterns in the data. Chapter 10 explores a contemporary, web-based niche literary form, Boys' love fiction, uncovering the feminist values and gender dilemmas embodied in it. Chapter 11 reviews the classic works in history, surveying the panorama of *Marx/Engels Collected Works* and tracing the evolution of their ideas about society.

Part VI continues to apply unsupervised machine learning methods to analyze media texts, with a particular focus on sentiment analysis. Chapter 12 examines the image of China in films outside of China, especially in Hollywood, while Chapter 13 compares this national image in films fromChinese mainland, Hong Kong Special Administrative Region (SAR), and Taiwan, Province of China. In addition to understanding the history and reality, as well as the change and development of this cultural image, causal analysis is also used to identify the socioeconomic factors behind these changes.

To help readers better understand the practical applications of machine learning methods in social science research, this book provides basic Python code examples in the appendix. These examples cover key analytical techniques such as regression, classification, topic modeling, word embeddings, and model interpretability, offering readers a hands-on reference for implementing and explaining machine learning models.

To the authors' knowledge, this is the first attempt to exhaustively address the application of machine learning technology in social science. Using a series of typical research cases, it illuminates the way forward on unsupervised and supervised machine learning methods, as well as big data in social science research. This book furthers the field of social science in three aspects.

First, in terms of computational social science, this book introduces key machine learning algorithms and their application scenarios, highlighting their ability to uncover latent indicators and enhance causal inference. By optimizing matching, instrumental variables, and quasi-experiments, and by enabling flexible estimation in high-dimensional settings, machine learning reduces model constraints, captures heterogeneity, and stabilizes causal effects—especially by constructing accurate counterfactuals and integrating complex confounders.

Second, in the context of cultural research across the social sciences, computational methods offer new ideas for dealing with large-scale literary and media data, thus adding to the theoretical understanding of the long-term interconnections between symbolic systems, communication media, and social reality. Machine learning methods enable researchers to capture the broader contexts and complex systemic dynamics of culture by drawing on extensive digital cultural resources that span wide spatial and temporal scales.

Third, for the social sciences more broadly, the rise of machine learning opens the door to new theoretical perspectives and research agendas. By extending the explanatory factors and dimensions of models, this approach revitalizes the sociological imagination and brings theoretical inquiry into dialogue with large-scale empirical analysis. It allows for the discovery of hidden social patterns, cultural trajectories, and emergent collective behaviors, deepening our understanding of issues such as inequality, power, and cultural change. In doing so, it helps the social sciences integrate macro structures with individual experiences across historical, contemporary, and future horizons.

References

Athey, Susan. 2018. Machine learning and causal inference for policy evaluation. The impact of machine learning on economics. In *The economics of artificial intelligence: An* agenda, ed. Ajay Agrawal, Joshua Gans, and Avi Goldfarb, 507–547. University of Chicago Press.

Barocas, Solon, and Andrew D. Selbst. 2016. Big data's disparate impact. *California Law Review* 104: 671.

Baumer, Eric P.S.., et al. 2017. Comparing grounded theory and topic modeling: Extreme divergence or unlikely convergence? *Journal of the Association for Information Science and Technology* 68 (6): 1397–1410.

Blei, David M., Andrew Y. Ng, and Michael I. Jordan. 2003. Latent Dirichlet allocation. *Journal of Machine Learning Research* 3: 993–1022.

Bonikowski, Bart, and Paul DiMaggio. 2016. Varieties of American popular nationalism. *American Sociological Review* 81 (5): 949–980.

Chen, Yunsong, Guangye He, and Fei Yan. 2021. *Understanding China through big data: Applications of theory-oriented quantitative approaches*. Abingdon and New York: Routledge.

Donoho, David. 2017. 50 years of data science. *Journal of Computational and Graphical Statistics* 26 (4): 745–766.

Goodfellow, Ian, Yoshua Bengio, and Aaron Courville. 2016. *Deep learning*. MIT Press.

Lazer, David, and Radford Jason. 2017. Data Ex Machina: Introduction to big data. *Annual Review of Sociology* 43 (1): 19–39.

Lazer, David, et al. 2009. Social science. Computational social science. *Science* 323 (5915): 721–723.

Li, Huang. 2012. *Statistical learning methods*. Beijing: Tsinghua University Press (In Chinese).

Martin, Travis, et al. 2016. Exploring limits to prediction in complex social systems. In *Proceedings of the 25th International conference on World Wide Web*, 683–694.

Mitchell, Tom. 1997. *Machine learning*. New York and London: McGraw-Hill.

Mohr, John W., and Petko Bogdanov. 2013. Introduction-topic models: What they are and why they matter. *Poetics* 41 (6): 545–569.

Molina, Mario, and Filiz Garip. 2019. Machine learning for sociology. *Annual Review of Sociology* 45: 27–45.

PART I

Basics of Machine Learning for Social Science

CHAPTER 2

Social Prediction: A New Research Paradigm Based on Supervised Machine Learning

1 Introduction

For Max Weber, sociology is a science that concerns itself with the interpretive understanding of social action as well as the causal explanation of its process and result (Weber 1968 [1921]: 4). His formulation exemplifies a broader orientation that has long shaped the social sciences: to describe and explain social processes and phenomena, to seek the meaning and interpretation of social actions, and to verify social hypotheses and theories. Consequently, description, interpretation, and statistical testing have become traditional and mainstream approaches within social scientific research.

In contrast, prediction seems to have had no role within the discipline for a long time. This phenomenon also widely exists in social sciences such as economics, political science, and social policy, which has not drawn concern or reflection. However, scholars have already emphasized that a causal interpretation must serve as the "basis for predicting social phenomena" (Hempel and Oppenheim 1948: 138). Hence, predictability is a necessary but not sufficient condition for the causal mechanism, as although predictability does not equate with causality, a prediction could be formed if there were causality. Based on this rationale, prediction should be regarded as a proper pursuit of the social sciences, particularly in fields such as sociology and economics, where the establishment of causality has long been a central concern. For example, in 2014, Duncan

Y. Chen et al., *Machine Learning in Social Science*,
https://doi.org/10.1007/978-981-95-6465-1_2

Watts published an article in the *American Journal of Sociology* to criticize the academic tradition of pursuing the meaning of "common sense" and ignoring the value of prediction (Watts 2014). Watts argued that if sociology is a science, sociologists' interpretations must be evaluated by scientific standards; that is, the science must be capable of making predictions.

Over the past century, social scientists have explored the meaning and explanation of society and social processes and devoted attention to providing theoretical guidance and evaluative examinations of social transformations. However, the social sciences pay significantly less attention to ex ante prediction than ex post facto evaluation and interpretation (Hofman et al. 2017). A series of papers on the topic of "prediction and its limits" has been published by *Science* (Jasny and Stone 2017). Although these articles came from different disciplines of social sciences such as economics, sociology, and political science, scholars' consensus was that in contrast to natural science, theories and data of social science were rarely used to make predictions. Martin et al. (2016) highlighted that the significant complexity of the social system and the limited information (the lack of data and models) have made social science research unable to make predictions over a long period.[1]

In the history of social science research, scientific practices for predicting social phenomena or processes have remained absent. However, the concept of "social prediction" has always lingered in the minds of scholars. As early as the 1940s, Kaplan (1940) proposed the concept of "social prediction," emphasizing that social science should predict social phenomena. In the 1980s, Chinese scholars also proposed this concept (Yan 1986). However, in both international and domestic academia, substantive prediction research in social science has not been fully developed, nor has it aroused academic resonance, due to limitations in data availability and econometric methods. The long-term absence of social prediction in empirical research impedes quantitative researchers as they seek to exert scientific power in influencing policy and promoting the discourse power of the media. Compared to scholars who emphasize theoretical criticism and interpretation, quantitative researchers are

[1] For example, the transformations in the Soviet Union and Eastern Europe are called the "Black Friday of social science." These historical events are such extremely rare cases that it is impossible to establish a dataset with sufficient historical samples. Therefore, scientific prediction based on data cannot be carried out.

even more cautious, conservative, and uninteresting due to their limited capacity for prediction and anticipation. Indeed, the public and governments would not be satisfied merely with concept refinement, process interpretation, and statistical estimation.

With the availability of multisource data and the advances of computer processing performance, social prediction has dawned on quantitative social science research, which is at the forefront of interdisciplinary research. Currently, quantitative research in social science has gradually met the three requirements for high-precision prediction: data, computing power, and algorithms. In particular, with the development of computer algorithms for specific data (Athey 2018), social scientists have been able to process large-scale social data, highlighting the academic value of social prediction (Hofman et al. 2017). The special issue of *Science* in 2017, which was devoted to predicting the social process, preliminarily sorted out this important developmental trend.

The rest of the article will review the historical development of the concept of social prediction and discuss the specific principles and methods of social prediction via algorithms. On this basis, the article will redefine social prediction in the contemporary era. In this sense, this article summarizes the disciplinary significance of social prediction from the perspectives of policy and academic significance and especially aims to present the main contribution fields and directions of social prediction for contemporary social research. Furthermore, this article discusses the paradigm significance of social prediction. Social prediction represents a new subparadigm of social science research from the methodological perspective rather than a strict ontology. With the emergence of big data and the improvement of computing power, the application of machine learning and the redefining of social prediction will boost the paradigm breakthrough of quantitative social science research and even social science research.

2 The History of Social Prediction

2.1 The Rise and Fall of Prediction

The prediction has involved logical and sequential consideration of natural and social phenomena since ancient times (Goodman 1983). However, it is a modern development that prediction has become a scientific category. The prediction of social phenomena and human behavior has long been compared with the prediction of natural phenomena or animal behavior but has been regarded as a more difficult task. As early as the 1940s, scholars suggested strengthening the work of prediction in social science and proposed the concept of social prediction (Kaplan 1940). Although Kaplan (1940) recognized the difficulty of prediction, he believed that social behavior was even more predictable than natural phenomena at the micro level.

However, since the mid-twentieth century, the development of social science has failed to make a substantial breakthrough in prediction. When Kaplan put forward the concept of prediction in social science, he predicted that it would be very challenging. In particular, there were four obstacles to be overcome: first, many influencing factors would be neglected; second, the sequence in the prediction may not be taken into account; third, it is difficult to capture accurate information on known variables; fourth, the complex association among social variables would be neglected (Kaplan 1940). Generally, these problems correspond to missing variables, logical chains, measurement errors, and the complexity of social phenomena in quantitative research in contemporary social sciences. Another development is the path model, which was popular in the 1970s and 1980s. The path model attempts to expose the implications of data and the complex associations among variables by including dozens of factors in the model. The method of variable packing is similar to the data mining model of machine learning, but the purpose and implementation of the path model differ significantly from those of machine learning.

In the Chinese academia of the humanities and social sciences, some scholars have proposed the concept of social prediction and carried out exploration based on early warning indicators of social stability; some of this work dates back to the 1980s (Yan 1986, 2005). In the *Sociology Dictionary* edited by Deng Zhiwei (2009), "social prediction" is defined as "speculation or analysis of possible social phenomena in the future... its purpose is to reveal the most important factors that determine the future development and the most important relationships of social phenomena, for decision-making reference." The dictionary even distinguishes "intuitive prediction" based on subjective experience and "quantitative prediction" based on data. Since the 1990s, scholars of the Chinese Academy of Social Sciences, namely, Xin Ru, Xueyi Lu, Peilin Li, Guangjin Chen, and Yi Zhang, have used the term "prediction" in a series of *Blue Books on Social Analysis and Prediction*. However, the related research methods primarily involve data displays of time trends, intuitive trend prediction, and traditional regression. In this sense, empirical prediction with scientific standards based on data is almost blank, although the concept of social prediction has been in use for a long time. Indeed, elaborations of its significance and difficulties are available in both international and Chinese academic publications.

The reasons for the poor development of social prediction are not complicated. Even in the twenty-first century, social scientists still cannot solve the problems posed by Kaplan (1940). Due to the great complexity of social processes, one requires sufficient data, complex models, and strong computer processing capacity to make an ideally accurate and precise social prediction, which are the three dimensions of information limitations mentioned in the introduction. Due to these three bottlenecks, social scientists can hardly practice prediction. Instead, these scientists have shelved the ambition of prediction since the second half of the twentieth century. Since the data, models, and computing power required for accurate prediction were not yet available, the entire social science community, especially quantitative research, has focused on the relationships among variables. That is, based on limited sample data, unbiased estimations of the pairwise relationships between variables are obtained using statistical models. The delicate implication of this compromise is that social scientists no longer have unrealistic confidence in social prediction as the early pioneers did. Instead, these scientists deliberately confined their work to analyzing the pairwise relationships between variables (Hofman et al. 2017; Athey 2018). In short, because of the bottlenecks of data, models, and computing power, most social scientists have long abandoned the scientific practice of prediction.

2.2 *Revisiting Prediction*

The abandonment of prediction has shaped the mainstream methods of quantitative research in the whole social science community. The primary efforts are spent determining the covariance between the independent variable X and the dependent variable Y through regression models. In other words, social scientists analyze whether the relationship between X and Y is statistically significant and has actual significance on economic and social scales based on certain statistical standards. They clarify whether and how the change of a unit of X is related to the change of Y. This correlation analysis, which focuses on covariance, cannot meet the ultimate academic mission of causal explanation. Thus, social scientists have started to use the analytical approach of parameter estimation to go beyond correlation analysis and reach causal inference. With the development of advanced econometric methods and the cautious application of experimental methods, some disciplines, such as economics, have shifted their mainstream quantitative analysis almost completely to causal inference based on the "counterfactual" framework in recent years, that is, they explore whether and how a change in X causes a change in Y through the observed social data (Pearl 2000; Rubin 1974). A similar disciplinary evolution occurred in sociology at the end of the twentieth century. Other disciplines such as statistics and econometrics provide ready-made methods and analytical models for causal inference in sociological analysis. Sociologists have contacted and introduced appropriate methods at an early stage (Morgan and Winship 2007; Brand and Xie 2007).

Can social scientists provide a satisfactory response to Max Weber's emphasis on explanatory mechanisms and causality when the relationship between social index X and social index Y can be identified? Although social scientists are still concerned and worried about the invasion of advanced econometric methods into the discipline, scholars at the forefront of the discipline have given a clear and determined answer that the covariant research of correlation analysis and causal analysis is insufficient to constitute a social explanation in terms of science. Many social explanations confuse understandability with causality, which does not meet the standard of scientific interpretation. If social scientists expect their interpretations to be scientifically legitimate, they must evaluate them according to scientific standards; that is, predictions must be made (Watts 2014: 313). To make research more scientific, he stressed that it is necessary to sacrifice some seemingly straightforward and reasonable view, so social scientists have to make the right and necessary choices between satisfying but unscientific stories and unsatisfying scientific explanations.

How can Watts' criticism be understood in relation to traditional quantitative methods in the social sciences? Watts directly engaged with Max Weber's view that research on social life should provide an interpretive understanding of social action ("verstehen" in German) and, through this understanding, offer a causal explanation of its processes and outcomes (Weber 1968 [1921]: 4). Watts argued that interpretive understanding and causal explanation were distinct. If an explanation was causal, it could support prior prediction, whereas interpretive understanding only needed to be reasonable and could be ex post. He emphasized that predictability was a necessary but not sufficient condition for establishing causal mechanisms and remained the most effective way to verify them. Yet many researchers overlook prediction or the improvement of predictive accuracy, claiming instead that prediction does not imply causality, that complex models lack generality, or that they offer little new insight. These concerns, however, miss the point: while prediction does not equal causation, causation can serve as a basis for prediction.

Watts' criticism almost targets the general approach of all empirical research, but his exposition of the relationship between causality and prediction is clear and accurate, conforming to the classic concept of causality (Hempel and Oppenheim 1948; Manski 2007). In a sense, Watts' view marks a rupture between the social sciences as empirical disciplines and the social sciences as part of the broader humanistic tradition. The tension between scientific and humanistic approaches has long existed across different fields (Chen 2017). Watts' argument introduces more rigorous scientific standards for empirical research in the social sciences.

In summary, prediction is a central component in realizing the scientific aims of quantitative social science research. Among correlation, causality, and prediction, correlation is the prerequisite for causality and prediction, while causality is a sufficient but unnecessary condition for prediction. If there was causality, an event must have been predictable, but not vice versa. Causality and prediction are both probabilistic at the social level, and they are both powerful approaches to comprehending social affairs. These concepts share the same foundation and same direction, and both are valued by empirical social science. The problem is that the discipline has been in a state of under-preparation for prediction for many years, although quantitative social science research has developed rather mature methods and models for correlation and causal analysis. When the research goal is to provide a mechanical explanation of X with respect to Y, the traditional method to identify causality is sufficient. However, if the research goal was to predict the probabilities and intensities of certain phenomena in the future based on the existing data and methods (which is often the practical requirement of the social governance process for social scientists), traditional tools cannot achieve this task. Thus, the social prediction must be put on the agenda.

3 The Realization of Social Prediction

With the development of machine learning, the emergence of large-scale social survey data and big data, and improved computer processing performance, the era of solving problems related to data, algorithms, and computing power and realizing social prediction has dawned. From the methodological perspective, the main approach to achieving social prediction is supervised machine learning.

3.1 Predictive Principle of Supervised Machine Learning

There are many specific methods for supervised machine learning, but the general model-fitting goal is quite different from the traditional model regression. The former category of methods aims at accuracy, that is, the difference between the prediction label and the real label is the smallest, while the latter type of procedure is meant to evaluate the impact of an independent variable on the dependent variable under the premise of controlling other variables (Athey 2018). Among numerous supervised machine learning algorithms, regularized regression based on linear models is widely used. Compared with the least squares model (OLS), the regularized regression model adds a penalty term into the regression coefficient. The unbiased estimation of the OLS regression coefficient β is

$$\hat{\beta}_{\mathrm{OLS}} = \mathrm{argmin}(y - X\beta)'(y - X\beta) = \left(X'X\right)^{-1}X'y$$

The regression coefficient of the regularized regression is

$$\hat{\beta}_{\mathrm{OLS}} = \ \mathrm{argmin}\left\{(y - X\beta)\prime(y - X\beta) + \lambda\left[(1 - \alpha)\beta'\beta + \alpha|\beta|\right]\right\}$$

When λ is 0, the penalty term is 0, which refers to an unbiased OLS regression; when λ is not 0 and α is 0, an L2 regularizer ($\sum P\ 1\beta 2\ J$) is added to the parameter, where the term refers to ridge regression. When λ is not 0 and α is equal to 1, an L1 regularizer ($\sum P\ 1|\beta_j|$) is added to the parameter, where the term refers to Lasso regression. The other cases are all elastic net regression. Therefore, ridge regression and Lasso regression can also be regarded as special cases of elastic net regression.

Here, we describe how regularized regression can obtain more accurate predictions than OLS. The error of a linear fitting of the model can be divided into three parts: bias, variance, and irreducible error. These errors represent the deviation between the fitting expectation and the real value, the dispersion of the fitting value, and the inevitable system noise, respectively. The deviation of OLS is constantly equal to 0 due to its inherent least sum of squares of residual errors, whereas the regularized regression model reduces variance and overall error by introducing bias to improve the model's prediction accuracy (Athey and Imbens 2016). The modeling of machine learning does not often consider theory. Generally, the inclusion of more variables helps to increase the prediction accuracy. Therefore, machine learning models can include seemingly unrelated variables and sacrifice the theoretical nature of the model. In general, there is a bias-variance tradeoff between introducing bias to improve the fitting accuracy of the model and continuing unbiased estimation to rely on previous theories, which directly reflects the difference between machine learning and traditional quantitative methods.

In addition to regularized regression based on linear models, other supervised machine learning methods have their own merits.[2] The input x is divided into many tree regions by the regression tree method, and then each output y is generated. Each node, i.e., each "leaf," corresponds to a prediction. The regression tree method divides the input X into many tree-like regions and generates the output Y, in which each node (or leaf) is a prediction. With ample branches in the regression tree, an accurate prediction of the whole sample can be generated. A neural network is a "black-box" algorithm designed to simulate the functioning of biological neural systems. The input–output layer and hidden layer of the algorithm are composed of several simple cells at the same level, and multiple groups of interactive hidden layers construct the whole neural network. By increasing the number of hidden layers to conduct layer-by-layer training and adding convolution, the stability and accuracy of the learning effect of the algorithm can be improved. A support vector machine (SVM) based on the VC dimension (Vapnik–Chervonenkis dimension) obtains the maximum-margin hyperplane to achieve binary classification. The non-linear classification task can also be realized

[2] Numerous algorithms have been developed by machine learning. This article focuses on the regularized regression method based on a linear model, since this method is the most similar to the traditional linear regression in social science. The method of exchanging deviation for precision can demonstrate the different functional orientations of machine learning and traditional quantitative models of sociology, economics, and political science, and the predictive advantages of machine learning.

by the kernel method. Bayesian classification adopts the classic Bayesian School of Statistics to classify samples by maximizing the posterior probability. Ensemble learning integrates multiple learning results to obtain a more comprehensive, stable, and strong supervised model. Furthermore, the bagging method reduces the variance of the classifications through multiple return sampling, and the boosting method uses the previous classification error to modify the weight of subsequent classifications, thereby optimizing the classification. Readers can find more information in relevant references (such as Mitchell 1997; Li 2012).

3.2 Redefinition of Social Prediction

Based on machine learning, we try to define social prediction in the context of contemporary social science. Thus, social prediction uses spatiotemporal data to demonstrate social phenomena or processes; machine learning based on appropriate algorithms can accurately quantify and measure unknown information to provide information and a basis for social decision-making and research. Machine learning encompasses both vertical prediction, which involves forecasting the future based on historical data, and horizontal prediction which uses sample data to make predictions about other data. Social prediction is an important part of computational social science. Computational social science is a new field of quantitative social science research that describes, explains, and predicts complex social phenomena and processes based on complex models and social computing tools. This field's research methods of social computing include social network analysis, simulation modeling, machine learning, and big data analysis. Among these methods, the combination of big data, machine learning, and social prediction has special advantages. While the massive background information on observation objects provided by big data offers considerable convenience for model training, big data can provide outliers on a large scale. With the help of machine learning analysis technology, these outliers may contribute to theoretical innovation and policy implementation.

4 The Disciplinary Significance of Social Prediction

Since social prediction can be achieved through machine learning, what is its main value as an emerging research field and methodological approach for the development of the social sciences? Based on our understanding of the discipline and recent literature, we classify the value of social prediction into three dimensions: academic, governance, and contextual significance.

4.1 The Academic Significance of Social Prediction

Because machine learning can process complex and diverse information content for social science and generate variable forms for analysis, it expands the research horizon of social science. In brief, social prediction based on machine learning has disciplinary significance for social science research in the following five respects.

First, the latent indicators of interest can be obtained through prediction. There are two types of data that are difficult to obtain through traditional surveys or big data in social science research. One type is the "subjective latent indicator," which often occurs because people are unwilling to disclose true individual information. The reasons include the sensitivity of the problem itself or social acceptance, such as personal unemployment, sexual orientation, venereal diseases, and religious beliefs. In the specific economic, social, and cultural context, this information is often deliberately hidden by respondents. At the social level, concealment prevents researchers or social governance officials from obtaining comprehensive, true, and accurate data about this type of information. The other problem is "objective latent indicators," that is, there are objectively complex data measurements or heterogeneous group classification indicators that are difficult to detect directly. These latent indicators can be found by machine learning, which will provide new dependent variables or independent variables for academic research.

For the subjective latent indicators, as long as some people in our data provide these indicators truly and accurately, a social prediction based on machine learning can use the input data as a training set to accurately predict the people who are not willing to provide information or provide distorted information (in a sense, the result of this process can be regarded as a supplement to the missing values). The prediction accuracy depends on the size and independence of the samples and the optimization of the algorithm models. He et al. (2018) used Baidu search index to predict the regional distribution data of AIDS in China and employed the dynamic panel pooled mean group model, based on the heterogeneity hypothesis, because the prediction accuracy would be reduced using the dynamic generalized method of moments. This model could make a more convincing and credible prediction when uncertainty was resolved by machine learning based on larger samples. For the objective latent indicators, unsupervised machine learning (UML) is often used in variable generation. For example, in economics, unsupervised machine learning is used to analyze satellite images and generate measurements of data indicators for forest harvesting, environmental pollution, and nighttime lighting (Donaldson and Storeygard 2016). Studies in sociology classify and analyze government documents (Mohr et al. 2013) and academic texts (McFarland et al. 2013). In addition, research on social network using unsupervised machine learning has also garnered the attention of scholars.

Second, theoretical hypotheses can be generated via prediction. In traditional quantitative methods, the essence of the model is to include new main explanatory variables to test new theoretical hypotheses. In addition to theoretical intuition, whether to add variables to the model from a statistical perspective depends on stepwise regression, partial least squares, and the standard comparison of AIC and BIC. Scholars have summarized 21 varieties of traditional variable selection methods (Castle et al. 2009). However, with the machine learning method, some brand-new means could be adopted to examine and expand the influencing factors of the model. We can discover new explanatory variables and dimensions, and develop new theoretical hypotheses. This process aligns with the idea of "bringing theory back" advocated by big data researchers (Luo et al. 2018).

For the explanatory variables, if the effect of an independent variable X on the dependent variable Y is evaluated, Varian (2014) proposes using the same machine learning algorithm to fit and predict Y when the variable is included and excluded and comparing the difference between the two fitting effects. If the fitting effect of the model containing X is better, a theoretically hypothesized covariant correlation or even causal relationship between X and Y can be posited, and this hypothesis can be verified using traditional quantitative methods. At the level of the explanatory dimension (i.e., a set of explanatory variables that are highly correlated conceptually and logically), machine learning can provide an important driving force for sociological imagination and realize the "precision difference analysis of grouped variables" method. The data can be labeled in advance, and all the variables in the data are combined and packaged into their respective explanatory dimensions without ready-made theoretical guidance, which is ultimately unified into the fitting process of machine learning. The prediction results of the same algorithm with and without an explanatory dimension are compared one by one. Thus, we obtain the predictive ability of an explanatory dimension for the dependent variable. Once a new explanatory dimension has a good ability to predict Y, we can examine the specific variables within this dimension and identify the most likely explanatory variable based on imagination and theory. In addition, the overall explanatory power or relevance of a new explanatory dimension to the dependent variables may trigger new thinking in the social sciences and even inspire new theories and hypotheses, that is, attempts to discover the overall influence of the new dimension.

Third, prediction facilitates the conduct of causal inference. In social science, the counterfactual framework, which defines the causal mechanism, is essentially speculation and simulation of the non-real world. Thus, when a certain influence is not applied or a certain processing factor is not changed, one asks what form the event will take. This problem is the precise problem at which machine learning is effective: constructing the state of an event that does not exist as accurately as possible with limited data (Athey 2015). Therefore, many studies have tried to apply machine learning methods to causal inference problems, especially in the counterfactual construction process and extensions of the selection model (Green and Kern 2012; Hazlett 2014; Imai and Ratkovic 2013).

For example, after the first-stage regression of the linear instrumental variable model, the endogenous explanatory variable X should be predicted, and the predicted value should be included in the main model (Chen 2011). The prediction process can be replaced by machine learning methods. Application cases include Lasso regression (Belloni et al. 2012), ridge regression (Carrasco 2012), and neural network methods (Hartford et al. 2016). Other examples are the prediction of propensity values in propensity score matching (PSM) and the logistic model used in the standard methods (Hu 2012). With machine learning methods, the model hypotheses and restrictions are reduced, and the causal effect estimation is stabilized. Existing application cases include the boosting method (McCaffrey et al. 2004), the neural network method (Westreich et al.

2010), and the regression tree method (Diamond and Sekhon 2013). For another example, regarding the heterogeneity in causal effect (Xie et al. 2012), the machine learning method can also greatly improve the accuracy of the estimation, which demonstrates that we can make more accurate predictions of the counterfactual state of treated or untreated individuals without excessive hypotheses and constraints in the estimation process of the parameter model.

Athey (2018) predicted that, in general, machine learning technology would draw increasing attention to causal inference problems. In the context of causal inference in social science, the vast majority of counterfactual constructions can be completed by machine learning methods, and the difference between a counterfactual construction and an actual occurrence can be tested quantitatively. In the process of constructing counterfactuals, the results of prediction with machine learning ought to be reported as well, which was mentioned by the review of machine learning published in *the Annual Review of Sociology* (Molina and Garip 2019).

Fourth, data proliferation can be realized by prediction. In empirical social surveys, randomly incomplete or missing sample data is a common but aggravating problem. The traditional processing methods are either deleting samples or supplementing data. Deleting data would not only reduce the sample size but also destroy the original sampling design. The method of supplementing data relies on subjective factors, mean values, or the prediction of traditional regression models with comprehensive information, though this method is well developed (Allison 2009). However, quantitative models are not good at making accurate predictions, while machine learning can undertake this task. For instance, some scholars have tested the supplemental performance of different machine learning methods based on 15 datasets and found that the performances of support vector machines and Naïve Bayesian methods were relatively optimal (Farhangfar et al. 2008). Other scholars have tried to use a Gaussian mixture model to estimate the potential contribution of data and supplement data through an extreme learning machine method (a single-layer neural network method) (Sovilj et al. 2016). Sovilj's study evaluated six different datasets and found that the accuracy of supplementing values through machine learning is higher than the accuracy of traditional methods. Based on existing research, the estimation of missing data values should adopt an appropriate machine learning method to achieve the best fitting effect, or at least report the fitting effect of machine learning estimation and other methods, among which the optimal result would be chosen.

Fifth, the prediction could promote theoretical innovation. Machine learning can provide powerful methods and new perspectives for scholars, helping them expand their theoretical horizons and generate new academic knowledge. In the current research of machine learning in the field of social science, whereas the results given by the algorithm are not the goal of the research, they are a source of discovery that inspires scholars to develop and innovate at the theoretical level, to promote existing theories and to put forward new hypotheses. For example, Kleinberg et al. used the machine learning method to study the case texts of New York state courts (Kleinberg et al. 2017). They first trained the regression tree model to predict the decision of "bail or release" in New York state court cases and explained the contradiction between the model prediction results and the actual judgments through quasi-random experiments. The research shows that the results of recent cases significantly influence the judge leading to more severe punishment for minor offenses. This discovery reveals potential factors affecting the judge's decision-making behavior from a new perspective and thus promotes the theoretical development of the social-psychological process of judicial judgment.

4.2 The Governance Significance of Social Prediction

It is one of the most traditional and basic topics of social science to predict economic and social processes and guide practice through research. However, neither an early intuitionistic prediction nor covariance research relying on traditional quantitative models can meet the real demands of economic and social prediction. At the forefront of contemporary social science, other disciplines have begun to explore the issue of social prediction. Among these disciplines, algorithm optimization and even prediction competition (to establish an open-source platform for different teams to participate and contribute algorithms to find the optimal machine learning model) have been applied in social governance, which is worthy of attention from policymakers and social scientists. Here are three cases closely related to social science.

First, this practice could benefit socially disadvantaged groups. Professor Salganik, a sociologist at Princeton University, and his colleagues used the big data of the "Fragile Families Challenge" project of Princeton University (the project tracks 5000 American children and obtains 54 million data points of their physical and mental health, cognitive ability, social-emotional ability, education and living conditions, family composition, family stability, and family economic status) to conduct an open-platform algorithm competition of machine learning with six aspects of the social results of children's performances, personalities, and life difficulties. More than 150 teams from 68 universities and scientific research institutes in seven countries have submitted prediction algorithms. In addition to applying the results of machine learning models to community services, these teams conduct in-depth analysis of special case data on outstanding children growing up in disadvantaged families to provide a decision-making basis for improving the living standards of children in these groups.[3]

Second, we have research on social inequality. Scholars from Imperial College of Technology published a paper in *Scientific Reports,* in which they used in-depth learning of street image data to present and analyze social, economic, environmental, and health inequalities in urban areas (Suel et al. 2019). The team focused on four British cities, including London, Birmingham, Manchester, and Liz, and used 525,860 pictures of London (corresponding to 156,581 postal codes) as the training set. Using the government's statistics on housing conditions, average income, mortality, and morbidity, these researchers made relatively accurate predictions of social stratification in the other three cities. This work's significance lies in training computer programs with visual signal tags in images of some characteristics of urban life (such as the housing quality and living environment) to predict inequality in cities without relevant data.

Third, we consider public health governance. In 2016, *American Economic Review* published a paper on improving urban governance by algorithmic competition (Glaeser et al. 2016). The authors cooperated with the Boston municipal government, Yelp (the largest review website in the U.S.), and Driviendata (a well-known machine learning and data science competition platform in the U.S. that is similar to Kaggle and TopCoder) to train algorithms with comment text data on Yelp to predict

[3] See more at http://www.fragilefamilieschallenge.org.

the possibility of violations of hygiene and health regulations of restaurants in the Boston area. The authors conducted out-of-sample tests of 23 submitted and complete algorithms and compared the predicted results with the actual results of 364 restaurants. Their results show that the efficiency of health inspections can be greatly improved by using the winning algorithm and machine learning to determine which restaurants are most likely to violate regulations and require inspection.

In many other fields, such as international politics, criminology, and public health, social prediction based on machine learning has also been employed. For example, Perry (2013) used the Random Forest method to predict the occurrence of violent conflicts in Africa. Berk (2012) used machine learning to predict the risk of crime in several studies. Kleinberg et al. (2015) used the Lasso regression model to predict which patients with medical insurance can obtain the most benefit from joint replacement surgery. To a large extent, these studies have opened up new areas of social exploration and provided important references and data templates for improving social governance.

5 The Paradigm Significance of Social Prediction

In the development of natural science, scholars in the scientific community use different paradigms in different stages (Kuhn 1962). In social science disciplines, an orthodoxy is similar to a paradigm in different historical stages. Therefore, social science has also undergone the development and evolution of its paradigm, which appears as a spiral rising from the conventional stage, through the crisis stage, and to the revolutionary stage ultimately culminating in a new conventional stage. When the development of social science steps into a specific stage and encounters problems that cannot be solved by the original methods, or new methods and information materials appear, a new paradigm will appear and gradually be accepted and recognized by the academic community. Certainly, the paradigm shift in social science research does not correspond to the kind of "paradigm revolution" described by Kuhn in the natural sciences, such as the subversion of Newtonian statics by relativity and the overthrow of Euclidean geometry by Riemannian geometry. Instead, social science presents a complex coexistence of the new and the old, as well as multiple dialogues.

Kuhn defined the paradigm more clearly at the end of his research career and summarized its content as three nested logical levels. Kuhn suggested that a paradigm refers to a prescriptive consensus of ontology and epistemology, a set of general rules of a theory or model, and a specific problem domain of a symbolic nature (Kuhn 1977). The three basic paradigms of contemporary social research are the empirical paradigm, the interpretive paradigm, and the critical paradigm, founded by Durkheim, Weber, and Marx, respectively. In the past hundred years, the social sciences, especially sociology, have evolved from speculation to a coexistence of speculative and empirical work. This transformation reflects the central position of two fundamental paradigms, interpretation and positivism, as well as the complementary role of the logical and objective perspective of social realism in relation to the individual reality and subjective differentiation emphasized by social nominalism. Within the empirical paradigm, qualitative interviews based on the field and quantitative analysis based on data complement each other, but there are significant differences in the epistemology, research rules, and problem domains. For example, qualitative analysis focuses on the depth of individual experience and theoretical refinement, while quantitative research focuses on sample size, causal mechanisms, theoretical verification, and falsification and emphasizes scientific attributes (Popper 1962). Therefore, qualitative work and quantitative work, in essence, constitute the subparadigm within the empirical paradigm.

With the rapid development of social prediction based on machine learning, the basic paradigm of empirical work will be split into three pieces from the original dual peaks of qualitative and quantitative work to a trilogy of qualitative work, quantitative work, and quantitative prediction. Compared with the traditional quantitative mechanism (correlation and causality), the paradigmatic differences in social prediction are evident in the following aspects.

First, in terms of epistemology, the black-box mechanism is introduced into prediction. Compared with traditional quantitative research that pursues explicit, clear, and theoretical explanations, the epistemological absolutism of prediction is weakened. Second, in terms of the problem domain, the prediction does not focus on the correlation and causal mechanisms of the cause and result, but rather takes the accurate estimation of the target variables as the goal. Third, in terms of the research method, the prediction reduces the dependence on theory and the focus on the counterfactual framework and instead relies on algorithms and data to train and test models. Fourth, in terms of the general rule, the prediction does not rely on the traditional hypothesis test rules and model identification techniques, such as the significance level of the regression coefficient. Instead, a series of new standards focusing on prediction accuracy are adopted, such as the F-score of accuracy and precision, the receiver operating characteristic (ROC) curve with the true positive rate (TPR) and false positive rate (FPR) as axes and the area under the curve (AUC) enclosed by the lower part of the curve.

Of course, if we adopt a more cautious attitude toward the understanding of a paradigm, it can be emphasized that the paradigm significance of social prediction lies in the fact that it has contributed to the subparadigm evolution of empirical research. In other words, the social prediction has experienced from qualitative work to qualitative plus quantitative work and then to a trilogy of qualitative work, quantitative correlation, and quantitative prediction.

6 The Ethical Implications of Social Prediction

The rise of social prediction has opened new frontiers for social science, but it also brings serious ethical challenges. These challenges do not only accompany technical progress but shape the very legitimacy of predictive research in social science. Three aspects are particularly important: privacy, bias, and the boundary between research and governance.

The first issue concerns privacy and consent. Predictive models in social research often rely on digital traces that contain sensitive personal information. The study using Baidu search queries to predict the regional distribution of AIDS in China illustrates both the promise and the risk (He et al. 2018). Search data provide timely signals of public health concerns, yet they also involve highly private queries that individuals never intended to share beyond the search engine. Even if such data are aggregated, the possibility of re-identification remains, raising doubts about whether participants retain meaningful control over their information. These dilemmas make clear that prediction cannot rely on technical efficiency alone; protocols of informed consent, data minimization, and secure handling are essential to preserve autonomy and trust.

The second issue is bias and inequality in predictive outcomes. Models trained on existing data inevitably mirror structural disparities. When Suel et al. (2019) used street-level images to predict socioeconomic inequality across British cities, the approach highlighted contrasts in urban living conditions, but it also risked fixing neighborhood reputations in ways that could stigmatize entire communities. Similar problems appear in crime and conflict prediction, where reliance on past records may reproduce earlier biases in policing or surveillance. These examples reveal that prediction is not a neutral reflection of society but an intervention that may reinforce disadvantage unless fairness tests and corrective measures are built into the research design.

The third issue concerns the boundary between academic research and governance applications. Work such as Glaeser et al. (2016)'s use of Yelp reviews to predict restaurant hygiene violations demonstrates how predictive models can improve efficiency in public administration. At the same time, the transfer of such tools into governance raises questions about transparency, accountability, and the risk of overreliance on algorithmic decision-making. Once models influence decisions with moral consequences, the line between technical guidance and normative judgment becomes blurred. In these contexts, social science must uphold its dual role as a provider of empirical tools and a critic of their use, ensuring that predictions are open to scrutiny and applied under conditions that respect social values.

In sum, the ethical implications of social prediction are inseparable from its scientific development. Protecting privacy, mitigating bias, and clarifying the boundary between research and governance are not optional concerns but necessary foundations for prediction to become a legitimate social science paradigm. By embedding these principles in both methodology and practice, social prediction can contribute to academic innovation and social welfare without compromising the trust on which the social sciences ultimately depend.

7 Conclusion

Prediction has always been an indispensable element of scientific methods. A prediction can verify and evaluate the applicability and effectiveness of existing theories. Although the process in which prediction drives interpretation has been widely used in physics and other natural sciences, it has not been widely used in social science. Indeed, the complexity of human society is much greater than that of nature, and the available data and computing tools in traditional social sciences are relatively lacking. In the past two decades, the rapid expansion of information and data in the network era has presented unprecedented opportunities for social science. As early as 2009, Lazer et al. predicted in *Science* that the era of computing social science would dawn (Lazer et al. 2009; Lazer and Jason 2017). In the past ten years, the network has undergone significant development, and research has accumulated rapidly. In accordance with Lazer's original expectation, a new wave is surging. Machine learning, which enables computers to process data in new ways, has been widely adopted. In summary, there is an urgent need for current academia to embrace machine learning and other trends, and this article intends to point out its future use.

Machine learning provides new assistance for the prediction research of social science and creates conditions for the formation of new paradigms in social science. This article first reviews the historical development of social prediction, discusses the current path of social prediction in relation to the principles and methods of machine learning, and provides theoretical considerations and empirical cases to demonstrate the value of prediction in social science. Machine learning is helpful in expanding the research horizon of social science, as it can obtain latent indicators, inspire theoretical hypotheses, generate causal inferences, realize data proliferation, and promote theoretical innovation. It presents a new paradigm in quantitative research for contemporary social research.

We fully realize that the data mining method on which social prediction relies cannot be perfect, and machine learning–based social prediction faces several fundamental limitations that must be acknowledged. A primary challenge lies in the "black-box" problem, whereby the internal mechanisms of algorithms such as deep neural networks remain opaque to both researchers and the public. This lack of interpretability may hinder social explanation, since understanding why a prediction occurs is as important as the prediction itself. Of course, the "black box" does not mean the model is completely unexplainable. An increasing number of interpretable machine learning algorithms are maturing, which can help us produce new theories from data and deepen the connection between causality and predictivity, as detailed in Chapters 6 and 7 of this book.

Equally critical is the sensitivity of machine learning models to data quality and bias. Unlike data generated in controlled laboratory settings, most social data arise from institutional processes, platform architectures, or self-reporting, which may neither be neutral nor random. For example, digital trace data may disproportionately represent younger, urban, or more affluent populations. Marginalized groups are often underrepresented or misclassified, making them particularly vulnerable to algorithmic misprediction. These imperfections can reproduce or even amplify existing social inequalities when fed into predictive systems. This sensitivity to the source data also points to a broader challenge: the issues of overfitting and weak generalizability. Models that perform well on historical or local data may fail when applied to new social contexts, undermining their reliability for long-term or cross-societal predictions. Overfitting to training data often yields deceptively high accuracy but poor real-world performance, limiting their value for long-term forecasting or cross-societal comparison. For social research, predictive models must therefore be contextualized and complemented by theory and qualitative insights rather than treated as universally portable tools.

Every method has its premises, assumptions, and limitations. The mission of social scientists is to ensure that these hypotheses are as close as possible to the specific research situation in a transparent, reasonable, and effective way and to make continuous progress on diminishing limitations. Therefore, Grimmer (2015) pointed out that data scientists should not only be computer scientists but also social scientists. Social prediction based on the black-box mechanisms of machine learning does not imply abandoning theoretical thinking and empirical knowledge; rather, these resources are essential for interpreting algorithmic results and dismantling opacity. In the process of dismantling the black box, the conclusions drawn from the black-box mechanism can and should be interpreted from the theoretical perspective and further verified by empirical methods. To address data quality and bias, social scientists should ask: who created these records and for what purpose? Which groups are overrepresented or absent? How do institutional practices shape what is observed? Such questions shift the focus from technical de-biasing to a deeper understanding of how data reflects and distorts the social world. Likewise, the problem of weak generalizability underscores the value of contextual knowledge. When a model that performs well in one setting fails elsewhere, this is not simply a statistical error but an insight from social science, revealing the boundaries of social processes and the significance of local conditions. The task of social science, therefore, is not to search for a universally perfect model, but to use theory to explain when and why models succeed or fail, turning limitations into opportunities for theoretical refinement.

New methods and paradigms will give rise to new problems and puzzles. In particular, the introduction of social prediction and machine learning may affect the theoretical depth and saturation of social science.

Similarly, the social sciences could potentially lose their humanistic feelings and theoretical concerns or even become a pure data mining game. Such concerns are understandable, but they do not constitute grounds for rejection and exclusion. Excessive worry often derives from the lack of a comprehensive understanding of new methods and new paradigms, and the lack of confidence in the strong theoretical tradition of social science and the diversified expression of the humanistic spirit. Since its establishment a century ago, the social sciences have maintained their strong vitality and attraction with their open vision, tolerant mind, and interdisciplinary spirit.

However, these worries and doubts are not baseless. It is exactly this kind of vigilance rooted in the hearts of social scientists that has enabled the leaders of disciplines, advocates of paradigms, reformers of thinking, and innovators of methods to always maintain the spirit of academic reflection, respect, and perseverance of the theoretical tradition at every critical historical juncture. In this sense, excellent social science research must exemplify the rational use of advanced methods, combined with humanistic feelings and theoretical concerns. Humanistic feelings, theoretical concerns, and methods of the times are indispensable to the academic background, historical heritage, and contemporary pulse of social science. Research without human feelings and theoretical concerns cannot obtain historical respect and academic depth even if it uses powerful methods and data. Furthermore, research without scientific research methods cannot reach a real historical height regardless of how strong its theoretical consciousness and humanistic spirit are.

Therefore, like the introduction and emergence of every new thing and new field in the history of a discipline's development, the introduction and emergence of machine learning and social prediction into the toolbox and thinking mode of social scientists will neither change the research merit of social science nor dim the traditional social research paradigms and methods. Causal inference in correlation research, big data, and computational social science represented by machine learning constitute three frontier quantitative research areas. Social scientists' constant inquiry into causal mechanisms, continuous pursuit of the breadth and depth of social information, and unremitting exploration of social processes and the certainty of social phenomena together constitute the historical drive and endogenous power of these three frontier areas. Some of these three frontier areas have elaborated their research themes, while others have just emerged. As new branches of the social sciences, these fields will be nourished by the historical tradition of the discipline and thrive.

References

Allison, Paul D. 2009. Missing Data. In *The SAGE handbook of quantitative methods in psychology*, ed. Roger E. Millsap and Alberto Maydeu-Olivares, 72–89. London: Sage.

Athey, Susan. 2015. Machine learning and causal inference for policy evaluation. In *Proceedings of the 21th ACM SIGKDD International Conference on Knowledge Discovery and Data Mining*, Sydney, NSW, Australia, 10–13 August.

Athey, Susan. 2018. The impact of machine learning on economics. In *The economics of artificial intelligence: An* agenda, ed. Ajay Agrawal, Joshua Gans, and Avi Goldfarb, 507–547. University of Chicago Press.

Athey, Susan, and Guido Imbens. 2016. Recursive partitioning for heterogeneous causal effects. *Proceedings of the National Academy of Sciences of the United States of America* 113 (27): 7353–7360.

Belloni, A., D. Chen, V. Chernozhukov, and C. Hansen. 2012. Sparse models and methods for optimal instruments with an application to eminent domain. *Econometrica* 80 (6): 2369–2429.

Berk, Richard. 2012. *Criminal justice forecasts of risk: A machine learning approach*, 27–41. New York: Springer.

Brand, Jennie E., and Yu Xie. 2007. Identification and estimation of causal effects with time-varying treatments and time-varying outcomes. *Sociological Methodology* 37 (1): 393–434.

Carrasco, Marine. 2012. A regularization approach to the many instruments problem. *Journal of Econometrics* 17 (2): 383–398.

Castle, Jennifer L., Xiaochuan Qin, and W. Robert Reed. 2009. How to pick the best regression equation: A review and comparison of model selection algorithms. Working Papers in Economics 09/13, University of Canterbury, Department of Economics and Finance.

Chen, Yunsong. 2011. The causal effect of social capital in the labor market: Identification challenges and strategies. *Chinese Sociological Review* 44 (2): 76–100.

Chen, Yunsong. 2017. Out of Fei Xiaotong's paradox: The dispute of methodology in Sociology. *Tsinghua Sociological Review* 7.

Zhiwei, Deng. 2009. *The dictionary of sociology*, 513. Shanghai: Cishu Press (in Chinese).

Diamond, Alexis, and Jasjeet S. Sekhon. 2013. Genetic matching for estimating causal effects: A general multivariate matching method for achieving balance in observational studies. *Review of Economics and Statistics* 95 (3): 932–945.

Donaldson, Dave, and Adam Storeygard. 2016. The view from above: Applications of satellite data in economics. *Journal of Economic Perspectives* 30 (4): 171–198.

Farhangfar, Alireza, Lukasz Kurgan, and Jennifer Dy. 2008. Impact of imputation of missing values on classification error for discrete data. *Pattern Recognition* 41 (12): 3692–3705.

Glaeser, Edward L., et al. 2016. Crowdsourcing city government: Using tournaments to improve inspection accuracy. *American Economic Review* 106 (5): 114–118.

Goodman, Nelson. 1983. *Fact fiction and forecast*, 114–118. Cambridge: Harvard University Press.

Green, Donald P., and Holger L. Kern. 2012. Modeling heterogeneous treatment effects in survey experiments with Bayesian additive regression trees. *Public Opinion Quarterly* 76 (3): 491–511.

Grimmer, Justin. 2015. We are all social scientists now: How big data, machine learning, and causal inference work together. *Political Science and Politics* 48 (1): 80–83.

Hartford, Jason et al. 2016. Counterfactual prediction with deep instrumental variables networks. arXiv: 1612.09596.

Hazlett, Chad. 2014. Kernel Balancing (KBAL): A balancing method to equalize multivariate distance densities and reduce bias without a specification search. MIT Unpublished Manuscript.

He, Guangye, et al. 2018. Using the Baidu search index to predict the incidents of HIV/AIDS in China. *Scientific Reports* 8 (1): 9038.

Hempel, Carl G., and Paul Oppenheim. 1948. Studies in the logic of explanation. *Philosophy of Science* 15 (2): 135–175.

Hofman, Jake M., Amit Sharma, and Duncan J. Watts. 2017. Prediction and explanation in social systems. *Science* 355 (6324): 486–488.

Hu, Anning. 2012. Propensity score matching and causal inference: A methodological review. *Sociological Studies* 27 (1): 221–242+246 (in Chinese).

Imai, Kosuke, and Marc Ratkovic. 2013. Estimating treatment effect heterogeneity in randomized program evaluation. *Annals of Applied Statistics* 7 (1): 443–470.

Jasny, Barbara R., and Richard Stone. 2017. Prediction and Its limits. *Science* 355 (6324): 468–469.

Kaplan, Oscar. 1940. Prediction in the social sciences. *Philosophy of Science* 7 (4): 492–498.

Kleinberg, Jon, et al. 2015. Prediction policy problems. *American Economic Review* 105 (5): 491–495.

Kleinberg, Jon, Annie Liang, and Sendhil Mullainathan. 2017. The theory is predictive, but is it complete? An application to human perception of

randomness. In *Proceedings of the 2017 ACM Conference on Economics and Computation*, 125–126.
Kuhn, Thomas S. 1962. *The structure of scientific revolutions*. Chicago: The University of Chicago Press.
Kuhn, Thomas S. 1977. *The essential tension*. Chicago: The University of Chicago Press.
Lazer, David, et al. 2009. Social science computational social science. *Science* 323 (5915): 721–723.
Lazer, David, and Radford Jason. 2017. Data Ex Machina: Introduction to big data. *Annual Review of Sociology* 43 (1): 19–39.
Li, Huang. 2012. *Statistical learning methods*. Beijing: Tsinghua University Press (In Chinese).
Luo, Jiade, Jifan Liu, Kunhao Yang, and Xiaoming Fu. 2018. Reintroducing theory into the triangle dialogue of big data, theory and prediction model. *Sociological Studies* 5: 1–19.
Manski, Charles F. 2007. Partial identification of counterfactual choice probabilities. *International Economic Review* 48 (4): 1393–1410.
Martin, Travis et al. 2016. Exploring limits to prediction in complex social systems. In *Proceedings of the 25th International conference on World Wide Web*, 683–694.
McCaffrey, Daniel F., Greg Ridgeway, and Andrew R. Morral. 2004. Propensity score estimation with boosted regression for evaluating causal effects in observational studies. *Psychological Methods* 9 (4): 403–425.
McFarland, Daniel A. et al. 2013. Differentiating language usage through topic models. *Poetics* 41 (6SI): 1–19.
Mitchell, Tom. 1997. *Machine learning*. New York and London: McGraw-Hill.
Mohr, John W., Wagner-Pacici. Robin, Ronald L. Breiger, and Bogdanov Petko. 2013. Graphing the grammar of motives in National security strategies: Cultural interpretation, automated text analysis and the drama of global politics. *Poetics* 41: 670–700.
Molina, Mario, and Filiz Garip. 2019. Machine learning for sociology. *Annual Review of Sociology* 45: 27–45.
Morgan, Stephen L., and Christopher Winship. 2007. *Counterfactuals and causal inference: Methods and principles for social research*, 15–31. New York: Cambridge University Press.
Pearl, Judea. 2000. *Causality: Models, reasoning, and inference*, 41–61. Cambridge: Cambridge University Press.
Perry, Chris. 2013. Machine learning and conflict prediction: A use case. *Stability: International Journal of Security and Development* 2 (3): 1–18.
Popper, Karl. 1962. *Conjectures and refutations: The growth of scientific knowledge*. New York: Basic Books.

Rubin, Donald B. 1974. Estimating causal effects of treatments in randomized and nonrandomized studies. *Journal of Educational Psychology* 66 (5): 688–701.

Sovilj, Du. šan, et al. 2016. Extreme learning machine for missing data using multiple imputations. *Neurocomputing* 174: 220–231.

Suel, Esra, et al. 2019. Measuring social, environmental and health inequalities using deep learning and street imagery. *Scientific Reports* 9 (1): 6229.

Varian, Hal R. 2014. Big data: New tricks for econometrics. *Journal of Economic Perspectives* 28 (2): 3–28.

Watts, Duncan J. 2014. Common sense and sociological explanations. *American Journal of Sociology* 120 (2): 313–351.

Weber, Max. 1968 [1921]. *Economy and society*. Translated and edited by G. Roth and C. Wittich. New York: Bedminster Press.

Westreich, Daniel, Justin Lessler, and Michele Jonsson Funk. 2010. Propensity score estimation: Neural networks, support vector machines, decision trees (CART), and meta-classifiers as alternatives to Logistic Regression. *Journal of Clinical Epidemiology* 63 (8): 826–833.

Xie, Yu, Jennie E. Brand, and Ben Jann. 2012. Estimating heterogeneous treatment effects with observational data. *Sociological Methodology* 42 (1): 314–347.

Yan, Yaojun. 1986. On social science and social prediction. In *Social science and contemporary society*, ed. Liu Zhongheng, 21–57. Shenyang: Liaoning People's Publishing House.

Yan, Yaojun. 2005. *Basic principles of social prediction*, 15–33. Beijing: Social Science Academic Press.

CHAPTER 3

Modeling Massive: Discovering Structure Using Unsupervised Machine Learning

1 Introduction

The social sciences' engagement with culture dates back to the work of Max Weber and Émile Durkheim. Yet under the influence of Enlightenment rationalism, culture was long treated as subordinate to social structure and lacked the status of an independent explanatory variable. The "cultural turn" that began in sociology in the late 1970s and 1980s reshaped this view within sociology and beyond. As a branch of sociology, cultural sociology explored art, literature, popular culture, and media, while extending to issues such as social stratification and politics, reframing culture as a social force shaping the real world. Its influence also extended to anthropology, political science, communication studies, and other branches of the social sciences. In the context of the linguistic turn, globalization, and the rise of new media, language, meaning, and individual agency have gained new importance. Globalization disrupted traditional understandings of culture, and digital media transformed how culture is created and circulated (Poster 2010). These changes have prompted social scientists to adopt computational approaches to capture the spatial and temporal dynamics of culture and to analyze large-scale patterns that earlier methods could not address.

In recent years, social computing technologies have created important opportunities for a paradigm shift in the study of culture across the social sciences. Quantitative research has evolved from descriptive statistics and the revelation of correlations between variables to the exploration of

Y. Chen et al., *Machine Learning in Social Science*,
https://doi.org/10.1007/978-981-95-6465-1_3

causal relationships among social phenomena, responding to social scientists' calls for the return of causality (Chen et al. 2021). With advances in machine learning, computer algorithms can now classify large-scale data and detect patterns that were previously difficult to observe. They enable the clustering of massive textual datasets, the analysis of themes and sentiments, and the identification of cultural explanatory variables that extend beyond traditional frameworks. In the era of big data, the use of diverse models and machine learning techniques has made culture both a subject of study and a source of theoretical insight. This development also gives new life to the cultural turn, which reaffirms the centrality of culture while moving beyond the limitations of extreme subjectivism and relativism.

This chapter begins with a historical overview of social science research on culture and introduces the classical methods of cultural study, represented by ethnography and qualitative content analysis. Then, with a contemporary focus, it introduces the application of emerging social computing methods in this field, using research from several important journals as examples. Finally, it introduces four methods for textual analysis through machine learning: LDA topic model, Word2Vec algorithm, named entity recognition, and sentiment analysis.

2 Traditional Cultural Research Methods

As early as 1958, Raymond Williams (1958: 25), one of the founders of cultural studies, stated, "Culture is one of the two or three most complicated words in the English language." The scope of culture is extremely broad. It is as ubiquitous and relevant as the air, but when it comes to defining the concept of culture, it will be blurred, like in the mist. The academic debate on this concept has never stopped. Under the influence of the cultural turn, numerous disciplines are involved in cultural studies (e.g., anthropology, linguistics, translatology, history, etc.), and no broad consensus has been reached until now. However, William Sewell (2005: 156–157) argues that the basic categories of culture can be identified: culture exists either as a defining aspect of theoretical concepts in social life or as people's concrete practices and behaviors. The former is a system of symbols and meanings, denoted as "culture" due to its abstract nature; the latter refers to the social practices of particular groups, denoted as "cultures" due to their actuality and their distinctions between groups (Geertz 1973; Sewell 2005: 164–165). However, the two categories are not contradictory, and the dialectical relationship between them counts for much in the research of cultural theory. Many definitions of culture include these two categories. For example, one of the definitions of the word "culture" in the *Oxford English Dictionary* is "the customs and beliefs, art, way of life and social organization of a particular country or group" (Stevenson 2010).

Although different disciplines approach these two categories in their own ways, social scientists share a concern with social reality and do not see culture only as an abstract system of symbols. They seek to understand how culture takes shape and functions in concrete contexts. The relationship between culture and structure has long been a central question in the social sciences. Pioneers such as Karl Marx, Max Weber, and Émile Durkheim all grappled with this relationship, though each understood it in markedly different ways. Marx saw consciousness as inseparable from material existence, arguing that it reflects the real conditions of life (Fromm 1971: 19). Culture, despite its creative potential, is ultimately subordinate to structure. Weber, in contrast, stressed the role of ideas, beliefs, and values alongside material interests in explaining historical change. He described his approach as *Kulturwissenschaft*, meaning cultural studies in English (Eberle 2016). For Weber, meaning formation is tied to power and domination; culture is a meaningful form of social action, and sociology is the study of this reality, giving culture and structure equal standing. Durkheim differed from both. Early in his work, he viewed culture as a product of social structure. Later, he recognized the independent force of belief and ritual in shaping social life (Alexander 2003). He treated culture as a collective representation capable of transcending individual behavior and linked it to the organization of society and the division of labor.

Cultural studies within the social sciences have continued to draw on the theories and methodologies of early pioneers. For instance, the structural functionalism that dominated American sociology after World War II until the 1960s was influenced by Marx and Durkheim, giving the values representing culture a functional status subordinate to structure without further elaboration of their meaning. The Chicago School in the late 1960s, represented by Herbert Blumer's theory of symbolic interaction, not only highlighted the constructive role of symbols for individual action but also achieved a revival of the interpretive paradigm. Another methodological contribution of the Chicago School is the development of grounded theory (GT), which informs its empirical research. As a qualitative research method, it runs counter to traditional positivism, and does not approach empirical facts by set research methods, but rather induces theories based on empirical facts, opening up another path for sociologists and anthropologists to study culture (Glaser and Strauss 2017). After structural functionalism lost its dominance, Weber's theory is back in the limelight. His approach to interpreting the meaning-making process and his formulation of how meaning affects actions, practices, and institutions fit the new horizons of social science research, and have even influenced a part of post-structuralist and postmodernist theories, including the cultural turn in sociology.

Although culture was an important research object in sociology at the very beginning, it was not until the cultural turn occurred that cultural sociology was formally established as a new branch of sociology. The real appeal of establishing cultural sociology lies in making necessary corrections to the long-standing marginal role of culture in sociology, breaking the grand narrative of structural functionalism, and adjusting value judgments based on scientific rationality. Influenced by semiotics, phenomenology, and linguistics, the autonomy of culture was elevated to an unprecedented level in the early stage of the discipline's establishment, and some scholars even believed that all social phenomena are composed of culture (Olick 2010: 97–108). Although the notion of cultural autonomy has since been reframed as a relative concept, the recognition of culture as a constitutive social force has been increasingly shared across the social sciences (2010: 99). As the interpretation of abstract cultural meaning becomes our focus, understanding culture in terms of other tangible things loses its meaning and is replaced by the study of how culture itself constantly reshapes the behavior of the real world (Sherwood 1993). After the cultural turn, culture came to be viewed not as a static element serving structural functions, but as a dynamic process in constant transformation. Consequently, space and time emerged as core dimensions of cultural analysis in the social sciences. At the theoretical level, the enduring question of culture is the relationship between the symbols, practices, and social structures that culture contains. How to strike a balance between structuralism and subjectivism is the constant goal of theorists such as Pierre Bourdieu and Anthony Giddens.

In the early years of cultural sociology's emergence, its purpose and features determined its rejection of scientism and macro theory, as well as its special emphasis on experience. So far, qualitative research methods, primarily based on field research (including participant observation and unstructured interviews), remain the mainstream approach in cultural sociology research. Among them, the ethnographic approach of anthropology is undoubtedly the best choice for cultural researchers when they aim to describe a certain kind of cultural practice. Both the Chicago School and the Birmingham School have made extensive use of ethnography, such as the fieldwork represented by the Chicago School. This trend is even more pronounced in the Birmingham School which specializes in cultural studies. For example, Williams applies historical ethnography to combine rural experiences in a series of literary works with his own experiences in *The Country and the City* (1973), adding life experiences to the images of rural and urban culture and giving culture a social significance. Similarly, Paul Willis in *Learning to Labour* (1977) used participatory ethnography, including listening, observing, and describing, to show how working-class youth reproduced structures of subordination through everyday acts of resistance. These studies illustrate how interpretive and experiential methods have shaped both cultural sociology and the broader social sciences in understanding culture as a lived and socially embedded process.

Ethnography has long been central to the study of cultural practices, from everyday interaction to artistic production and consumption. When attention shifts from the process of production to the cultural object itself, experience becomes crucial to understanding its social meaning. Methods such as qualitative content analysis and discourse analysis, drawing on traditions in literature and art studies, allow researchers to examine how meanings are constructed through language, imagery, and form. When content analysis directly engages with the object, causality gives way to participation, and the observer's perception becomes part of the process, revealing the internal logic and social meaning of the cultural form (Abbott 2007). By engaging directly with cultural texts and artworks, these approaches reveal how aesthetic experience connects to broader social structures and values. They also extend the interpretive tradition of cultural research, treating art and literature not merely as representations but as social facts with emotional and symbolic power (Bourdieu 1993; Abbott 2007; De la Fuente 2007).

From the above review, it is clear that cultural research in the social sciences combines both subjective and objective dimensions. It values interpretation and understanding while maintaining the empirical spirit of scientific inquiry. Methods such as ethnography, content analysis, and discourse analysis examine how cultural practices interact with social life. These qualitative approaches have at times been questioned for relying too heavily on interpretation, for offering limited causal explanation, and for struggling to capture how culture changes over time. In response, newer forms of quantitative cultural research have begun to address these limits. Rather than describing culture mainly in the manner of traditional anthropology or focusing on textual meaning as in literary studies, they treat culture as something that can be measured, modeled, and used to explain social outcomes. Social computing is central to this development. It makes it possible to move from local and small-scale observation to large-scale analysis of structure and stratification, opening new possibilities for the study of culture across the social sciences.

3 Computational Approaches in Cultural Research

Quantitative methods have advanced cultural research within the social sciences in two key ways: through innovations in statistical modeling and the emergence of computer algorithms capable of processing big data. With the introduction of advanced econometric models such as hierarchical linear models, non-linear approaches including logistic regression, and methods for causal identification, simple correlation analysis has evolved into causal inference, enabling clearer identification of relationships between social indicators (Chen et al. 2021). Yet for cultural research, the expansion of analytical tools alone is insufficient to transform its paradigm. When facing hard-to-capture cultural phenomena, algorithms are more objective tools than personal feelings, as they can transform the phenomena into data and models allowing culture to be causally analyzed together with other social phenomena and novel possibilities of cultural-structural interaction to be explored. With the help of cloud computing and cloud storage technologies, the data resources available to social scientists have expanded dramatically. For example, the 2019 version of Google Books has digitized more than 15 million books published between 1500 and 2019, forming a corpus of over 600 billion words, which is estimated to account for about 15% of all books ever published in human history.[1] By analyzing it in comparison with realistic behavioral data, the impact of cultural meanings on social reality can be verified from a macro diachronic perspective, bridging the gaps in traditional methods. In Chen et al. (2020)'s study, examining the relationship between the frequency of suicide terms in books and actual suicide rates deepens understanding of the role of cultural and media autonomy.

Beyond classical causal inference, cultural research in the social sciences increasingly adopts mixed methods. The complexity of culture demands approaches that combine close interpretation with empirical analysis, connecting culture with society, subjectivity with objectivity, and micro behavior with macro structure. Bourdieu's *Distinction* (1984) remains a foundational example: it integrates textual description, interviews, and participatory observation with the analysis of large-scale survey data using Multiple Correspondence Analysis (MCA) to map social space and lifestyle. The richness of Bourdieu's data and his use of non-traditional statistical tools provide a lasting methodological model for cultural social science (Holt 1997). Later scholars have extended this view, arguing that no single method or dataset can claim full objectivity and that the binary divide between qualitative and quantitative methods should be replaced with more integrated, multidimensional approaches (Majima and Moore 2009). While concerns persist about the reduction of cultural complexity through coding, researchers increasingly recognize that humanistic interpretation is not the only legitimate mode of cultural analysis (Lee and Martin 2015). The potential of computational and quantitative methods can therefore no longer be ignored.

The blurring of qualitative and quantitative boundaries has also driven the development of non-traditional descriptive analysis. Social computing, through big data and algorithms, allows culture to be measured and analyzed at scale. Interdisciplinary studies now use big data to explore social reality in cultural products. For example, researchers have compiled datasets of fiction across languages and periods to analyze gendered language, finding that collective terms such as person or people more often reference men than women (Bailey et al. 2022). Others have used probabilistic models to trace the evolution of love narratives in fiction, revealing that higher economic development correlates with more frequent representations of love (Baumard et al. 2022). In a study

[1] See https://books.google.com/ngrams/info for an introduction to Google Books Ngram.

published in the journal *Cultural Sociology*, Harvey (2009) applied a 3D digital city model of Manchester that combined quantitative data, imagery, and statistics to reconstruct the city's social geography, showing how digital visualization can generate new cultural narratives.

At the macro level, machine learning has further expanded the analytic horizon. Machine learning algorithms were born for "how to learn to solve problems without explicit programming." They can automatically update and upgrade empirical features of sample data to cluster or predict the data. Among the subfields related to machine learning, data mining and clustering are related to unsupervised machine learning, which can mine and cluster a large number of texts and images, helping us quickly understand the themes and features of these cultural objects without understanding and reading them one by one and greatly shortening the research time. Although some scholars worry that such methods overlook the aesthetic and interpretive dimensions of art, they provide a necessary complement to traditional close reading. As a form of distant reading, they help reveal long-term trajectories and recurrent patterns in cultural production that remain inaccessible through conventional methods.

Alongside methodological innovations in macro-level text analysis (Jockers 2013), *Poetics*, a leading journal of cultural studies, launched a special issue in 2013 that introduced topic models based on machine learning. The studies clustered textual themes and linked them to social factors such as author gender, nationality, and publication date, demonstrating how topics become measurable variables (Jockers and Mimno 2013). Another study compared the conceptual vocabularies of two academic communities to reveal how each constructs its understanding of the world (Marshall 2013). As scholars increasingly analyze large-scale datasets from the Internet, social media, and digitized archives, the capacity to work with data at scale becomes indispensable (Mohr and Bogdanov 2013). Such approaches enable both macro-level analyses of cultural patterns and focused examinations of smaller cultural domains, extending the reach of traditional interpretive methods.

The emergence of social computing methods has brought culture and society closer together. In the era of big data, it is possible to accurately measure cultural behaviors, images, and texts, allowing them to be correlated with other traditional social indicators as an independent variable and tested for causality. These novel techniques help achieve the goal of the cultural turn in the new period, that is, to observe traditional social issues such as social stratification and social networks from the perspective of culture and through the approaches of culture, as well as to bridge the individual social behavior and the macro social structure. In this way, new theories can emerge from systematic data analysis, continuing the original spirit of grounded theory in exploring how meaning, action, and structure intertwine.

4 Introduction of Unsupervised Machine Learning Methods

Text is a vital carrier of views, values, social activities, and historical traces of human society, and textual content analysis has long been a crucial method in cultural research. As archaeologists apply fossils to interpret history, textual content analysis researchers often collect and analyze various forms of written materials, such as books, newspapers, and poems, to explore social behaviors, cultural trends, and historical phenomena. Using machine learning methods to analyze textual materials can help social scientist avoid the challenges of subjectivism and relativism.

Textual content analysis often requires systematic, objective, and quantitative analysis. Traditional content analysis methods often require researchers to start from specific research questions. Then, they need to sample from the documents and quantify the document features by reading them manually according to a pre-drafted coding system. The limitations of this approach are as follows. First, the sheer size of the textual material makes manual reading impractical, and the errors that accompany sampling are equally difficult to avoid. Second, the researcher must determine the research question and coding method in advance, which means that the researcher's awareness and experience could have a great impact. Along with more digitized information and more accurate and automated natural language processing algorithms, we can identify the latent cultural structure of massive amounts of texts from the historical perspective and explore cultural development at a macro level.

Text analysis based on machine learning is achieved through unsupervised machine learning, as it is suitable for unstructured data sets without labels. When the covariate matrix is available and the explained variable is not, the algorithm will calculate the distance between different samples based on the given covariate information, and cluster the samples. This section introduces four unsupervised machine learning methods for textual analysis: LDA topic model, Word2Vec algorithm, named entity recognition, and sentiment analysis. They can all be used to analyze the structure and contents to obtain further information about the deep connotation of the text, while each has its advantages. In addition to the case of Chinese poems presented in the section of the LDA, cases of other methods are in Chapters 10–13 of this book.

4.1 Topic Model

The LDA topic model is an important method for text analysis, which can automatically identify latent topic information in a large-scale text corpus and quantitatively measure the focus of the text. LDA is a three-level hierarchical Bayesian model for document topic generation with unsupervised machine learning techniques (Blei et al. 2003). The application of LDA is based on three nested concepts: the text set to be modeled (the "corpus"), an item in the corpus (a "document"), and a word in the document (a "term"). Thus, documents are nested in the corpus, and the terms are nested in the documents. This model assumes that the corpus contains multiple topics. Each topic is defined as the probability distribution of fixed words, whereas each document selects a topic with a certain probability, and a certain word is selected from this topic with a particular probability. A corpus is described as a probability distribution of potential topics, whereas each topic is a probability distribution of terms. Subsequently, data analysis is performed using the joint distribution to calculate the conditional distribution (a posteriori distribution) of the hidden variable (subject structure) given a specific observed variable (word in the document). The formula is expressed as follows:

$$p(\beta_{1:K}, \theta_{1:D}, z_{1:D}, w_{1:D}) = \prod_{i=1}^{K} p(\beta) \prod_{d=1}^{D} p(\theta_d) \left(\begin{matrix} \prod_{n=1}^{N} p(z_{d,n}|\theta_d) \\ p(w_{d,n}|\beta_{1:K}, z_{d,n}) \end{matrix} \right)$$

In this formula, $\beta_{1:K}$ represents all topics and β_K represents the distribution of the words for the Kth topic. $\theta_{1:D}$ represents all documents, θ_d is the proportion of the topic in the dth document, and $\theta_{d,k}$ reflects the proportion of the Kth topic in the dth document. All of the topics of the dth document are z_d, and $z_{d,n}$ is the topic of the nth word in the dth document. Furthermore, all of the words in the dth document constitute w_d, and $w_{d,n}$ is the nth word in the dth document. Compared with a simple co-occurrence analysis, the LDA topic model reveals the underlying semantic relationships between words, even if the words never appear together in a document. Unlike other topic cluster models, the LDA topic model uses a distinct mixed-membership approach that allows a document to span various topics, ensuring the accuracy of the analysis.

We take the analysis of ancient Chinese poems as an example. Through the LDA topic model, we discovered 10 topics in *Complete Poetry Collection of Tang Dynasty* (2011), which contains around 48,900 poems: (1) sorrow of parting evoked by the landscape; (2) women's love and bitterness; (3) bosom friends across time; (4) Zen born from the forest and wind; (5) frontier of war; (6) idyllic leisure; (7) rites and music to praise; (8) seclusion as drifting clouds; (9) lessons from history; (10) immortal in Taoism. If the temporal dimension is introduced into the calculation of topic proportion, the panorama of cultural development and the features of different periods can be further examined, as shown in Fig. 1.

For example, poems with the topic of "rites and music to praise" were most prosperous in the height of the Tang Dynasty, around 700

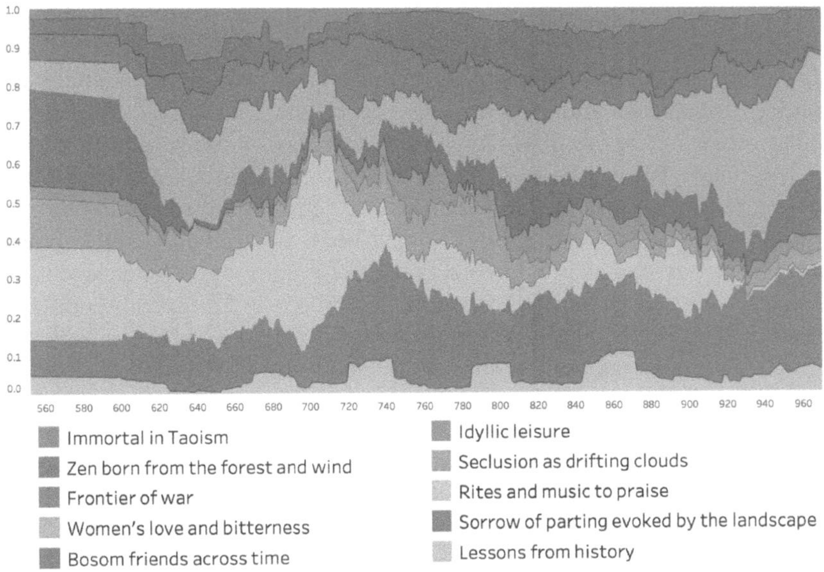

Fig. 1 The temporal trend of poetry topics in Tang Dynasty2

A.D., when the political, diplomatic, and economic development of this dynasty was at its peak. The trends of pilgrimages from various countries also gave rise to a culture of poems, music, and rituals in praise of the monarch. In contrast, during the Middle and Late Tang Dynasty, the topic of "rites and music to praise" gradually declined, replaced by the flourishing of "women's love and bitterness" since poets needed to express their worries. Moreover, the topic of "Zen born from the forest and wind" can be linked to the prevailing Buddhism in the Tang dynasty as a proxy for measuring religious culture. Thus, combining the cultural characteristics discovered by the topic model with indicators of the social and historical context can make up for the lack of a macroscopic view in cultural research and accurately quantify the relationship between culture and society. The relevant research is further presented in Chapters 10–13 of this book.

4.2 Word2Vec Algorithm

Word2Vec is Google's open-source algorithm toolkit. It transforms unstructured text data into high-dimensional vector data, measures the similarity between words, and predicts the context (Yao et al. 2017). Word2Vec includes continuous bag of words (CBOW) and skip-gram algorithms, both of which are generated by a shallow neural network model, calculating and normalizing the cosine similarity between the input vector of the input word (the current word) and the output vector of the target word (the context of the current word). After the word segmentation, stemming, and stop-words removal, the two algorithms transform each word into a high-dimensional vector. The CBOW model takes the context of a certain word as the training input, the keyword itself as the training label, and predicts the central word through the context. On the contrary, the Skip-gram model takes a certain word in the sentence as the training input, and its context as the training label, and applies the input keyword to predict its context (Mikolov et al. 2013).

This section illustrates the application of the CBOW algorithm in the Word2Vec model, using the social concept polarization phenomenon in the "pseudo-environment" of the Internet as an example. The topic "which is more effective between traditional Chinese medicine and Western medicine" has been controversial in China's Internet community. We analyzed this topic based on two data sources, one from China's largest Internet Q&A community "Zhihu," an equivalent to the website Quora, and the other from China's largest instant social media "WeChat," whose functions are equivalent to WhatsApp. First, we crawled all the answers under the questions containing both "traditional Chinese medicine" and "western medicine" on Zhihu, with a total of 8162 answers under 44 questions obtained, totaling more than 2.08 million words, with a time span from 2012 to 2021. Then, 735 articles related to traditional Chinese medicine and Western medicine were obtained from the "official account" of WeChat, a mini program for publishing long articles, totaling more than 2.34 million words, spanning from 2014 to 2021.

Each word is converted into a 256-dimensional vector during modeling, and the dimension of each word vector is reduced using Google's embedding projector tool before mapping them into 3D space in different time periods. In this space, each point is a vector space position of a word. The denser the local point groups, the greater the difference between the semantics of the representative words, and the stronger the perspective polarization. Figures 2 and 3 show certain polarization. Evidently, two opposing word groups have appeared in the text about traditional Chinese medicine on both Zhihu and WeChat as a whole in recent years.

More importantly, the time characteristics of polarization can be clearly seen in the spatial distribution of word embeddings, as shown in Figs. 4

Fig. 2 Word vector polarization in Zhihu from 2012 to 2021

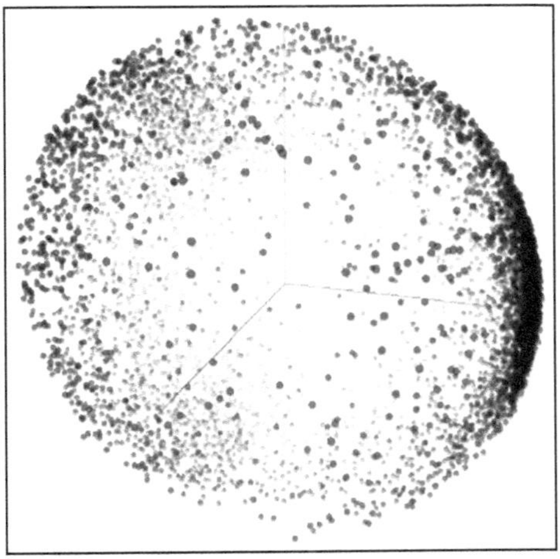

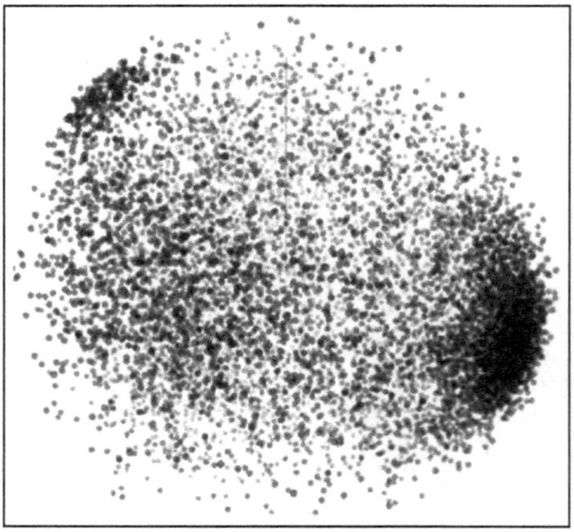

Fig. 3 Word vector polarization in WeChat from 2014 to 2021

and 5. First, word embedding is gradually polarized over time. Second, the spatial distribution of word embeddings is roughly divided into two periods, with an even distribution before 2015 and apparent polarization after 2015. Furthermore, there is a turning point in 2020 for WeChat. The distribution characteristics of Figs. 3 and 4 are obviously the integrated results of uniform distribution in earlier years and polarization in recent years.

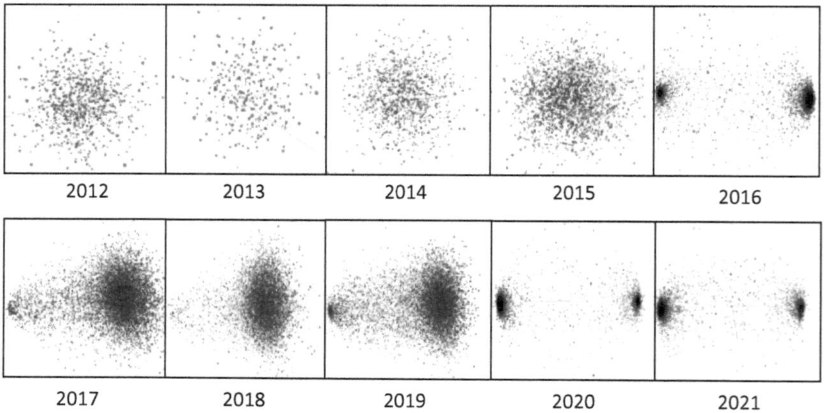

Fig. 4 Spatial distribution of word vector of "Traditional Chinese Medicine and Western Medicine" in Zhihu

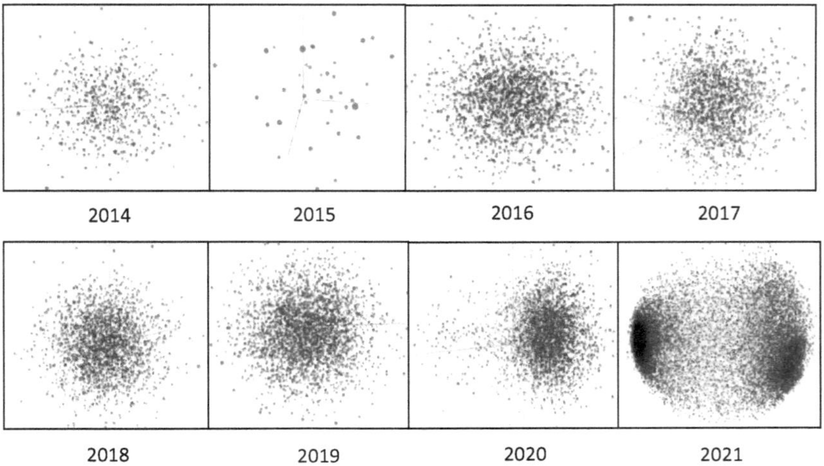

Fig. 5 Spatial distribution of word vector of "Traditional Chinese Medicine and Western Medicine" in WeChat

For Skip-gram model, it is worth mentioning that, in addition to calculating the similarity between the input vector of the input word and the output vector of the target word, there is another way to conduct this algorithm: calculating the cosine similarity between the input vector of the input word (the current word) and the input vector of the target word (the words similar to the current word). This IN-IN vector produces words with similar functions as the target word, while the IN–OUT vector gives words that often co-occur with the target word in the context (Nalisnick et al. 2016). The research using Skip-gram IN–OUT vector algorithm is further presented in Chapters 10, 12, and 13 of this book.

4.3 *Named Entity Recognition*

Named entity recognition (NER) is the tool for locating and categorizing important and proper nouns in a text, mainly including names of people, places, organizations, and time. As a fundamental technique for the automatic extraction of text information, NER, although simple, can accurately identify the subject, object, or adverbial in a sentence, and these entities often contain the most important information, such as time, place, and person.

The tool used for this analysis is the Stanford Named Entity Recognizer, developed by the Natural Language Processing Group at Stanford University, which uses linear-chain conditional random field (CRF) sequence models (Finkel et al. 2005). This Java-based system uses CoNLL, MUC-6, MUC-7, ACE, and other named entity corpora for mixed model training. By utilizing one or more machine learning sequence models to label entities, it can automatically identify names of people, places, and organizations in sentences in a given corpus, and achieves outstanding performance in many applications.[2] The relevant research is further presented in Chapter 11 of this book.

4.4 *Sentiment Analysis*

Sentiment analysis involves analyzing, processing, drawing conclusions, and reasoning about sentiments in subjective texts. The text suggests various emotional tendencies among different people, which researchers can use to analyze the public's views or evaluations of a specific issue. We conducted the sentiment analysis via Google's Cloud Natural Language platform, which employs machine learning algorithms to reveal the emotional meaning of the text. The platform allows users to run sentiment analysis on uploaded texts through its application programming interface (API). After inputting text information, the model can determine the overall attitude expressed in the text, represented by a tone between −1.0 (negative) and +1.0 (positive). Scores in the negative range signify negative sentiments, while positive numbers denote positive sentiments. The greater the absolute value, the stronger the sentiment; the closer the number gets to zero, the more neutral the sentiment is (Garvey and Maskal 2020). The relevant research is further presented in Chapters 12 and 13 of this book.

5 Conclusion

Culture has long been a central concern across the social sciences. Since the cultural turn, two distinct approaches have shaped cultural research: on the one hand, qualitative researchers who focus on the hermeneutic approach emphasize the understanding and interpretation of cultural

[2] See https://nlp.stanford.edu/software/CRF-NER.html for details of this tool.

meanings, hoping to present the interaction between society and culture in depth through fieldwork and literature analysis, but are inevitably challenged by relativism; on the other hand, quantitative researchers who believe in the positivism of social science are committed to data analysis to ensure the objectivity of cultural research, but they are limited to small samples and individual-level analysis, ignoring the magnitude and continuity of culture. The reason for this phenomenon is that the abstract culture at the macro level cannot be observed and analyzed through microscopic investigations. In addition, the vast number of cultural forms that have emerged as material entities, such as fiction, historical archives, media, government documents, academic journals, etc., only allows the researcher to scan a limited amount of material in a short amount of time. In this case, the contribution of big data and machine learning technology is to provide indicators of cultural volumes that are difficult to be exhausted by traditional qualitative research and cultural characteristics that are difficult to be measured by quantitative research. Thus, researchers can extract topic structures or cultural information from cultural histories or databases spanning a huge time–space scale, construct measurable indicators of cultural meaning, and explore how explicit social structures influence implicit cultural features in a macro-distant reading.

This chapter does not reject traditional methods in cultural research but rather emphasizes the importance of big data and machine learning in opening new directions for the social sciences. Given the unstructured nature of vast amounts of cultural data, big data computing, which specializes in text mining, has a natural fit with cultural research. We call for a synthesis of traditional qualitative methods and emerging machine learning technologies for analysis, a data-driven approach that draws on the visualization tools and indicator descriptions of big data to generalize and discover sociocultural patterns in texts and form theories, or a quantitative calculation of unstructured text to realize the operationalization of cultural hidden indicators and empirical tests.

Nonetheless, big data and machine learning pose substantial methodological and epistemological challenges for social scientists. Although algorithms operate autonomously, every stage of the analytical process remains shaped by human decisions. Critical decisions such as the selection and curation of the corpus, the specifics of data preprocessing, the choice of a particular model, and the tuning of its hyperparameters (like the number of topics) are all subject to the researcher's discretion.

Each of these choices can alter the results to some extent. Furthermore, the outputs of unsupervised models, such as topic clusters or word embeddings, represent statistical patterns that require informed interpretation. Assigning meaningful social labels to abstract clusters of words is a fundamentally hermeneutic act that reintroduces a significant degree of subjectivity. Also, the lack of a ground truth makes model validation a profound challenge. Unlike supervised machine learning, where a model's predictive accuracy can be tested against known outcomes, there is no single correct thematic structure for a corpus. This makes it difficult to assess whether the result genuinely corresponds to meaningful, real-world cultural categories or are simply artifacts of the algorithm's statistical assumptions.

Computational approaches also raise ethical and political concerns. The large-scale use of digital traces and cultural archives involves issues of privacy and consent, as individuals may not expect their expressions to be permanently stored or analyzed. Algorithms may further reproduce structural biases already present in the data. For instance, when topic modeling is applied to the Tang poetry corpus, the dominance of male literati and the scarcity of women's voices and folk traditions mean that the results reproduce an already partial cultural record. When cultural models are extended beyond academia, they may also shape governance or platform practices in ways that constrain openness and diversity. These challenges do not diminish the value of computational approaches but highlight that methodological innovation must be accompanied by sustained ethical reflection and responsibility.

In an era of unprecedented cultural production and digital transformation, social computing offers significant potential to expand the scope of social scientific inquiry, reconstruct disciplinary discourse, and foster paradigm shifts. Yet its legitimacy depends not only on technical advancement but also on the social sciences' capacity to uphold ethical standards, address bias, and remain critically engaged with the cultures and societies they seek to understand.

References

Abbott, Andrew. 2007. Against narrative: A preface to lyrical sociology. *Sociological Theory* 25 (1): 67–99.

Alexander, Jeffrey C. 2003. *The meanings of social life*. Oxford: Oxford University Press.

Bailey, April H., Adina Williams, and Andrei Cimpian 2022. Based on billions of words on the internet, people = men. *Science Advances* 8 (13): eabm2463.

Baumard, Nicolas, Huillery Elise, Hyafil Alexandre, and Safra Lou. 2022. The cultural evolution of love in literary history. *Nature Human Behaviour* 6 (4): 506–522.

Blei, David M., Andrew Y. Ng, and Michael I. Jordan. 2003. Latent Dirichlet allocation. *Journal of Machine Learning Research* 3: 993–1022.

Bourdieu, Pierre 1984. *Distinction: A social critique of the judgement of taste.* Trans. Richard Nice, London: Routledge & Kegan Paul.

Bourdieu, Pierre. 1993. *The field of cultural production: Essays on art and literature, edited and introduced by Randal Johnson.* New York: Columbia University Press.

Chen, Yunsong, Fei Yan, Guangye He, and Wei Yan. 2020. The werther effect revisited: Do suicides in books predict actual suicides? *Poetics* 81: 101441.

Chen, Yunsong, Guangye He, and Fei Yan 2021. *Understanding China through big data: Applications of theory-oriented quantitative approaches.* Abingdon; New York: Routledge.

De La Fuente, Eduardo 2007. The "new sociology of art": Putting art back into social science approaches to the arts. *Cultural Sociology* 1 (3): 409–425.

Eberle, Thomas S. 2016. Qualitative cultural sociology. In *The Sage handbook of cultural sociology*, ed. David Inglis, et al., 237–254. London: Sage Publications.

Finkel, Jenny R., Trond Grenager, and Christopher Manning. 2005. Incorporating non-local information into information extraction systems by Gibbs sampling. In *Proceedings of the 43rd annual meeting of the association for computational linguistics* (ACL'05), 363–370.

Fromm, Erich. 1971. *Marx's concept of man.* New York: Frederick Ungar.

Garvey, Colin, and Chandler Maskal. 2020. Sentiment analysis of the news media on artificial intelligence does not support claims of negative bias against artificial intelligence. *Omics (Larchmont, N.Y.)*, 286–299.

Geertz, Clifford. 1973. *The interpretation of cultures: Selected essays.* New York: Basic Books.

Glaser, Barney G., and Anselm L. Strauss. 2017. *The discovery of grounded theory: Strategies for qualitative research.* New York: Aldine de Gruyter.

Harvey, Penny. 2009. Between narrative and number: The case of ARUP's 3D digital city model. *Cultural Sociology* 3 (2): 257–276.

Holt, Douglas B. 1997. Distinction in America? Recovering Bourdieu's theory of tastes from his critics. *Poetics* 25 (2): 3–120.

Jockers, Matthew L. 2013. *Macroanalysis: Digital methods and literary history.* Baltimore: University of Illinois Press.

Jockers, Matthew L., and David Mimno. 2013. Significant themes in 19th-century literature. *Poetics* 41 (6): 750–769.

Lee, Monica, and John Levi Martin. 2015. Coding, counting and cultural cartography. *American Journal of Cultural Sociology* 3 (1): 1–33.
Majima, Shinobu, and Niamh Moore. 2009. Introduction: Rethinking qualitative and quantitative methods. *Cultural Sociology* 3 (2): 203–216.
Marshall, Emily A. 2013. Defining population problems: Using topic models for cross-national comparison of disciplinary development. *Poetics* 41 (6): 701–724.
Mikolov, Tomas et al. 2013. Efficient estimation of word representations in vector space. arXiv:1301.3781.
Mohr, John W., and Petko Bogdanov. 2013. Introduction-topic models: What they are and why they matter. *Poetics* 41 (6): 545–569.
Nalisnick, Eric et al. 2016. Improving document ranking with dual word embeddings. In *Proceedings of the 25th International Conference Companion.*
Olick, Jeffrey K. 2010. What is "the relative autonomy of culture"? In *Handbook of cultural sociology*, ed. John R. Hall, et al., 97–108. London: Routledge.
Poster, Mark. 2010. The cultural turn: Language, globalization, and media. In *Handbook of cultural sociology*, ed. John R. Hall, et al., 45–46. London: Routledge.
Sewell Jr, William H. 2005. *Logics of history: Social theory and social transformation.* Chicago; London: University of Chicago Press.
Sherwood, Steven J. 1993. The British are coming...Again! The hidden agenda of "cultural studies". *Contemporary Sociology* 22 (3): 370–375.
Stevenson, Angus, eds. 2010. *Oxford dictionary of English.* Oxford University Press.
Tang, Guizhang. 2011. *Complete poetry collection of Tang Dynasty.* Beijing: Zhonghua Book Company (in Chinese).
Williams, Raymond. 1958. *Culture and society: 1780–1950.* New York: Columbia University Press.
Williams, Raymond. 1973. *The country and the city.* London: Chatto and Windus.
Willis, Paul E. 1977. *Learning to labour: How working class kids get working class jobs.* Farnborough, Hants: Saxon House.
Yao, Yao, et al. 2017. Sensing spatial distribution of urban land use by integrating points-of-interest and Google Word2Vec model. *International Journal of Geographical Information Science* 31 (4): 825–848.

PART II

Measuring the Unmeasurable

CHAPTER 4

Unspeakable Violence: Predicting the Incidence of Intimate Partner Violence

1 Introduction

Domestic violence refers to violence or other abusive behaviors that occur within the household and includes violence against partners, children, teenagers, and the elderly. Recently, increasing worldwide research attention has been focused on a type of domestic violence known as intimate partner violence (IPV) (Garcia-Moreno et al. 2006; Adams et al. 2012). IPV is typically defined as any behavior, such as physical attacks, sexual coercion, psychological abuse, or controlling behavior, that causes physical, psychological, or sexual harm to others in an intimate relationship, which is usually a marital relationship (Krug et al. 2002; Stewart and Chandra 2017). Research has shown that women are more likely than men to suffer from domestic violence, most often perpetrated by their male partners (Swan et al. 2008). According to the World Health Organization, in 2018, approximately 30% of women worldwide had experienced physical and/or sexual violence from an intimate partner or husband in the previous 12 months (World Health Organization 2021). In addition, the stress and anxiety caused by lockdowns during the coronavirus disease 2019 pandemic have led to an impending crisis of domestic violence (Chandan et al. 2020). In China studies using local samples have estimated that the incidence rate of IPV ranges from 20 to 25% (Xu et al. 2005), yet a nationwide estimate has not been determined.

A crucial problem faced by researchers aiming to empirically analyze IPV is the large amount of missing data. This problem is particularly

Y. Chen et al., *Machine Learning in Social Science*,
https://doi.org/10.1007/978-981-95-6465-1_4

pronounced in Asian societies, such as China, where traditional and patriarchal norms mean that women tend to conceal their partners' violence toward them and are reluctant to report IPV experiences. This is consistent with feminist theory, which posits that domestic violence is the result of a patriarchal system that enables men to control women and thus strengthen their dominant position in society (Brookman et al. 2017; Hamberger et al. 2017). Thus, if a culture overemphasizes aggressive masculinity and patriarchal norms, there is an increased probability that domestic violence that occurs within this society will not be reported, especially violence experienced by women (Mshweshwe 2020). Previous research has determined that there are several reasons why domestic violence is not reported, such as concerns about privacy, a fear of reprisal or stigmatization, or a desire to protect the offenders. Consequently, substantial portions of data on certain types of domestic violence remain missing, which means that data analyses yield systematic underestimates of the number of domestic violence cases. Thus, it is challenging for researchers and policymakers to determine the real incidence rate of domestic violence.

Thus far, only survey-based analyses have been used to estimate domestic violence (Cui et al. 2012), with missing data problems addressed by the use of listwise deletion or various imputation methods, such as mean imputation and multiple imputation. However, listwise deletion and mean imputation have been criticized as leading to biased or less accurate estimates. For example, the multiple imputation method, which has been widely used, is based on a missing at random (MAR) assumption that may not hold for domestic violence data, as victims may be too ashamed to admit having suffered from domestic violence (Felson et al. 2002). To solve this problem, the current study used advanced machine learning methods to interpolate missing data and thereby obtained accurate estimates of the percentages of Chinese women who have suffered from domestic violence. Machine learning methods have been proven to be more powerful than other methods for obtaining missing data, as the flexibility and complexity of these methods enable them to capture higher-order interactions between data and thus generate better predictions (Pantanowitz and Marwala 2009; Jerez et al. 2010; He et al. 2013). Thus, this chapter used six machine learning algorithms to analyze data from the Third Wave Survey on the Social Status of Women in China (TWSSSCW 2010) and to estimate the incidence rates of three types of IPV: physical violence, verbal violence, and cold violence.

2 Method

2.1 *Survey and Sample*

The data were obtained from the TWSSSCW 2010, the most recent nationally representative survey conducted by the All-China Women's Federation and the National Bureau of Statistics of China. It included a wide range of questions on family, gender relations, health and well-being, and domestic violence (including IPV). The TWSSSCW 2010 used multi-stage random stratified probability-proportional-to-size sampling to ensure that its sample was representative of the general population at the province/municipality, street, and neighborhood levels. The survey comprised a sample of 26,166 respondents, but due to the research question of our study, we limited our sample to women and men who were married. Thus, the sample we used in our analysis comprised 23,597 married women and men.

2.2 *Measures*

Three types of IPV were used as the dependent variables, namely physical violence, verbal violence, and cold violence. In the TWSSSCW 2010, respondents were asked: "Has your partner beaten you?", "Has your partner insulted you?", and "Has your partner constantly ignored you?" Responses were recorded on a 4-point scale ("never," "occasionally," "sometimes," or "often"). We dichotomized the three variables to measure whether respondents suffered IPV. As frequencies expressed as "occasionally," "sometimes," or "often" are similar and vague in meaning, we collapsed these frequencies into one category. Table 1 shows that 1.22% of men and 2.83% of women reported experiencing physical violence; 4.88% of men and 6.32% of women reported experiencing verbal violence; and 8.46% of men and 9.49% of women reported experiencing cold violence. The overall percentage of missing data was 6.95%. Figure 1 shows the demographic distributions of missing data on the respondents' experiences of IPV. Respondents who were female, from urban areas, and had low education levels were more likely not to have supplied complete responses to questions on IPV than other female respondents, which suggested that IPV data were more likely to be missing from the answers of this subgroup of respondents.

To estimate the missing values, we analyzed the values of 611 variables from the dataset that covered a wide range of topics related to aspects

Table 1 Descriptive statistics of IPV and missing cases

	All sample	*Men*	*Women*
Physical violence (%)			
No	95.95	46.57	49.38
Yes	4.05	1.22	2.83
Verbal violence (%)			
No	88.79	42.90	45.90
Yes	11.21	4.88	6.32
Cold violence (%)			
No	82.05	39.34	42.71
Yes	17.95	8.46	9.49
Proportion of missing cases (%)	6.95	2.41	4.54
Observations (n)	23,597	11,063	12,534

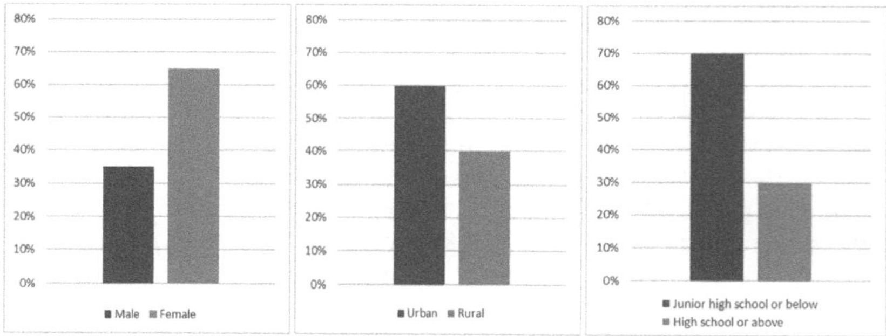

Fig. 1 Social and demographic distributions of cases with missing IPV data

such as respondents' health, educational levels, employment status, family backgrounds, gender ideology, leisure activities, political participation, religious affiliation, housework hours, and insurance enrollment status.

2.3 *Imbalanced Data Problem*

As shown in Table 1, the dataset was highly imbalanced, as only a small proportion of respondents reported having experienced IPV. For instance, in the case of physical IPV, there are 21,067 class 0 samples indicating that individuals were never beaten by their spouses, but the class 1 samples, which represent those who were beaten, total only 889, accounting for approximately 4% of the class 0 samples. Similar imbalances were observed for verbal and psychological abuse. In the machine learning process, the majority class often dominates the learning process, making classifiers difficult to recognize minority classes. For example, if a learning algorithm were to adopt a simple approach and predict all 21,956 samples as class 0, indicating no spousal abuse, it would achieve an accuracy of 96%. However, this contradicts our goal of identifying genuine cases of IPV. Therefore, although ignoring the minority class is economical and efficient in algorithm processing of data imbalances, the resulting model bias in practical applications is immeasurable.

It is necessary to use strategies before applying machine learning algorithms to mitigate the degree of data imbalance, generally in two main directions: (1) increasing the number of minority class samples through oversampling and (2) reducing the majority class samples through under sampling. Since each method has its advantages and disadvantages depending on different application scenarios and data structures, we chose typical methods such as Random Over Sampler and SMOTE for oversampling, Random Under Sampler-ensemble and K-means for under sampling, and SMOTE-ENN, which combines both oversampling and under sampling, for model training. We then compared the performance of each model. The 21,956 non-missing samples were split into a training set and a validation set in a 70%–30% ratio, maintaining the original dataset's distribution of two categories of IPV in both the validation set and training set. The training set was then resampled, and a Random Forest algorithm was used to train the classifier, with the validation set used to measure the classifier's generalization effect.

Table 2 exemplifies the performance of models under different sampling methodologies using "physical violence" as a reference. In terms of evaluation metrics, we calculated accuracy, recall, confusion matrices, AUC values, ROC curves, and detection error tradeoff (DET) curves for a comprehensive assessment of each model. Accuracy (Acc) represents the proportion of correctly predicted samples out of the total samples, providing a straightforward reflection of model prediction effectiveness. However, it lacks significance in scenarios of imbalanced sample distribution. Recall (Rec), also known as the true positive rate, reflects the proportion of positive cases correctly identified among all actual positives. The confusion matrix visually contrasts the discrepancies between actual outcomes and predictions, where TN, FN, FP, and TP respectively stand for true negatives, false negatives, false positives, and true positives. The

ROC curve illustrates the tradeoff between the true positive rate and the false positive rate across different thresholds, with the AUC ranging from 0.5 to 1, where higher values indicate better model performance. Similarly, the DET curve plots the false negative rate against the false positive rate at various thresholds, with a smaller AUC indicating a lower overall error probability and thus superior model performance. Since ROC and AUC are used to evaluate the overall performance of classifiers and are less sensitive to class imbalances, they are suited for the algorithms used in this study. In contrast, Rec is more informative than Acc when focusing on class 1 samples, especially when their number is significantly lower than that of class 0 samples. Accordingly, in this research, we prioritized AUC and Rec as the main evaluation metrics, supplemented by Acc and the confusion matrix, to select the best-performing machine learning classification model.

Regarding accuracy, the SMOTE algorithm performed the best, achieving accuracies of 0.96 and 0.95 in the test and validation sets, respectively; SMOTE-ENN followed closely but also showed good results with 0.95 in the training set and 0.94 in the validation set. However, the recall of SMOTE was only 0.33 in the training set and 0.16 in the validation set, and SMOTE-ENN also underperformed, as evidenced in the confusion matrix where these two algorithms frequently misclassified class 1 samples as class 0. This suggests that although these sampling models addressed the issue of sample balance, the trained models still tended to neglect minority class samples and erroneously categorize cases into

Table 2 Fitness statistics for the dependent variable "physical violence" in various sampling methods

	T-Acc	*V-Acc*	*T-Rec*	*V-Rec*	*TN*	*FN*	*FP*	*TP*
ROS	0.88	0.85	0.95	0.53	5457	863	126	141
SMOTE	0.96	0.95	0.33	0.16	6229	91	224	43
RUS-ensemble	0.72	0.71	0.95	0.77	4499	1821	62	205
K-means	0.28	0.27	1.00	0.96	1543	4777	11	256
SMOTE-ENN	0.95	0.94	0.47	0.25	6096	224	200	67

Note T-Acc = accuracy in training set, V-Acc = accuracy in validation set, T-Rec = recall in training set, V-Rec = recall in validation set. TN = true negative, FN = false negative, FP = false positive, TP = true positive, ROS = random oversampling method, SMOTE = synthetic minority oversampling technique, RUS-ensemble = random under sampling ensemble method, SMOTE-ENN = SMOTE-edited nearest neighbor method the majority class. In terms of recall, the K-means method exhibited the highest recall, reaching 1 and 0.96 in the test and training sets, respectively, but its accuracy was only 0.28. The confusion matrix also indicated that this classifier erroneously predicted a large number of class 0 samples as class 1. ROS sampling showed good accuracy and recall in the training set, but the validation set recall was not satisfactory. Overall, the classifier under RUS-ensemble sampling exhibited the best overall performance, with an accuracy of 0.72 and a recall of 0.95 in the training set, and accuracies of 0.71 and recalls of 0.77 in the validation set, showing a relatively even prediction performance across categories in the confusion matrix.

Figure 2 displays the ROC and DET curves for "Physical Violence" under different sampling methods. The ROC curves in the left graph lie well above the diagonal, indicating that predictions made by the algorithms significantly outperform random predictions; the classifier under RUS-ensemble sampling achieves the largest area. The DET curve on the right also shows that RUS-ensemble sampling yields the fewest errors. Therefore, in subsequent predictions, we employ the Random Under Sampler-ensemble method to train our models. We randomly select an equal number of majority class samples as there are minority class samples, combine them with all minority class samples, and train a classifier. This process is repeated 500 times, training 500 classifiers in total, and using these 500 base classifiers to predict each case, yielding 500 outcomes. Ultimately, a majority voting method is applied to adopt the most frequently occurring class from the predictions as the final classification for each case.

2.4 Algorithm and Parameter Selection

Building upon the Random Under Sampler-ensemble sampling technique, we compared the performance of six classification algorithms: Random Forest, AdaBoost (Adaptive Boosting Ensemble), Gaussian Naïve Bayes, Support Vector Machine (SVM), Logistic Regression, and Neural Network. We continued to use the question "Has your spouse ever beaten you?" as a case study, partitioning the 21,956 non-missing samples into training and validation sets in a 70%–30% split. Table 3 presents the model evaluation metrics for "Physical Violence" under different algorithms, and Fig. 3 displays the corresponding ROC and DET curves.

Random Forest achieved an accuracy of 0.75 and a recall of 1 on the training set, and an accuracy of 0.71 and a recall of 0.75 on the validation

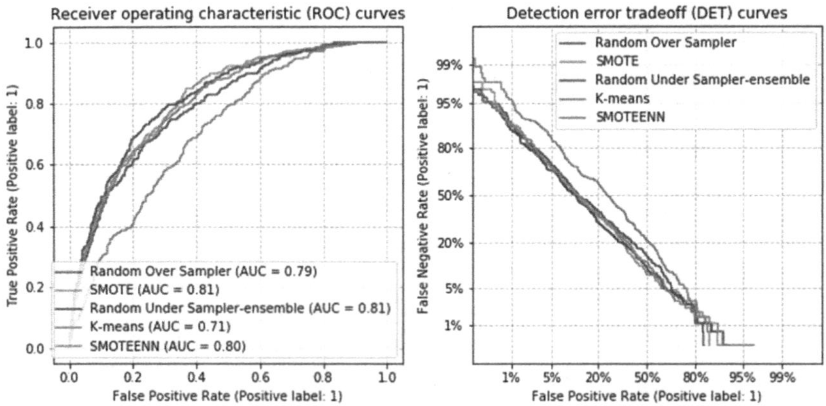

Fig. 2 ROC and DET curves for different sampling methods for the dependent variable "physical violence"

Table 3 Fitness statistics for the dependent variable "physical violence" in various algorithms

	T-Acc	*V-Acc*	*T-Rec*	*V-Rec*	*AUC*	*Proportions*
Random Forest	0.75	0.71	1	0.75	0.81	7.10%
AdaBoost	0.80	0.79	0.81	0.63	0.80	5.38%
Gaussian NB	0.58	0.58	0.86	0.72	0.71	7.00%
SVM	0.82	0.80	0.88	0.58	0.81	7.73%
Logistic	0.79	0.77	0.86	0.59	0.78	6.45%
Neural network	0.82	0.78	1.00	0.58	0.79	10.59%

Note T-Acc = accuracy in training set, V-Acc = accuracy in validation set, T-Rec = recall in training set, V-Rec = recall in validation set, AUC = Area Under the ROC Curve, Proportions = physical violence rate in full data

set. It also exhibited greater explanatory power and a lower error rate on the ROC and DET curves compared to the other models, demonstrating generally better performance. The SVM algorithm's AUC was equivalent to that of Random Forest at 0.81, and it also showed a higher accuracy. However, its recall on the validation set was only 0.58, indicating that the combination of this algorithm and the resampling method did not resolve the algorithmic bias caused by data imbalance. AdaBoost was close to Random Forest, with a slightly higher accuracy and a slightly lower

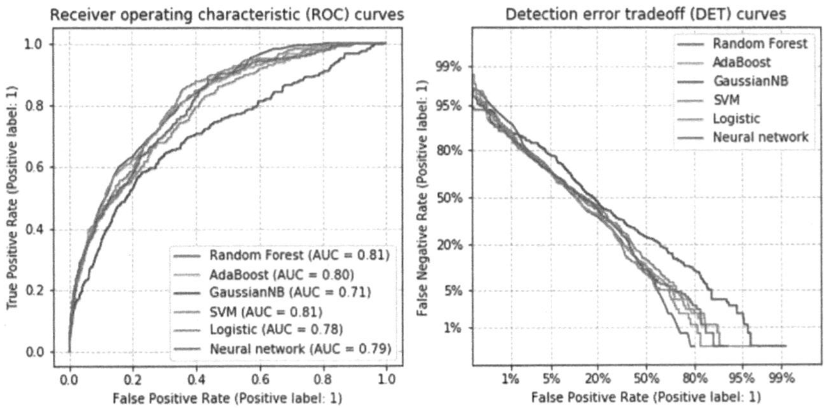

Fig. 3 ROC and DET curves for different algorithms for the dependent variable "physical violence"

recall, and its AUC value under the ROC curve was marginally lower than that of Random Forest. Gaussian NB was the least satisfactory among the six algorithms; the confusion matrix showed that it incorrectly predicted nearly half of the class 1 samples as class 0, yielding the lowest AUC value at 0.71 and the highest error rate under the DET curve. Both Logistic Regression and Neural Network had generally lower recall rates in the validation set, at 0.59 and 0.58 respectively, with average AUC values of 0.78 and 0.79. Taken together, considering all evaluation metrics comprehensively, we propose to employ the Random Forest algorithm for the final prediction of missing values.

The Random Forest algorithm is a supervised machine learning method for classification. It generates an ensemble of decision trees, and these then vote for the most popular class. The growth of each tree in the ensemble is governed by random vectors. First, a random vector Θk is generated for the kth tree; it is independent of the previous random vectors Θ1,..., Θk−1, but has the same distribution. Then, a tree is grown using the training set and Θk, which results in a classifier h (x, Θk). After a large number of decision trees have been generated, these trees vote for the most popular class. Thus, a Random Forest algorithm is a classifier that consists of a set of tree-structured classifiers {h (x, Θk), k = 1,...}, where {Θk} are independent identically distributed random vectors and each tree casts a unit vote for the most popular class at input x (Breiman

2001). This can be expressed by the following formula:

$$Hx = \arg\max \sum_{i=1}^{k} I(h_i(x) = Y)$$

where $H(x)$ represents the Random Forest model, $h_i(x)$ is a single tree-structured classifier, and Y is the output variable or target variable.

Constructing a Random Forest classifier involves tuning numerous hyperparameters. Although Scikit-learn provides default settings for this classifier, tailoring training hyperparameters specifically for the dataset can significantly enhance model performance. The objective of hyperparameter tuning is to balance the bias and variance of the classifier ensemble within reasonable limits. For Random Forest, increasing the number of decision trees (n estimators) can substantially reduce the overall model variance without affecting the bias and variance of individual sub-models, although there is a ceiling effect on performance improvements. Considering computational efficiency, we increased the number of sub-models from the default value of 100 to 500. For each sub-decision tree within the Random Forest, reducing the maximum number of features considered during splits (max features) introduces additional randomness into the model, which decreases the correlation between sub-models and enhances generalization capability, although too few features can increase the model's bias. Furthermore, a deeper maximum tree depth (max depth) results in more complex sub-models, lowering the overall model bias but potentially increasing the variance among sub-models or leading to overfitting.

Thus, we employed a grid search method to identify the optimal hyperparameter settings within a specific range. We set the "maximum number of features" between 20 and 45 and "maximum tree depth" between 5 and 30, training a model at every five-unit interval, producing 36 different hyperparameter combinations. To avoid the randomness inherent in proportional division of test and validation sets, we applied a more rigorous ten-fold cross-validation approach. The selection criterion for the optimal model was based on the composite evaluation metric, the AUC value.

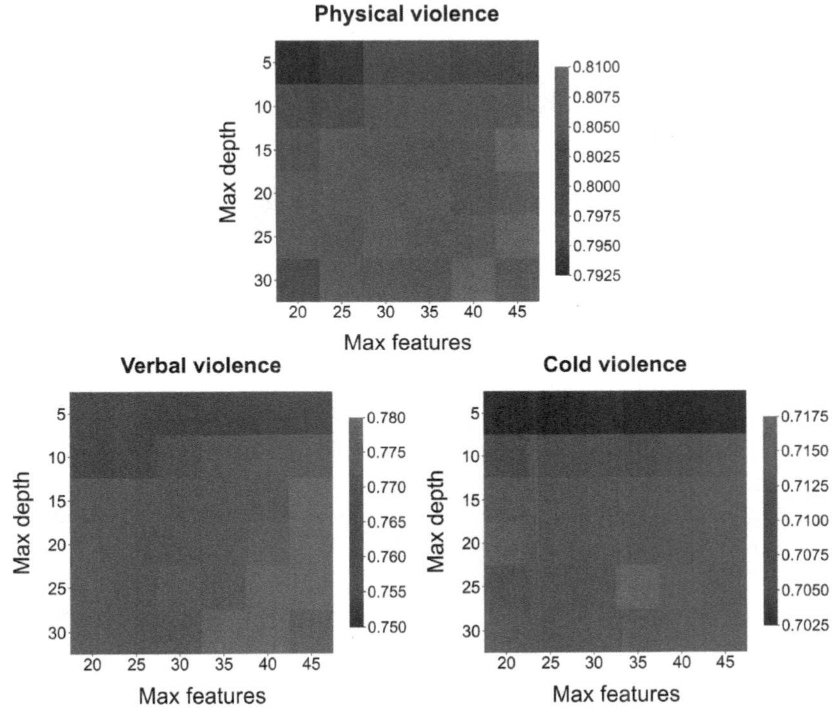

Fig. 4 AUC metrics for different hyperparameter settings of the Random Forest algorithm

Figure 4 displays the grid search results for three different issues, with each grid representing a hyperparameter combination. The color of each grid indicates the average AUC value of the ten-fold cross-validated model under that hyperparameter setting, with lighter colors denoting better model performance. For "Physical Violence," the optimal hyperparameters were a maximum depth of 25 and maximum features of 45, achieving an average AUC value of 0.811. For "Verbal Violence," the combination of a maximum depth of 20 and maximum features of 45 yielded the highest average AUC value of 0.781. For "Cold violence," the best performance was observed with a maximum depth of 25 and maximum features of 35, where the model achieved an average AUC value of 0.719.

3 Results

Table 4 shows that the Random Forest classifier analyzed 1,641 missing cases of physical violence, of which 854 and 787 were classified as "No" and "Yes," respectively. Thus, the incidence rate of physical violence was 7.10% in the data imputed via the Random Forest algorithm, which was greater than the rate (4.05%) in the original raw dataset (i.e., without imputation). Similarly, the Random Forest classifier analyzed 1,643 missing cases of verbal violence and classified 860 and 783 cases as "No" and "Yes," respectively. This equated to an incidence rate of verbal violence of 13.74%, which was greater than the original incidence rate of 11.21%. Finally, the Random Forest classifier analyzed 1,645 missing cases of cold violence and classified 546 and 1,099 cases as "No" and "Yes," respectively. This equated to an incidence rate of cold violence of 21.35%, which was greater than the original incidence rate of 17.95%.

Figure 5 shows the joint distributions of IPV in different sex groups and confirms that the missing data imputed by the Random Forest algorithm revealed that there were much higher incidence rates of IPV, especially among women, than previously determined. This suggests that the incidence rates of IPV may be underestimated if missing data are not considered. After the analysis of the dataset that contained the imputed

Table 4 Fitness statistics and predicted outcomes of the Random Forest algorithm

	Physical violence	*Verbal violence*	*Cold violence*
T-Acc	0.75	0.77	0.86
V-Acc	0.71	0.68	0.63
T-Rec	1	1	1
V-Rec	0.75	0.72	0.68
AUC	0.81	0.78	0.72
Predicted frequencies			
No	854	860	546
Yes	787	783	1099
Proportions in non-missing data	4.05%	11.21%	17.95%
Proportions in predicted missing data	47.96%	47.65%	66.81%
Proportions in full data	7.10%	13.74%	21.35%

Note T-Acc = accuracy in training set; V-Acc = accuracy in validation set; T-Rec = recall in training set; V-Rec = recall in validation set; AUC = area under the ROC curve

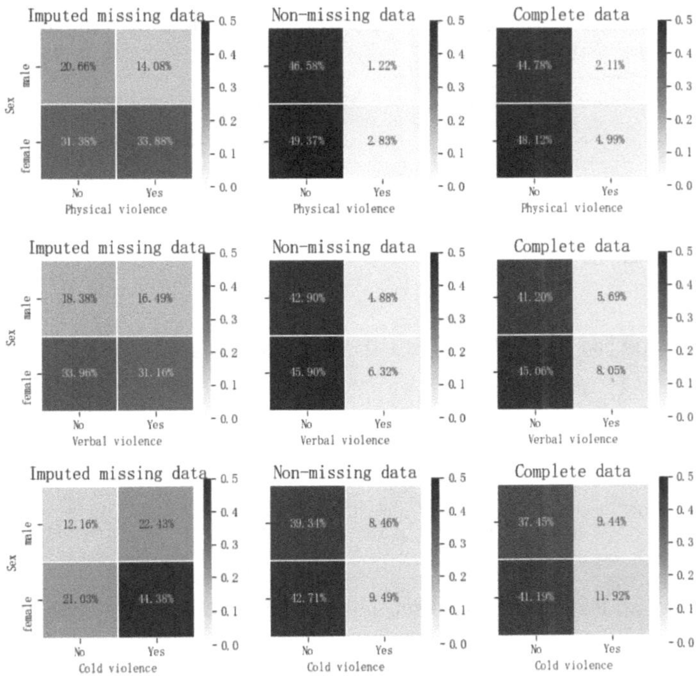

Fig. 5 Joint probability distributions of sex and IPV

missing data, the incidence rate of physical violence increased from 2.83% to 4.99% for women, and from 1.22% to 2.11% for men; the incidence rate of verbal violence increased from 6.32% to 8.05% for women, and from 4.88% to 5.69% for men; and the incidence rate of cold violence increased from 9.49% to 11.92% for women and from 8.46% to 9.43% for men.

4 Robustness and Heterogeneity Analyses

To test the robustness of our findings, we examined whether using different training sets would yield similar results. Previous research has shown that the tendency of respondents to report IPV is associated with their gender ideology. A more patriarchal ideology holds that men are more capable than women, and thus men should predominate in roles of

Table 5 Results from the Random Forest algorithm processing of different training sets

Training data	*Training sample*	*Physical violence*			*Verbal violence*			*Cold violence*		
		Men	*Women*	*Total*	*Men*	*Women*	*Total*	*Men*	*Women*	*Total*
Original incomplete data	–	1.22%	2.83%	4.05%	4.88%	6.32%	11.21%	8.46%	9.49%	17.95%
Complete data with imputations	21,956	2.11%	4.99%	7.10%	5.69%	8.05%	13.74%	9.43%	11.92%	21.35%
Complete data, excluding respondents with patriarchal gender ideology	18,290	2.23%	5.31%	7.54%	5.80%	8.38%	14.18%	9.31%	11.82%	21.13%

leadership and authority. Consequently, men and women who cleave to a patriarchal gender ideology are more likely to conceal having suffered IPV: men due to fear of stigmatization, and women due to their desire to protect the offenders. We used the following question to measure patriarchal gender ideology: "Do you think that women are less capable than men?" We assumed that respondents who answered in the affirmative tended to have a patriarchal gender ideology and were therefore more likely to provide unreliable answers to the IPV questions. We therefore excluded this group of respondents, and repeated our analyses using the Random Forest algorithm. Reassuringly, the results were highly consistent with those of the main analysis (see Table 5).

5 Conclusion

In recent years, the problem of domestic violence, especially IPV, has received increasing attention from academics and policymakers worldwide, as it is regarded as an important predictor of couples' health, well-being, and quality of life. However, missing data on certain types of domestic violence presents a substantial challenge for researchers performing IPV studies. The pattern of these missing data is missing not at random because these missing data are largely related to IPV. For example, people may fail to disclose having suffered IPV due to concerns about privacy, a fear of reprisal or stigmatization, or a desire to protect the offenders. Therefore, the traditional methods used to deal with datasets that are missing data, such as listwise deletion and multiple imputation, are not suitable for dealing with datasets that are missing IPV data because these methods are based on missing completely at random or missing at random assumptions. Indeed, we found that the incidence rates of physical, verbal, and cold violence were underestimated if we performed listwise deletion of cases with missing values prior to analysis. Thus, we used innovative machine learning methods to predict the missing data on the incidence rates of three types of IPV: physical violence, verbal violence, and cold violence.

We therefore compared the performance of various machine learning methods and selected the optimal method—the Random Forest algorithm—to impute missing data. We found that analysis of datasets containing imputed data led to increased incidence rates of physical violence (7.10%), verbal violence (13.74%), and cold violence (21.35%), compared to those obtained from datasets without imputed data (4.05%, 11.21%, and 17.95%, respectively).

These results highlight the necessity and advantages of using machine learning methods to address the missing data problem in IPV research. This chapter reveals that more effective tools must be designed to enable the accurate estimation of incidence rates of domestic violence and demonstrates the need for more empirical research to further advance the understanding of IPV, using machine learning to obtain missing data.

References

Adams, Adrienne E., et al. 2012. The impact of intimate partner violence on low-income women's economic well-being: The mediating role of job stability. *Violence against Women* 18 (12): 1345–1367.

Breiman, Leo. 2001. Random forests. *Machine Learning* 45: 5–32.

Brookman, Fiona, Edward R. Maguire, and Mike Maguire, eds. 2017. *The handbook of homicide*. Wiley.

Chandan, Joht Singh et al. 2020. COVID-19: A public health approach to manage domestic violence is needed. *The Lancet Public Health* 5 (6): e309.

Claudia, Garcia-Moreno., et al. 2006. Prevalence of intimate partner violence: Findings from the WHO multi-country study on women's health and domestic violence. *The Lancet* 368 (9543): 1260–1269.

Cui, Yi et al. 2012. A current situation survey and influential factors of domestic violence in seven provinces and cities of China. *Chinese Journal of Clinical Psychology* 20 (3): 360–362.

Felson, Richard B., et al. 2002. Reasons for reporting and not reporting domestic violence to the police. *Criminology* 40 (3): 617–648.

Hamberger, L. Kevin., Sadie E. Larsen, and Amy Lehrner. 2017. Coercive control in intimate partner violence. *Aggression and Violent Behavior* 37: 1–11.

He, Haibo, Yuan Cao, Yi Cao, and Jinyu Wen. 2013. Ensemble learning for wind profile prediction with missing values. *Neural Computing and Applications* 22 (2): 287–294.

Jerez, José M., et al. 2010. Missing data imputation using statistical and machine learning methods in a real breast cancer problem. *Artificial Intelligence in Medicine* 50 (2): 105–115.

Krug, Etienne G., et al. 2002. The world report on violence and health. *The Lancet* 360 (9339): 1083–1088.

Linda, Mshweshwe. 2020. Understanding domestic violence: Masculinity, culture, traditions. *Heliyon* 6 (10): e05334.

Pantanowitz, Adam, and Marwala, Tshilidzi. 2009. Missing data imputation through the use of the Random Forest algorithm. In *Advances in computational intelligence*, 53–62. Berlin, Heidelberg: Springer.

Stewart, Donna E., and Prabha S. Chandra. 2017. WPA international competency-based curriculum for mental health providers on intimate partner violence and sexual violence against women. *World Psychiatry* 16 (2): 223.

Swan, Suzanne C., et al. 2008. A review of research on women's use of violence with male intimate partners. *Violence and Victims* 23 (3): 301–314.

World Health Organization. 2021. Violence against women prevalence estimates, 2018: global, regional and national prevalence estimates for intimate partner violence against women and global and regional prevalence estimates for non-partner sexual violence against women.

Xu, Xiao, et al. 2005. Prevalence of and risk factors for intimate partner violence in China. *American Journal of Public Health* 95 (1): 78–85.

CHAPTER 5

Hidden Identities: Predicting Sexual Minority Orientation Among Youth

1 Introduction

Across the globe, rights movements for sexual minorities have advanced at an unprecedented pace over the past few decades in Western countries and many other regions (Ghaziani et al. 2016). Despite this, individuals with sexual minority identities in most cultures are relegated to lower status and even marginalized as a distinct social group. Compared to sexual majorities, members of sexual minorities are segregated geographically (Gross 2012), socially, and psychologically, and are constantly exposed to the discriminatory tastes of the heterosexual majority (USAID 2014; Lee et al. 2016; Wang et al. 2019).

While most of the existing literature on sexual minorities has been conducted in the Western world, research focusing on sexual minorities in China is relatively scarce (UNDP 2016). Owing to negative stereotypes and devaluation, sexual minority identities often result in antipathy (i.e., disgust), and even blame attributions and justification of unfair social treatment (O'Donohue and Caselles 1993; USAID 2014; UNDP 2016). Such long-standing stigmas and moral condemnation make individuals with sexual minority orientation reluctant to disclose their inherent sexual orientation, leading to a high percentage of missing values and downward-biased estimates in information obtained from traditional social surveys. For example, in the U.S., the relevant statistics from the Centers for Disease Control and Prevention (CDC) have shown that an estimated 4% of adults identify as members of a sexual minority.

Y. Chen et al., *Machine Learning in Social Science*,
https://doi.org/10.1007/978-981-95-6465-1_5

However, if we look at items relevant to same-sex sexual behavior and same-sex attraction, the number of individuals who reported having same-sex sexual behavior experience, and same-sex attraction has increased to about 8.2% and 11%, respectively (Gates 2011). This, to some degree, implies that the question relevant to sexual minority orientation may suffer from severe underestimation. A report from the American College Health Association showed that in 2006, 10% out of 33,000 undergraduates were identified as sexual minorities in the U.S. (Postsecondary National Policy Institute 2018). In China, the paucity of reliable data that can identify the sexual minority group and its associated needs contributes significantly to the invisibility of the sexual minority population in the eyes of academia as well as critical social programs (Cao and Lu 2014; Hu 2016; Xu et al. 2017).

To address the challenges of estimating the size of China's sexual minority population, this research, based on the Beijing College Students Panel Survey (BCSPS), aims to estimate the genuine percentage of sexual minorities among Chinese youth in Beijing using machine learning methods. We used Random Forest, an ensemble learning approach for classification and regression, to predict the sexual orientation of those who didn't respond to the survey question. Given that the size of sexual minorities is considerably smaller than that of heterosexual people, the standard Random Forest classifier tends to be biased toward the majority class. To mitigate the bias, we adopted repeated random subsampling methods (Khalilia et al. 2011). To evaluate model performance, we compared the results of bagging, boosting, Gaussian Naïve Bayes support vector machine (SVM), and Logistic Regression classifiers. Results from multiple machine learning classifiers and different sets of covariates generally show that the actual percentage of sexual minorities among Beijing college students is nearly twice as large as that obtained from traditional social survey data, such as the BCSPS. Through our research, we paid particular attention to protecting individuals' information security. All results that are presented in the paper reflect the group trend rather than personal traits.

2 Materials and Methods

2.1 Data

The analysis is based on the Beijing College Students Panel Survey (BCSPS) conducted by the Survey and Data Center of Renmin University in China. The first wave of data was collected in 2009. Using stratified random sampling, college students from 15 universities in Beijing were selected, with a response rate of around 93%. Since then, the follow-up surveys have been conducted each year until 2013. In the fourth-wave survey, there was a question relevant to respondents' sexual orientation. It asked the surveyed college students to report their sexual orientation and provided four items to choose from ("heterosexual," "homosexual," "bisexual," and "not sure"). As Table 1 shows, among the 4043 samples, 3684 students identified themselves as heterosexual and 115 identified themselves as sexual minorities (homosexual or bisexual), or belonging to a sexual minority. According to this, the percentage of sexual minorities among college students in Beijing is around 3.03% if we deleted 244 samples with missing values on sexual orientation (i.e., 156 declined to respond and 88 chose "not sure"). However, as mentioned above, many of the 244 students who did not explicitly respond to the question about their sexual orientation are very likely to be sexual minorities, given the lurking stigma toward sexual minorities in China (Wang et al. 2019).

The fourth wave of BCSPS contains 910 variables for 4043 respondents, providing comprehensive information about demographic characteristics, academic performance, and socioeconomic attributes, which offer us an opportunity to predict missing values on sexual orientation. However, including all 910 variables in the predicting models would

Table 1 The frequency and percentage for sexual orientation in the BCSPS

	Frequency	*Percentage (%)*	*Sexual minority rate (%)*
Heterosexual	3684	91.12	
Homosexual	49	1.21	3.03 (N = 3799)
Bisexual	66	1.63	
Not sure	88	2.18	Missing value
Refuse to answer	156	3.85	
Sum	N = 4043	100	

Table 2 Descriptive analysis of major demographic factors

Sex (Biological)	Freq	Percent	*University Tier*	Freq	Percent
Male	2124	52.54	Top 3 Universities	1150	28.44
Female	1919	47.46	Project 985 Universities	750	18.55
Ethnic Group	*Freq*	*Percent*	Project 211 Universities	686	16.97
Han Chinese	3588	88.99	Others	1457	36.04
Manchu	133	3.3	Current Age	*Freq*	*Percent*
Hui	94	2.33	$\leq$ 20 (Min = 19)	24	0.59
Mongol	48	1.19	21–23	2198	54.37
Others	180	4.45	24–26	1793	44.35
Party Affiliation	*Freq*	*Percent*	$\geq$ 27 (Max = 29)	28	0.69
Communist Party of China	1490	37.05	Hukou	*Freq*	*Percent*
Communist Youth League of China	2223	55.27	Urban Hukou	2894	71.58
Others	4	0.1	Rural Hukou	1128	27.9
No Party Affiliation	305	7.58	Unspecified Hukou	21	0.52

introduce substantial redundancy. Accordingly, we used a Lasso regression algorithm (Tibshirani 1996; Lantz 2015) to select 337 sexuality-related variables to perform prediction, including individual family background, educational performance, mental and physical health, as well as indices of social behavior, which, to a large degree, ensures the comprehensiveness of variables that could capture the differences in characteristics between individuals with sexual majority and minority orientation. As a robustness check, we also ran prediction models using all 910 predictors. Because of space constraints, we do not present the statistics of all predictors of sexual orientation, which are available upon request. Instead, in Table 2 we present the major demographics of the samples and other selected attributes.

2.2 *Imbalanced Problem*

As shown, the dataset is highly imbalanced with respect to sexual orientation, which is unsurprising because the percentage of sexual minorities is much smaller than that of heterosexual people worldwide. In our data, the imbalance ratio is approximately 1:32 (115/3684), and the percentage of sexual minorities is 3.03% (115/3799). If one is using a standard prediction algorithm, the highly imbalanced data may lead to under-prediction of the minority group because most classifiers assume that training and testing data are drawn from the same distribution. In this vein, it is not easy to prepare appropriate data for training and testing, which leads to a biased prediction (Provost 2000). Taking sexual orientation as an example, if 99% of people declare themselves to be heterosexual, a standard machine learning algorithm (such as a Naïve Bayes classifier or a decision tree) can hardly do better than the 99% accuracy achieved by a trivial classifier that labels everyone as heterosexual. That is, when applying machine learning on highly imbalanced datasets, the built-in goal to maximize the accuracy of the learning algorithm will inevitably under-predict the minority class, as this is the "intelligent" solution for the algorithm. To address this, a common practice is to rebalance the training sets by resampling, boosting, bagging, or conducting repeated random subsampling (Japkowicz and Stephen 2002).

In this chapter, we applied the repeated random subsampling approach to address the imbalanced data problem. That is, we partitioned the training data into subsamples using 6-split, 12-split, 24-split, and 32-split of the original sexual majority respondents, respectively. By doing so, each subsample ends up containing a less imbalanced data set than the original one (the one with an imbalance ratio of around 1:32). For the 6-split subsample, the number of sexual majority participants is 614 (the original number = 3684/6). As a result, the imbalance rate is 1:5.34 (115:(3684/6)). Similarly, for the 12-split subsample, the number of sexual majority participants is 307, and the imbalance ratio is 1:2.67 (115:(3684/12)). For the 24-split subsample, the number of sexual majority participants is 153 and the imbalance ratio is 1:1.33 (115:(3684/24)). Finally, the 32-split subsample contains an equal number of instances from the sexual minority and sexual majority (115:115), with the imbalance ratio being 1. Note that the 32-split approach is 1:1-resampling, following Khalilia, Chakraborty, and Popescu (Khalilia et al. 2011) by partitioning the training data into subsamples with each subsample containing half the sexual minority and half the sexual majority, except for the last subsample (in some cases). We also experimented with repeated random subsampling by replicating sexual minority cases six, twelve, and twenty-four times. This approach reduced the imbalance in each subsample compared with the original dataset. However, due to the introduced repeated samples, the overfitting problem emerged, so we did not present the relevant results in this chapter.

In Random Forest, a forest itself consists of an ensemble of decision trees which could output a classification, where the output is predicted using the mode of observations in the terminal nodes. In this chapter, the splitting decision is based on the Gini index, a measure of node purity. It is given by the following formula:

$$Gini = 1 - \sum\nolimits_{k=0}^{k} P_k{}^2$$

where P_k is the probability of being classified as class k in a node. Thus, the Gini index takes values in [0,1], where 0 indicates that all elements are of the same class. In decision tree construction, splits are chosen to minimize the Gini index. The Gini index measures the distribution of class labels in nodes. A smaller value of the Gini index suggests a purer node. A split is valid only when the Gini index for a child node is less than that for the parent node.

Random Forest has the reputation of being insensitive to the training hyperparameters (Palmer et al. 2007); to choose the maximum number of features for a split, we followed standard practice by taking the square root of the number of our variables ($18 \approx \sqrt{337}$) for each individual tree. We followed the rule of thumb to set 50 as the number of trees for the Random Forest algorithm.

2.3 *Sample Splitting*

In this chapter, we developed an N-fold cross-validation using the whole available BCSPS data. We chose 6, 12, 24, and 32 (1:1) as split times (T_i) to create an upgrade trend for the sexual minority rate. For each splitting turn, we first separated the samples for learning ($N_l = 3799$) and the samples for predicting ($N_p = 244$). And then, the learning sample was further divided into N_l sexual majority set ($N_{l0} = 3684$) and sexual minority set ($N_{l1} = 115$). For the sexual majority set, we randomly sorted the N_{l0} set and partitioned it into T_i subsamples. Every N_{l0} subsample has an equal number of unrepeated samples except the last N_{l0} subsamples of 24 and 32 splits (they contain 165 and 119 samples respectively). For the sexual minority set, the data points are sampled without replacement.

To generate subsamples for prediction, we combined each subsample from N_{l0} with N_{l1}. By doing this, each subsample of the sexual majority sample was selected once, while the sexual minority sample was selected T_i times. For each subsampling set, we randomly sorted the data and took

30% as the validation set, and the remaining 70% as the training set, where the 30/70 ratio was chosen by trial and error.

For each round, we trained the model on the training set and validated it on the validation set. Based on this, we predicted the missing sexual orientation in N_p samples using a "major voting" approach. That is, an individual would be labeled as a member of the sexual minority if that individual received more than half the votes among T_i subsamples for prediction. Otherwise, the individual would be classified as heterosexual. To make the final decision, the aforesaid process would be repeated 100 times, and each time a different random seed would be selected. In the end, to choose between the numbers of splits, the average ROC curve and the AUC for the classifier would have been calculated and compared. The analytical scheme is drawn in Fig. 1.

As mentioned before, we do two sets of predictions with RF, one using 337 predictors obtained from Lasso, and the other using all 910 predictors. To evaluate the performance of the Random Forest model, we compared the results of 24-split subsampling with the other five algorithms. We used the default hyperparameters for bagging, boosting, Naïve Bayes, and Logistic Regression. For SVM, the linear kernel was used. We

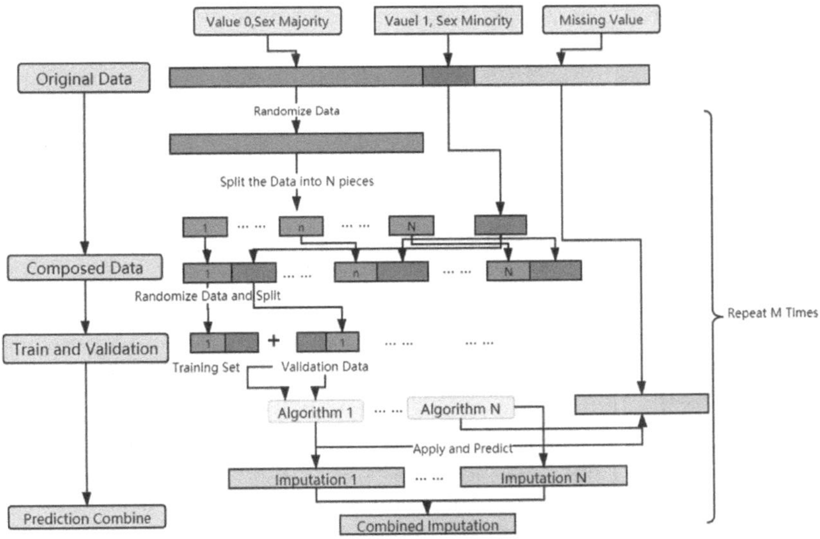

Fig. 1 Missing value imputation of sexual minority orientation

performed machine learning classification using the Scikit-Learn toolkit driven by Python.

Considering that sexual minorities are more likely to experience victimization and bullying and mental health difficulties globally due to the heavy stigma that surrounds them (Sterzing et al. 2014), students with sexual minority orientation may also have higher levels of psychological distress if compared to students with heterosexual orientation. Based on the newly imputed data, we then examine the psychological well-being and gender attitudes between college students with sexual majority orientation and sexual minority orientation.

3 Results

3.1 Primary Results

We present the results below in Table 3 using 337 variables to predict sexual orientation using a resampling Random Forest approach. As seen from the tables below, when using the 6-split subsample, the results of the Random Forest prediction show 43 out of the 244 respondents who did not report their sexual orientation are likely to be sexual minorities. As for the 12-split and 24-split subsamples, the Random Forest approach inferred that 78 and 116 out of 244 vacancy samples are likely to be sexual minorities. Note that the results from the 24-split experiment are obtained from a relatively balanced number of sexual minority and majority cases across all training sets. When it comes to the 32 splits experiment using fully balanced data (115 vs. 115), the Random Forest approach inferred that 131 of them are likely to be sexual minorities.

According to the metrics, the Random Forest predictors tend to obtain higher accuracy for the sexual majority samples in the presence of highly imbalanced data. For example, the validation accuracy is above 0.976 when fitting the Random Forest model onto the original dataset, while its counterpart of the 32-split subsample is merely 0.633. Meanwhile, the failed prediction of sexual orientation for the sexual minority group decreased as the split number increased. When it comes to the no-split experiment, the ratio of mistakenly predicting sexual minority people as sexual majority people is as high as 29.6% (=34/115). In contrast, the ratio decreased to 7.9% (=9/115) when using the 32-split data.

Considering that many sexual minorities were most likely to withhold their sexual orientation, and that the Random Forest algorithm

Table 3 Results from Random Forest predictors using different splitting strategies (337 control variables)

Random Forest	*Maj: Min*	*Majority = 0 (N = 3684)*		*Minority = 1 (N = 115)*		*Vacancy (N = 244)*	
	(Mean)	*0*	*1*	*0*	*1*	*0*	*1*
No split	3684:115	3684	0	34	81	223	21
6 splits	614:115	610	4	26	89	201	43
12 splits	307:115	301	6	14	101	166	78
24 splits	153:115	145	8	8	107	128	116
32 splits (1:1)	115:115	107	8	9	106	113	131

Random Forest	*Train Acc*	*Val Acc*	*Train F1*	*Val F1*	*AUC*
No split	0.9947	0.9763	0.9537	0.4940	0.9568
6 splits	0.9902	0.8322	0.9810	0.5647	0.9735
12 splits	0.9968	0.7843	0.9960	0.6327	0.9788
24 splits	0.9954	0.7134	0.9953	0.6865	0.9858
32 splits (1:1)	0.9985	0.6334	0.9985	0.6276	0.9822

relies more on the information of control variables rather than adjusting strategy to make accurate predictions when the data are more balanced in terms of sexual orientation, we adopt the results obtained from 24 splits. This choice is further supported by key validation statistics, including a higher AUC and F1 score. In this vein, the corresponding estimated percentage of sexual minorities among Beijing college students is 5.71% (= (115 + 116)/4043) rather than 3.03%. Therefore, the original estimation of the rate of sexual minorities among Beijing college students based on traditional surveys is nearly half of the actual value, which is substantially downward-biased.

3.2 *Robustness Check*

To assess the robustness of the results, we also used all 910 variables to predict sexual orientation, and report the relevant results in Table 4. Comparing the results obtained from the 910 variables in Table 4 with those from the 337 variables in Table 3, we found that, overall, the predicted frequency of suspected sexual minorities is slightly lower than that reflected in Table 3. As Table 4 shows, in the 6-split subsample, there are 26 suspected sexual minorities among 244 respondents who did not report their sexual orientation. When further using the 12-, 24-, and 32-split subsamples, the Random Forest approach inferred that 54, 108, and 128 of 244 missing cases, respectively, were likely to be sexual minorities, respectively.

In terms of validation accuracy of the Random Forest model and the ratio of the false positive of heterosexual people, we observe that the validation accuracy of the Random Forest predictors using the entire variable set on the original dataset is 0.965, which is lower compared with the Random Forest using 337 variables. Correspondingly, the ratio of mistakenly predicting suspected sexual minorities as sexual majorities is a bit higher and reaches 0.322 (=37/115). Furthermore, looking at the Random Forest results on the 32-split subsamples, these two numbers are 0.661 and 0.087 (=10/115), respectively.

By comparing the AUC and Val F1 results across different splits of subsamples, the 24-split is still preferred. Although the AUC of 24-split is slightly smaller than the 12-split, the difference (0.0015) is negligible. Moreover, AUC is problematic in highly imbalanced data (this circumstance). So F1 score should be given more weight. Therefore, based on the Random Forest results obtained from the 24-split, the corresponding

Table 4 Results from Random Forest predictors using different splitting strategies (910 control variables)

Random Forest	*Maj: Min*	*Majority = 0 (N = 3684)*		*Minority = 1 (N = 115)*		*Vacancy (N = 244)*	
	(Mean)	*0*	*1*	*0*	*1*	*0*	*1*
No split	3684:115	3684	0	37	78	244	0
6 splits	614:115	614	0	28	87	218	26
12 splits	307:115	305	2	18	97	190	54
24 splits	153:115	145	8	10	105	136	108
32 splits (1:1)	115:115	145	8	10	105	116	128

Random Forest	*Train Acc*	*Val Acc*	*Train F1*	*Val F1*	*AUC*
No split	0.9967	0.9645	0.9690	0.4910	0.9305
6 splits	0.9920	0.8379	0.9845	0.4818	0.9723
12 splits	0.9953	0.7824	0.9942	0.5536	0.9824
24 splits	0.9980	0.6611	0.9980	0.6177	0.9809
32 splits (1:1)	0.9997	0.6076	0.9997	0.6032	0.9787

percentage of suspected sexual minorities among Beijing college students is 5.52% (= (115 + 108)/4043).

To cross-validate the results, we also used and compared the results from Bagging, AdaBoost, Gaussian NB, SVM, and Logistic Regression methods with the results from the Random Forest approach. For brevity, we only present the results obtained from the 24-split subsamples with 337 control variables (the results from the other types of subsamples are available upon request). As shown in Table 5, by applying these competitive classifiers, the estimated percentage of suspected sexual minorities among Beijing college students ranges from 3.03% to 5.96%. The smallest estimate is generated by SVM. As mentioned earlier, the data are highly imbalanced in terms of sexual orientation; an SVM classifier trained on a dataset as such often produces models that are biased toward the majority class. Accordingly, as anticipated, almost no people are classified into a sexual minority among the 244 non-respondents using SVM. The largest estimate is generated by a boosting classifier, followed by a bagging classifier, where an estimated 126 and 116 individuals are likely to be sexual minorities, respectively.

Table 5 Comparing bagging, boosting, Gaussian NB, and SVM (24 splits subsample 337 control variables)

Algorithms	*Maj: Min*	*Majority = 0 (N = 3684)*		*Minority = 1 (N = 115)*		*Vacancy (N = 244)*	
	(Mean)	*0*	*1*	*0*	*1*	*0*	*1*
Random Forest	*153:115*	*145*	*8*	*8*	*107*	*128*	*116*
Bagging	153:115	145	8	9	106	128	116
AdaBoost	153:115	131	22	24	91	118	126
Gaussian NB	153:115	138	15	99	16	218	26
SVM	153:115	153	0	19	96	244	0
Logistic	153:115	129	24	68	47	176	68

Algorithms	*Train Acc*	*Val Acc*	*Train F1*	*Val F1*	*AUC*
Random Forest	*0.9954*	*0.7134*	*0.9953*	*0.6865*	*0.9858*
Bagging	0.9954	0.7134	0.9953	0.6865	0.9829
AdaBoost	0.8720	0.6555	0.8697	0.6391	0.9087
Gaussian NB	0.5680	0.6101	0.4254	0.3836	0.5560
SVM	1	0.6494	1	0.3937	0.9812
Logistic	0.6049	0.5786	0.5832	0.5183	0.6243

Among five alternative classifiers, bagging prevails, as it has the highest validation accuracy, the lowest false positive rate of heterosexual people, and is high in both ROC and Val F1. Note that Random Forest, which combines the concepts of bagging and random selection of features, is an extension of bagging (Khalilia et al. 2011). Such results are thus in accordance with expectations. Based on the results from the bagging classifier, 116 out of 244 individuals are likely to be sexual minorities, which is consistent with the Random Forest classifier. In this analysis, we choose Random Forest over bagging because, compared with bagging, Random Forest can attenuate tree correlation by injecting more randomness into the tree-growing process, which largely increases the predictive power. Moreover, Random Forest also has a better out-of-the-box performance. As Probst et al. (2019) demonstrated, the Random Forest algorithm has the least variability in their prediction accuracy when tuning among popular machine learning algorithms. To further show the performance of classification models, the ROC curves of Random Forest with different split strategies and different algorithms are drawn in Fig. 2.

Furthermore, considering that some sexual minorities may deliberately report they are heterosexual people, we excluded samples who declared themselves as heterosexual people but were predicted as sexual minorities in the validation set during the first round. Note that this doesn't necessarily indicate that these samples are sexual minorities who provide fake answers but only suggests they have a higher probability of being sexual minorities compared to others. We then took the remaining samples to make the prediction on the missing samples. The 24-split Random Forest model with 337 variables shows that the percentage of sexual minorities

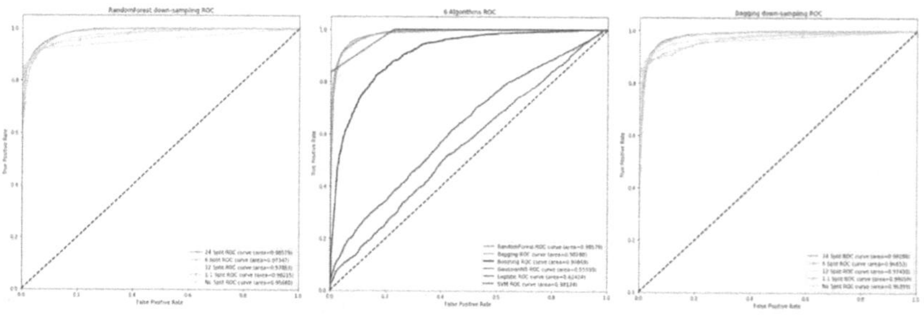

Fig. 2 ROC curves of Random Forest with different split strategies and different algorithms

becomes 5.61%,[1] which changed little compared to our general finding. The convergent trend remains consistent.

4 Conclusion

In the past decade, profound social transformations have caused the emergence of a broad sociopolitical climate that is gradually more accepting of sexual minorities in many countries (Lane 2007). Despite the overall shift toward reduced discrimination and greater acceptance, it would be premature to claim the imminent demise of societal stigma and individual prejudice against the sexual minority population. Being "invisible" in mainstream society becomes a living strategy for many sexual minorities in China. The perceived stigma may drive biased responses, particularly when using traditional survey methods, as sexual minorities often feel reluctant to disclose their sexual orientation, leading to a high percentage of missing values. To overcome such barriers, we adopt Random Forest imputation, a machine learning approach to infer the sexual orientation of non-respondents based on survey questions from BCSPS. After filling out those missing values, the percentage of college students with sexual minority orientation increased from 3.03% to 5.71%, which is a bit higher than the official estimation (2–4%) based on the first nationwide survey of sexual behavior in China conducted in 1998–99 (Wong 2015). The results remain consistent if alternative classifiers are adopted.

Regarding our result, one doubt may arise as we didn't distinguish "not sure" and "refuse to answer" but simply took them as "missing value." While different implications may link to these answers,[2] this doesn't challenge our findings. First, as respondents in the fourth-wave BCSPS are all senior-year college students, people who don't understand the meaning of terms are rare. Second and most importantly, our models are trained to give the best prediction for samples' sexual orientation without predefining their sexual preferences. If based on the training set, these models get the ability to predict an individual's sexual orientation, then ideally, they can figure out whether an individual is a sexual/

[1] We only took a one-round test as a robust check to back up our major results.

[2] Although "refuse to answer" clearly belongs to missing value, people choose "not sure" can also result from their unfamiliarity with the meaning of terms including "heterosexual," "homosexual," and "bisexual."

gender majority or minority in any cases within the dataset. A valid prediction model independently predicts individuals' sexual orientations without researchers' influence.

Still, there are some limitations worth discussing. First, this analysis only provides a crude estimation of the percentage of college students with a sexual minority orientation without further differentiating specific types; especially, it does not capture gender minorities (e.g., transgender) and some subtypes of sexual minorities, namely pansexual or asexual (Suen and Chan 2020). Our coding scheme which only contains two values: 1-yes, 0-no, ensures that we still could capture those people but with lower precision. Considering the sensitivity of the sexual orientation issue, the data that involves sexual orientation is rare in China. Besides, most of the survey data relevant to sexual minorities are collected using the snowball sampling strategy; the data created are a non-probability sample which has no societal representativeness. BCSPS data is actually the only publicly available and regional representative dataset that has information about sexual orientation. It is one of the few data that has the potential to provide an accurate inferring of the sexual minority community, though the measurement of sexual orientation is far from ideal.

Second, extrapolating the sexual minority proportion in this analysis is based on the assumption that respondents reported their real sexual orientation. Note that due to the stigmatized social status of sexual minorities, respondents' answers might be biased toward prevalent social norms, which are more acceptable to mainstream society. This means there may be some sexual minorities who deliberately hide their true sexual orientation by intentionally giving inaccurate responses. It is therefore likely that our estimation of the percentage of sexual minorities is still underestimated. In other words, our results provide a conservative estimation of the sexual minority of college students in Beijing. Nevertheless, as the BCSPS is a large-scale social survey with stratified random sampling and a clear commitment to protect respondents' information security, sexual minorities generally have little need to deliberately pretend they are heterosexual people in an anonymous questionnaire. Furthermore, our robustness check by expelling samples who declared heterosexual preference but were predicted as sexual minorities in the first round shows little change occurred compared with the general findings.

Third, as the results show, the training accuracy is much higher than the validation accuracy, which implies that our Random Forest classifier may suffer from an overfitting problem. However, Breiman (2001) claimed that the Random Forest algorithm does not overfit, as it can generate an internal unbiased estimate of generalization error when more trees are added to the model. There is significant controversy surrounding this subject. Some other scholars have shown that as the forest building progresses, it is the generalization error variance rather than the bias itself that would decrease to zero in the Random Forest (Tang and Ishwaran 2017). In this research, by adopting a Lasso regression algorithm, we largely reduce the size of the variable sets for estimation, which, to some degree, has down-weighted bias arising due to an overfitting problem.

Finally, another potential source that may lead to biased estimation is the fact that our assessment is based on a one-item question: "What is your sexual orientation?" Considering the sensitivity of this question, substantial inaccuracies may occur. A more accurate estimate might be achieved by incorporating prevalent sexual orientation tests (including the Kinsey scale test, the Epstein Sexual Orientation Inventory (ESOI), Storm's sexual orientation test with quadrants, and even list experience) into our approach. It is also worth noting that this study is limited to assessing the sexual orientation of college students in Beijing, but does not seek to estimate the number of gender minorities.

In spite of some deficiencies, the methods we used to predict the potential sexual minorities have undoubtedly been a breakthrough. Our effort helps increase the visibility of sexual minorities, which in turn will enhance the health and well-being of the sexual minorities and serve to protect their rights, which are so important in achieving equality in society and before the law.

References

Breiman, Leo. 2001. Random forests. *Machine Learning* 45: 5–32.

Cao, Jin, and Xinlei Lu. 2014. A Preliminary exploration of the gay movement in Mainland China: Legacy, transition, opportunity, and the new media. *Signs* 39 (4): 840–848.

Gates, Gary J. 2011. *How many people are lesbian, gay, bisexual and transgender?* Retrieved from UCLA School of Law: http://williamsinstitute.law.ucla.edu/wp-content/uploads/Gates-How-Many-People-LGBT-Apr-2011.pdf.

Ghaziani, Amin, Verta Taylor, and Amy Stone. 2016. Cycles of sameness and difference in LGBT social movements. *Annual Review of Sociology* 42 (1): 165–183.

Gross, Larry. 2012. *Up from invisibility: Lesbians, gay men, and the media in America*. Columbia University Press.

Hu, Yang. 2016. Sex ideologies in China: Examining interprovince differences. *Journal of Sex Research* 53 (9): 1118–1130.

Japkowicz, Nathalie, and Shaju Stephen. 2002. The class imbalance problem: A systematic study. *Intelligent Data Analysis* 6 (5): 429–449.

Khalilia, Mohammed, Sounak Chakraborty, and Mihail Popescu. 2011. Predicting disease risks from highly imbalanced data using Random Forest. *BMC Medical Informatics and Decision Making* 11 (1): 51.

Lane, Jan-Erik. 2007. A new cultural cleavage in post-modern society. *Brazilian Journal of Political Economy* 27 (3): 375–393.

Lantz, Brett. 2015. *Machine learning with R*. Birmingham: Packt Publishing.

Lee, Ji Hyun, et al. 2016. Discrimination, mental health, and substance use disorders among sexual minority populations. *LGBT health* 3 (4): 258–265.

O'Donohue, William, and Christine E. Caselles. 1993. Homophobia: Conceptual, definitional, and value issues. *Journal of Psychopathology and Behavioral Assessment* 15 (3): 177–195.

Palmer, David S., et al. 2007. Random Forest models to predict aqueous solubility. *Journal of Chemical Information and Modeling* 47 (1): 150–158.

Probst, Philipp, Anne-Laure. Boulesteix, and Bernd Bischl. 2019. Tunability: Importance of hyperparameters of machine learning algorithms. *Journal of Machine Learning Research* 20: 1–32.

Provost, Foster. 2000. Machine learning from imbalanced data sets 101. *AAAI Technical Report*. https://www.aaai.org/Papers/Workshops/2000/WS-00-05/WS00-05-001.pdf.

Postsecondary National Policy Institute. 2018. *LGBTQ students in higher education*. Retrieved from Postsecondary National Policy Institute: https://pnpi.org/wp-content/uploads/2021/05/LGBTQStudentsinHigherEducation_PNPI_May2021.pdf

Sterzing, Paul R., Wendy F. Auslander, and Jeremy T. Goldbach. 2014. An exploratory study of bullying involvement for sexual minority youth: Bully-only, victim-only, and bully-victim roles. *Society for Social Work and Research* 5: 321–337.

Suen, Yiu-tung, and Randolph Chun Ho Chan. 2020. A nationwide cross-sectional study of 15,611 lesbian, gay and bisexual people in China: Disclosure of sexual orientation and experiences of negative treatment in health care. *International Journal for Equity in Health* 19 (1): 46.

Tang, Fei, and Hemant Ishwaran. 2017. Random Forest missing data algorithms. *Statistical Analysis and Data Mining* 10 (6): 363–377. https://doi.org/10.1002/sam.11348.

Tibshirani, Robert. 1996. Regression shrinkage and selection via the Lasso. *Journal of the Royal Statistical Society Series B-Methodological* 58 (1): 267–288.

UNDP. 2016. *Being LGBTI in China: A national survey on social attitudes towards sexual orientation, gender identity and gender expression*. https://www.asia-pacific.undp.org/content/rbap/en/home/library/democratic_governance/hiv_aids/being-lgbti-in-china-a-national-survey-on-social-attitudes-towa.html.

USAID. 2014. *Being LGBT in Asia: China country report*. https://www.usaid.gov/documents/1861/being-lgbt-asia-china-country-report.

Wang, Yuanyuan, et al. 2019. Discrimination against LGBT populations in China. *The Lancet Public Health* 4 (9): e440–e441.

Wong, Day. 2015. Sexual minorities in China. In *International encyclopedia of social and behavioral sciences*, 2nd ed., ed. James D. Wright, 734–739. Oxford: Elsevier.

Xu, Wenjian, et al. 2017. Internalized homophobia, mental health, sexual behaviors, and outness of gay/bisexual men from Southwest China. *International Journal for Equity in Health* 16 (1): 36.

PART III

Developing Theories

CHAPTER 6

Computing Grounded Theory: Algorithm-Based Approach to Deriving Theories

1 Introduction

Quantitative analysis was previously a general designation for the analysis and research of numerical data (Scott and Marshall 2009: 538). But it has been increasingly framed in a single dimension with the deductive method as logic, theoretical (hypothesis) verification as purpose, statistical inference as the paradigm, especially the binary separation of qualitative and quantitative studies. Undoubtedly, the method of hypothesis testing has shattered the pure philosophical speculation involving unsocial phenomena. But it seems to gradually lose the initiative of theory production and development. To be specific, new concepts and theories are constantly observed, discovered, and refined by qualitative researchers, thus forming the "precursor" of the theoretical development frontier. On the contrary, quantitative researchers can only conduct post hoc statistical tests on existing theories or hypotheses derived from the literature and from researchers' own interpretive assumptions. Quantitative researchers focusing on Karl Popper (2005)'s definition of science tend to overlook the value of data and models for directly enlightening theory and the application possibility of inductive logic for quantitative research since they get indulged in self-appreciation of the importance of falsification testing in most cases.

Is there a new methodological path through which quantitative researchers can, like their qualitative counterparts, directly contribute to the development of theoretical hypotheses rather than merely performing

Y. Chen et al., *Machine Learning in Social Science*,
https://doi.org/10.1007/978-981-95-6465-1_6

post hoc statistical tests? Large quantities of unsubstantiated or even absurd hypotheses may be produced from brainstorming variable lists randomly or even via the pairwise correlations of $N \times (N - 1)$ variables in ergodic form. Moreover, problems such as quantitative restriction, selective combination, and multicollinearity of control variables cannot be addressed through the implementation of the cyclical tests for various X–Υ combinations based on the traditional regression model. As a result, the direct application of data and models in the direct midwifery of theory has been considered impossible among quantitative scholars for quite a long period of time.

However, with the abundance of social survey data on a large scale and the application of methods such as machine learning in social science research, possibilities have been discovered. In this chapter, a generation method for quantitative theory was proposed based on large amounts of data and machine learning models (algorithm model). In practical terms, quantitative analysis was conducted on a series of X to Υ predicting capabilities through supervised machine learning for the given Υ and a large number of explanatory variables X. Many factors with strong predictability can be explored and filtered using the logical correlation between causality and predictability, which is directly referential for the theoretical hypothesis. In addition, Υ attempts to be prepared with one or more new factors that have potential theoretical value, further helpful for social scientists to generate, develop, and revise theories. As a typical method for computational social science, its logical foundation has achieved the same result by the core principle of "grounded theory (GT)," a famous method for qualitative research. Data were coded and interpreted by breaking the preconception of theory, and without any theoretical hypothesis, so that the generation path from empirical to theoretical research can be opened by breaking the logic of "deduction verification." It is named the computing grounded theory (CGT).

2 Limit of Falsification

2.1 *Hypothesis Testing and Scientific Ring*

The development of quantitative social science research has expanded a century from the initial simple data description to contingency tables, and from various regression models to causal inference methods. In the past four decades, the fundamental model for quantitative social science research was built on the basis of questionnaire data. And the multiple linear regression was adopted to statistically infer whether explanatory variables are correlated or causal with the explained variables. This development process from formation to maturity is a process during which research paths are constantly solidified, and the traditional quantitative study is fast developed. That is, the relatively standardized "template" format has been adopted by mainstream social science journals at home and abroad. A traditional quantitative article that conforms to the standard should be composed of problems, references, assumptions, measurements, data, methods, analyses, and conclusions, with these closely interlocked parts forming a connecting link between what comes before and what goes after. In fact, Wells and Picou (1981) also made similar conclusions regarding the hypothesis-testing model upon analyzing the contents of the *American Sociological Review* (1936–1979). Furthermore, the conventional paradigm of quantitative research is not unique to sociology but is also widely applied across other social sciences such as economics, political science, and psychology. In these fields, quantitative analysis typically follows the principle of statistically testing theoretical propositions by falsifying their corresponding null hypotheses.

Testing existing theories is not the entirety of theoretical work in the social sciences. In *Scientific Logic in Sociology*, Walter L. Wallace (1971: 18, 23) proposed the concept of the "scientific ring," arguing that social research advances through a continuous, reciprocal cycle of theory construction and empirical testing (Fig. 1). Although the traditional quantitative paradigms of hypothesis testing apparently center on the right half of the "scientific ring," the process of theoretical construction to testing is a complete path followed by social science research institutes. And theoretical construction has seemingly become an exclusive mission of qualitative research, while theoretical verification is taken as a pattern by quantitative research due to the distinction formed between quantitative and qualitative research. Therefore, qualitative research is utilized for the proposal of theories as it is considered "inductive," "understanding," "humanistic," and "historical context," whereas quantitative research featuring "deductive," "objective," "positivist," and "of natural law" are for theoretical verification. Quantitative research, however, tends to be assumed under the limitation of existing common senses of theories and research, leaving it challenged by "the verification of common senses with complex methods" and "the mediocrity of research topics" in most cases.

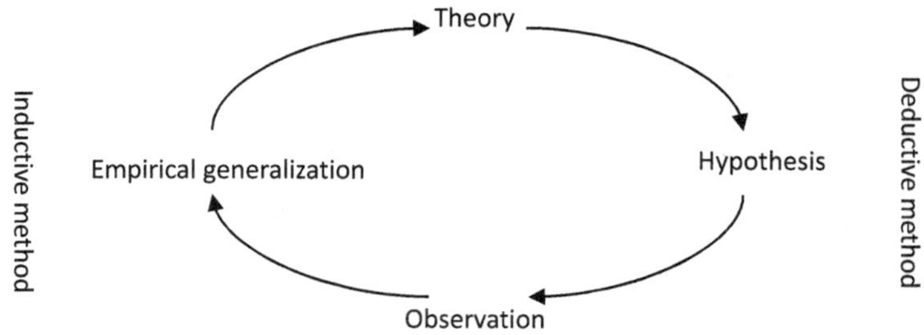

Fig. 1 Two logics of Wallace's "Scientific Ring"

As Robert K. Merton noted, empirical research has gone far beyond the passive function of the testing theory. It has four functions performed during the development of shaping theory, including the creation, revision, transformation, and clarification of theory rather than merely confirming or refuting assumptions (Merton 1968). The theory is empirically inspected, which is seen as a preconceived view of existing theoretical study and common sense. However, quantitative research increasingly neglects the need to rediscover theory from ongoing social realities and to examine how it interacts with existing theoretical frameworks (Glaser 2008).

2.2 *Historical Origin of the Hypothesis-Testing Objective*

The paradigm of hypothesis testing, which was derived from the tradition of optimistic methodology, was strengthened after the normative institutionalization movement of quantitative research by the Colombian school. Both Lazarsfeld and Samuel Stouffer advocated the purpose orientation and scientific movement of theory should be verified with empirical materials. *Social Research to Test Ideas,* written by Stouffer, is a drive for popularizing the method of validating theory with data in the quantitative study community. This methodological tradition is aimed at the traditional theoretical discourse featuring a lot of metaphysical speculation and untested assertions. In addition, it is seen as an "empty statement," unable to improve the reliable judgment about social facts. Therefore, it is excluded from accurate scientific knowledge. A "positive personality" has been formed gradually among quantitative social scientists in academic edification and method training. They require themselves to constantly revise their minds about society, and view research as a work constantly approaching reality through theoretical construction. Besides, they are devoted to upgrading the research on social science and its effectiveness in answering substantive questions (Pawson 2000).

The hypothesis-testing quantitative paradigm is a disciplinary consensus collectively formed across academic disciplines, by which the gap between theory and experience can be bridged to secure the scientific conclusion. Beyond all questions, there is solid cognitive and methodological support behind it that plays a decisive role in scientific and standardized quantitative research. On the other hand, there may be varied subjective preferences for interpretation; however, any form of interpretation can be placed above another for no scientific basis (Domingos 1999). If the analysis path of "theory first-data validation" is taken for granted without reflection, the methodology that was once a power for knowledge liberation can easily be translated into a restraint impeding theoretical production creativity. The hypothesis-testing paradigm should have consisted of first theory proposing and then testing. Note that these two parts are equally important. The depth and comprehensibility of qualitative data are more conducive to the actual process of research in social science. Based on this, theoretical hypotheses were proposed directly using C. Wright Mills' concept of sociological imagination. Quantitative data features high simplification as a numerical index, and its mathematical statistics that are inherently associated cannot be discovered directly by humans through the combination of vision and brain functions. Therefore, in-depth development has been achieved in both qualitative and quantitative paradigms in their respective fields of expertise. Qualitative researchers are indeed becoming more skillful at proposing theoretical hypotheses, while quantitative researchers are becoming more skillful at conducting complex statistical testing and even causal inference.

But in fact, the most original interpretation of the laws between data indicators can be achieved with the help of simple quantitative logic tools such as statistical software. By doing so, a possible theoretical direction or potential causal mechanism can be acquired, which then can be used for more stringent statistical tests. This is the actual process of theory production for traditional quantitative research. For instance, Lazarsfeld advocated that the strict quantitative program should be relaxed for data analysis. "Undiscovered results should be searched for and possible assumptions should be looked for in simple distribution of variables." Hartwig and Dearing (1979) also emphasized multiple times that the two principles of suspicion and openness should be insisted on, that is to say, we should be open to unexpected patterns of data categories. Moreover, data information should be used to the maximum extent, criticizing the non-openness of quantitative studies. Simply, new findings, obtained from the data, will not be expressed by many researchers based on the real research process. On the contrary, new theories are proposed through literature review and plain related statements from existing theories. In this way, their theories are often "dressed up" as theoretical assumptions that have existed, as though these assumptions had been made before data analyses. After that, they are affirmed in line with the logic of the hypothesis test (Glaser 2008: 15). Such great emphasis has been put on the standardized paradigm of theory verification by the academic community, as if the assumption must be located in the existing theory. Only in this way can the author's understanding of the field be highly manifested, making the article reasonable.

2.3 *Consequences of Hypothesis Testing*

Knowledge-creating capacity can be restrained from two aspects by the "hypothesis testing" of quantitative studies.

(1) **Absence of theoretical production in quantitative study.** Social science covers the entire process from the generation to the verification of theories. A fine division of labor has been formed gradually in the academic community for a long time due to the imbalance of quantitative study in the generation and verification of theories. Furthermore, a common impression is formed between practitioners and onlookers, that is, empirical research cannot generate theories, and is used for theoretical verification. The theory, instead, shall be obtained from the researchers' imaginations (Merton and Barber 2011). In turn, the division of labor is further strengthened by this impression, that is, theoretical verification is what social scientists engaging in empirical research shall do, with the theory provided by specialized theoretical workers. Besides, theory creation and hypothesis inspiration are regarded as the exclusive mission of qualitative research for some scholars. Possible explanations are proposed in qualitative research through exploratory work. While quantitative research is to verify the universality and scientific validity of explanations. Due

to these impressions and actual orientations of scientific research, common prosperity has been promoted among different research paradigms, resulting in the postposition and even absence of quantitative study in the journey of scientific discovery. To be concrete, the assumptions which are deduced from existing theories have been logically verified by quantitative researchers. Based on this, the existing theories have been made more refined, with the rare production of new theoretical constructions. In other words, it is more difficult for those fewer and fewer quantitative researchers to propose theories and concepts.

(2) **Losing insight in quantitative research due to its dependence on common sense.** The theories or assumptions, which are verified by quantitative study, basically stem from the simple derivation of existing theories or the basic knowledge and inspiration of social scientists. Some scholars, such as Popper (1962), advocated "free imagination superior to empirical observation." By doing so, bold hypotheses are encouraged with rigorous verification. In fact, the problems of quantitative study are still mostly confined to the elaboration of existing theories, or verifying social common sense with the use of complex methods, slowly spawning bonsai-style research. Duncan Watts directly targeted the paradigm crisis of the current social science research for its too much reliance on common sense (Watts 2014). As the possibility is taken to consider possible future events, preference will be shown for those explanations of known results while overlooking other possibilities. The paradox lying in common sense is its ability to help us understand the world on the one hand, but to weaken our ability to understand as well (Watts 2011). Whether common sense is scientific, on the one hand, needs to be challenged and affirmed by social scientists with the mission of "breaking away from common sense" (Becker 2008). But on the other hand, possible explanatory variables have to be selected from the stereotypes and data channels of existing common sense while seeking data with the establishment of assumptions. Conservative common sense and mainstream theories are unconsciously reproduced by scientists who are dedicated to theoretical verification. Therefore, they will lose insight in the face of the rapidly changing social structure in China and social order across the world.

3 Computing Grounded Theory

3.1 Developing Theory Using Proposed CGT

Given a dataset of N variables, we can theoretically propose and test as many as $N \times (N-1)$ hypotheses. In the real world of theory generation, we focus on a limited number of Υ as dependents, given our research interests and accumulation of prior knowledge of social sciences. Here, for simplicity, we limit our framework to the scenario where target Υ is clearly set. Given a certain Υ, implementing CGT to propose a new hypothesis of Υ proceeds over the following five steps.

(1) Data preparation. Possessing sufficient data of sufficient quality is the basis of CGT because machine learning models depend on high-quality training data. Otherwise, even the most performant algorithms can be rendered useless, and the resulting model may perform poorly. Rich secondary data, especially large survey data, are obviously an effective choice. Note that we can also use text data to perform CGT; however, to implement this, we must treat each word in a document as a feature.
(2) Model training. A machine learning model must be trained to predict the target variable. Here, any complex algorithm is acceptable regardless of whether the algorithm itself is interpretable, and a good model can make the results more scientific.
(3) Predictability comparison. Model-agnostic methods can be used to interpret black-box models to uncover potentially important variables. These variables frequently have a relatively significant impact on the prediction outcome or accuracy.
(4) Robustness test. Here, we use different data sets, hyperparameters, and machine learning algorithms to determine whether the analysis results are stable.
(5) Theory induction. In this step, we convert empirical variables to more abstract theoretical propositions. The proposed CGT can be used to create, develop, and correct theories. Note that the entire process can be both iterative and interactive, where each step can be repeated by adjusting and adding data.

These five steps comprise the framework of the proposed CGT (Fig. 2).

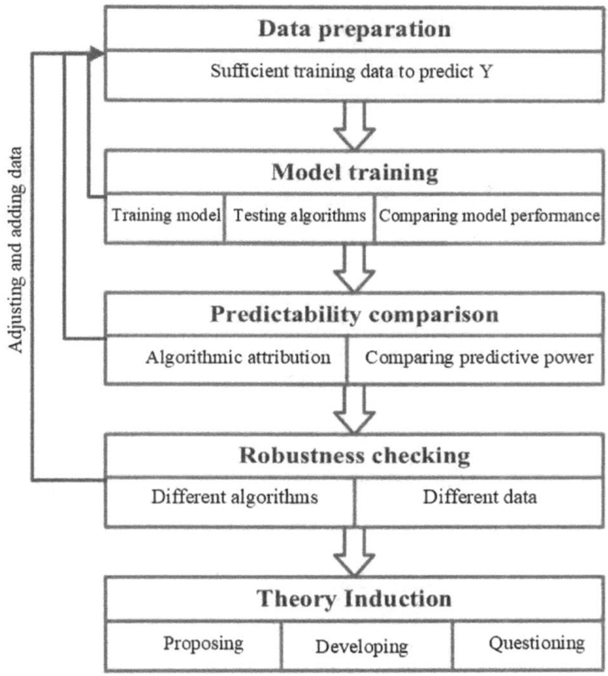

Fig. 2 Framework of proposed CGT

The reason we describe the proposed method as a special form of GT is primarily related to the fact that the logic of developing theory with the proposed CGT can be traced back to the origins of traditional GT. The proposed CGT differs from traditional GT in that machine learning is used to process data (rather than managing documents manually). Similar to traditional GT, the strategy of the proposed CGT is also data-led and is free of preexisting theoretical assumptions. Unlike traditional GT, where text is coded manually to generate theories, CGT method seeks new and strong predictors of Y to inspire a hypothesis using a machine learning model. In this regard, algorithm-based computing in CGT plays a similar role in laying the foundation to inspire new theories as the manual text coding process in the traditional GT. The former is a black-box machine learning process, and the latter depends on one's intellectual capacity and academic formation.

3.2 Logical Premise of Computing Grounded Theory

CGT is a theoretical production method rooted in a clear logic, which is totally different from Mills' thinking mode that calls for changing the perspective from personal life experience to social issues. Although they are created from theories, the former obtains theoretical inspiration from a series of association combinations that are most likely to approach the causal mechanism data variables based on the predicting capability using algorithms. The latter obtains concepts and theories from personal life experience as per the macro transition of mental understanding. The algorithm presents a clear and systematic logic, even in a black-box process of machine learning. And the vague and scattered inspiration of personal thinking is dependent on time, space, personal academic vision, quality, and even talent in most cases. The following two aspects are the logical premises for CGT.

(1) **Inductive Logic Rooted in the Grounded Theory**

Since the GT was developed based on a reflection of empirical research on the paradigm of testing quantitative hypotheses, Glaser, one of its founders, pointed out that social research overemphasized theoretical verification rather than the previous step of concept discovery and assumptions associated with the research field. In such a context, more efforts in closing the gap between theoretical and empirical research can be seen in improving the method of testing theory, whereas narrowing the gap from the theoretical level has hardly been studied (Glaser 2008: 7). Glaser advocated that the theoretical energy frozen by overemphasis on verification theory should be released from theories among data (Glaser 2008: 8). Based on this, Glaser and Strauss established the fundamental principle of GT, directly creating a theory from empirical materials through step-by-step induction and then comparing it with existing theories and research references. Apparently, avoiding preconceived ideas or guesses before the research is essential for ensuring the effectiveness of "rooting." In fact, opening the generation path from empirical research to theoretical research by breaking the logic of "deduction verification" is the core principle of the grounded theory. This is also the reason why the method of directly generating theories from quantitative data proposed is called "computing grounded theory." Theories are created from processing data with computational social science methods such as machine learning.

Glaser emphasized that the GT is a universal methodology applicable to both qualitative and quantitative data. Quantitative and qualitative data without fundamental conflicts in purpose and ability can be a benefit to the generation and verification of theories since Glaser even believed that all is data (Glaser 2008: 17). But people found that the GT is more suitable for qualitative research with its practical development. Strauss, another proposer, even regarded the theory as the "exclusive tool" of qualitative research (Strauss and Corbin 1994). It's easy to understand the reason behind. First, qualitative research collects data that is more systematic and detailed than that from quantitative research as it is directly oriented to the empirical reality featuring complex and changing, which was also recognized by Glaser (Glaser 2008: 18). Second, humans cannot directly encode quantitative data without appropriate algorithm models due to the highly concise expression of numerical indicators. And the traditional regression model for quantitative research cannot handle the above task due to the high requirements of appropriateness for the algorithm model.

Glaser elaborated on the steps and examples of quantitative calculation in *Doing Quantitative Grounded Theory* to break the stereotype that GT is applicable to qualitative data only. Being confined to the limitations of the times, his idea was similar to the one-click traversal process. That is, the rough indexes reflecting the positive and negative changes of variable relations are computed among all possible two variables. If the variables are always related to a series of variables, a potential theory model will be formed when these variables are put together and reasoned to analyze research results. Next, refined analysis is conducted, namely, three or more variables are analyzed to further saturate the categories by developing their attributes, so as to achieve a more intensive theory (Glaser 2008: 54). The question remains: there are no clear rules for selecting model-independent variables for control variables or potential explanatory variables included in the Y model, although the relationship between X and Y can be fitted iteratively from a logical point of view with the help of a mainstream regression model after more control variables are added into the combination of two variables. In particular, many problems, such as insufficient degrees of freedom or collinearity with respect to linear regression models, will occur when the number of independent variables becomes large to some given extent. In this regard, Lazarsfeld's solution mentioned above is to relax the strict quantitative procedure. Therefore, in general, Glaser's quantitative rooting theory is logical and feasible. Meanwhile, the rooting theory has become a symbol of qualitative research since no suitable model could be used in a standardized and convincing manner at that time.

(2) Predictable Logic of Causality

The predictability and causal mechanism between social phenomena are two different but highly related categories. The confirmation of causality has long been regarded as a foundational principle across the social sciences. Max Weber, one of the pioneers of modern social science, defined sociology as a science that provides causal explanations of social processes and outcomes (Weber 1968: 4). His definition laid the groundwork for a causal-analytic tradition that continues to shape research across the social sciences. Within this framework, theory building can be understood as the formulation of hypotheses about causal relations among social indicators. By deductive reasoning, dependent variables in such models must be predictable for independent variables, since predictability is "necessary but not sufficient" for the establishment of causality and can also be seen as the most basic means to verify underlying mechanisms (Watts 2014; Hempel and Oppenheim 1948; Manski 2007).

Most social scientists, however, pay little attention to prediction because of the constraints of mathematical statistics and traditional regression models. In fact, the use of prediction and the application of predictive results to generate knowledge have received limited attention even at the forefront of contemporary quantitative research. Instead, social scientists focus more on endogenous issues in an attempt to push quantitative research from traditional statistical correlation to causal inference. This is a crucial step, yet it remains focused on testing existing theoretical hypotheses rather than directly generating theory from data and reasoning. Social scientists normally use evasive words or emphasize that prediction is not equal to cause and effect while ignoring the logic that cause and effect must be predictable in discussing the concepts of cause and effect, correlation, and prediction. Or they highlight the complex regression model with too many independent variables, or criticize that the algorithm model that can predict data cannot be explained because of its black-box process. In response to the above points of view, Watts summarized and severely criticized these arguments one by one (Watts 2014).

Fully utilizing the important relationship between prediction and causality is one of the logical foundations of CGT. In other words, causality is a sufficient rather than a necessary condition for prediction, indicating that X is a strong candidate for being a cause of Y if an X can well predict Y. The probability of forming a cause and effect is always far higher than that without predictability, although the relationship is only "possible" rather than "inevitable." With the direct prediction relationship of X and Y, it is possible to propose a hypothesis that X affects Y. Moreover, if we have some existing research on the causes of Y that are contained in these causes, it is possible to propose a new theory $X-Y$ for the predictability between $X-Y$. This possibility of being verified tends to be high if there are some intuitive mechanisms.

Social scientists gradually cut the academic purport to the analysis of the relationship between two variables while discarding social prediction (Hofman et al. 2017; Athey 2018). In such a context, it is of great significance for quantitative research to push forward the direct production of theories with the predictive ability of machine learning. But the premise that cause and effect must be predictable forms the basic logic of reverse thinking. In that case, we should first explore the predictive relationship between all possible and actually influencing factors X and Y variables, rather than simply deriving a seemingly understandable possible explanation chain from existing theories or personal inspiration while explaining the dependent variable Y to discover hypotheses and theories.

3.3 Machine Learning for Prediction

Here, we discuss why we focus on machine learning models rather than regression models. Breiman (2001) divided statistical modeling techniques into data models and algorithmic models. With data models, social sciences ask whether a particular coefficient in an idealized model is statistically significant rather than asking whether a given theory can predict some outcomes in the real world (Hoffmann et al. 2021). However, algorithmic models represented by machine learning provide a better alternative to obtaining effective predictions. The implicit epistemological assumption behind machine learning is that the intrinsic mechanism of data is unknown, and the key point is to develop a pattern that can predict Y by X. Algorithmic models tend to adopt non-linear, non-parametric methods that adjust model complexity through one or more hyperparameters, and this flexibility often results in good predictive performance (Molnar et al. 2020). Machine learning allows data to be distributed in any shape without satisfying any assumptions. Thus, we expect that this freedom from usage limits will improve the ability to gather data in at least two ways.

First, the complex relationships of models are more in line with real social situations. Real situations are far less straightforward than simple ideal models (Kaplan 1940). However, machine learning is driven by the real data distribution; thus, it can break limitations imposed by preset assumptions and ideal models. We should predict at first, then understand at second (Breiman 2001).

Second, machine learning algorithms can consider thousands of unique variables in a single model simultaneously (Linthicum et al. 2019). Including more explanatory variables can potentially help us gain more comprehensive and complex information from the models. Using machine learning models, we can strengthen our theoretical reasoning and empirical judgment by identifying new explanatory variables and dimensions (Chen et al. 2020).

Note that algorithm models are imperfect. Scholars tend to question the limited explanatory power of algorithm models. However, a growing body of evidence in machine learning literature suggests that an increasing number of methods to "disassemble the black box" have been developed in order to improve the interpretability and explanatory power of algorithm models (Ribeiro et al. 2016). These techniques enable the large-scale application of machine learning to social science research.

Doshi-Velez and Kim (2017) stated that understanding the black-box models of machine learning is an effective way to discover data-driven factors. Here, we apply the SHapley Additive exPlanations (SHAP) approach by Lundberg and Lee (2017) to introduce specific paths to explain the black box of our model. The SHAP value was initially introduced by Lloyd Shapley in 1953, and its original purpose was to handle the distribution of rewards in cooperative games. Essentially, it reflects the average expected marginal contribution of each player after all possible combinations have been considered, and it is an important indicator for determining the distribution of collective interests for all players (Chen and Guestrin 2016; Lundberg and Lee 2017). The classical formula to calculate the SHAP value of each participant i is as follows:

$$\phi_i = \sum_{S \subseteq N \backslash \{i\}} \frac{|S|!(|N| - |S| - 1)!}{|N|!}(v(S \cup \{i\}) - v(S)) \tag{1}$$

where ϕ_i is SHAP value of each participant; N is the set of all participants, and |N| is the number of participants in set N. S is one combination of participants, which is a subset of N, and $S \subseteq N\backslash\{i\}$ represents all subsets of set N after deleting feature i. $v(S \cup \{i\}) - v(S)$ is the marginal effect of the general benefit including participant i minus the marginal effect of the general benefit excluding participant i, and this marginal effect will occur $|S|!(|N|$-$|S|$-1)! times after considering all $|N|!$ permutations.

Due to the difficulty of calculating ϕ_i in the above equation with classical SHAP values, Lundberg and Lee (2017) recently proposed a tree SHAP value algorithm for GBT models as a measure of feature attribution value based on game theory. SHAP is also used to interpret the results of a machine learning model. In the interpretability of a machine learning model, the participant is the feature value used for prediction, the general benefit is the difference between the predicted result of each sample and the overall mean, and the purpose of the explanation is to explore the contribution of each feature to the difference in the predicted result and the overall mean, which can be positive or negative. Here, assume we have $2N$ subsets S and must train $2N$ models for N features because machine learning involves a large number of features. To improve computational efficiency, data scientists have developed SHAP algorithms, e.g., the Kernel SHAP method and the Tree SHAP method. Additional details about the tree SHAP algorithm can be found in the literature (Lundberg and Lee 2017; Lundberg et al. 2020).

The SHAP value is a powerful explanation tool for developing theory using a data-grounded approach. It satisfies efficiency, symmetry, dummy, and additivity simultaneously by fully considering the interactions among variables (Winter 2002). The SHAP value also satisfies three desirable properties, i.e., local accuracy, missingness, and consistency (Lundberg and Lee 2017). It can also provide explanations for comprehensible tree models and more complex ensemble models, and can reflect the direction, magnitude, and specific mode of the effect of each feature (Aas et al. 2021). Thus, in this chapter, the SHAP value model is used as the explanatory tool.

3.4 Recommended Technical Standards for Computing

Supervised machine learning and attribution algorithms are involved in the technical process of CGT. But there is no unified standard for machine learning, especially for the machine learning training methods used in social science. Therefore, the top 60 highly cited papers in social science were selected as machine learning keywords from the core collection of Web of Science. To be concrete, "machine learning" was first taken as the theme word with retrieval research direction as papers in *Business Economics, Society, Education, Educational Research, Social issues, Government law, Social Sciences,* and other topics. On this basis, papers of the core collection of Web of Science were limited to ensure the quality of the papers before ranking them according to the number of papers cited. Then, 60 empirical studies involving machine learning for detailed statistics were selected through manual reading. In general, problems predicted in the 60 papers involve a variety of economic, demographic, and cultural issues such as financial stocks, bond ratings, poverty, credit, suicide, depression, employment, population, personality, academic performance, and court decisions.

After that, representative documents were summarized and information used by these training models for predicting was sorted out, such as the number of characteristic variables used for prediction, the number of samples used for training models, the type of dependent variables predicted, and the final accuracy rate of the model. In this way, a detailed experience reference standard can be provided for CGT and the general application of model training for social science machine learning. Details of the proposed methods are shown in Table 1. These standards are for recommendation purposes only, and a more reliable basis can be acquired from further data research.

(1) **Sample size.** More training samples indicate more information, and a greater contribution to the improvement of the accuracy of model recognition. In theory, it is sufficient when the model prediction performance is not improved with the rising sample size. According to the statistical results in the literature, the maximum number of samples used can reach up to 30 million, with a median of 1888. Among them, the median of literature samples was 11,196 after 2015. The author suggested that the sample size for exploratory analysis should be no less than 2000, with the sample

Table 1 Detailed statistical methods for empirical research on machine learning

	Minimum	*Maximum*	*Average*	*Median*	*Standard*
Sample size	30	32959773	682660	1888	4394722.67
Number of features	6.00	1821	148.12	22.50	361.36
Model prediction effect	0.36	0.97	0.78	0.79	0.12
Algorithm	Random Forest	29%	Target variables	Binary	70%
	Support vector	26%			
	Neural network	17%		3 to 10 Classes	20%
	Gradient boosting trees	15%			
	Others	14%		More than 10 Classes or Continuous	10%

size for empirical calibration no less than 10,000, according to the sample size of the current mainstream social survey questionnaire data on the premise of ensuring the availability of numerous survey data and the prediction accuracy. CGT is an exploratory analysis with a not high prediction accuracy, so the sample size should be no less than 2000.

(2) **Sample balance.** The sample size should be adjusted according to the number of categories and the difficulty of the variables to be predicted. Of particular note is that the sample size for rare categories shall not be too small. In a machine learning task with 10% as class 1 samples and 90% as class 0 samples, for instance, the algorithm will prefer to assign 0 to avoid making mistakes as much as possible in the prediction process. Imbalanced samples should be resampled to balance all kinds of samples. For specific methods, please refer to the discount and proliferation method proposed by scholars to predict sexual minorities (Chen et al. 2022). The *Υ* object involved in CGT may be either a balanced sample or an imbalanced sample, which should be processed as per the actual situation.

(3) **Number of Features.** The number of model characteristics is the number of *x* variables for training. 1821 variables were used at most, with a median of 22.5 according to the statistical results. On the one hand, more abundant *X* variables will bring better training results. On the other hand, features with high dimensions may lead to excessive data noise with reductions in the training efficiency and prediction effectiveness of the model. For CGT, few *X* values are obviously not conducive to finding a new potential theory, whereas hundreds or more variables can be obtained from large social questionnaires. Therefore, we recommend that the number of model characteristics should be higher than 100 on the basis of not affecting the performance of the model, being roughly 10 times that of traditional regression models.
(4) **Algorithm model selection.** Random Forest is the most used algorithm among the 60 papers, accounting for 29%, followed by support vector machine, accounting for 26%. And neural network and gradient lifting algorithms account for 17% and 15%, respectively. It is worth noting that more than one algorithm has been adopted in most of the papers with the model performance results compared. Therefore, it is recommended to compare the prediction performance and grounded results of various algorithms and test the robustness of the model's interpretability by comparing the root results of different models based on the best model selected as far as possible during grounded computation.
(5) **Model prediction effect.** The highest prediction effect is approximately 0.97 in the literature collected, with a median accuracy of 0.79. Note that the accuracy of model prediction is affected by many factors, such as whether social problems can be predicted, whether the predicted variables are continuous variables or categorical variables, the number of categories, whether the relationship between data and dependent variables is sufficient to support prediction, whether the distribution of different types of data is balanced, data noise, and whether model selection and hyper-parameter setting are appropriate. The accuracy of the model prediction is the premise of the effectiveness of CGT. Thus, it is suggested that, considering that the prediction variables (dependent variables) in the existing papers are binary in most cases, the accuracy rate of the model for grounded computation should be

greater than 0.8 if it is binary variables, and can be appropriately reduced if it is a continuous variable.

4 Conclusion

Explanatory analysis and accurate prediction of social phenomena have long been central concerns of the social sciences. In a 2021 Nature article, Jake Hofman, Duncan Watts, et al. once again called for the integration of explanation and prediction within computational social science. They proposed a conceptual framework consisting of four quadrants: descriptive modeling, explanatory modeling, predictive modeling, and integrative modeling (Hofman et al. 2017). They argued that research combining explanation and prediction approaches in the fourth quadrant remains limited, despite its considerable theoretical potential.

Building on this framework, CGT represents a new attempt to integrate explanation and prediction within the integrated modeling quadrant. It offers an alternative path for quantitative research in the social sciences and serves as a valuable complement to Mills' concept of the sociological imagination. While sociological imagination emphasizes shifting and deepening perspective through personal experience, CGT provides a data-driven capacity to generate theory by algorithmically processing data at a scale and complexity beyond individual cognition. In this sense, rather than viewing the black-box process of machine learning as a limitation, it should be understood as a necessary means of translating complexity into analyzable forms. Through data and algorithm-based operations, machine learning produces simplified representations of the immense complexity of social life. These simplified forms allow researchers to deconstruct and compare intricate social mechanisms through attribution algorithms, thereby generating new theoretical insights and expanding the capacity for reasoning beyond traditional data models.

Scientific research assisted by machine learning has advanced to the forefront of multiple disciplines. *Nature* once highlighted the significance of artificial intelligence (AI) based on the algorithmic model in science with a cover story titled "AI-guided intuition." Researchers have identified potential relationships among the mathematical components of machine learning models and sought to interpret them through attribution techniques, aiming to propose concrete pathways for guiding scientific intuition and hypothesis formation. This process parallels, in some sense, the logic of computational grounding discussed in this chapter. Unlike the natural sciences, where such algorithmic insights often refine existing theories, the grounded approach introduced here represents one of the first systematic attempts to assist the theoretical production of quantitative social science through machine learning. However, data generated from social phenomena are far more complex and voluminous, posing greater challenges for explanation and interpretation.

While recognizing that algorithms and data can contribute to the development of theory, this chapter does not deny the value of traditional quantitative methods in social science. The toolkit of quantitative research has become increasingly refined, progressing from association analysis to causal inference, and from social prediction to algorithmic attribution. Each method represents an important part of quantitative inquiry, with its own assumptions, advantages, limitations, and appropriate research contexts.

CGT seeks to generate new hypotheses by moving beyond long-established theoretical frameworks and conventional reasoning, rather than replacing existing theories. It regards theory derived from data as a scientific intermediary that precedes empirical testing by quantitative researchers. This position emphasizes complementarity rather than opposition between data-driven insights and theoretical validation.

We accept the view that everything can be treated as data, but we reject the extreme claim that data alone constitute knowledge. As Merton pointed out, empirical findings do not contribute to the accumulation of knowledge unless they are incorporated into general theoretical propositions. CGT should therefore serve as a method for theoretical dialogue, knowledge production, disciplinary development, sociological imagination, and reflection on public affairs.

At the same time, we recognize that new analytical methods will inevitably bring new problems. CGT faces as many challenges as it creates opportunities for knowledge production:

(1) Limits of data scope. We can never fully capture the dynamics of social life, as many variables remain unobserved. Although broadening the data dimension of analysis is one of CGT's key goals, this effort is like "dancing with the shackles of data availability." The insights and discoveries generated by CGT are inevitably confined by the information already contained in the data. Broadening data

coverage is possible, but identifying the point of saturation requires both accumulation and continuous exploration.

(2) Limits of social prediction. Social prediction forms the foundation of CGT, yet there has always been criticism that doubts the predictability of complex social phenomena (Sherden 1998; Taleb 2010). CGT may not apply to all research scenarios, especially those dominated by randomness or affected by the absence of adequate data and models. The inherent unpredictability of complex social systems makes this limitation inevitable.

(3) Challenges of model attribution. Researchers often ignore information inconsistent with their prior knowledge because confirmation bias is difficult to avoid in the process of learning. The variable relationship found by CGT may contradict prior knowledge or resist interpretation due to the complex interactions and emergent mechanisms among models. This may result in explanations that are less satisfying yet remain scientifically valid.

(4) Heterogeneity within CGT. The researchers' position in knowledge production has shifted from the front end to the back end of the research, while data and models have assumed a central role. For example, the Rashomon effect exemplifies this challenge: different results may arise not only from distinct prediction algorithms but also from variations in attribution methods applied to machine learning models. Such heterogeneity calls for careful cross-verification.

(5) Correlation without causality. The relationships between grounded variables identified by CGT indicate their relative contribution to prediction, but not necessarily causal links. Therefore, future research should deepen the analysis of causal mechanisms and the underlying chains of influence.

However, the maturity of any scientific approach requires a long process of continuous testing, refinement, and validation by both practice and the scholarly community. Similarly, the computing grounded approach still has much to be explored and improved. Future work should focus on developing clearer methodological standards and guidelines, expanding its range of applications, strengthening its reliability with unstructured data, establishing closer dialogue with statistical and causal inference methods, and advancing its degree of programmatic automation.

As an emerging paradigm that integrates the reasoning and logic of qualitative inquiry into quantitative research, CGT deserves greater attention, openness, and sustained practice. More empirical studies are needed to test, refine, and extend its applicability in contemporary social research. Only when this approach contributes to generating new concepts and theories for modern social science can its full potential and inherent limitations be properly understood.

References

Aas, Kjersti, Martin Jullum, and Anders Løland. 2021. Explaining individual predictions when features are dependent: More accurate approximations to Shapley values. *Artificial Intelligence* 298: 103502.

Athey, Susan. 2018. *The impact of machine learning on economics*. In Ajay Agrawal, Joshua Gans, and Avi Goldfarb eds, The economics of artificial intelligence: An agenda. Chicago: University of Chicago Press.

Becker, Howard S. 2008. *Tricks of the trade: How to think about your research while you're doing it*. Chicago: University of Chicago press.

Breiman, Leo. 2001. Random forests. *Machine Learning* 45: 5–32.

Chen, Tianqi and Carlos Guestrin. 2016. XGBoost: A scalable tree boosting system. In *Proceedings of the 22nd ACM SIGKDD International Conference on Knowledge Discovery and Data Mining*, San Francisco, CA, USA, 785–794.

Chen, Yunsong, Fei Yan, Guangye He, and Wei Yan. 2020. The Werther effect revisited: Do suicides in books predict actual suicides? *Poetics* 81: 101441.

Chen, Yunsong, Guangye He, and Guodong Ju. 2022. The hidden sexual minorities: Machine learning approaches to estimate the sexual minority orientation among Beijing college students. *Journal of Social Computing* 3 (2).

Domingos, Pedro. 1999. The role of Occam's razor in knowledge discovery. *Data Mining and Knowledge Discovery* 3 (4).

Doshi-Velez, Finale, and Been Kim. 2017. Towards a rigorous science of interpretable machine learning. *arXiv preprint arXiv:* 1702.08608.

Glaser, Barney G. 2008. *Doing quantitative grounded theory*. Mill Valley: Sociology Press.

Hartwig, Frederick, and Brian E. Dearing. 1979. *Exploratory data analysis*. USA: Sage.

Hempel, Carl G., and Paul Oppenheim. 1948. Studies in the logic of explanation. *Philosophy of Science* 15 (2): 135–175.

Hoffmann, Sabine, et al. 2021. The multiplicity of analysis strategies jeopardizes replicability: Lessons learned across disciplines. *Royal Society Open Science* 8 (4): 201925.

Hofman, Jake M., Amit Sharma, and Duncan J. Watts. 2017. Prediction and explanation in social systems. *Science* 355 (6324): 486–488.

Kaplan, Oscar. 1940. Prediction in the social sciences. *Philosophy of Science* 7 (4): 492–498.

Linthicum, Kathryn P., Katherine Musacchio Schafer, and Jessica D. Ribeiro. 2019. Machine learning in suicide science: Applications and ethics. *Behavioral Sciences & the Law* 37 (3): 214–222.

Lundberg, Scott M., and Su-In Lee. 2017. A unified approach to interpreting model predictions. *In 31st Conference on Neural Information Processing Systems (NIPS 2017)*, Long Beach, CA, USA.

Lundberg, Scott M., et al. 2020. From local explanations to global understanding with explainable AI for trees. *Nature Machine Intelligence* 2 (1): 56–67.

Manski, Charles F. 2007. Partial identification of counterfactual choice probabilities. *International Economic Review* 48 (4): 1393–1410.

Merton, Robert K. 1968. *Social theory and social structure*. New York: Simon and Schuster.

Merton, Robert K., and Elinor Barber. 2011. *The travels and adventures of serendipity*. USA: Princeton University Press.

Molnar, Christoph, Giuseppe Casalicchio, and Bernd Bischl. 2020. Interpretable machine learning-a brief history, state-of-the-art and challenges. *Joint European conference on machine learning and knowledge discovery in databases*. Cham: Springer.

Pawson, Ray. 2000. Middle-range realism. *European Journal of Sociology* 41 (2): 283–325.

Popper, Karl. 1962. *Conjectures and refutations: The growth of scientific knowledge*. New York: Basic Books.

Popper, Karl. 2005. *The logic of scientific discovery*. New York: Routledge.

Ribeiro, Marco Tulio, Sameer Singh, and Carlos Guestrin. 2016. Why should I trust you? Explaining the predictions of any classifier. In *Proceedings of the 22nd ACM SIGKDD International Conference on Knowledge Discovery and Data Mining*, 1135–1144.

Scott, John, and Gordon Marshall. 2009. *A dictionary of sociology*. USA: Oxford University Press.

Sherden, William A. 1998. *The fortune sellers: The big business of buying and selling predictions*. New York: Wiley.

Strauss, Anselm, and Juliet Corbin. 1994. *Grounded theory methodology: An overview. Handbook of qualitative research*. USA: Sage.

Taleb, Nassim Nicholas. 2010. *The black swan: The impact of the highly improbable*. New York: Random House.

Wallace, Walter L. 1971. *The Logic of Science in Sociology*. Chicago: Transaction Publishers.

Watts, Duncan J. 2011. *Everything is obvious: Once you know the answer.* Australia: Currency.

Watts, Duncan J. 2014. Common sense and sociological explanations. *American Journal of Sociology* 120 (2): 313–351.

Weber, Max. 1968[1921]. *Economy and society*, trans. and ed. G. Roth and C. Wittich. New York: Bedminster Press.

Wells, Richard H., and J. Steven Picou. 1981. *American sociology: Theoretical and methodological structure.* USA: University Press of America.

Winter, Eyal. 2002. The shapley value. *Handbook of game theory with economic applications* 3: 2025–2054.

CHAPTER 7

Applications of Computing Grounded Theory: Revisiting Subjective Well-Being

1 Introduction

In the age of big data and algorithmic modeling, a fundamental question in the social sciences remains unresolved: how can we generate new theories directly from empirical data, especially when prior knowledge is limited or contested? This chapter applies the methodological framework of computing grounded theory (CGT) , which aims to bridge this gap by integrating machine learning algorithms with model-agnostic interpretability techniques, enabling the identification of potential explanatory variables and the theoretical interpretation of social patterns from large-scale survey data. Unlike traditional grounded theory, which relies primarily on qualitative coding and human interpretation, CGT leverages computational power to detect hidden structures in high-dimensional data and estimate the relative importance of each variable through Shapley Additive exPlanations (SHAP).

To demonstrate the practical utility of CGT, we focus on subjective well-being (SWB) as a case study. As a long-standing and richly studied domain in the social sciences, SWB offers an ideal testing ground for evaluating whether CGT can move beyond established predictors and uncover "new" explanatory factors. Using data from the 2017 China General Social Survey (CGSS2017), we train machine learning models to predict SWB and estimate the SHAP values of all potential predictors. We then extend our analysis globally by applying the same framework to World

Y. Chen et al., *Machine Learning in Social Science*,
https://doi.org/10.1007/978-981-95-6465-1_7

Values Survey (WVS) data from over 80 countries, thereby exploring both universal and context-specific mechanisms shaping subjective well-being.

By comparing findings across national and global contexts and testing the CGT method in diverse domains such as fertility intention and political satisfaction, this chapter illustrates not only the explanatory potential of data-driven theory generation but also its scalability and adaptability. Our results indicate that CGT can enrich existing theoretical frameworks (e.g., U-shaped happiness theory, relative deprivation) while also producing novel propositions (e.g., family distance theory). Through this, we highlight the broader promise of CGT as a theory-generative methodology for the computational social sciences.

2 The Subjective Well-Being of Chinese People

To verify the usefulness and potential of the proposed CGT in terms of developing theories, we consider subjective well-being, which is a widely and extensively researched topic in social science research, as an example dependent variable to find its most powerful predictors that can be expected to serve as a pool where potential "new" explanatory variables for subjective well-being can be located.

Subjective well-being has been a classic topic in social science research since the 1950s (Glatzer 2000; Campbell 1976), and prior research has shown that the level of subjective well-being is closely related to a wide range of individual attributes, including wealth (Easterlin 1973; Quoidbach et al. 2010; McBride 2010), life satisfaction (Gundelach and Kreiner 2004; Luchesi et al. 2018), health (Kushlev et al. 2020; Jo 2016; Steptoe 2019), and education (Michalos 2017). With the CGT method and the richness of CGSS data, we expect to locate new predictors for subjective well-being that have not been addressed in previous studies, which will allow us to propose new theories of subjective well-being.

2.1 Data and Variables

Our preliminary data comprise 12,582 samples collected by the National Survey Research Center, Renmin University of China, from the CGSS2017. For each sample, we extracted the value of 783 variables from the CGSS2017 survey questionnaire, including comprehensive information about the class identity, social status, and social network of the samples. The target Y variable in this study, i.e., "subjective well-being," is based on survey question A36: "In general, how happy would you say you are?" The responses are on a five-point scale: (1) very unhappy, (2) unhappy, (3) neutral, (4) happy, and (5) very happy. All other variables (other than the target variable) in the dataset are the predictor variables. To improve prediction accuracy while maintaining the ability to develop theories, we dichotomized the target variable "subjective well-being" by recoding "very unhappy, unhappy, and neutral" as class zero and kept "happy" and "very happy" as class one. We further converted categorical variables into the one-hot encoding format while removing the outliers of ordinal and interval variables. Note that we discarded variables with greater than 30% missing values and we filled the remaining missing values with the median.

In addition, the number of samples from class one was much greater than the number of samples from class zero, which may cause deviations in predictions. Thus, we employed the Random Over-Sampling method (Menardi and Torelli 2014) to increase the size of the sample set for class zero such that it was equal to that of class one.

2.2 *Assessing the Predictive Power of a Feature*

We employed a gradient boosting tree algorithm, i.e., eXtreme Gradient Boosting (XGBoost) for the modeling task. Here, the number of the sub-decision trees was set to 1000, and the other hyperparameters took default values in our model (i.e., learning rate = 0.1, max depth = 10, gamma = 0, reg alpha = 0, reg lambda = 1). We randomly divided the data into training (70%) and test (30%) sets and considered precision, recall, and the F1-measure (also referred to as the F-score) to evaluate the quality of the model. The precision, recall, and F1-measure results are presented and discussed extensively in Sect. 4. In summary, the model's prediction accuracy was 0.92, the recall rate was 0.86, and the value of the F1-measure was 0.92; thus, we consider that the model exhibited good overall performance.

We employed SHAP, a feature attribution method, to analyze the interpretability of the model's predictions about subjective well-being and to identify the factors contributing most to the results. Here, for each sample, we calculated the SHAP value for each predictor variable. With these SHAP values, we can identify the marginal contributions of the predictor variables when predicting "subjective well-being." Generally, if the SHAP value is positive, including it will lead to an increase in the result of the predicted value. In contrast, a negative SHAP value will lead to a decrease in the predicted result. Then, for each predictor variable, we obtain the mean SHAP value. By directly comparing the mean SHAP values between predictor variables, we can identify the contributions of all predictor variables to the overall model and arrange the values in descending order.

2.3 *Results of Chinese subjective Well-Being on CGT*

Figure 1a shows a bar plot of the top 20 factors extracted by the SHAP method that contribute most to predicting subjective well-being. These factors were measured according to the mean of the absolute value of the marginal SHAP value for all individuals with different feature values. Figure 1b shows specific details about the influence and distribution of different predictors on the target variables in the form of a scatter plot, where each point in Fig. 1b represents a real sample, and its color represents the magnitude of the feature value of each sample in a single row. Here, the larger the feature value, the redder the color of the point. In Fig. 1b, the horizontal axis is the SHAP value, where a positive SHAP value indicates that the predicted effect on subjective well-being is positive (and vice versa). Here, as more points have the same SHAP value, the cross-sectional area of the "honeycomb" increases, and the thicker it appears. Generally, this graph can reflect the mode and magnitude of the interaction between variables, as well as the distribution of related cases. Taking the "sense of fairness" as an example, the scatterplot shows that individuals with a higher sense of fairness (i.e., a positive SHAP value) tend to be concentrated on the right side of the horizontal axis, and individuals with a low sense of fairness (i.e., a negative SHAP value) tend to be concentrated on the left side of the horizontal axis. This means that the sense of fairness typically has a positive impact on subjective well-being.

Figure 1a also shows that the "sense of fairness" has a SHAP value of 1.4; thus, it contributes the most to the prediction of subjective well-being, followed by the "health" variable with a SHAP value of 0.8. Figure 1b further shows the changing trend in SHAP values for some typical variables through the scattered points. In fact, the identified 20 factors span a wide range of domains, including psychology, economics, sociology, and political science. These areas are to some extent considered key issues in the discussion of factors that affect subjective well-being in existing theoretical and empirical studies (Diener 2009; Diener et al.

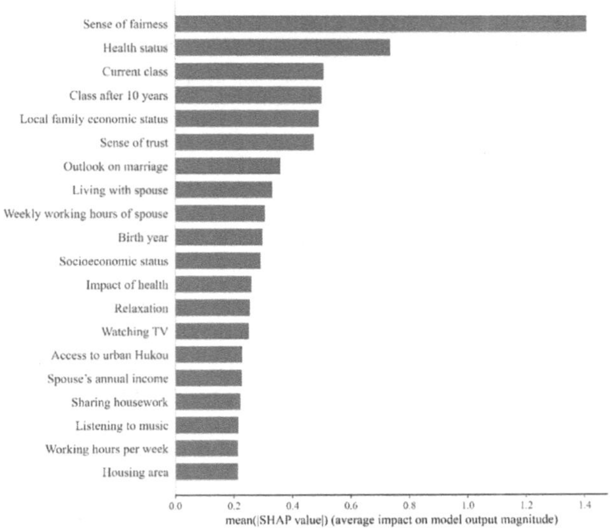

(a) Bar plot

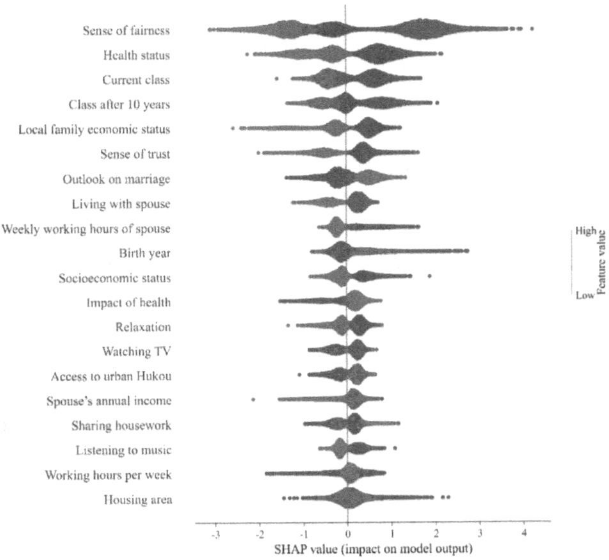

(b) Beeswarm plot

Fig. 1 Top 20 factors of predicted marginal effects on subjective well-being

2018). The results that are generally consistent with existing theories motivated us to propose a new theory; however, the results that contested existing theories cannot be ignored and should motivate us to reconsider previous studies.

2.4 Proposing a New Theory

Figure 1b shows that the weekly working hours of a spouse (WHS) strongly predict subjective well-being. Its contribution to the prediction of subjective well-being is even higher than that of age, socioeconomic status, health, and a set of variables (gender, education, income, etc.) that have long been known to influence subjective well-being (Mookerjee and Beron 2005; Michalos 2017; Diener and Oishi 2000). However, in the context of marriage and family, previous studies on subjective well-being have primarily focused on marital status, marriage matching, and family support (Stack and Eshleman 1998; Chapman and Guven 2016; Rogers and White 1998; North et al. 2008; Lu and Lin 1998), thereby generally neglecting the potential role of WHS.

Thus, the data-grounded CGT method allowed us to discover something new, e.g., subjective well-being may be affected by one's spouse. We suspect that there may be an important link between WHS and subjective well-being, which we refer to as "family distance." Note that previous studies paid little attention to the correlation between WHS and subjective well-being; however, our data-grounded results exhibited an interesting n-shaped curve correlation between WHS and subjective well-being (Fig. 2g). If a person's spouse works more than 70 hours a week, the person's subjective well-being will increase; otherwise, it will decrease. This contrasts with the curve showing the relationship between respondents' own weekly work hours and well-being. We have controlled other variables, e.g., income, meaning that the results should reflect the net effect of WHS; thus, we can explain this result from the perspective of family distance: greater family distance provides spouses with greater personal space, which may help reduce family conflicts.

In summary, we found that appropriate family distance can improve well-being. Instead, a distance too far or too close will impair the well-being.

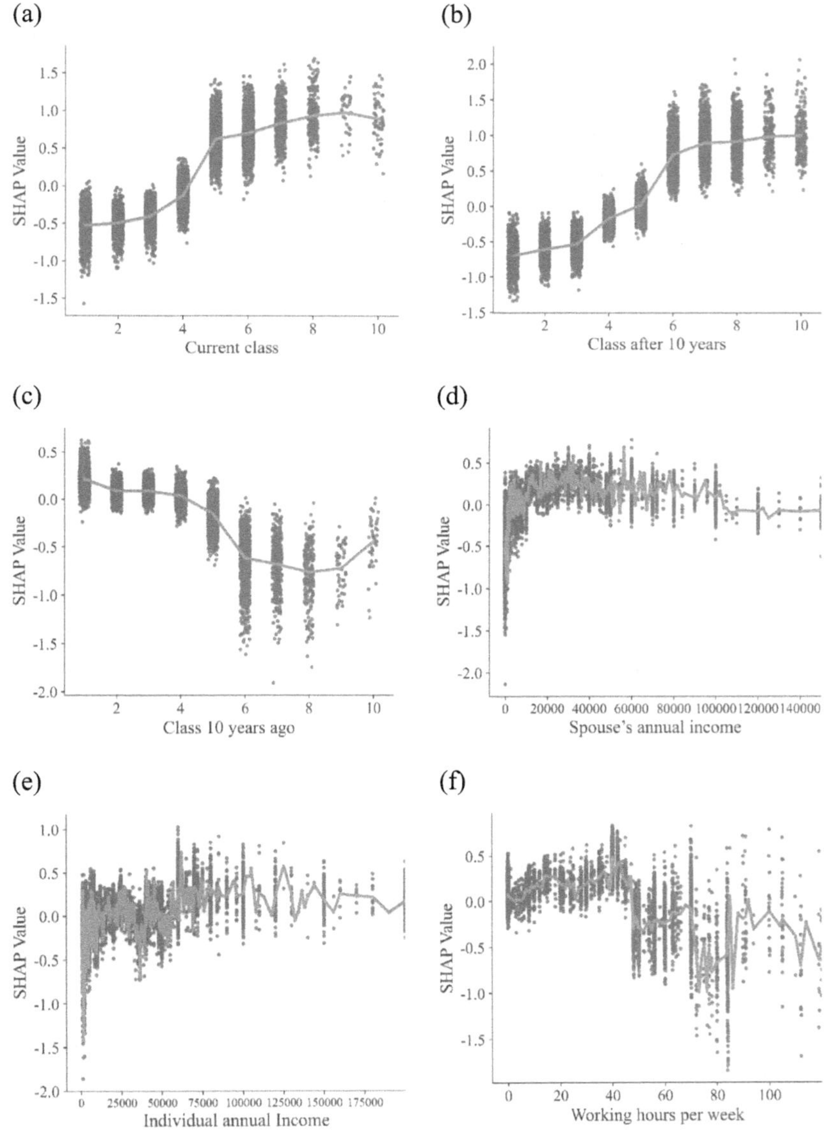

Fig. 2 Partial dependence plot of SHAP values for typical predictor features

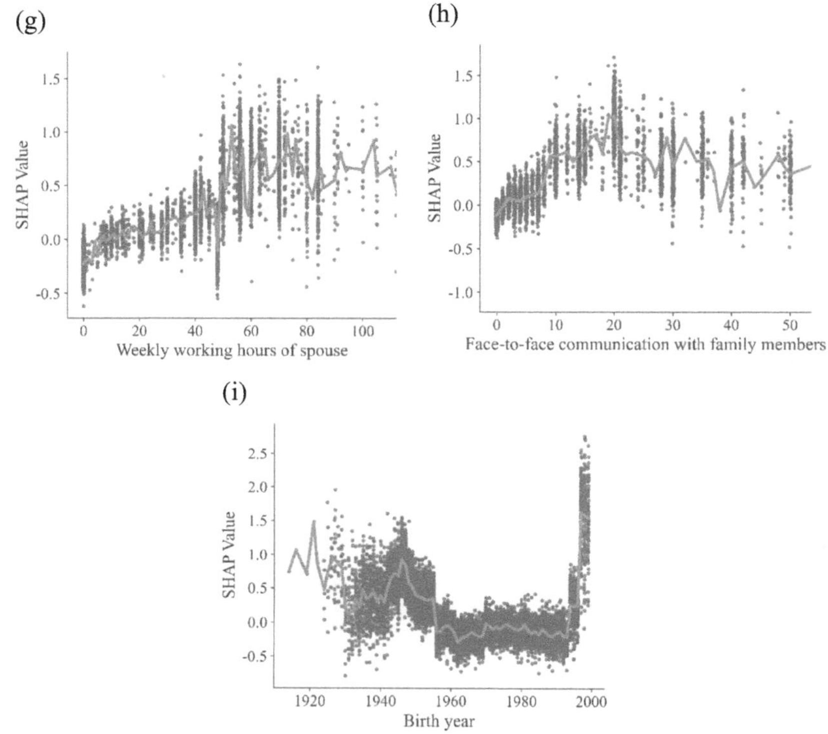

Fig. 2 (continued)

2.5 *Expanding Existing Theories*

Many studies have demonstrated that age and socioeconomic status variables best characterize subjective well-being levels (e.g., Campbell 1976; Clark et al. 2008; Diener et al. 1993; FitzRoy et al. 2014; Larson 1978; Vera-Villarroel et al. 2012). Our findings indicate that some of the CGT findings are in line with prior research. For example, as shown in Fig. 2a–e, higher socioeconomic status results in higher subjective well-being. Note that this result is consistent with classical research in the fields of economics (Easterlin 2003; Frey & Stutzer 2010; Kozma & Stones 1983) and social status (Anderson et al. 2012; Cameron 1975; Veenhoven 2015). Relevant studies into the theoretical perspectives of relative deprivation and tunnel effect have also confirmed that horizontal social comparison and subjective social mobility expectations have significant impacts on subjective well-being (Senik 2009; Hirschman and Rothschild 1973).

Beyond this consistency, our results are crucial to providing supplementary insights about preexisting theories. Early studies regarding the interaction between age and subjective well-being concluded that age had little or no influence on subjective well-being (Hervás 2009). However, the results of an increasing number of studies are in alignment with the U-shaped subjective well-being theory, where higher levels of subjective well-being are experienced before our twenties and after our fifties (Blanchflower and Oswald 2008; Graham and Ruiz Pozuelo 2017; Frijters and Beatton 2012; Inglehart et al. 2008; Swami et al. 2009). As shown in Fig. 2i, our results also demonstrate a U-shaped relationship between a person's birth year and their subjective well-being. People born between 1955 and 1995 are less happy than people born before 1955 and after 1995. We suggest the postponement may result from the national circumstances of China (for example, modernization and market economy transformation) and the cohort effect, which deserve further investigation in the future.

In addition, subjective socioeconomic status indicators, e.g., current class and class after ten years, exhibit a Z-shaped ladder distribution, as shown in Fig. 2a and b. Followed by this distribution, the SHAP values are nearly fixed within a certain range but change rapidly after reaching a turning point to finally become flat again. There are no significant internal disparities within the grades 1–3 current class group and the grades 5–10 current class group; however, conversion from the former to the latter leads to significant differences due to the key turning point that occurred in grades 4–5. A similar effect of the key breakpoint also occurs between the class expectations of grades 1–5 and grades 6–10. Thus, we propose that turning points are the key issues for the conversion of subjective well-being. Classical relative deprivation theory about subjective well-being has established that subjective well-being results from the comparison (Knies et al. 2008; Veenhoven 1991; Verme 2013). In our study, a significant finding is that the effects of comparisons appear to be discrete and separated by the turning points, through which individuals are classified into different hidden groups, and the comparisons between individuals from different groups have significant impacts on subjective well-being.

The above examples demonstrate that the proposed CGT can draw conclusions that are consistent with existing research without a prior knowledge base, can make contributions to understanding social phenomena, and drive theoretical progress by identifying new evidence.

2.6 *Complex Relationships*

To draw further information from the data-grounded approach, we explore the heterogeneity of prediction results. Many previous studies about subjective well-being that employed traditional quantitative methods were performed under linear assumptions (Frey and Stutzer 2010; Stack and Eshleman 1998; Veenhoven 2015). In other words, the models employed simply consider a one-way linear relationship and assume homogeneity while ignoring heterogeneity effects (for example, there are large differences in the effects on different individuals). However, our data-grounded approach allows us to recognize complex relationships in our models and identify the effects of heterogeneity.

Traditional quantitative methods are primarily based on the comparison of the overall mean among different groups, and they do not consider the distribution of samples within a group. Here, a homogeneous effect means that well-being has the same effect on people of the same group, and the ingroup variance of the SHAP value is small. A heterogeneous effect means that the effect of well-being on the same group of people varies greatly, and the ingroup variance of the SHAP value is huge. Figure 2f (working hours per week) shows that the SHAP values of working hours (ranging from zero to 40 hours) are between −0.5 and 0.5, following a relatively uniform distribution, which means that the effect of weekly working hours on well-being is homogeneous. However, the SHAP values for working hours ranging from 70 to 80 hours are between −1.5 and 0.1, which embodies a large heterogeneity effect on well-being. Generally, this suggests that people with shorter working hours are happier than those with longer working hours; however, longer working time can sometimes bring more subjective well-being.

2.7 *Robustness Test*

Many researchers have noticed the Rashomon effect of algorithms: Internal heterogeneity caused by different hyperparameter settings of the same model and external heterogeneity caused by different algorithmic models (D'Amour 2021; Breiman 2001), which may lead to different results. Thus, we must ensure that the CGT models and explanatory models are robust; otherwise, the confidence and reliability of the models will be implausible. Therefore, we tested the robustness of our data-grounded models according to three aspects.

(1) **Different datasets**. Robust grounded methods do not vary greatly when the size and composition of the data change. Here, we employed the bootstrap sampling method to randomly select 50, 60, 70, 80, 90, and 100% of the original data.
(2) **Different predictive algorithms**. Data-grounded results should be similar when using different predictive machine learning algorithms. Here, we compared the data-grounded results generated by five algorithms, i.e., the XGBoost, CatBoost, LightGBM, Gradient-Boosting, and Random Forest algorithms.
(3) **Different algorithm hyperparameters**. We replaced the original values of all hyperparameters in the XGBoost algorithm with various other values and compared the results. These hyperparameters (Fig. 3) included the maximum depth, regularization coefficient, learning rate, and subsample ratio.

First, we obtained the mean absolute SHAP values of all models under the abovementioned conditions. We then calculated the Pearson correlation coefficients for each pair based on the mean absolute SHAP values. The results are shown in Fig. 3. Generally, the results of these models are highly similar, i.e., most correlation coefficients between any two models are greater than 0.95, and the significance of the correlation coefficients is 0.000. In particular, the heterogeneity of the data and internal heterogeneity of the algorithm parameters are minimal. Only the pairs that included the Random Forest algorithm showed small heterogeneity in the correlation coefficients, although the correlation coefficient was greater than 0.88. We also calculated the Spearman rank correlation coefficient according to the ordering of the importance of SHAP values under each condition. The results were very similar to those obtained in terms of the Pearson coefficient.

Generalization error, including a researcher's degrees of freedom and the model's algorithmic constraints, is an inherent feature of the modeling process. Generally, simple models do not necessarily outperform complex ones in terms of generalizability. However, complex machine learning

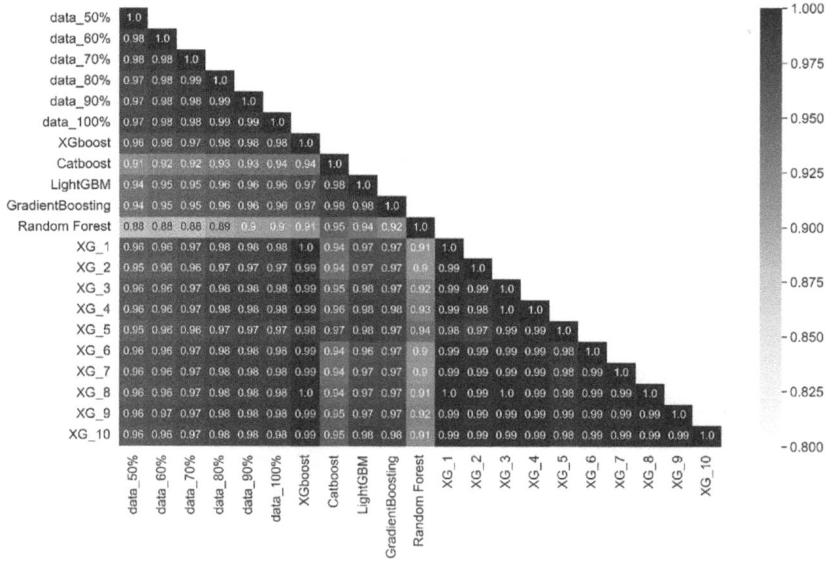

Fig. 3 Results of the robustness test

techniques can reduce generalization errors significantly using ensemble methods, e.g., bagging and boosting (Skurichina and Duin 2002). Here, our data-grounded method is a type of complex ensemble model with 1000 decision trees. In addition, reviewing multiple models for cross-validation and ensuring normative standards for the training and interpretation processes of machine learning models (D'Amour et al. 2020) is a feasible means to improve the reliability and validity of data-grounded methods. In summary, in the case of well-being, our data-grounded method is sufficiently robust.

3 The Subjective Well-Being of People Worldwide

In addition to analyzing the factors influencing subjective well-being in China, we used data from the WVS Wave 7 (2017–2022) to further explore the key factors influencing subjective well-being worldwide. First, we conducted the CGT method on subjective well-being using data from

94,278 respondents across 80 countries. The top 20 factors influencing subjective well-being are illustrated in Fig. 4.

Globally, the top three factors influencing subjective well-being are "Satisfaction with financial situation," "How much freedom of choice and control," and "Secure in neighborhood." This indicates that financial situation, freedom of choice, and a secure residential environment are common keys to subjective well-being worldwide.

In general, the factors influencing subjective well-being worldwide can be broadly categorized into the following dimensions.

(1) **Material and Security**

(1) satisfaction with financial situation (Ranking 1st)
(2) Secure in neighborhood (Ranking 3rd)
(3) Gone without a cash income (Ranking 9th)
(4) Gone without needed medicine or treatment (Ranking 11th)

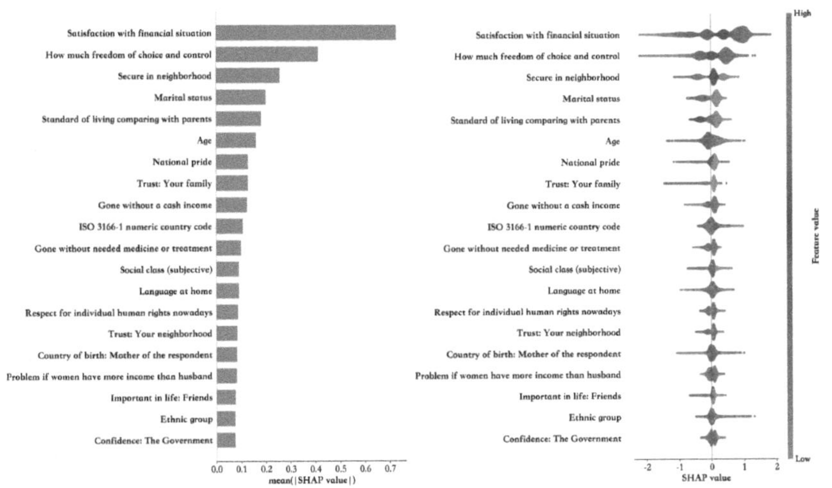

Fig. 4 Top 20 factors of predicted marginal effects on subjective well-being (WVS)

(2) **National and Political**

(1) How much freedom of choice and control (Ranking 2nd)
(2) National pride (Ranking 7th)
(3) ISO 3166-1 numeric country code (Ranking 10th)
(4) Language at home (Ranking 13th)
(5) Respect for individual human rights nowadays (Ranking 14th)
(6) Country of birth: Mother of the respondent (Ranking 16th)
(7) Ethnic group (Ranking 19th)
(8) Confidence: The Government (Ranking 20th).

(3) **Family and Social Relationships**

(1) Marital status (Ranking 4th)
(2) Trust: Your family (Ranking 8th)
(3) Trust: Your neighborhood (Ranking 15th)
(4) Problem if women have more income than husband (Ranking 17th)
(5) Important in life: Friends (Ranking 18th)

(4) **Social Comparison**

(1) Intergenerational upward comparison: Standard of living compared with parents (Ranking 5th)
(2) Horizontal social status comparison: Social class (subjective) (Ranking 12th)

We further explored whether there are differences in the factors influencing subjective well-being across countries. We selected Japan and Russia from Asia, the UK and Germany from Europe, the U.S. from North America, Brazil from South America, Nigeria from Africa, and Australia from Oceania to investigate whether there are differences in the factors influencing subjective well-being in different regions. The analysis results are shown in Fig. 5a–h.

According to Fig. 5, there are both similarities and differences in the factors influencing subjective well-being across countries, as follows:

"Satisfaction with financial situation" is almost universally the most important factor influencing subjective well-being across all countries, except for Australia. In Russia, economic conditions are highly valued,

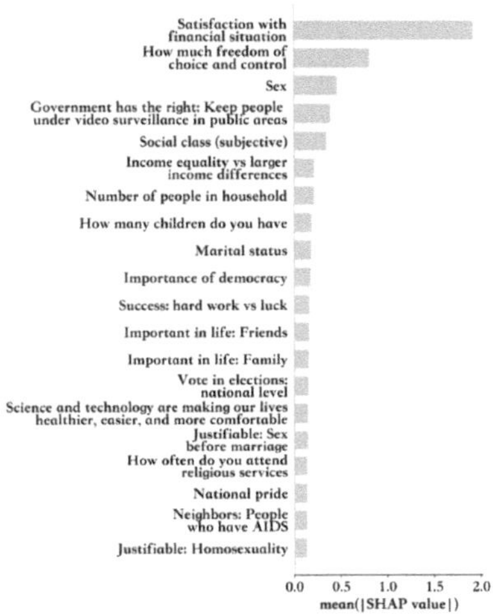

(a) Japan

(b) Russia

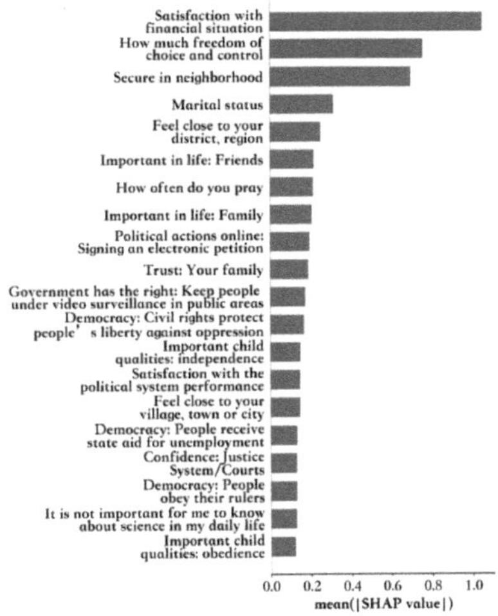

(c) the U.S.

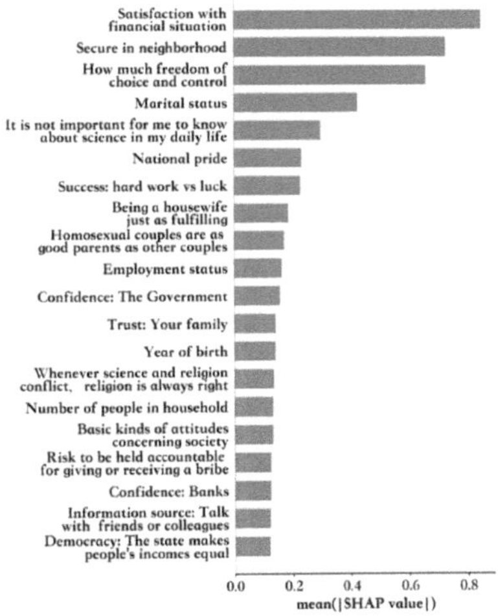

(d) the UK

Fig. 5 Top 20 factors of predicted marginal effects on subjective well-being (8 countries)

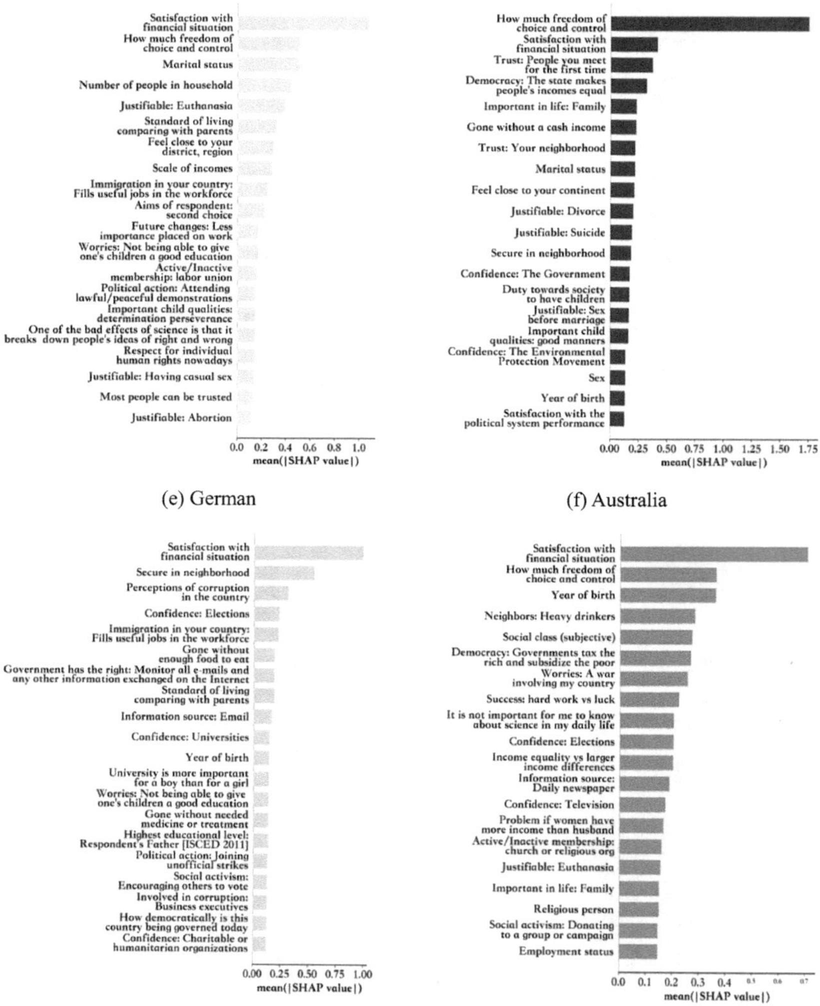

(e) German

(f) Australia

(g) Nigeria

(h) Brazil

Fig. 5 (continued)

with satisfaction with financial situation and income level ranking as the top two factors influencing subjective well-being, while "Gone without a cash income" and "Gone without enough food to eat" also appear among the top factors.

In contrast, in Australia, "how much freedom of choice and control" is the most important factor influencing subjective well-being, with democracy and trust in the political system also ranking high, reflecting a high emphasis on individual autonomy and freedom of will in society. Also, confidence in environmental protection movements ranks 16th, which may reflect Australians' increasing concern for sustainable development and environmental protection.

In the UK and the U.S., "Secure in neighborhood" is a critical factor influencing subjective well-being, ranking 2nd and 3rd, respectively. However, unlike the focus on family gender norms and employment in the UK, Americans' subjective well-being is more closely related to political and democratic values, such as "How much freedom of choice and control" (Ranking 2nd); "Feel close to your district, region" (Ranking 5th); "Political actions online: Signing an electronic petition" (Ranking 9th); "Government has the right: Keep people under video surveillance in public areas" (Ranking 11th); "Democracy: Civil rights protect people's liberty against oppression" (Ranking 12th); "Satisfaction with the political system performance" (Ranking 14th); "Feel close to your village, town, or city" (Ranking 15th); "Democracy: People receive state aid for unemployment" (Ranking 16th); and "Democracy: People obey their rulers" (Ranking 18th).

For developing countries, distinctive features exist in the factors influencing subjective well-being. For example, in Nigeria, material and security needs occupy a crucial position, with "Secure in neighborhood" ranking 2nd, "Gone without enough food to eat" and "Gone without needed medicine or treatment" ranking 6th and 14th. Additionally, corruption, elections, and education are closely related to subjective well-being, such as "Perceptions of corruption in the country," "Confidence: Elections," "Involved in corruption: Business executives," "Confidence: Universities," "University is more important for a boy than for a girl," "Worries: Not being able to give," and "Highest educational level: Respondent's Father." For Brazil, "Neighbors: Heavy drinkers" and "Worries: A war involving my country" are unique factors influencing subjective well-being.

Furthermore, gender is a critical factor influencing subjective well-being in Japan, ranking 3rd, but not in other countries, which means women's subjective well-being is significantly higher than men's. Additionally, "Number of people in household" and "How many children do you have" are closely related to subjective well-being (ranking 7th and 8th) in Japan, with higher subjective well-being often associated with more cohabiting family members or children.

4 Five Values of CGT

We tested other predictor variables and different datasets in a more abundant way, made a similar analysis of the "fertility desire" for the CGSS2017 data and variables such as "government satisfaction," "weight," and "donation behavior" for the CFPS2018 data.[1] Under the corroboration and inspiration of plentiful empirical results, five application values of CGT were summarized.

4.1 Directional Focusing

The traditional quantitative analysis emphasizes whether there is a statistically significant relationship between two variables, yet with less concern for the importance of such a relationship in the research problem. As Duncan Watts pointed out in the journal Nature, for any research theme, there exists a large number of competing interpretations in social sciences, and they always have inconsistencies and contradictions (Watts 2017). He also pointed out that this paradox is caused by the fact that social science is too concerned with theoretical progress rather than starting from research issues. The data-grounded approach is a solution to such a contradiction with its research-oriented predictive logic. Hence, the variables mined can be directly sorted according to the marginal effect of the impact.

[1] In the CGSS2017 data, "How many children would you like to have without policy restrictions?" is the question corresponding to fertility willingness, and the answer is a continuous variable. In the CFPS2018 data, "Evaluation of the city and county government" is the question corresponding to government satisfaction, and the answer is an ordinal variable ranging from 1 (worse than before) to 5 (great achievement). "What is your weight?" is the question corresponding to weight, and the answer is a continuous variable. "Have you donated money personally to any organization or individuals in the past 12 months?" is the question corresponding to the donation behavior, and the answer is yes/no.

This means that the effect of variables can be directly compared among hundreds of possible factors with a focus on the principal contradiction affecting the research question.

For example, we found that large numbers of indicators related to the spouses of the study subjects were ranked at the forefront in the grounded test for subjective well-being. Furthermore, their spouses' working time and annual income have greater impacts on the subject's subjective well-being compared with their own working time, annual income, and educational level. It indicates that family structure and division of labor, especially more refined marriage relationships, should be the research priority of social psychology. In terms of fertility willingness, the offspring's fertility willingness is significantly affected by the family background of the study subjects, such as the father's education level and whether the mother works as a farmer, which has not been fully considered in the existing theoretical paradigm of fertility research. Conversely, fertility willingness is less influenced by factors traditionally emphasized in social science research, such as gender, urban and rural areas, income, education level, and social security. It can directly guide in refocusing the theoretical focus of fertility research (Fig. 6).

4.2 *Inspired Discoveries*

Compared with traditional data models, the algorithm-oriented machine learning method can overcome limitations of model form and variable selection, with considerations of various interactions between variables. By breaking the limitation of the number of independent variables and the relationship, it is possible for us to completely think and expand the affecting factors of explanatory variables using a new method. Rich data can guide researchers to obtain inspiration for new theoretical hypotheses from the levels of discovering new explanatory variables and new explanatory dimensions. We stress that new research opportunities may arise if data are grounded with empirical results which are unexpected or contradict prior theoretical or general knowledge. The proposed method can be called free imagination of data in comparison with researchers' "subjective" free imagination for the hypothesis.

For instance, previous studies have paid little attention to the influence of spouses' working time on well-being. But the grounded data reveal that the spouse's weekly working time plays a crucial role in one's subjective well-being. In the meantime, the influencing manner shows an

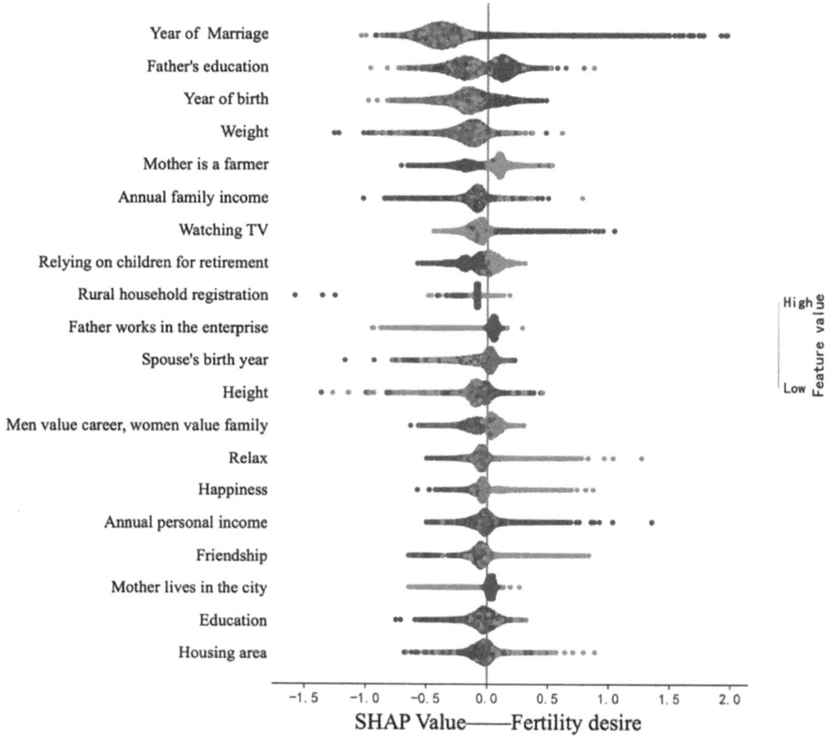

Fig. 6 Top 20 factors of predicted marginal effects on fertility desire

interesting phenomenon of n-shaped distribution, that is, the longer the spouse works, the more monotonically the subjective well-being increases before 70 hours, with a downward trend after 70 hours. This is totally contrary to the U-shaped effect of the respondent's weekly working time and well-being. Why does this paradox arise? The extended working time of spouses is accompanied by higher household income and greater freedom of family space, thereby lowering the risk of conflict among family members, according to our speculations. Hard work brought by working time has a negative effect on oneself, while having a positive spillover effect on the family. Or we found that the number of underage children is significantly negatively associated with subjective well-being, which is significantly different from our common sense that the more

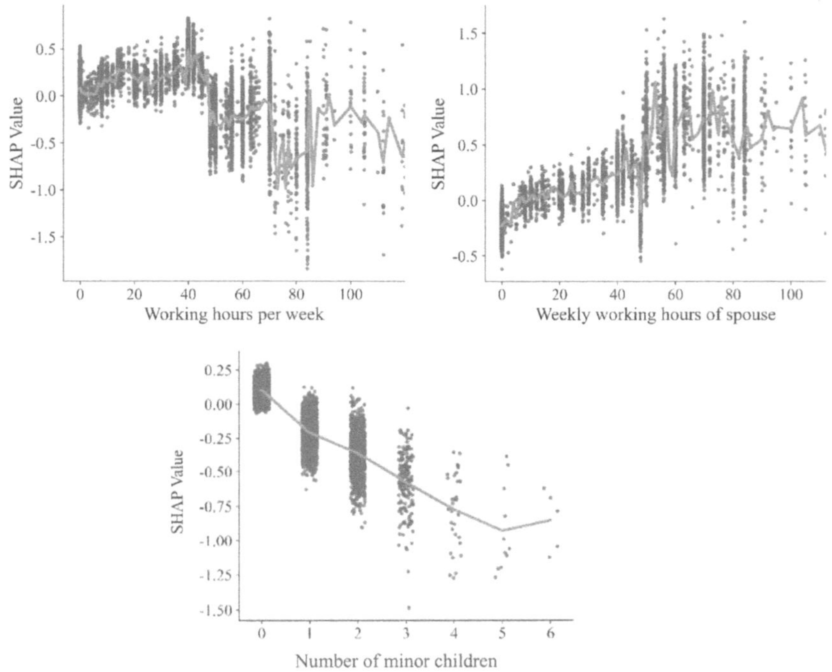

Fig. 7 Partial dependence graph of the SHAP value for heuristic discovery

children, the more blessings and finding subjective well-being in suffering (Fig. 7).

4.3 *Details Clarification*

A simple but interesting classic case was cited by Varian. The Logistic model showed that age was nearly unrelated to rescue with a negative coefficient in an analysis of the rescued passengers on the Titanic. But the real social scenario is that the elderly and children are evacuated preferentially, causing a U-shaped relationship between age and whether they are rescued (Varian 2014). Whether there exists a non-linear relationship, in general, is identified in the traditional way through the scatter plot and the smooth line graph. Then independent variables are converted into a linear relationship upon squaring with polynomial regression. But it is worth noting that such a method is applicable only to preliminary exploration and hypothesis-first confirmatory analysis. The complex relationship between variables is fully expected by the data-grounded theory through fitting data with models. The SHAP value can meticulously reflect how the marginal effect varies with the characteristic value within a possible influence feature for its calculation of the marginal effect for each case and feature. By doing so, the linear shackles of the traditional econometric model can be completely broken to capture more detailed data.

For instance, the more detailed mining is embodied concretely in the following three points: First, the non-linear relationship. A sharp increase in subjective well-being is observed among the group born before 1955 and after 1995, from the perspective of the relationship between age and subjective well-being. Evidently, there is a clear depression among the group born between 1955 and 1995. This "U-shaped" distribution is consistent with the recent literature on age and well-being with major breakthroughs (Blanchflower and Oswald 2008; Frijters and Beatton 2012). And similar typical cases are "厂-shaped" distribution between income and subjective well-being, and the ladder-shaped distribution between stratum and subjective well-being. Second, the homogeneity-heterogeneity effect between samples. Taking the impact of "working hours per week" on subjective well-being as an example, the SHAP values of cases with working hours of 0–40 hours are between −0.5 and 0.5, presenting a more uniform distribution. Working hours have more homogeneous impacts on subjective well-being. Whereas the SHAP value of the case with working hours of 70–80 hours is distributed between −1.5 and −0.1, exerting a great heterogeneous effect on subjective well-being. Evidently, people with shorter working hours are generally happier, whereas people with longer working hours may be happier or less fortunate. It can be observed that subjective well-being is affected by other important interaction variables, together with working hours. Third, the effect of imbalance. The influence of a variable on subjective well-being is not distributed in equilibrium by the zero line of SHAP. Take the influence of the "stratum 10 years ago" on subjective well-being as an example. The case point and mean line are obviously unevenly distributed below the zero line of SHAP, indicating that there is an extremely limited positive effect of low stratum on subjective well-being 10 years ago, but a significantly negative effect of high stratum on subjective well-being 10 years ago. Variables with such imbalanced impacts should be highlighted in the study.

4.4 *Theory Verification*

As a matter of fact, data-grounded and traditional quantitative analysis methods oriented to hypothesis testing can be mutually complemented and verified. If social scientists expect their interpretation to be scientifically legitimate, the interpretation must be evaluated as per scientific standards, and the prediction must be conducted (Watts 2014). Among correlation, causation, and prediction, correlation is a prerequisite for judging causality and making predictions, and causality is a sufficient but not necessary condition for predicting. This means that A can be surely utilized to predict B if the regression model proved a significant correlation or causal relationship between variables A and B. When put in the data-grounded, A must also have a larger contribution value to the average marginal effect predicted by variable B. Otherwise, A can be reasonably believed to only have a weak correlation or causality with B, but in fact, it is of little significance. Conversely, it is reasonable to suspect that there may be a non-linear relationship between the variables or a large heterogeneity between the samples if the relationship between the two variables in the regression analysis is not significant, with a large contribution value in the prediction. In this way, the ideal linear relationship cannot be fitted. In that case, the data can be further processed and adjusted based on feasibility conditions, so as to re-perform the regression or causal inference in the sense of the traditional model.

Taking the effect of TV watching time on weight as an example, longer hours spent watching TV are generally associated with increased weight due to sedentary behavior accompanied by eating habits. The CGT analysis on weight shows that TV watching time has a significant influence on weight gain. Since it has a high marginal effect on weight prediction, those with longer TV watching time might gain more weight (Fig. 8).

4.5 *Governance Effectiveness*

Social science is a practical science. Both the public and policymakers eagerly expect scholars to provide guidance from macro governance to

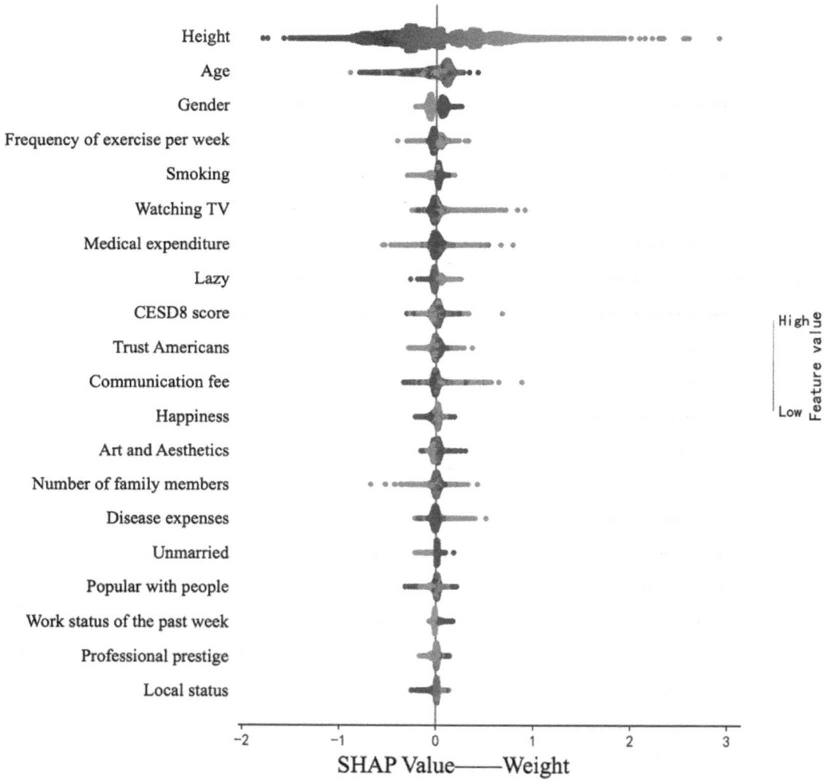

Fig. 8 Top 20 factors of predicted marginal effects on weight

personal destiny, rather than merely being satisfied with concept extraction, process interpretation, and statistical judgment. In such a context, the mission of quantitative social science research should be extended to identify the key possible intervention factors and make suggestions for serving a country's top priorities from theoretical verification. The machine learning algorithm, based on the problem orientation of social prediction, fully considers the emergence and interaction of multi-cause, common-cause, and complex phenomena of social phenomena. Also, the interpretability algorithm fully guarantees the accuracy of the prediction, the possible results of the prediction, and the distribution of contributions between the various predictors. In the pursuit of the basic goal of social governance effectiveness, identifying the crucial intervention variables is practical for social governance through continuously simulating social phenomena that do not exist.

Concerning local government satisfaction, the main factors affecting government satisfaction are explored through the data-grounded approach. Although the public services provided by the government involve aspects such as transportation, public security, education, housing, social security, and employment, from the data results, medical problems have the greatest impact on government satisfaction compared with other government functions. It is concretely manifested in the three major aspects of the medical conditions, medical costs, and medical level, presenting a diminishing relationship in terms of importance. The data-grounded approach reflects the most common and urgent conditional needs of the broad masses of people in a simple, direct, and reliable manner, which plays a data reference role for policymakers to address the most concerning national affairs through resource allocation. Moreover, the grounded analysis of donation behavior indicates that donation behavior is greatly impacted by citizens' reading behaviors and the use of mobile Internet. In other words, citizens' empathy and the generation of positive interactions that are beneficial to society will be greatly stimulated by means of creating a sound cultural infrastructure and an Internet communication environment. It can be extended broadly both at the macro and micro levels. Similar research on issues such as unemployment rate, crime rate, quality of education, and deviant behavior can be conducted to assist and intervene in social governance (Figs. 9 and 10).

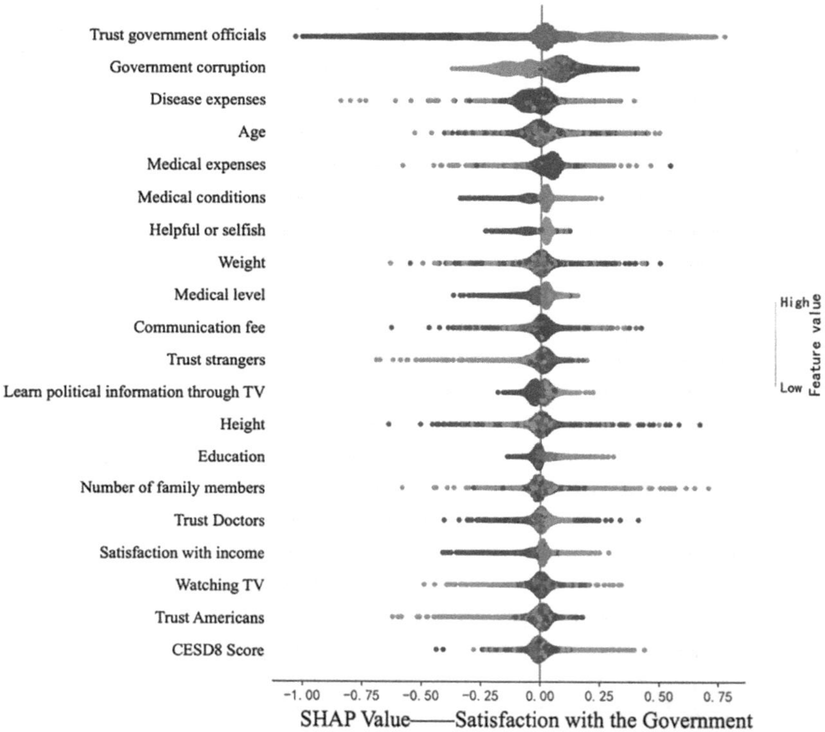

Fig. 9 Top 20 factors of predicted marginal effects on satisfaction with the government

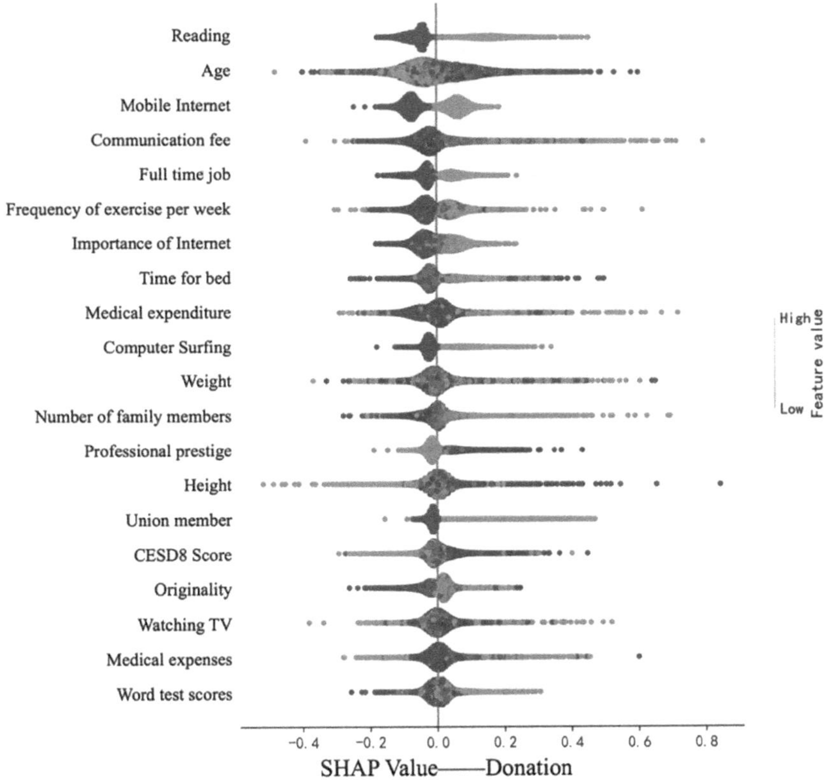

Fig. 10 Top 20 factors of predicted marginal effects on donation

5 Conclusion

In this part, we proposed CGT, an algorithm-based approach to identifying potential patterns of relationships among key variables from large survey data. CGT has addressed a fundamental issue in data-driven methods, i.e., how to generate theories using quantitative data when prior knowledge is limited or contested. Using machine learning methods, SHAP values, and a dataset about subjective well-being from the CGSS2017 survey, we have demonstrated that the proposed CGT is valid and reliable in terms of extracting predictor variables that contribute the most to prediction and thereby inspire the proposal of new theories.

Our results suggest that new hypotheses and theory revision and development can be derived directly from a dataset and algorithms. For example, the "family distance theory" states that the appropriate distance between couples can lead to positive impacts on subjective well-being. In addition, relative to subjective well-being research in terms of demographics and socioeconomics, we have demonstrated that our results can add new thoughts to existing theories, e.g., supplementing the U-shaped subjective well-being theory (i.e., we found considerable age postponement in the Chinese context compared to the findings of previous western studies in which higher levels of subjective well-being are experienced before our twenties and after our fifties) and the relative deprivation theory (we found that the effects of comparisons for classical relative deprivation theory appear to be discrete and separated by turning points). In addition, through comparative analysis, our cross-national comparisons also revealed the differences in the importance ranking of the impact of different countries on subjective well-being. Taken together, the results of this chapter demonstrate the potential benefit of machine learning and model-agnostic methods to analyze socioeconomic issues and highlight the unlimited possibilities of the data-grounded approach to test and generate theories. Moreover, in the future, along with the increasing amount of data information and data dimensions available in the digital era, CGT will be of even greater value in developing relevant theories.

References

Anderson, Cameron, et al. 2012. The local-ladder effect: Social status and subjective well-being. *Psychological Science* 23 (7): 764–771.

Blanchflower, David G., and Andrew J. Oswald. 2008. Is well-being U-shaped over the life cycle? *Social Science & Medicine* 66: 1733–1749.

Breiman, Leo. 2001. Statistical modeling: The two cultures (with comments and a rejoinder by the author). *Statistical science* 16(3): 199–231.

Cameron, Paul. 1975. Mood as an indicant of subjective well-being: Age, sex, social class, and situational differences. *Journal of Gerontology* 30 (2): 216–224.

Campbell, Angus. 1976. Subjective measures of well-being. *American Psychologist* 31 (2): 117–124.

Chapman, Bruce, and Cahit Guven. 2016. Revisiting the relationship between marriage and wellbeing: Does marriage quality matter? *Journal of Subjective Well-Being Studies* 17 (2): 533–551.

Clark, Andrew E., Paul Frijters, and Michael A. Shields. 2008. Relative income, subjective well-being, and utility: An explanation for the Easterlin paradox and other puzzles. *Journal of Economic Literature* 46 (1): 95–144.

D'Amour, Alexander. 2021. Revisiting Rashomon: A comment on "The Two Cultures." *Observational Studies* 7 (1): 59–63.

D'Amour, Alexander, et al. 2020. Underspecification presents challenges for credibility in modern machine learning. *Journal of Machine Learning Research* 23 (226): 1–61.

Diener, Ed. 2009. Subjective well-being. *The Science of Well-Being* 95 (3): 542–575.

Diener, Ed, et al. 1993. The relationship between income and subjective well-being: Relative or absolute? *Social Indicators Research* 28 (3): 195–223.

Diener, Ed, Shigehiro Oishi, and Louis Tay. 2018. Advances in subjective well-being research. *Nature Human Behaviour* 2 (4): 253–260.

Easterlin, Richard A. 1973. Does money buy subjective well-being? *The Public Interest* 30: 3.

Easterlin, Richard A. 2003. Explaining happiness. *Proceedings of the National Academy of Sciences* 100 (19): 11176–11183.

FitzRoy, Felix R., et al. 2014. Testing the tunnel effect: Comparison, age and subjective well-being in UK and German panels. *IZA Journal of European Labor Studies* 3 (1): 1–30.

Frey, Bruno S., and Alois Stutzer. 2010. *Happiness and economics: How the economy and institutions affect human well-being*. Princeton University Press.

Frijters, Paul, and Tony Beatton. 2012. The mystery of the U-shaped relationship between subjective well-being and age. *Journal of Economic Behavior & Organization* 82 (2–3): 525–542.

Glatzer, Wolfgang. 2000. Happiness: Classic theory in the light of current research. *Journal of Subjective well-being Studies* 1 (4): 501–511.

Graham, Carol, and Julia Ruiz Pozuelo. 2017. Subjective well-being, stress, and age: How the U curve varies across people and places. *Journal of Population Economics* 30 (1): 225–264.

Gundelach, Peter, and Svend Kreiner. 2004. Happiness and life satisfaction in advanced European countries. *Cross-Cultural Research* 38 (4): 359–386.

Hervás, Gonzalo. 2009. Psicología Positiva: Una introducción. *Revista Interuniversitaria De Formación Del Profesorado* 66: 23–41.

Hirschman, Albert O., and Michael Rothschild. 1973. The changing tolerance for income inequality in the course of economic development: With a mathematical appendix. *The Quarterly Journal of Economics* 87 (4): 544–566.

Inglehart, Ronald, et al. 2008. Development, freedom and rising subjective well-being. A global perspective (1981–2007). *Perspectiveson Psychological Science* 3: 264–285.

Jo, Myoung-Ju. 2016. The factors related to subjective well-being among nursing students. *The Journal of Korean Academic Society of Nursing Education* 22 (2): 182–190.

Knies, Gundi, et al. 2008. Keeping up with the Schmidt's–an empirical test of relative deprivation theory in the neighbourhood context. *Journal of Contextual Economics-Schmollers Jahrbuch* 1: 75–108.

Kozma, Albert, and Michael J. Stones. 1983. Predictors of happiness. *Journal of Gerontology* 38 (5): 626–628.

Kushlev, Kostadin, et al. 2020. Does subjective well-being improve health? Evidence from a randomized controlled trial. *Psychological Science* 31 (7): 807–821.

Larson, Reed. 1978. Thirty years of research on the subjective well-being of older Americans. *Journal of Gerontology* 33 (1): 109–125.

Lu, Luo, and Yu Yi Lin. 1998. Family roles and subjective well-being in adulthood. *Personality and Individual Differences* 25 (2): 195–207.

Luchesi, Bruna Moretti, et al. 2018. Factors associated with subjective well-being in the elderly persons living in the community. *Archives of Gerontology and Geriatrics* 74: 83–87.

McBride, Michael. 2010. Money, subjective well-being, and aspirations: An experimental study. *Journal of Economic Behavior & Organization* 74 (3): 262–276.

Menardi, Giovanna, and Nicola Torelli. 2014. Training and assessing classification rules with imbalanced data. *Data Mining and Knowledge Discovery* 28 (1): 92–122.

Michalos, Alex C. 2017. Education, subjective well-being and wellbeing. In *Connecting the quality of life theory to health, well-being and education*, 277–299. Springer.

Mookerjee, Rajen, and Krista Beron. 2005. Gender, religion and subjective well-being. *The Journal of Socio-Economics* 34 (5): 674–685.

North, Rebecca J., Charles J. Holahan, Rudolf H. Moos, and Ruth C. Cronkite. 2008. Family support, family income, and subjective well-being: A 10-year perspective. *Journal of Family Psychology* 22 (3): 475.

Quoidbach, Jordi, et al. 2010. Money giveth, money taketh away: The dual effect of wealth on subjective well-being. *Psychological Science* 21 (6): 759–763.

Rogers, Stacy J., and Lynn K. White. 1998. Satisfaction with parenting: The role of marital subjective well-being, family structure, and parents' gender. *Journal of Marriage and the Family*, 293–308.

Senik, Claudia. 2009. Direct evidence on income comparisons and their welfare effects. *Journal of Economic Behavior & Organization* 72 (1): 408–424.

Skurichina, Marina, and Robert PW. Duin. 2002. Bagging, boosting and the random subspace method for linear classifiers. *Pattern Analysis & Applications* 5 (2): 121–135.

Stack, Steven, and J. Ross Eshleman. 1998. Marital status and subjective well-being: A 17-nation study. *Journal of Marriage and the Family* 527–536.

Steptoe, Andrew. 2019. Happiness and health. *Annual Review of Public Health* 40 (1): 339–359.

Swami, Viren, et al. 2009. Psychometric evaluation of the tagalog and German subjective subjective well-being scales and a cross-cultural comparison. *Social Indicator Research* 93: 393–406.

Varian, Hal R. 2014. Big data: New tricks for econometrics. *Journal of Economic Perspectives* 28 (2): 3–28.

Veenhoven, Ruut. 1991. Is subjective well-being relative? *Social Indicators Research* 24 (1): 1–34.

Veenhoven, Ruut. 2015. Social conditions for human subjective well-being: A review of research. *International Journal of Psychology* 50 (5): 379–391.

Vera-Villarroel, Pablo, et al. 2012. Money, age and subjective well-being: Association of subjective wellbeing with socio-demographic variables. *Revista Latinoamericana De Psicología* 44 (2): 155.

Verme, Paolo. 2013. The relative income and relative deprivation hypotheses: A review of the empirical literature. *World Bank Policy Research Working Paper* (6606).

Watts, Duncan J. 2014. Common sense and sociological explanations. *American Journal of Sociology* 120 (2): 313–351.

Watts, Duncan J. 2017. Should social science be more solution-oriented? *Nature Human Behaviour* 1 (1): 0015.

PART IV

Identifying Causality

CHAPTER 8

Enhancing Traditional Methods of Causal Inference Using Machine Learning: Optimizing Matching, Instrumental Variables, and Quasi-Experiments

1 Introduction

Despite ongoing advancements in quantitative analysis methods, many empirical studies are limited by research design, data quality, and model setup. As a result, they often rely on regression analysis to explore relationships between variables, leaving causal relationships unclear. On the one hand, scholars such as Stephen Morgan and Christopher Winship argue that social explanation must be grounded in a counterfactual framework, in which causal relationships are delineated through regression models (Morgan and Winship 2007). On the other hand, scholars such as Aage Sørensen, Raymond Boudon, Jon Elster, and Peter Hedström stress the importance of research design that integrates social mechanisms, social processes, and statistical inference (Hedström 2005, 2008). Despite their differing emphases, these scholars share a consensus that understanding explanatory mechanisms or making causal inferences should be central to social science research. Causal inference provides a framework that transcends mere associations, allowing for a deeper understanding of the mechanisms underlying observed phenomena. Establishing causal relationships is critical for evaluating interventions, understanding behavior patterns, and predicting policy outcomes across disciplines such as economics, sociology, and political science.

Y. Chen et al., *Machine Learning in Social Science*,
https://doi.org/10.1007/978-981-95-6465-1_8

Random assignment is generally considered the gold standard for causal inference. However, due to its high costs and the ethical challenges associated with its implementation, this method is often difficult to apply in practical research. Most social science research relies on observational data, but such data—often the only available resource—are susceptible to endogeneity bias, where the explanatory variables are systematically related to the error term in the research model. This relationship can result in biased estimates of the true causal effect (Chen 2011; Chen and Volker 2016). To address this challenge, researchers need to employ statistical analysis methods that minimize such biases. Common methods for causal inference include regression analysis, propensity score matching (PSM), instrumental variables (IVs), regression discontinuity, and difference-in-differences (DID) (Angrist and Pischke 2014; Chen et al. 2021; Chen 2022). Regression analysis adjusts for observable confounding variables using statistical control strategies, whereas PSM creates a quasi-experimental design by balancing covariate distributions between treatment and control groups. IVs leverage exogenous tools to isolate variation in explanatory variables, whereas regression discontinuity uses institutional thresholds to establish quasi-randomization conditions. Finally, DID eliminates time-invariant confounders by comparing changes over time. Collectively, these methods reconstruct counterfactual inference frameworks using various identification strategies, advancing the field of quantitative analysis in social science from simple association research to more rigorous causal inference.

Table 1 summarizes common causal inference methods, along with their premises, advantages, and disadvantages. Most causal inference methods rely on data models, assuming that the data follow a specific functional distribution $f(x)$ (e.g., linear regression models); they estimate the parameters of $f(x)$ based on sample data and model structures (Breiman, 2001). However, the validity of such data models is based on idealized assumptions, including the relationships between variables and data distributional properties necessary for parameter estimation. Consequently, data must meet certain criteria, such as adhering to linear or basic functional relationships and being limited to a certain number of variables. In reality, the complex interactions between social mechanisms and variables often cannot be adequately captured by such idealized parametric models. If a model does not accurately represent the actual data-generating process, research conclusions may be biased. Thus, although the aforementioned causal inference methods have been developed and applied to empirical studies over the past few decades, they undoubtedly have several limitations, including the following.

1. **Reliance on Strong Assumptions:** Most causal inference methods depend on assumptions that are difficult to verify or satisfy, such as assumptions regarding relevance and exogeneity of IVs, local randomization in regression discontinuity, parallel trends in DID, and conditional independence assumption in PSM. These assumptions limit the applicability of these methods.
2. **Covariate Limitations:** Traditional causal inference methods rely on precise control of covariates to accurately isolate causal effects. Missing key covariates can introduce confounding bias, negatively affecting the identification of causal effects. By contrast, including too many covariates can lead to the "curse of dimensionality," increasing model complexity and resulting in unstable parameter estimates.
3. **Assumption of Data Relationships:** Traditional causal inference methods often depend on pre-specified equations that define relationships between variables. For instance, linear regression assumes that causal relationships are linear and that error terms follow a normal distribution. In practice, these assumptions are frequently difficult to meet. Parametric models can make it challenging for researchers to accurately capture the functional forms of treatment status, covariates, and their impact on outcomes. Deviations from these assumptions can result in biased and inconsistent estimates of causal effects.
4. **Heterogeneity Analysis Limitations:** Traditional methods typically assume that causal effects are consistent across different groups, known as the average treatment effect (ATE) assumption. However, in reality, various groups may respond differently, leading to significant causal heterogeneity. Such heterogeneity is particularly evident in diverse populations, but traditional methods often struggle to effectively capture and analyze it, limiting their application in personalized and group-differentiated research.

Furthermore, machine learning algorithms have come under scrutiny Sfor the challenges in interpreting and clearly identifying causal relationships using these algorithms. The primary goal of these algorithms is to achieve

Table 1 Premises, advantages, and disadvantages of common causal inference methods

Method	*Premise*	*Advantages*	*Disadvantages*
Randomized experiment	Random assignment of treatment variables	Gold standard for causal inference	High cost / ethical limitations
Linear regression	Model assumption, conditional independence	Simple and interpretable	Strong assumption dependence, difficult to incorporate many variables, struggles with non-linear/ complex interactions
Instrumental variables	Exogeneity and relevance assumptions of IV	Addresses unobserved confounders	Difficult to find instruments, weak instruments, local average treatment effect
Propensity score matching	Conditional independence assumption, accurate estimation of propensity scores	Suitable for handling high-dimensional confounders	Relies on accurate estimation of propensity scores, matching difficulties, struggles with unobserved confounders
Regression discontinuity	Local randomization assumption at threshold	Controls for unobserved confounders near the threshold	High data requirements, only applicable to samples near the threshold
Panel regression	No unobserved time-varying confounders	Controls for time-invariant confounders	High data requirements, cannot control for time-varying confounders

(continued)

Table 1 (continued)

Method	*Premise*	*Advantages*	*Disadvantages*
Differences in differences	Parallel trend assumption, no time-varying unobserved confounders	Controls for time-invariant confounders	High data requirements, hard to satisfy/verify assumptions
Synthetic control	Treatment group and synthetic control group are highly similar	Data-driven weighting reduces subjective selection bias in the control group	Requires a large control group for synthesis, requires long observation periods, weight settings are sensitive

predictive accuracy, which can prioritize correlations over causal relationships. Consequently, establishing causal relationships between features and predicted variables becomes less important. An increasing amount of research indicates that errors in machine learning algorithms can entail significant risks, including unstable model predictions, biased decisions, and difficulties in implementing interventions, with spurious correlations between variables being a primary source of such risks (Cui and Athey 2022).

In recent years, the integration of machine learning with causal inference has emerged as a prominent research focus (Chen et al. 2020). Researchers have been examining the new opportunities and challenges that machine learning presents in identifying causal relationships. For example, Varian posits that a crucial step in any causal analysis involves estimating counterfactuals, that is, predicting outcomes in the absence of treatment. The author suggests that the powerful techniques employed in machine learning may help better estimate counterfactuals, thereby strengthening causal inference (Varian 2016). Brand et al. contend that machine learning can address potential biases in estimating causal effects and identify heterogeneous causal effects in four ways: general causal effect identification, heterogeneous causal effects, causal mediation, and spatiotemporal interference (Brand et al. 2023). In this chapter, we discuss the fundamental principles and advantages of integrating machine learning algorithms into counterfactual causal inference. We also detail how various causal inference methods can be integrated with machine learning algorithms, highlighting their applicable scenarios, advantages, and disadvantages.

2 Machine Learning's Contribution to Causal Inference

The introduction of machine learning has enabled the development of novel analytical tools for causal inference. In machine learning models, data are no longer used simply to fit predefined idealized models and estimate specific parameters. Instead, by leveraging datasets, machine learning modifies the model's complexity using non-linear and non-parametric approaches with one or more hyperparameters to learn patterns and approximate inherent relationships within the data. This evolution enables machine learning to support causal inference research in several ways.

(1) Breaking Model and Variable Constraints: Better Control of Confounding Variables and Fitting Non-Linear Relationships

A key advantage of machine learning is its ability to analyze high-dimensional variables and perform feature selection. In traditional model analysis, including unnecessary covariates may introduce noise, while omitting crucial ones may lead to bias. As a result, traditional analytical models often struggle with variable selection, which can be influenced by subjective choices aimed at achieving statistical significance (Fafchamps and Labonne 2017). However, machine learning allows for the inclusion of a large number of potential covariates, from which selected key variables can be identified from a global optimal perspective through regularization processing or information grouping. This approach minimizes the constraints of model selection regarding the number of confounding variables and the researcher's subjective biases.

In causal inference, non-parametric machine learning methods can help researchers address biases stemming from model specification and variable selection. Researchers often lack knowledge about the functional form of how treatment status and covariates influence outcomes (Brand et al. 2023). When a causal model fails to accurately represent the true data-generating process, the estimated causal effect may be inaccurate. Non-parametric machine learning methods do not make strict assumptions about the distribution of data; instead, they learn directly from the data to identify relationships between variables. The advantage of this approach lies in its ability to adapt to complex data structures, including non-linear relationships and complex interactions among variables (Mullainathan and Spiess 2017), rather than forcing the data to conform to a predetermined model form (Chen and Chen 2024).

This flexibility in capturing variable relationships is particularly crucial when working with high-dimensional data, where variable relationships in high-dimensional space can be more complex and challenging to represent using simple parametric models. Consequently, traditional causal inference methods, which often rely on these simpler models, can be enhanced by using machine learning models, thereby improving the analytical power of causal inference methods, particularly in scenarios involving numerous confounding variables and unknown complex relationships among them.

(2) **Breaking Interaction Constraints: Heterogeneity of Causal Effects**

In causal inference, researchers are concerned not only with the ATE but also increasingly with the heterogeneity of treatment effects, particularly the conditional average treatment effect (CATE). This heterogeneity reflects the varying effects experienced by different individuals or subgroups receiving the same treatment. Traditional quantitative research methods analyze treatment effect heterogeneity by incorporating interaction terms into parameter equations. However, the following challenges remain: first, numerous factors may contribute to heterogeneity in treatment effects, but not all can be included in a regression equation; second, the specific forms of interaction terms may not satisfy the assumptions underlying the parametric equations. Polynomial and multivariable complex interactions often arise, but they are difficult to estimate effectively using parametric models (Hu et al. 2021). In addition to interaction terms, Xie et al. developed propensity score-based methods to evaluate treatment effect heterogeneity by consolidating the variables that may cause heterogeneity into a single propensity score. This approach analyzes how treatment effects change as the propensity score varies (Xie and Wu Xie and Xiaogang 2005; Xie et al. 2012). Although this method mitigates problems related to interaction terms and their specifications, it can only highlight the existence of heterogeneity in treatment effects without examining the specific factors driving such heterogeneity (Hu et al. 2021).

Machine learning offers a novel approach for evaluating and validating treatment effect heterogeneity. First, machine learning can uncover sources of variation that may have been previously overlooked (Lundberg et al. 2022; Shu and Ye 2023). Using data-driven techniques, this method automatically selects covariates that significantly interact with the intervention variable. Second, certain machine learning algorithms can estimate treatment effects for each individual, providing flexible explanations for the variations in treatment effects across individuals.

(3) **Breaking Assumption Constraints: Data-Driven Discovery of Better Research Findings**

In practice, causal inference methods often require researchers to devise innovative research designs. This may include selecting suitable confounding variables to control for biases caused by endogeneity or identifying an IV that ensures exogeneity while being highly correlated with the independent variable. A high degree of creativity and analytical skills is required to accomplish tasks such as finding a control sample that satisfies the parallel trend assumption for the DID method or identifying a critical breakpoint where before-and-after samples for a continuous variable are similar. Good instruments and control groups often arise serendipitously; in addition to skillful data usage, they require a high standard of design inspired by the researcher's ingenuity and analytical experience (Chen 2012a, 2012b). However, this inspiration depends on the researcher's talent, timing, experience, and imagination, making it difficult to replicate due to its inherent instability. Moreover, especially in quasi-experimental designs for constructing control groups, the complexity of high-dimensional variable matching implies that the resulting data cannot be assessed solely based on the researcher's experience and intuition. In these situations, machine learning, using an operational logic of "fitting data with algorithms" rather than "fitting data to a model," is rooted in the data itself. It enables researchers to uncover the most fundamental and authentic relationships, thus enhancing the design of causal inference research.

3 Machine Learning and Causal Inference Techniques

This section mainly discusses how machine learning can be effectively integrated with various causal inference techniques at three specific methodological levels: matching, IV, and quasi-experimental.

3.1 Machine Learning + Matching

(1) **Propensity Score Matching**

The propensity score was first introduced by Rubin and Rosenbaum in 1983 to tackle the problem of matching with multiple covariates (Rosenbaum and Rubin 1983). It aims to simplify the complex matching problem by employing a "dimensionality reduction" strategy that transforms it into a more straightforward matching problem based on an index. In the context of causal inference, the propensity score represents the conditional probability that an individual is affected by an independent variable, given that observed confounders are controlled (Hu 2012). If two samples have identical propensity scores, yet one receives treatment, and the other does not, the observed difference can be attributed solely to random factors. Machine learning contributes to PSM in two primary ways.

First, machine learning improves the estimation of propensity scores. Traditional methods for calculating propensity scores are generally parametric, relying on logit or probit models that estimate scores based on numerous confounding variables. However, several challenges arise in practice. First, researchers find it difficult to account for all relevant covariates that could influence the treatment effect. Due to data and model limitations in terms of the number of variables, researchers typically select potential confounding factors manually when estimating propensity scores. This approach raises concerns about reliability, where omitting a significant confounding variable can lead to omitted variable bias, similar to issues encountered in linear regression. A more reliable alternative is to use all available covariates for estimation, but this necessitates additional model-fitting strategies to avoid sparse data bias and non-convergence. Second, researchers often struggle to determine the functional relationship between covariates and the intervention variable. Once they identify the necessary covariates for estimating the propensity score, they must select an appropriate method for the estimation. Mainstream parametric methods generally assume a specific parameter equation between models, and researchers must make many decisions regarding the functional form of the variables, such as whether to incorporate quadratic, cubic, or higher-order terms for covariates and whether to include interaction terms. Ideally, these model-setting decisions would be supported by robust theory. However, in most studies, this type of theoretical foundation is lacking. As a result, predictive models for propensity scores, similar to linear regression, are always at risk of model misspecification.

The propensity score essentially predicts the likelihood of an intervention effect. Compared with traditional models, machine learning methods excel in prediction (Chen et al. 2021). As a result, researchers have proposed leveraging machine learning methods to estimate propensity scores (Hill and Su 2013). When employing machine learning to predict the intervention variable, researchers are not bound by strict constraints regarding collinearity among independent variables. They can use complex "black-box" models, such as Random Forest and gradient boosting, which significantly enhance modeling flexibility and predictive accuracy. Studies comparing Logistic Regression (with all main effects) to machine learning techniques—including classification and regression trees (CART), pruned CART, and ensemble methods such as bagged CART, Random Forest, and boosted CART—have shown that Logistic Regression often performs suboptimally under conditions of moderate non-additivity and non-linearity. In contrast, ensemble methods significantly reduce bias, making them more effective in such scenarios (Lee et al. 2010; Westreich et al. 2010).

Second, machine learning improves the matching of control groups. Traditional matching methods calculate propensity scores and group samples based on their similarity to create balanced control and treatment groups, thereby eliminating selection bias and estimating causal effects. Common matching methods include nearest neighbor, radius, and kernel matching. However, these methods have certain limitations: if a significant difference in propensity score distributions exists between the treatment and control groups (e.g., a high proportion of individuals with extreme propensity scores), some samples may be excluded due to a lack of suitable matches. This exclusion reduces the effective sample size and introduces bias due to selective sample exclusion. Even if inverse probability weighting is applied to retain all samples, individuals with propensity scores close to 0 or 1 may receive large weights, leading to unstable estimates.

Machine learning offers innovative solutions for PSM. For instance, some studies have suggested using generative adversarial networks (GANs) to enhance PSM (PSSAM-GAN). This method generates synthetic samples that can be paired with unmatched instances, creating artificial treatment matches and thus rebalancing the data (Ghosh et al. 2021). The model optimizes both the generator (which generates synthetic data matching the distribution of real samples) and the discriminator (which differentiates between real and synthetic samples) during adversarial training. This process effectively generates samples that fill the matching gaps in the original data, thereby reconstructing the overlap between treatment and control groups in the feature space.

(2) **Algorithmic Matching**

PSM achieves causal inference through covariate dimensionality reduction. However, machine learning provides a more direct solution by accurately matching high-dimensional covariates without relying on propensity score estimation. A representative method is the causal Random Forest (Athey et al. 2019; Wager and Athey 2018), which improves upon traditional Random Forest models. This approach recursively partitions the sample feature space, creating subgroups within local areas where covariates are homogeneous. It directly matches individuals with similar characteristics but different intervention statuses while estimating counterfactual differences. Its technical implementation involves the following seven steps.

(a) **Data Splitting:** First, the dataset is split into two independent parts: one for creating decision trees (training data) and the other for estimating treatment effects (estimation data). Known as the "honesty" principle, this separation ensures that the same data are not used for both fitting the model and estimating causal effects, thereby reducing overfitting and bias.

(b) **Tree Construction**: Numerous decision trees are constructed within the training subset. Each tree is constructed by recursively splitting the data into subsets based on covariate values that most effectively distinguish treatment effects based on treated and untreated observations. The splitting criterion is specifically designed to maximize heterogeneity in treatment effects rather than focusing on prediction accuracy as in traditional Random Forest models.

(c) **Variable Selection**: At each split in a tree, a random subset of covariates is selected for consideration for splitting. This randomness in variable selection enhances the diversity of trees in the forest and aids in exploring various causal pathways.

(d) **Leaf Estimation**: For each leaf in the trees built from the training data, the ATE is estimated by comparing the outcomes of treated and untreated groups within that leaf. This localized estimation approach determines potential heterogeneity in treatment effects across subpopulations.

(e) **Aggregation**: Once the trees are built, the causal effect for an observation in the estimation set is predicted by averaging the estimates from all trees where the observation falls into the corresponding leaf. This aggregation reduces the variance of the estimated treatment effects by leveraging the ensemble learning approach.

(f) **Validation**: The treatment effects estimated from the estimation data are validated or cross-validated using various statistical measures to evaluate their accuracy and reliability. This step is essential for ensuring that the model generalizes well to new data.

(g) **Refinement**: Based on the validation results, model hyperparameters such as the number of trees, tree depth, or the minimum number of observations per leaf may be adjusted to optimize model performance.

In addition to matching covariates in structured data, machine learning can directly match unstructured, high-dimensional data, such as text and images, to form experimental and control groups. Although these data types are rich in causal information, they present challenges for traditional matching methods owing to their high-dimensional sparsity and implicit semantics. For instance, in the case of text data, the framework for machine learning matching involves the following two key technical steps (Mozer et al. 2020).

(a) **Choice of text representation**. This involves converting unstructured text into structured feature vectors using techniques such as topic modeling and word embedding.
(b) **Choice of distance metric**. Appropriate distance functions must be designed to evaluate semantic similarity between texts (Mozer et al. 2020). For example, Roberts et al. (2020) proposed a text matching strategy called topic inverse regression matching, which employs a suitable topic model to represent text and then matches texts into control and treatment groups based on these features. This allows researchers to effectively and transparently address confounding factors present in the text (Roberts et al. 2020).

3.2 *Machine Learning + Instrumental Variables*

(1) **Non-linear Estimation of Instrumental Variables**

A common method for addressing endogeneity issues involves using IVs. Let us suppose we want to study the causal relationship between x_1 and y, but an endogeneity problem exists because the error term ε is correlated with x_1. In this case, we can search for an IV z, which is external to the model and influences only the dependent variable y through its impact on the independent variable x_1. If the IV z is correlated with the independent variable x_1, an incremental change in z will cause an exogenous shock to x_1. If a causal relationship exists between x_1. and y, this shock from z inevitably affects y. Under a series of assumptions, as long as we can demonstrate that the indirect shock of z on y is statistically significant, we can infer that x_1 has a causal impact on y.

A common method for estimating IVs is two-stage least squares (2SLS). This method comprises two stages. In the first stage, a regression analysis is conducted with the endogenous variable x_1 as the dependent variable and the IV z as the independent variable to obtain the predicted value of x_1, denoted as $\hat{x_1}$. In the second stage, a second regression analysis is performed with y as the dependent variable and the predicted value of x_1 from the first stage, $\hat{x_1}$, as the independent variable. The first stage effectively assesses the predictive power of the exogenous IV on the endogenous variable. Typically, the first stage is analyzed using a parametric regression model. However, if the relationship between the IV and the intervention variable is not entirely linear, this traditional approach may not yield accurate results. In such cases, machine learning can be advantageous.

In addition, when multiple endogenous variables are present in a model, an equal number of valid IVs is needed, which poses practical challenges. To address these issues, researchers have introduced a deep learning-based estimation method known as Deep IV. This approach can be regarded as an extension of the 2SLS method for non-linear models. In the first stage, both IVs and other exogenous variables are used as inputs, with a deep network employed to predict the conditional distribution of the endogenous variable. In the second stage, the predicted distribution from the first stage, along with other exogenous variables, is input into another deep network to predict the dependent variable (Hartford et al., 2017). Deep IV uses deep neural networks to model the relationship between the endogenous variable and IVs, as well as the relationship between the endogenous variable and dependent variables. This enables effective causal inference even in complex non-linear scenarios.

(2) **Identifying Potential Instrumental Variables**

The greatest challenge in using IVs is selecting the appropriate instrument. Researchers often struggle with how to choose an ideal IV that ensures both exogeneity and relevance. Inappropriate IVs, such as weak instruments, not only fail to correct biases in causal estimates but may also lead to decreased estimation efficiency due to larger standard deviations. Although a potential pool of IVs exists to consider—such as exogenous variables from natural phenomena, empirical variables used in other studies, and synthetic variables derived from data aggregation—these options may have varying degrees of issues. Machine learning can assist researchers in identifying the most suitable IVs from the numerous possibilities. For example, Belloni et al. (2012) recommend using the Lasso algorithm to select IVs that are most relevant to the intervention variable from a large pool.

3.3 *Machine Learning + Quasi-Experiments*

Machine learning can also enhance quasi-experimental methods, such as DID, synthetic control, and regression discontinuity design (RDD), by aiding in the identification of suitable control groups. In executing DID, the crucial task is to find a control group that displays a trend similar to that of the treatment group before the intervention. Machine learning can analyze large datasets using clustering analysis, matching algorithms, and dimensionality reduction techniques to identify control groups with pre- and post-intervention trends that closely resemble those of the treatment group, thus improving the accuracy of causal effect estimation. For synthetic control methods, a synthetic control group is created by selecting a set of untreated units and combining them using a weighted method; the aim is to make this synthetic group as similar as possible to the treatment group across several key variables predicting the intervention effect before the intervention (Abadie et al. 2010). The challenge in synthetic control is how to assign weights to each potential control unit so that the linear combination of these weights most accurately reproduces the characteristics of the treatment group before the intervention. When the relationship between treatment and control groups is complex or when the dimensionality of pre-intervention data is very high, the allocation and calculation of weights become constrained by the number of variables and the model structure. By combining machine learning techniques, researchers can apply non-parametric or semi-parametric methods to flexibly model the relationship between treatment and control groups.

Machine learning can also play a significant role in RDD, which involves identifying a precise cutoff or threshold beyond which a unit receives treatment when a continuous variable exceeds this threshold. Traditionally, the selection of this cutoff is based on theory or prior experience, which can introduce selection bias. In addition, in cases in which high-dimensional covariates exist before and after the cutoff, determining the cutoff position through mere observation can be challenging. To address this, Herlands et al. (2018) proposed a data-driven machine learning approach that automatically identifies and verifies potential cutoff points, offering a more objective and accurate method for cutoff selection.

4 Causal Machine Learning Use Cases

Given that different causal inference methods are suitable under different scenarios, the question of how researchers choose a causal inference method remains unanswered. Figure 1 illustrates the process of choosing the appropriate causal inference method based on different data conditions and research objectives. The circles represent judgment conditions leading to different methods, the blue rectangles represent commonly used traditional causal inference methods, and the yellow rectangles denote methods in which machine learning can complement causal inference. In general, the choice of causal inference methods depends on the following four key considerations.

(1) Can Potential Confounding Variables Be Observed?

When preparing to perform causal inference, researchers must first consider whether potential confounding variables can be observed. This decision affects the choice of causal inference method. If confounding variables can be observed, meaning that the conditional independence assumption (CIA) is satisfied, researchers can control for these variables to achieve causal inference. A second key issue then arises: whether linear regression, PSM, or other CIA-based methods should be used. In cases in

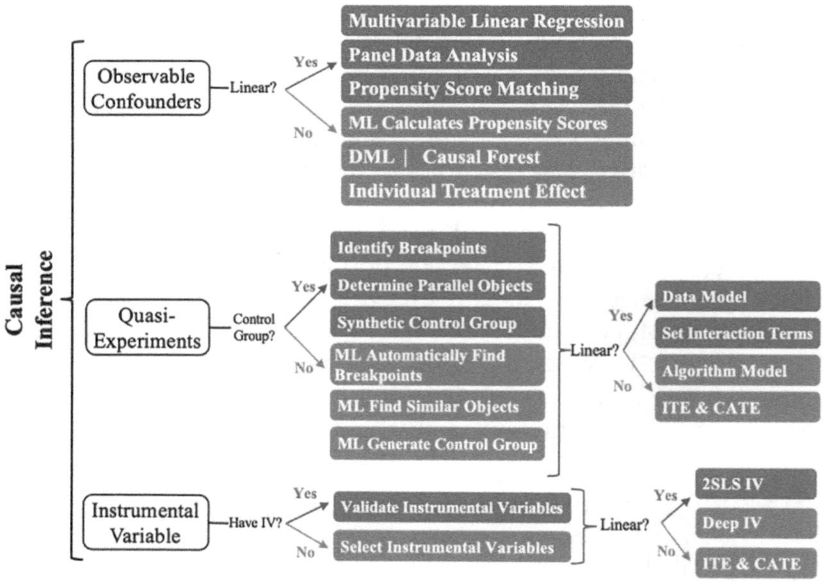

Fig. 1 A new perspective on causal inference based on machine learning (*Note* The blue in the figure represents commonly used traditional methods of causal inference, while the yellow represents how machine learning can complement causal inference).

which significant confounding variables cannot be observed or measured, researchers should consider some form of randomization to break the correlation between the target variable and unmeasured confounders. This can involve employing quasi-experimental methods such as regression discontinuity, DID, or synthetic control to simulate the random assignment of treatment and control groups. Alternatively, IVs can be employed to introduce exogeneity and indirectly measure causal relationships. Here, machine learning plays a role by leveraging data-driven reverse logic, which flexibly captures complex data relationships. This aids in tasks such as identifying suitable cutoff points for regression discontinuity, selecting control groups that meet parallel trends assumptions for DID, or fitting a counterfactual control group for synthetic control.

(2) **Is the Relationship Between Variables Linear? Are Confounding Variables Low-Dimensional?**

These issues are essential for determining whether traditional causal inference methods or machine learning approaches should be employed. When confounding variables are observable and few in number, and when the relationships between variables are straightforward, researchers can use multiple linear regression, panel analysis, and traditional PSM (Chen and Yan 2018; Fu et al. 2024). However, when many confounding variables result in the "curse of dimensionality" or when the functional form of the relationships is complex or unknown, machine learning algorithms should be considered. Applications include using machine learning for calculating propensity scores, causal forests for direct matching, or double machine learning (DML) for mitigating confounding effects (note that DML principles will be introduced in Chapter 9). When observable confounders are not satisfied, machine learning can complement causal estimation methods by fitting data before and after the cutoff for regression discontinuity or by improving two-stage estimation for IVs through deep learning.

(3) **Should Average Heterogeneity or Individual Heterogeneity Be Estimated?**

In general, traditional regression models are effective for estimating the ATE and for identifying targeted subgroups based on research objectives such as CATE. By contrast, machine learning algorithms can estimate individual treatment effects, enable the detection of CATE and also provide a more nuanced understanding of heterogeneity in causal effects across various groups. Additionally, machine learning can assist researchers in discovering sources of variation that were previously overlooked. Researchers should select the appropriate method for heterogeneity analysis based on their specific research needs while considering whether the interaction forms of variables are straightforward and well-defined.

(4) **Is It Necessary to Estimate the Confidence Interval?**

Traditional causal inference methods generally yield accurate estimates of confidence intervals, but this is not always the case for methods based on machine learning. In statistics, confidence intervals are typically derived from parameter estimates of the model, which are based on assumptions about data distribution. These assumptions are used to compute the standard errors of the parameters, which in turn inform the confidence interval. However, many machine learning models do not have a clear parametric form and often involve a large number of parameters, making it difficult to provide direct estimates of parameter uncertainty. Nonetheless, machine learning can still provide confidence intervals in some cases, such as through DML, where the residual regression method combined with traditional regression models can generate significant estimates and confidence intervals. In addition, machine learning techniques can estimate the distribution of prediction results through methods such as bootstrap sampling and cross-validation, which can be used to determine confidence intervals. However, the confidence intervals obtained from these methods reflect the model's variance and thus are not based on distribution assumptions, indicating that they measure uncertainty about the model's results.

Considering these four questions helps researchers better understand the role of machine learning in causal inference and assists them in selecting the most suitable method based on their research context and objectives. However, emphasizing that each method has its own assumptions and issues is important. No one can be 100% certain that all confounding variables can be observed; similarly, no one can prove the strict exogeneity of an IV. Accordingly, researchers cannot guarantee that assumptions such as the similarity of breakpoints or parallel trends will always hold. No universally "best" or "applicable" method exists. The value of understanding and comparing methods lies in enabling researchers to carefully weigh the pros and cons; the best method is the one most suited to the current context.

5 Conclusion

The combination of machine learning and causal inference has opened new avenues for social science research, providing effective tools to address the challenges of complex data environments and identify causal relationships. Traditional causal inference methods—such as regression analysis, PSM, IVs, and DID methods—have been widely applied in theory and practice. However, their application is limited by strict model assumptions, incomplete variable selection, difficulties in fitting non-linear relationships, and challenges in determining heterogeneous effects. The introduction of machine learning, with its unique non-parametric modeling capabilities, high-dimensional data processing capacity, and data-driven analysis approach, has effectively expanded the applicability and analytical depth of causal inference. Machine learning demonstrates significant advantages in controlling for confounding variables, handling non-linear relationships, identifying heterogeneous causal effects, and optimizing counterfactual construction.

However, the combination of machine learning and causal inference cannot completely replace traditional methods; rather, it supplements and extends them. While machine learning improves prediction accuracy, it also faces challenges such as insufficient data, limited model interpretability, and unstable confidence interval estimates. Therefore, researchers must balance the suitability of traditional methods with machine learning approaches based on specific research contexts while focusing on combining theoretical assumptions with data-driven analysis.

In the future, the development of causal inference methods must drive innovative applications of machine learning while deepening its integration with social science theories. Researchers must focus on individualized effects and heterogeneous analysis when exploring causal relationships, promoting the widespread application of causal inference in areas such as policy evaluation, intervention effectiveness testing, and social mechanism discovery. This interdisciplinary integration can inject momentum into causal inference research and offer valuable insights for both practical and theoretical advancements in social science. In summary, the intersection of machine learning and causal inference is a field rich with potential, and its evolution will yield more flexible, precise, and comprehensive analytical tools and methods for social science research, aiding in resolving more complex social problems and policy issues.

References

Abadie, Alberto, Alexis Diamond, and Jens Hainmueller. 2010. Synthetic control methods for comparative case studies: Estimating the effect of California's tobacco control program. *Journal of the American Statistical Association* 105 (490): 493–505.

Angrist, Joshua D., and Jörn-Steffen Pischke 2014. *Mastering metrics: The path from cause to effect*. Princeton: Princeton University Press.

Athey, Susan, Julie Tibshirani, and Stefan Wager. 2019. Generalized random forests. *The Annals of Statistics* 47 (2): 1148–1178.

Belloni, A., D. Chen, V. Chernozhukov, and C. Hansen. 2012. Sparse models and methods for optimal instruments with an application to eminent domain. *Econometrica* 80 (6): 2369–2429.

Brand, Jennie E., Xiang Zhou, and Yu Xie. 2023. Recent developments in causal inference and machine learning. *Annual Review of Sociology* 49 (1): 81–110.

Breiman, Leo. 2001. Statistical modeling: The two cultures (with comments and a rejoinder by the author). *Statistical Science* 16 (3): 199–231.

Chen, Yunsong. 2012a. Logic, imagination and interpretation: The application of instrumental variables for causal inference in the social sciences. *Sociological Studies* 6: 192–216+245–246 (In Chinese).

Chen, Yunsong. 2012b. Do networks pay off among internal migrants in China? An instrumental variable analysis. *Chinese Sociological Review* 45 (1): 28–54.

Chen, Yunsong. 2011. The causal effect of social capital in the labor market: Identification challenges and strategies. *Chinese Sociological Review* 44 (2): 76–100.

Chen, Yunsong. 2022. *Causal effects of social capital: Labor markets and beyond*. London: Palgrave Macmillan.

Chen, Yunsong, and Beate Volker. 2016. Social capital and homophily both matter for labor market outcomes-evidence from replication and extension. *Social Networks* 45: 18–31.

Chen, Yunsong, and Fei Yan. 2018. International visibility as determinants of foreign direct investment: An empirical study of Chinese provinces. *Social Science Research* 76: 23–39.

Chen, Yunsong, Fei Yan, Guangye He, and Wei Yan. 2020a. The Werther effect revisited: Do suicides in books predict actual suicides? *Poetics* 81: 101441.

Chen, Yunsong, Guangye He, and Fei Yan. 2021. *Understanding China through big data: Applications of theory-oriented quantitative approaches*. Abingdon, New York: Routledge.

Chen, Zhuo, and Yunsong Chen. 2024. Computing grounded theory: A quantitative method to develop theories. *The Journal of Chinese Sociology* 11 (1): 17.

Cui, Peng, and Susan Athey. 2022. Stable learning establishes some common ground between causal inference and machine learning. *Nature Machine Intelligence* 4 (2): 110–115.

Fafchamps, Marcel, and Julien Labonne. 2017. Using split samples to improve inference on causal effects. *Political Analysis* 25 (4): 465–482.

Fu, Zhihui, Shukai Liu, Guodong Ju, Wen Ma, and Yunsong Chen. 2024. Instrumental Guanxi culture and inbound urban migration in China: A prefecture-level analysis using online search data. *The China Quarterly* 260: 1040–1058.

Ghosh, Shantanu, et al. 2021. Propensity score synthetic augmentation matching using generative adversarial networks (PSSAM-GAN). *Computer Methods and Programs in Biomedicine Update* 1: 100020.

Hartford, Jason, Lewis Greg, Leyton-Brown Kevin, and Taddy Matt. 2017. Deep IV: A flexible approach for counterfactual prediction. In *International Conference on Machine Learning*, 1414–1423. PMLR.

Hedström, Peter. 2005. *Dissecting the social: On the principles of analytical sociology*. Cambridge: Cambridge University Press.

Hedström, Peter. 2008. Studying mechanisms to strengthen causal inferences in quantitative research. In *The Oxford Handbook of Political Methodology*, ed. J. M. Box-Steffensmeier, H. E. Brady, and D. Collier. New York: Oxford University Press.

Herlands, William et al. 2018. Automated local regression discontinuity design discovery. In *Proceedings of the 24th ACM SIGKDD International Conference on Knowledge Discovery & Data Mining*, 1512–1520.

Hill, Jennifer, and Yu-Sung Su. 2013. Assessing lack of common support in causal inference using Bayesian nonparametrics: Implications for evaluating the effect of breastfeeding on children's cognitive outcomes. *The Annals of Applied Statistics* 1386–1420.

Hu, Anning. 2012. Propensity score matching and causal inference: A methodological review. *Sociological Studies* 27(1): 221–242+246 (In Chinese).

Hu, Anning, Xiaogang Wu, and Yunsong Chen. 2021. Analysis of heterogeneous treatment effect: New opportunities and challenges with machine learning techniques. *Sociological Studies* 36 (1): 91–114+228 (In Chinese).

Lee, Brian K., Justin Lessler, and Elizabeth A. Stuart. 2010. Improving propensity score weighting using machine learning. *Statistics in Medicine* 29 (3): 337–346.

Lundberg, Ian, Jennie E. Brand, and Nanum Jeon. 2022. Researcher reasoning meets computational capacity: Machine learning for social science. *Social Science Research* 108: 102807.

Morgan, Stephen L., and Christopher Winship. 2007. *Counterfactuals and causal inference: Methods and principles for social research*, 15–31. New York: Cambridge University Press.

Mozer, Reagan et al. Matching with text data: An experimental evaluation of methods for matching documents and of measuring match quality. *Political Analysis* 28 (4): 445–468.

Mullainathan, Sendhil, and Jann Spiess. 2017. Machine learning: An applied econometric approach. *Journal of Economic Perspectives* 31 (2): 87–106.

Roberts, Margaret E., Brandon M. Stewart, and Richard A. Nielsen. 2020. Adjusting for confounding with text matching. *American Journal of Political Science* 64 (4): 887–903.

Rosenbaum, Paul R., and Donald B. Rubin. 1983. The central role of the propensity score in observational studies for causal effects. *Biometrika* 70 (1): 41–55.

Shu, Xiaoling, and Yiwan Ye. 2023. Knowledge discovery: Methods from data mining and machine learning. *Social Science Research* 110: 102817.

Varian, Hal R. 2016. Causal inference in economics and marketing. *Proceedings of the National Academy of Sciences* 113 (27): 7310–7315.

Wager, Stefan, and Susan Athey. 2018. Estimation and inference of heterogeneous treatment effects using Random Forests. *Journal of the American Statistical Association* 113 (523): 1228–1242.

Westreich, Daniel, Justin Lessler, and Michele Jonsson Funk. 2010. Propensity score estimation: Neural networks, support vector machines, decision trees (CART), and meta-classifiers as alternatives to Logistic Regression. *Journal of Clinical Epidemiology* 63 (8): 826–833.

Xie, Yu, and Xiaogang Wu. 2005. Reply to Jann: Market premium, social process, and statisticism. *American Sociological Review* 70 (5): 865–870.

Xie, Yu, Jennie E. Brand, and Ben Jann 2012. Estimating heterogeneous treatment effects with observational data. *Sociological Methodology* 42 (1): 314–347.

CHAPTER 9

Double Machine Learning for Causal Inference on High-Dimensional Data: A Flexible and Robust Approach to Causal Estimation

1 Introduction

Double machine learning (DML) is a causal inference method developed by Professor Chernozhukov and colleagues at MIT in 2018 (Chernozhukov et al. 2018). This method responds to the limitations of traditional multiple linear regression models, particularly with regard to model specification and covariate selection. Non-linear relationships between variables and the presence of numerous covariates can lead to issues such as multicollinearity and dimensionality, resulting in estimation bias. Furthermore, commonly used causal inference methods face challenges, such as the difficulty in satisfying the parallel trends assumption in the difference-in-differences (DID) approach and the large data requirements of propensity score matching (PSM). Given a large number of observable confounding variables, DML can effectively address the shortcomings of traditional causal analysis methods. This method is particularly suitable for validating causal relationships based on multiple variable indicators and non-linear patterns.

In recent years, improvements in related technologies and application software have led to the increased use of DML in the social sciences. This chapter aims to introduce the causal analysis method of DML in the clearest and most accessible manner. Furthermore, it seeks to provide a comprehensive review of its various applications and extensions, defining

Y. Chen et al., *Machine Learning in Social Science*,
https://doi.org/10.1007/978-981-95-6465-1_9

its boundaries and offering new insights for researchers in the social sciences to enhance their causal analysis methods. This chapter compares DML with other causal inference methods, highlighting the distinctions, connections, advantages, and disadvantages of DML and situating it within the broader evolution of causal inference methods. This comparison will assist researchers in selecting the most suitable method based on their data and research topics.

The second section of this chapter outlines the basic assumptions and methodological principles underlying DML for estimating the average treatment effect (ATE), emphasizing the importance of using residuals for causal inference. The third section explores the extended applications of DML, which include estimating treatment effect heterogeneity, analyzing causal mediation effects, handling panel data, and processing unstructured data. The fourth section compares DML with traditional causal inference methods such as general regression analysis, IVs, and PSM, summarizing the scenarios in which DML excels, as well as its advantages and limitations. To enhance readers' understanding of DML's practical applications, the fifth section explains in detail the specific operational process and analysis outcomes of DML, illustrated through a case study examining the effects of "parental academic expectations" on "children's academic performance." This chapter concludes with a summary of the content and reflections on the future application of DML methods.

2 Double Machine Learning

2.1 Use Cases and Prerequisites of Double Machine Learning

Confounding variables are a crucial concept in causal inference as they are related to both the independent (treatment) and dependent variables. In the counterfactual framework, accurately computing the causal effect between the treatment and control groups requires effective control of all potential confounding variables. Failing to consider these confounding variables may result in a spurious correlation between the independent and dependent variables (Chen & Fan 2010), complicating the accurate assessment of their "net effect." When confounding variables are observable, traditional causal inference methods typically employ one of two strategies: incorporating confounding variables as control variables in the statistical model or using PSM to estimate causal relationships.

Although these two methods help reduce confounding bias to some extent, each has significant limitations. The first method, which involves directly including confounding variables in the regression model, assumes that a specific (e.g., linear) relationship exists between the confounding variables and both the independent and dependent variables—an assumption that may not always hold. Moreover, if too many confounding variables are included, multicollinearity issues may arise, compromising the stability and interpretability of the model. The second method of PSM simplifies the problem by reducing multiple confounding variables to a single propensity score. Although this method can mitigate the effects of multicollinearity to some extent, model selection and parameter estimation for the propensity score are also fraught with uncertainty (Draper 1995). More importantly, both methods struggle with effectively identifying the specific confounding variables that lead to causal effect heterogeneity and quantifying how this heterogeneity manifests (Hu et al. 2021).

DML offers a new approach for addressing confounding variables. DML is designed to estimate causal effects between independent and dependent variables when a large number of confounding variables are observable. When many observable confounding variables exist and modeling their effects on treatment and outcome variables through parametric models proves challenging, DML leverages the advantages of machine learning techniques and traditional causal inference methods. It constructs confidence intervals to approximate unbiased estimates of the ATE and enhances causal inference by handling high-dimensional data, relaxing functional assumptions, and analyzing conditional ATE (CATE).

However, the DML method infers causal relationships between variables through model-based control of confounding variables. This is based on the fundamental assumption that all confounding variables are observable; that is, it follows the conditional independence assumption (CIA). If this assumption is violated and key confounding variables are omitted, the resulting estimates will be biased. Nonetheless, the continuous advancement of large-scale social surveys and big data technologies has enriched available data resources. This wealth of information includes not only traditional structured indicators but also unstructured data, such as text and images, which can be integrated into the analysis framework as potential confounding variables. This increase in data richness significantly improves the conditions for meeting the non-confounding assumptions required by DML, creating a more favorable foundation for achieving unbiased causal effect estimation.

2.2 *Basic Principles of Double Machine Learning*

The principles of DML have been thoroughly explained by Chernozhukov et al. (2018). Here, we provide a brief introduction. Consider a dependent variable y, an independent variable (treatment variable) x, and a set of high-dimensional confounding variables w, where both x and y are related. When w is high-dimensional and the relationships between w, x, and y are non-linear, regression models become inadequate. If machine learning is directly applied to model the relationships between w, x, and y, the estimated treatment effect θ_0 for x, is often biased for two main reasons.

(1) Regularization Bias: Regularized machine learning methods introduce penalty terms to constrain model complexity, which may cause parameter estimates to deviate from their true values.

(2) Overfitting Bias: A model that is too complex may capture noise or random fluctuations in the training data instead of learning the true underlying structure, resulting in good performance on the training data but poor performance on unseen data.

DML addresses regularization bias by orthogonalizing the residuals. This process ensures that the residuals are independent of the confounding variables, effectively isolating the net effect of the treatment variable on the outcome variable. The calculation involves two stages.

In the first stage, two machine learning models are used to estimate the effects of the confounding variables w on the outcome variable y and independent variable x, respectively, to obtain the estimates $\hat{g}(W)$ and $\hat{m}(W)$. The residuals E_y and E_x of the two prediction models are then computed.

In the second stage, the residual E_x is used as an explanatory variable and E_y as the dependent variable. A model is then built to estimate the ATE of x on y. The specific steps are as outlined below.

a. Use the **confounding** variables w and fit the outcome variable y using any machine learning model to obtain the residual E_y:

$$E_y = Y - \hat{g}(W), \qquad \hat{g}(W) = E(Y|W). \tag{9.1}$$

b. Use the confounding variables w and fit the independent variable x using any machine learning model to obtain the residual E_x:

$$E_x = X - \hat{m}(W), \qquad \hat{m}(W) = E(X|W). \tag{9.2}$$

c. Use any model to fit E_y as a function of E_x and estimate the treatment effect θ, where θ is the average causal effect of x on y:

$$E_y = \theta_0 * E_x + \varepsilon \tag{9.3}$$

The orthogonalization of the residuals helps eliminate the confounding influence of w on both y and x, thereby reducing the effects of regularization-induced bias and enhancing the robustness of causal effect estimation. These residuals represent the parts of the outcome and treatment variables that remain unexplained after controlling for confounding variables. Here, E_y represents the unexplained part of the outcome variable after controlling for confounding variables, effectively removing the correlation between y and w; E_x denotes the unexplained part of the treatment variable after controlling for confounding variables, effectively removing the correlation between x and w. When residuals E_y and E_x are utilized, the effects of confounding variables can be effectively removed, bringing the remaining correlation closer to a causal relationship.

Simultaneously, DML reduces overfitting bias through a process known as cross-fitting. For example, before analysis, we divide the total sample into two parts, S_1 and S_2. In the first stage, we use S_1 to train the two machine learning models and then use S_2 to estimate the two residuals. We then proceed to the second-stage estimation to calculate the causal effect θ_1. Next, we use S_2 to train the two machine learning models and employ S_1 to estimate the two residuals and the causal effect θ_2. The final causal effect θ is the average of θ_1 and θ_2. A similar approach can be employed using K-fold cross-validation to enhance the robustness of the estimate by splitting the data into k parts, repeating the estimation k times, and obtaining the final causal effect estimate as

$$\theta = \frac{\theta_1 + \theta_2 + \ldots + \theta_k}{K} \tag{9.4}$$

When the two core steps of residual orthogonalization and cross-validation are combined, the causal effect estimated by DML is nearly unbiased (Chernozhukov et al. 2018). Even if one of the models, such as the treatment probability model or the outcome model, is incorrectly specified, the DML method still ensures consistent causal effect estimates. This robustness stems from Neyman orthogonality, a property that renders estimates insensitive to local errors in nuisance parameters, thereby improving the model's robustness in real-world applications (Neyman 1959). Additionally, DML is highly flexible: it accommodates both categorical and continuous variables, and allows researchers to apply various appropriate models in the prediction and estimation processes of the first and second stages. During the pure prediction task in the first stage of DML, researchers can select the most suitable machine learning algorithm based on the characteristics of the independent and dependent variables, whether that involves a classification model or a regression model. When dealing with high-dimensional confounding variables, models with regularization and variable selection capabilities, such as Lasso, Elastic Net, or decision trees, should be prioritized. In cases with complex relationships and numerous confounding variables, more advanced ensemble learning methods or neural network models are recommended to achieve more accurate predictions (Chen et al. 2021). As long as accurate predictions are obtained, the complexity or interpretability of the model itself need not be the primary concern.

In the second stage of DML, researchers may choose either parametric or non-parametric models to estimate causal effects depending on the specific circumstances. The chosen model will directly influence the statistical properties of the final estimate. For instance, if linear ordinary least squares (OLS) regression is applied, the estimated average causal effect will be linear and accompanied by corresponding confidence intervals, making it particularly suitable for cases in which the independent variable is binary. However, when the independent variable is continuous and the true causal relationship is non-linear, linear models may introduce bias. In such scenarios, researchers should consider using polynomial regression models or non-parametric options, such as the causal Random Forest (Athey et al. 2019). Non-parametric models tend to capture complex non-linear relationships more effectively and can generate confidence intervals for estimates using bootstrap sampling methods. However, the confidence intervals derived from bootstrap sampling primarily reflect model variance rather than bias and are more reliable under large sample conditions.

3 Causal Extensions of Double Machine Learning

3.1 *Evaluation of Treatment Effect Heterogeneity Using Double Machine Learning*

A significant advantage of DML is its ability to flexibly evaluate CATE, allowing for the analysis of the heterogeneity of treatment effects across groups or conditions. This analysis mainly occurs in the second stage of DML, where heterogeneity is captured through the inclusion of interaction terms or by employing algorithmic models to estimate CATE. The method used and results obtained upon evaluating treatment effect heterogeneity in DML depend on whether a data model or an algorithmic model is used in the second stage.

When a data model is employed for this analysis, the methodology resembles traditional regression techniques. Interaction terms between the independent variable residuals (E_x) and the moderating variables are included in the second-stage regression equation. The treatment effect heterogeneity is revealed by estimating the coefficients of these interaction terms. This method has a clear and straightforward model structure, making it easy to understand and interpret. In addition, it provides confidence intervals and significance test results for treatment effect heterogeneity, making it suitable for cases with a limited number of moderating variables. However, challenges arise when many sources of variation in treatment effects are present. This approach struggles with adding numerous interaction terms to the model and accurately determining the specific form of these interaction terms (e.g., linear, quadratic, cubic, or higher-order interactions) (Hainmueller et al. 2019). Moreover, because data models predefine the relationships between variables, they may fail to capture the complex and diverse non-linear heterogeneity across groups. Consequently, data models are more suitable for cases with fewer interaction variables, primarily used to assess the significance and overall direction of variations, rather than for cases including numerous moderating variables or for depicting heterogeneity differences across groups in detail.

Second, when an algorithmic model such as Causal Forest or Random Forest is used in the second stage of DML, the basic principle is to incorporate both the independent variable residuals (E_x) and other variables that may influence variations in treatment effects in the model. By employing interpretable machine learning techniques such as the SHAP value (Lundberg and Lee 2017), we can quantify the impact of each moderating variable on the prediction results for individual cases, thereby assessing the heterogeneity of treatment effects. A key benefit of using an algorithmic model to estimate CATE is its ability to rank the importance of moderating effects based on data-driven method. This approach automatically identifies significant moderating variables and effectively captures non-linear relationships among the moderating effects across groups. However, a notable limitation of this method is that due to the complexity of the machine learning model structure, the explanation for the treatment effect heterogeneity is post hoc; that is, it cannot be directly derived from the model's parameters but is instead assessed by observing changes in model output in response to changes in input features. In addition, an algorithmic model for computing CATE generally does not provide direct estimates of the uncertainty associated with each moderating variable's parameters, such as significance levels.

3.2 *Double Machine Learning for Mediation Effect Analysis*

In addition to evaluating the heterogeneity of treatment effects, the DML method can be applied to causal mediation analysis. Farbmacher et al. (2022) proposed a method that combines causal mediation analysis with DML to estimate the indirect effect of an independent variable through mediating variables as well as its direct effect. This method can be implemented using the medDML function in the causal weight package in R. The core idea is to estimate natural direct and indirect effects within the potential outcome framework. The specific procedure involves using machine learning algorithms (such as Lasso regression or Random Forest) to estimate the distribution of the treatment variable (i.e., treatment probability or propensity score), the conditional distribution of the mediating variable (given the treatment variable and covariates), and the conditional expectation of the outcome variable (given the treatment variable, mediating variable, and covariates). Based on these estimations, direct and indirect causal effects are computed using efficient score functions (Tchetgen et al. 2012). Throughout the process, sample splitting and cross-fitting techniques are employed to mitigate model overfitting bias, ensuring the reliability of the estimated results. Similar to the nature of DML, using the DML framework for mediation effect analysis offers multiple forms of robustness, allowing for relatively accurate estimates even when one of the models for treatment probability, conditional distribution of the mediating variable, or conditional expectation of the outcome variable is incorrectly specified.

3.3 Double Machine Learning for Estimating Causal Temporal Effects

The next concern is regarding how DML handles panel data. Panel data can indeed be treated as cross-sectional data, enabling a straightforward DML analysis based on the aforementioned steps. However, this approach presents certain challenges. First, although DML reduces overfitting bias through cross-fitting, this step relies on the independent and identically distributed (i.i.d.) assumption for the observed values. Because data from the same sample at different time points in panel data are often correlated, these correlated data can end up in different training and test sets, heightening the risk of overfitting in the machine learning model. Second, cross-sectional DML analysis considers only the effects of contemporaneous treatment variables and confounding variables on the current outcome variable, neglecting the temporal effects of causality. In other words, the current outcome variable may be affected by past independent and dependent variables; similarly, current confounding variables may be influenced by past independent variables. As a result, estimates of causal effects could be biased (Fuhr & Papies 2024).

Accordingly, some studies have examined how DML can be improved for handling panel data and estimating dynamic effects. Lewis and Syrgkanis (2020) combined Rubin's structural nested mean model (SNMM) with DML by incorporating sequential g-estimation from the SNMM into the DML framework. Using a sequential residualization method, they first estimated the residuals for each period and then constructed a strongly convex objective function. The regression analysis starts from the last time point, proceeding backward and removing the treatment effect for each time point (Lewis & Syrgkanis 2020). Bodory et al. (2022) combined semi-parametric efficient estimation of dynamic treatment effects under sequential conditional independence with DML, employing machine learning-based dynamic treatment propensity scores (which predict the probability of treatment given covariates and past treatment history) and conditional means (given treatment history, covariates, and past outcomes) to estimate dynamic temporal treatment effects. Fuhr and Papies (2024) discovered through simulation tests that directly applying DML to panel data that violates the i.i.d. assumption does not result in significant errors. However, by incorporating time averages of the independent and covariate variables into the machine learning predictions of outcomes and treatments, they were able to model unobserved heterogeneity. This adjustment shifts the DML assumption from "no unobserved confounding variables" to "no time-variant unobserved confounding variables" (Fuhr & Papies 2024).

3.4 Double Machine Learning and the Application of Unstructured Data

Structured data typically comprise indicators obtained by researchers through operationalization. However, in social science research, images, text, and other types of data can also contain substantial information. Because DML operates without strict assumptions regarding variable dimensions or distributions, researchers can theoretically incorporate unstructured data, such as text and images, into their models for analysis. On the one hand, unstructured data may act as important confounding variables, which researchers can directly convert into high-dimensional vectors using word-, sentence-, or image-embedding models. These can then be fed into DML for first-stage predictions to acquire residuals for estimating causal effects. On the other hand, if the goal is to interpret unstructured data, researchers should treat these data as independent variables or attributes for heterogeneity analysis. This process involves first converting the unstructured data into operationalized indicators relevant to the dimensions of interest before conducting DML analysis.

For example, Dube et al. (2020) employed the DML method to estimate labor supply elasticity in the online labor market, specifically on the MTurk platform. They treated labor compensation as the independent variable and the time interval between job vacancies as the dependent variable, analyzing the causal effect of compensation on hiring. However, factors such as job type, difficulty, and requirements also significantly influenced the results; these factors were often overlooked in traditional analytical methods due to the challenge of operationalizing them as structured indicators. To address this, the authors converted textual data, such as job titles, descriptions, and keywords, into phrase statistics, topic distributions, and Doc2Vec sentence embeddings. They used these high-dimensional vectors in a Random Forest model to predict both the independent and dependent variables, thereby estimating the causal effect of wages on job vacancies (Dube et al. 2020).

4 Double Machine Learning and Other Causal Inference Methods

Although DML is a relatively new approach to causal inference, it shares similarities with established methods for estimating causal effects. This section reviews DML methods, highlighting their advantages and disadvantages via comparisons with other causal inference techniques.

4.1 Double Machine Learning and Linear Regression Models

Controlling for confounding variables that affect both X and Y through traditional linear regression is a widely adopted method for causal inference. However, the primary distinction between DML and regression models lies in their treatment of residuals. DML orthogonalizes residuals to eliminate the effects of confounding variables using machine learning, whereas linear regression models establish relationships between confounding variables through predefined parameter equations. In essence, DML uses algorithmic models to control for confounding variables, whereas regression models rely on data models. When a substantial number of variables are included, particularly when the number of control variables approaches the sample size, or when the relationships among the variables are non-linear, traditional data models may fail. By contrast, algorithmic models are more adept at handling complex, high-dimensional data scenarios (Chen & Chen 2024; Breiman 2001b). Moreover, when estimating the heterogeneity of treatment effects, traditional regression models can incorporate interaction terms. However, when the nature of these effects is non-linear, regression models may struggle to provide accurate estimations. Despite these differences, DML and traditional regression methods share some commonalities. Following residual orthogonalization, if individual treatment effects are not investigated or if few moderating variables exist, OLS or other linear models can be applied to the residuals. This approach enables the evaluation of the average causal effect and derivation of significance tests and confidence intervals for the causal effect.

4.2 Double Machine Learning and Propensity Score Matching

The propensity score represents the probability that an individual is affected by the independent variable. PSM helps mitigate endogeneity bias caused by confounding variables or sample selection by matching individuals with similar propensity scores; DML and propensity score methods are similar to some extent. Both operate under the conditional independence assumption, meaning that they assume that confounding variables are observable and measurable, thus making the potential outcome independent of the treatment condition given the observed characteristics. In addition, calculating the propensity score involves predicting the independent variable using confounding variables, a process that parallels the first stage of DML, where confounding variables are employed to predict the independent variable. Both approaches address the limitations of performing direct regression with respect to the number of variables and the linearity assumption. However, the key difference is that DML computes the residuals from the predicted independent variable, whereas PSM uses matching to construct control and treatment groups. DML is more advantageous than the PSM when the independent variable is continuous, as it does not require matching within a "common support" region. Furthermore, when estimating treatment effect heterogeneity, DML can more flexibly identify the confounding variable that drives the heterogeneous effects and can reveal specific effect differences between different groups.

4.3 Double Machine Learning and Instrumental Variables

The IV method infers the causal effect of the independent variable on the dependent variable indirectly by introducing an exogenous instrument unrelated to the error term but associated with the independent variable (Chen 2012a; Chen & Xu 2024). Researchers typically exercise theoretical and empirical judgment when identifying an appropriate instrument before conducting a two-stage regression (Chen 2012b; Fu et al. 2024). From another perspective, the residuals used in DML also align with the logic of IVs. The residuals E_x obtained by predicting the independent variable with confounding variables can be understood as an IV for the independent variable X. These residuals are highly correlated with X but uncorrelated with other confounding variables, establishing their exogeneity; they affect Y only through X. The residual E_y in DML can also be understood as the purified dependent variable Y. It is highly correlated with Y and uncorrelated with other confounding variables. Regressing E_y on E_x in this case actually removes the effects of all confounding variables, thus revealing the net effect of the independent variable on the dependent variable. Hence, the DML process effectively functions by creating an instrument E_x derived from machine learning predictions, as opposed to relying on natural instruments.

Compared with traditional causal inference methods that rely on the CIA, such as linear regression and PSM, DML transcends the limitations related to the number of variables and their relationships inherent in traditional regression models. It mitigates the bias caused by insufficient control variables and avoids the "curse of dimensionality" that arises from redundant control variables. Moreover, DML can effectively avoid model misspecification problems. Unlike PSM and other machine learning methods that struggle to estimate confidence intervals, DML circumvents these difficulties. As a methodological framework, DML is capable of integrating any model within the two-stage estimation process. By orthogonalizing residuals and employing cross-validation, it yields accurate causal estimates. This flexibility allows DML to combine the strengths of both algorithmic models and data models, making it better suited to different data characteristics and research requirements.

5 Empirical Example

This section illustrates the effects of parental academic expectations on children's academic performance to demonstrate how DML can be used to estimate causal effects between these two variables. The selection of this case is driven by two considerations. First, parental expectations and children's academic performance are classic topics in educational studies and are common concerns in Chinese families, making them ideal for comparing traditional and contemporary methods. Second, although existing studies (e.g., Yamamoto & Holloway 2010) have established a significant relationship between parental academic expectations and children's academic performance and have also examined moderating factors such as family economic status, gender, and urban-rural differences, they fall short in quantifying the relative magnitudes of these moderating effects or the heterogeneity of effects through complex non-linear relationships between groups. Moreover, the magnitude of the effects may vary across learning stages, exhibiting temporal heterogeneity. Thus, this section describes how the DML method can be used to tackle these complex confounding variables, capture group and time heterogeneity, and showcase the distinct advantages of this method in this context.

5.1 Data and Variables

The data used in this chapter are derived from the China Education Panel Study (CEPS) baseline survey of 2013–2014 and the follow-up survey of 2014–2015, both conducted by the China Survey and Data Center at Renmin University of China. The dataset includes two waves of panel data, with samples from seventh graders during the baseline survey and eighth graders during the follow-up. In total, 19,532 valid data entries were obtained. The dependent variable, "raw scores from the 2013/2014 mid-term exams," was calculated as the sum of students' scores in Chinese, mathematics, and English, represented as a continuous variable. The independent variable was "What expectations do your parents have for your academic performance?" with responses ranging from "No special expectations," "Average level in class," "Above average," to "Top five in class," recorded each as an ordinal variable (1–4, respectively). To control for confounding variables, the model includes all survey variables with missing values no higher than 10%, totaling 119 variables. Categorical variables such as job type were converted into dummy variables, and missing values for other variables were imputed using the median.

5.2 Average Treatment Effect Estimation

Table 1 presents the estimations of the ATE of "parental academic expectations" on "children's academic performance" using various methods. First, we evaluated the causal relationship using traditional methods. Model 1 employs a general mixed regression (OLS) method to analyze the two-year data, whereas Model 2 uses a fixed effects (FE) model for the same dataset. Both models account for factors such as gender, household registration, whether the child is an only child, family economic conditions, whether the child resides at school, relationship with parents, and parental education level. Both models reveal a positive and statistically significant effect of the independent variable on the dependent variable. However, because both models include a limited number of control variables and cannot address time-varying confounders, we suspect that

Table 1 Average causal effects estimated by different models

Model	*ATE*	*Stderr*	*Ci_lower*	*Ci_upper*
Model_1 (OLS)	28.938***	0.602	27.758	30.117
Model_2 (FE)	4.907***	0.642	3.649	6.164
Model_3 (RF+OLS)	16.803***	0.456	15.848	17.758
		0.481		
Model_4 (XGBoost +OLS)	14.409***		13.514	15.303
Model_5 (RF+lasso)	16.934***	0.437	16.077	17.791
Model_6 (XGBoost +lasso)	14.175***	0.399	13.392	14.957
Model_7 (RF+CF)	17.423***	0.712	16.028	18.818
Model_8 (XGBoost +CF)	13.874***	0.538	12.818	14.929

Note +p<0.1, *p<0.05, **p<0.01, ***p<0.001 (two-tailed test)

other important omitted variables could influence the causal relationship between the two variables. Therefore, we used the DML method to estimate the ATE between the independent and dependent variables, controlling for the 119 other variables identified as confounders in the survey.

To test the validity of the DML analysis, we cross-validated the robustness of the estimated effects using six models in both stages of DML. In the first stage, we used either Random Forest or XGBoost to estimate the independent and dependent variables while considering confounders. In the second stage, we applied OLS regression, Lasso regularization, or causal forests to regress the residuals, allowing us to estimate both the magnitude and significance of the effects of the independent variable on the dependent variable. The OLS and Lasso models computed confidence intervals through statistical inference, whereas causal forests use the bootstrap method. All models undergo five-fold cross-validation. The results of these analyses are detailed in Models 3–8, which show that the various DML models consistently exhibit considerable robustness in estimating the causal relationship between the two variables. All models indicate that "parental academic expectations" positively influence "children's academic performance," with this effect being significant at the 99.9% level. This finding suggests a stable causal relationship exists after controlling for over a hundred confounding variables and considering non-linear relationships.

In estimating the ATE, both traditional causal inference methods and DML analysis yield significant results. The key differences between these approaches are as follows: OLS is significant when controlling for a limited number of observable confounding variables, FE is significant when controlling for both a limited number of observable confounding variables and unobservable confounders that remain constant over time, and DML is significant when controlling for high-dimensional observable confounding variables. In general, the latter two methods offer greater power. If DML's primary advantage in estimating average effects lies in its ability to exclude more confounding variables, subsequent analyses will demonstrate DML's supplementary advantages over traditional causal inference methods. These advantages include managing treatment effect heterogeneity while accommodating non-linear relationships and addressing temporal variations in causal effects.

5.3 Heterogeneity of Causal Effects

After establishing the causal effect, a question arises whether we can further analyze the differences in impact across different groups. A common analytical approach is to incorporate interaction terms into the regression model or estimate how the treatment effect varies with individual propensity scores (Hu et al. 2021). However, the use of interaction terms can be limited by their inherent constraints, and analyzing propensity scores does not provide insight into the specific factors that contribute to treatment effect heterogeneity. Both approaches fall short of identifying the factors that most significantly affect causal heterogeneity and the non-linear influence across different groups. This section explains the use of DML to determine the magnitude and specific manifestations of variable heterogeneity. We investigated the following nine demographic and family background-related moderator variables: the child's gender (male or female), household registration type (agricultural, non-agricultural or resident households), whether the child is an only child (yes or no), family economic conditions (very poor, relatively poor, average, relatively affluent or very affluent), whether the child lives at school (yes or no), relationship with father (not close, average or very close), relationship with mother (not close, average or very close), father's education level (from never attended elementary school to attended graduate school on a scale of 1–9), and mother's education level (from never attended elementary school to attended graduate school on a scale of 1–9). This analysis helps elucidate the differences in treatment effects across these nine groups.

Machine learning provides a flexible approach for estimating the heterogeneity of statistical effects by assessing individual causal effects. In this analysis, we employed the causal forests model in the second stage of DML, incorporating the nine moderator variables mentioned above. We also used the SHAP interpretability method to detail the varying influences of "parental academic expectations" and "children's academic performance" across groups. Figure 1(a) displays the average absolute SHAP values of all cases for each moderator variable, ranking the overall effect of these nine variables on causal heterogeneity. Figure 1(b) provides the details of the moderation of each moderator variable under each case. Here, each point represents an individual case, with colors indicating the magnitude of the feature value X for that variable (darker reds correspond to larger values). The horizontal axis represents the SHAP value's magnitude; a greater number of points sharing the same SHAP value suggests a wider distribution for that particular row. Figure 2 presents the macroscopic feature impact chart of SHAP values across the full sample, illustrating the specific moderating effects of the nine variables. In this chart, blue points represent individual samples, with the horizontal and vertical axes representing the values of the relevant moderator variable and the magnitude of the moderating effect or SHAP value, respectively. The yellow line indicates the mean value of the moderating effect within the relevant group (i.e., the CATE).

Data analysis results reveal that, among the nine moderator variables, gender is the most significant factor. This finding underscores that gender differences exert the most significant influence on the strength of the causal relationship between X and Y. As illustrated in Figs. 1(b) and 2(a), the SHAP value for males is notably higher than that for females, suggesting that parental academic expectations have a greater effect on boys' academic performance than on that of girls. Previous studies have indicated that boys may encounter more adaptive challenges in school environments compared with girls, leading to greater difficulties in fulfilling the "student" role (Downey & Vogt Yuan 2005). By contrast, girls tend to better meet the expectations of diligent study from both school and family and are more comfortable embracing the role of the "good student."

Parental education level is a crucial variable in moderating the effects of academic expectations on academic performance. Data show that the mother's education level has a slightly greater influence than the father's in this regard. The mother's education level ranks second among the

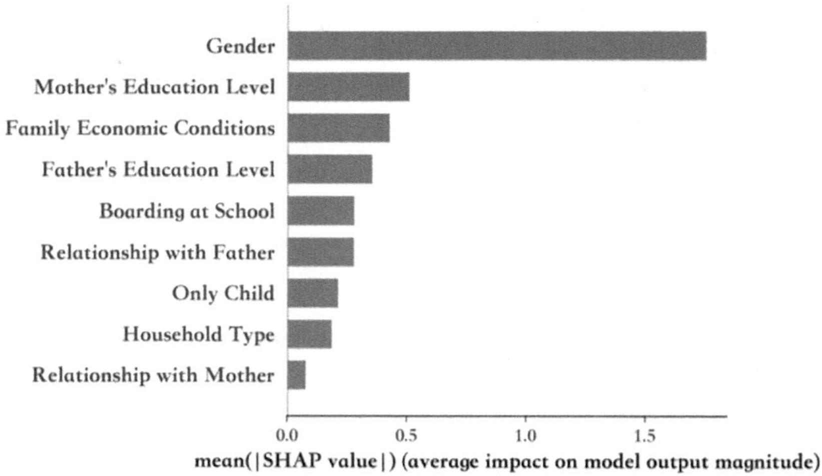

(a)

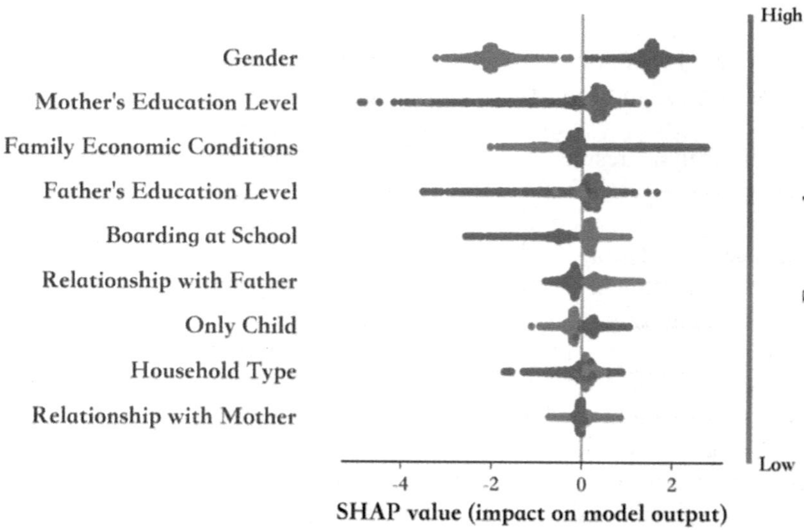

(b)

Fig. 1 Ranking of the magnitude of heterogeneity in treatment effects

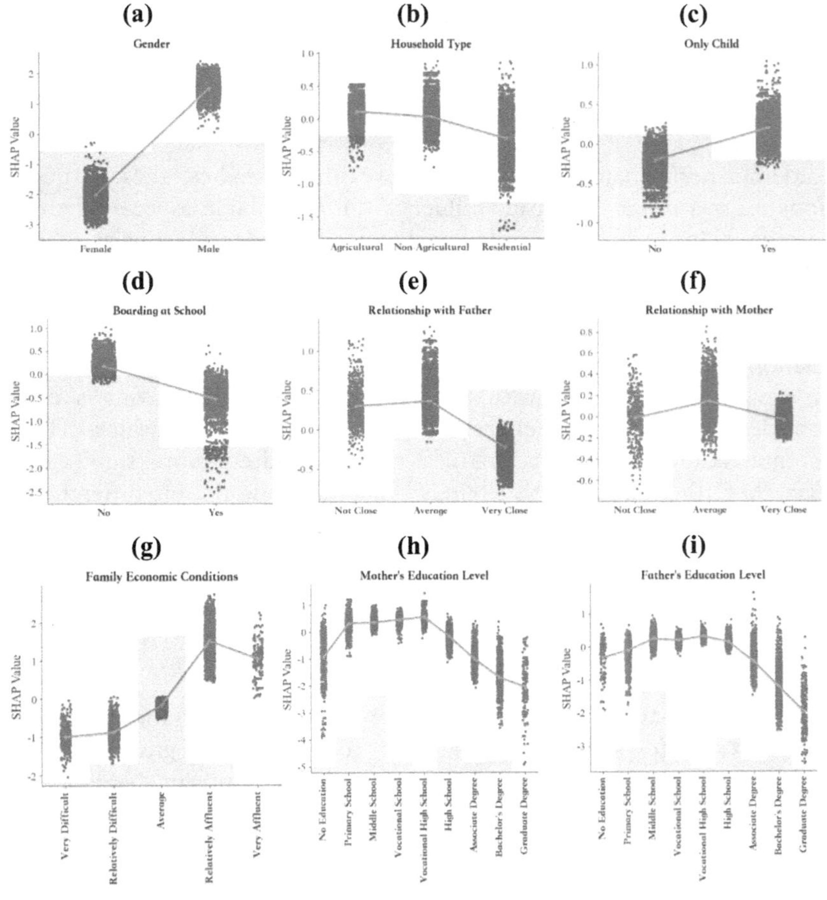

Fig. 2 SHAP value macroscopic feature impact chart for moderator variables

variables in terms of moderating effect, whereas the father's education level ranks fourth. The inter-group ATE shows a trend in which both parental education levels exhibit increasing and then decreasing moderating effects. For parents whose education is at or below the vocational high school level, the moderating effect either increases or remains stable as their education level rises. However, once parental education reaches high school or higher levels, the moderating effect decreases.

This suggests that the effectiveness of family educational support does not follow a linear trajectory but involves complex interactions.

Family economic conditions rank third among the nine variables influencing the causal relationship. In families with challenging economic conditions, parental academic expectations have less effect on children's academic performance. However, in wealthier families, these expectations exert a more significant influence. Other notable aspects of group heterogeneity include the following: first, for students living at school, parental academic expectations exert less impact on academic performance; thus, non-residential students are more affected by these expectations compared with their residential counterparts. Second, a closer relationship with parents tends to weaken the effect of academic expectations on performance, with father-child relationships having a more considerable moderating effect than mother-child relationships. Third, parental academic expectations affect only children more significantly than they do children with siblings. Finally, no significant difference is observed in how parental academic expectations affect academic performance across household registration types or varying degrees of closeness to the mother.

5.4 *Temporal Differences in Causal Effects*

Considering that the effects of parental academic expectations on children's academic performance may vary over different grade levels in middle school, we used two-period panel data comprising baseline and follow-up surveys to examine whether this causal effect changes as students advance through grades. Table 2 presents the analytical results. The table shows that the causal effects in both periods are statistically significant. However, when students first enter middle school in grade 7, the average causal effect of parental academic expectations on children's academic performance is 7.266, which is significantly lower than the average causal effect of 15.994 in grade 8. This indicates that as students progress through grades, the positive effects of parental academic expectations on their academic performance become more pronounced. A possible explanation for this finding is that as students gradually adapt to the middle school learning pace and environment, parental expectations begin to have a greater effect: in grade 7, students may still be adjusting to the new learning model and social dynamics, and parental expectations may not yet have fully translated into genuine motivation for learning or

Table 2 Dynamic causal effect estimates at different time points

Model	*ATE*	*Stderr*	*Zstat*	*Ci_lower*	*Ci_upper*
Grade 7	7.266***	0.729	9.970	5.837	8.694
Grade 8	15.994***	0.740	21.626	14.544	17.443

Note +p<0.1, *p<0.05, **p<0.01, ***p<0.001 (two-tailed test)

into specific parenting styles that affect academic performance. By grade 8, when students are more familiar with school life, parental expectations are more likely to be internalized and transformed into tangible learning outcomes through external discipline.

6 Conclusion

Machine learning, which leverages a large number of variables and non-linear relationships, offers new insights for causal inference methods. This chapter introduces the emerging causal inference method of DML. The core idea of DML is to use many confounding variables, operating under the assumption that all confounders are observable, and apply machine learning algorithms to compute the residuals of independent and dependent variables separately. Through residual orthogonalization and cross-fitting, DML allows for the estimation of nearly unbiased causal effects. This chapter also reviews the applications of the DML method in analyzing causal effect heterogeneity, causal mediation effects, and causal time effects and in handling unstructured data. In addition, by contrasting DML with traditional methods such as regression, PSM, and IVs, the study clarifies the role of DML. Finally, this chapter employs two rounds of panel data from CEPS to validate the causal relationship between "parental academic expectations" and "children's academic performance" and discusses group heterogeneity and temporal differences in causal effects from multiple perspectives.

As an emerging statistical technique, the DML method for causal inference offers several unique advantages, particularly in the following areas:

First, DML can effectively control for a large number of confounding variables while fitting non-linear relationships. In the first stage of DML, two machine learning algorithms are employed to account for confounding variables, overcoming the limitations of traditional regression models in terms of the number of variables and their pre-established relationships. This approach reduces estimation bias from insufficient control variables and also avoids the "curse of dimensionality" derived from redundant control variables. Consequently, it minimizes model misspecification issues and clarifies the causal relationship between independent and dependent variables.

Second, DML excels in analyzing causal heterogeneity, estimating time-varying causal effects, and handling unstructured data. When exploring treatment effect heterogeneity, the second stage of DML uses machine learning models to automatically identify significant moderating effects, facilitating theoretical insights. By estimating individual-level causal effects, DML can flexibly illustrate the specific forms of treatment effect heterogeneity. When estimating time effects, DML captures how causal effects evolve, revealing the temporal dynamics of causal effects, which can support policy research and social governance decisions. In addition, DML can incorporate unstructured data, such as text and images, as potential confounding variables, enriching the analysis with valuable information.

Finally, DML enhances analytical accuracy through Neyman orthogonality and cross-fitting. Neyman orthogonality ensures that the estimates remain robust to local errors in nuisance parameters. Even when some models are wrongly specified or perform poorly, DML provides relatively consistent and reliable causal effect estimates. Furthermore, by reducing model-fitting bias through cross-fitting within the data, DML significantly improves the robustness of the resulting estimates.

However, DML has certain limitations and challenges. First, it requires that all confounding variables be observable. In practice, even with the inclusion of a large number of potential confounders, some key variables may still be omitted. When this occurs, the estimated causal effects can become biased, necessitating careful consideration of the confounders for inclusion. Second, if few confounders are observable or critical ones are omitted, DML may be less applicable than other causal inference methods, such as DID, regression discontinuity, or IVs, which can effectively manage confounders through research design. Researchers can also integrate the DML framework with methods such as DID and IVs to leverage experimental designs or exogenous variables for more robust estimates. Third, DML employs machine learning techniques to fit residuals and uses cross-fitting to reduce bias, making it particularly suited to handling high-dimensional data and large sample sizes. This requirement places higher demands on the richness of the data. Fourth, effective machine learning predictive models depend on careful model selection and hyperparameter tuning, often resulting in increased computational workloads and complex tuning processes. Furthermore, different algorithms and parameter settings can yield varying analytical results, leading to the methodological dilemma of "same data, different conclusions." Finally, if complex machine learning models are employed in all stages of DML, researchers must rely on post hoc explanations, which can make DML less interpretable and straightforward compared with traditional data models.

Causal inference methods using machine learning extend beyond DML alone; however, DML is notable for its relatively loose assumptions. In the context of increasingly sophisticated secondary data and big data measurement technologies, DML offers a more flexible and reliable solution for complex causal inference challenges. More importantly, DML serves as a robust estimation framework for causal inference methods, and its data-driven approach enables the exploration of key heterogeneity features of causal impact mechanisms and non-linear relationships involving group and time heterogeneity. This capability not only inspires and refines theoretical hypotheses but also encourages the formulation of new questions, the discovery of new phenomena, and a deeper understanding of complex causal mechanisms within social phenomena. However, current applications of DML in social science largely focus on the verification of average causal effects, with few studies investigating its potential in areas such as causal effect heterogeneity, causal mediation mechanisms, time effects analysis, and the examination of unstructured data. These represent significant opportunities for DML's future application in social science research. Looking ahead, research should aim to optimize the DML technical framework and advance the development of related programming languages or software packages for DML and its extended applications. In addition, the integration of DML with various quasi-experimental causal inference methods and relevant social research topics should be emphasized. By fostering productive interaction between theory verification and inspiration, as well as promoting a bidirectional relationship between theory and methods, DML can offer more comprehensive and effective computational tools for studying causal mechanisms in the social sciences.

References

Athey, Susan, Julie Tibshirani, and Stefan Wager. 2019. Generalized random forests. *The Annals of Statistics* 47 (2): 1148–1178.

Bodory, Hugo, Martin Huber, and Lukáš Lafférs. 2022. Evaluating (weighted) dynamic treatment effects by double machine learning. *The Econometrics Journal* 25 (3): 628–648.

Breiman, Leo. 2001b. Statistical modeling: The two cultures (with comments and a rejoinder by the author). *Statistical Science* 16 (3): 199–231.

Chen, Yunsong. 2012a. Logic, imagination and interpretation: The application of instrumental variables for causal inference in the social sciences. *Sociological Studies* 6: 192–216+245–246 (In Chinese).

Chen, Yunsong. 2012b. Do networks pay off among internal migrants in China? An instrumental variable analysis. *Chinese Sociological Review* 45 (1): 28–54.

Chen, Yunsong, and Xiaoguang Fan. 2010. The endogeneity problem review in quantitative analysis: A review of estimating causal effects of social interaction. *Chinese Journal of Sociology* 30 (4): 91–117.

Chen, Yunsong, and Xu Qi. 2024. *Causal inference in social science*. Beijing: Peking University Press.

Chen, Yunsong, Guangye He, and Fei Yan. 2021. *Understanding China through big data: Applications of theory-oriented quantitative approaches*. Abingdon, New York: Routledge.

Chen, Zhuo, and Yunsong Chen. 2024. Computing grounded theory: a quantitative method to develop theories. *The Journal of Chinese Sociology*, 11 (1), 17.

Chernozhukov, Victor, et al. 2018. Double/debiased machine learning for treatment and structural parameters. *Econometrics Journal* 21: C1–C68.

Downey, Douglas B., and Anastasia S. Vogt Yuan. 2005. Sex differences in school performance during high school: Puzzling patterns and possible explanations. *Sociological Quarterly* 46 (2): 299–321.

Draper, David. 1995. Assessment and propagation of model uncertainty. *Journal of the Royal Statistical Society Series B: Statistical Methodology* 57 (1): 45–70.

Dube, Arindrajit, et al. 2020. Monopsony in online labor markets. *American Economic Review: Insights* 2 (1): 33–46.

Farbmacher, Helmut, et al. 2022. Causal mediation analysis with double machine learning. *The Econometrics Journal* 25 (2): 277–300.

Fu, Zhihui, Shukai Liu, Guodong Ju, Wen Ma, and Yunsong Chen. 2024. Instrumental Guanxi culture and inbound urban migration in China: A prefecture-level analysis using online search data. *The China Quarterly* 260:1040–1058.

Fuhr, Jonathan, and Dominik Papies. 2024. Double machine learning meets panel data—Promises, pitfalls, and potential solutions. *arXiv preprint* arXiv: 2409.01266.

Hainmueller, Jens, Jonathan Mummolo, and Yiqing Xu. 2019. How much should we trust estimates from multiplicative interaction models? Simple tools to improve empirical practice. *Political Analysis* 27 (2): 163–192.

Hu, Anning, Xiaogang Wu, and Yunsong Chen. 2021. Analysis of heterogeneous treatment effect: New opportunities and challenges with machine learning techniques. *Sociological Studies* 36 (1): 91–114+228 (In Chinese).

Lewis, Greg, and Vasilis Syrgkanis. 2020. Double/debiased machine learning for dynamic treatment effects via g-estimation. arXiv preprint arXiv:2002.07285.

Lundberg, Scott M. and Su-In Lee. 2017. A unified approach to interpreting model predictions. In 31st Conference on Neural Information Processing Systems (NIPS 2017), Long Beach, CA, USA.

Neyman, Jerzy. 1959. Optimal asymptotic tests of composite statistical hypotheses. In *Probability and statistics*, ed. U. Grenander. New York: Wiley.

Tchetgen, Eric J. Tchetgen, and Ilya Shpitser. 2012. Semiparametric theory for causal mediation analysis: Efficiency bounds, multiple robustness, and sensitivity analysis. *Annals of Statistics* 40 (3): 1816.

Yamamoto, Yoko, and Susan D. Holloway. 2010. Parental expectations and children's academic performance in sociocultural context. *Educational Psychology Review* 22 (3): 189–214.

PART V

Modeling Topics

CHAPTER 10

Modeling Gender Consciousness: Women Authors' Creation in Boys' Love Fiction

1 Introduction

There is no other literature that reflects the current ethos in China like constantly updated and edited online fiction. The open online space welcomes women with different interests to gather, providing them with the chance to express their thoughts and even forge a digital feminism (Chang & Tian, 2021). Among the various genres of women's literature, Boys' Love (BL) fiction is an unconventional one, primarily focusing on the romance between men but typically created by and for heterosexual women. That is, BL fiction does not always reflect the reality of gay men, and the opposite gender of its author and protagonists produces an imaginary male-male love (Zhou et al., 2018). In contemporary China, BL fiction's rapid development as an important women's culture makes it relevant to their consciousness (Tian, 2020a).

Although it originated in Japan, BL fiction shares similar features to slash fiction[1] in the West. BL fiction is influenced by literary aestheticism from Europe; therefore, it is also referred to as tanbi, meaning "to indulge in beauty" (Kurihara & Kakinuma, 1993: 325–335). During the 1990s, Japanese BL fiction became known in Chinese mainland through Taiwanese translations. Inspired by them, Chinese women authors began

[1] Slash fiction also focuses on fictional male-male romantic or sexual relationships, but is mostly fan fiction based on existing literary or film works, whereas the BL fiction we studied is original and standalone unrelated to any existing work.

Y. Chen et al., *Machine Learning in Social Science*,
https://doi.org/10.1007/978-981-95-6465-1_10

to create original BL works online. The high number of Internet users in China facilitated an exponential increase in these stories, as well as the creation of several influential communities and websites devoted to BL fiction. The most well-known BL website is Jinjiang Literature City (JLC) (http://www.jjwxc.net), established in 2003. As of December 2021, JLC had seen over 80,000 BL fiction stories and 50.95 million registered users, with women accounting for 91% of the users.[2]

The existing studies discussed BL works from Europe, America, Chinese mainland, Taiwan, Thailand, and Japan (Pagliassotti, 2008; Feng, 2013; Mizoguchi, 2015; Chiang, 2016; Zhang & Dedman, 2021), including BL comics, novels, movies, and TV dramas (Martin, 2012; Wong, 2020; Ng & Li, 2020; Xu & Tan, 2021). Research on Chinese BL fiction investigated gender politics constructed by BL fandom groups. As an epitome of neoliberal feminism, BL authors and readers explored their subjectivity, while also resisting or conforming to official discourse and state authority (Tian, 2020b). When discussing the cultural attributes of Chinese BL fiction, researchers mostly regarded it as a modern or postmodern counterculture against Confucianist cultural norms (Chang & Tian, 2021), while paying less attention to its possible patriarchal remnants in the traditional culture and clan system. In addition, the relevant literature primarily adopted qualitative methods, such as interviews, questionnaires, and textual analysis of representative works. Although their conclusions have greatly enriched our understanding of gender perspectives in BL novels, their research objects were always within their visible range, causing them to easily ignore works that were not popular but did have a certain impact on the author and the reader.

Tracing the origin of BL fiction, Japanese BL fiction had two characteristics, namely the Western story background and tragic plots (Mizoguchi, 2015:26-27). These aligned with the pursuit of supreme beauty and sensory pleasure under aestheticism. Following two decades of growth, Chinese BL fiction has already departed from its Japanese ancestor and developed its own tastes. As an article in *The New York Times* stated, BL fiction in China is too large to be considered a subculture in comparison with its Japanese counterpart (Tatlow, 2014). Besides, owing to the Chinese government's anti-pornography campaign, nowadays, no sexual scenarios appear on legal websites (Yang & Xu, 2017). The resulting

[2] See http://www.jjwxc.net/aboutus/.

unique and implicit depiction of love is like "slow-burn heat" (Luskey, 2019), making BL stories close to mainstream popular culture. In this study, we aimed to map the topics of Chinese BL fiction, analyzing whether they were defined by China's cultural features.

BL fiction has already become an increasingly prosperous women-centered culture in China that involves millions of women authors. We are interested in understanding their consciousness in literary works. Although there do exist male authors and readers of BL fiction, the data show that its authors and audiences have primarily been heterosexual women (Pagliassotti, 2008). This phenomenon produces a contradiction: the market of BL fiction belongs to women, but the main protagonists are men, constructing both feminist and patriarchal ideas. Therefore, we further explored the contents of Chinese BL fiction from women authors' perspectives, specifically the paradoxical gender consequences brought by Chinese traditional ethics.

We adopted unsupervised machine learning text analysis methods to analyze the titles and introductions of 72,548 Jinjiang's original BL fiction pieces from 2003 to 2019. Text analysis methods could scan extensive amounts of text macroscopically, finding objective and universal patterns (Grimmer & Stewart, 2013; Cui, 2018; Eads et al., 2020). In this study, we applied the LDA topic model to classify the fiction topics and word vector technology to analyze the context of keywords related to gender and same-sex relationships synchronically and diachronically. These analyses answered two questions: (1) What topics and contents do Chinese women BL authors prefer? (2) How do the gender concepts of Chinese culture affect the topics and contents of BL fiction?

2 Gendered Perspective

Elaine Baruch (1991:9) stated in her work *Women, Love, and Power* that great love literature could help us look for the transcendence of gender polarization and disrupt the hierarchically structured male/female binary system. In a sense, BL fiction is "great love literature" from its readers' and authors' perspectives. This genre can be considered a breakthrough of the "male gaze," which constructs the "female gaze" through consuming male erotica (Meyer, 2013).

The majority of studies about male-male romance have suggested gender, especially the impact of gender description on readers' intention and their identity (Yi, 2013; Nagaike & Suganuma, 2013). For the former, scholars such as Pagliassotti (2008) found that the "pure love" gender-absent dimension in the stories, which avoided one-dimensional characters of women and heterosexual "boring narratives," was the primary attraction for the audience. Furthermore, Zsila et al. (2018), using an online survey, proved that sexual titillation, visual imagery, and aesthetics explained readers' preference for BL fiction.

Other researchers have focused on the authors' intentions conveyed by the text of the fiction. When Jenkins (1992: 191) researched slash fiction, similar to BL fiction in China, he considered that the transition of these stories from male homosocial desire to homoerotic passion was an exploration of alternatives to traditional masculinity. Since BL fiction was often associated with women's literature, Takemiya (1993), a Japanese BL manga artist, believed that BL works negated the subservient gender role imposed on women, helped women liberate themselves from the oppression of male power, and facilitated feminist ideals. A Chinese scholar went further by invoking Michel Foucault's constructivism to argue that women created a heterotopia through BL to compete for political space and resist patriarchy (Zheng, 2016). These studies presented the feminist significance of BL fiction.

However, recent studies have increasingly analyzed the anti-feminist features of BL stories. For example, Zhou, Paul, and Sherman (2018) studied the heterosexual romantic ideal in BL fiction and found that power differences persist in relationships between men. In particular, the fixed couple of seme (the attacker in Japanese, referring to the penetrator in sex) and uke (meaning the receiver in Japanese, referring to the penetrated in sex)[3] imitates the typical male-woman relationship that produces unequal power. Han (2020) also highlighted that Chinese BL authors often allow male protagonists to behave like heterosexual women in the male-male relationship, while women were absent in these relationships. This phenomenon suggests that the burden of sexual objectification cannot disappear easily. "The male gaze would not be simply inverted to produce a straightforward female gaze" (Burston & Richardson, 1995: 32), which means the female gaze could not consume the other gender as

[3] Men's physiological characteristics determine that there must be distinct roles in sexual behavior. However, different from the real situation, the roles of seme and uke in BL fiction are relatively fixed, and they rarely exchange roles with each other, thus producing unequal power.

completely as the male gaze can. Therefore, it is unreasonable to assume that feminist thoughts completely dominate the female gaze.

Although there are controversies surrounding the feminist features of BL fiction, it is undeniable that power-related issues remain crucial in the study of gender within BL fiction, not only as a reflection of gender power against patriarchy, but also as a manifestation of resistance to authority and mainstream culture. As Foucault (1979: 48) points out in *The History of Sexuality*, pleasure and power are linked by complex mechanisms and devices of excitation and incitement while they seek, overlap, and reinforce each other. When women BL authors enjoy their erotic desire through the two male protagonists, their pleasure is also associated with power. Indeed, some researchers considered that gender power and political power could work together. From the authors' side, Xu and Yang (2013) focused on a particular branch, father-son incest, which, in their perspective, reflected the resistance of Chinese women authors to the "authoritarian" government. From the government's side, Bai (2022) analyzed the regulation of pornography in BL works and pointed out that this seemed to be objective censorship that was contextually and structurally gendered. However, interpreting any narrative about imbalanced power relationships solely as a political metaphor might be unfounded. At the very least, an alternative explanation could be that BL works on legal websites, which do not contain any substantial political implications due to self-regulation. Consequently, for the unseen political threat of BL works, the government endeavored to reduce the pornographic content inside rather than simply ban this genre.

Shifting from a political focus, given China's rich ancient history, systematic ethics, and literary heritage, it is likewise reasonable and theoretical to hypothesize that the traditional culture may have greatly influenced women's writing. Considering that Chinese BL fiction is embedded within Chinese culture, some long-standing patriarchal values—including the importance of marriage and the continuity of a clan through reproduction—may help to explain the content of BL fiction. Therefore, the context of Chinese traditional culture should be explored when analyzing gender power in Chinese BL fiction's literary creation.

3 Data and Methods

We implemented text mining methods to explore the unstructured text data of BL fiction. This methodology was chosen for the following three reasons: (1) We planned to obtain an entire picture of Chinese women BL authors' literary creation, which could only be achieved with large-scale text analysis, and any part of the data enables further representative studies. (2) Compared with questionnaire surveys and qualitative thematic analysis, text mining of Chinese BL fiction is more objective in exploring the fiction topics and gendered expressions in the fictional stories. (3) Different from quantitative methods that use computer programs to search texts for keywords, the LDA topic model and word vector technology of text mining methods explore the meaning of the text by fully considering the relations between terms (DiMaggio et al., 2013).

We selected JLC as the data source, which is the largest and most well-known online platform for BL fiction creation in China and globally. Various studies have used cases and data from JLC. Several have focused on the site's profit model (Jiang and Kuang, 2016), whereas others have examined the feminist implications for Chinese women's literature (Feng, 2009). This website features strong interactivity. Since its fiction is mostly serialized, readers' preferences strongly influence the story's completion. Like sponsors, online reading communities offer authors emotional and financial incentives through comments and rewards (Tian and Adorjan, 2016). Their support even forms a "gift economy" that provides authors with the opportunity to contract with JLC and publish commercially, thus earning both popularity and commercial benefits (Wei, 2014).

To deal with the sample selection problems that may exist in previous studies and include works with lower visibility in the study, we analyzed titles and introductions of all 72,548 BL fiction pieces published since the foundation of Jinjiang in 2003. To make our topic more focused, we excluded fan fiction, so only original and stand-alone stories were entered into the database. We counted the number of Jinjiang original BL fictional works by year, as shown in Fig. 1. This number increased every year, save for a slight decrease between 2014 and 2016 due to the Chinese government's most extensive anti-pornography campaign.

Due to the data protection protocol of the paid main body on JLC, we could not extract and archive all complete texts of the 72,548 BL fiction pieces. Rather, we explored the information-rich titles and introductions (written by the author and containing a blurb and a plot synopsis) to

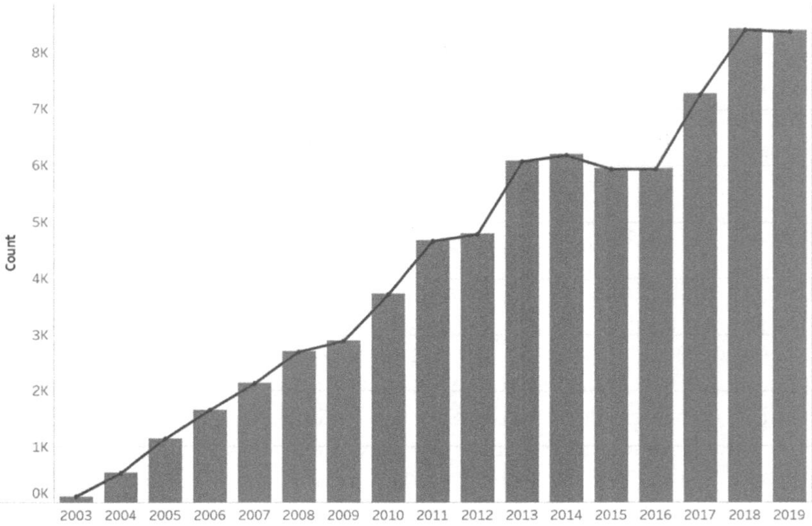

Fig. 1 Numbers of BL fictional works from JLC by year

explore specific content. According to the French literary critic Gérard Genette (1997: 1-2), the title and the introduction are the work's paratexts. Similar to a "vestibule," they provide the reader with the choice of either stepping inside or abandoning the text. Currently, online fiction is typically mass-produced and formulaic. When readers search for fiction, titles and introductions are essential in attracting readers through quick scanning and picking. More importantly, titles and introductions written by the authors can precisely capture what the author intends most to express, which is more efficient and precise in collecting the gender-related attitudes of the authors than the complete fiction texts. That is, the authors have already presented us with the plots and highlights of their stories, which are obviously better than those acquired using other methods such as machine learning.

The topics of BL fiction reflect the author's preferences and interests, which focus on a macroscopic level. Consequently, topic choices reveal the level of relevance to Chinese culture and social reality, as well as the aspirations projected by women authors onto the male protagonists. Therefore, we applied the LDA topic model to cluster the topics using fiction titles and introductions. We also adopted the Word2Vec model of word embedding techniques to predict specific keyword contexts in BL fiction titles and introductions. The keywords were related to gender and same-sex relationships. See Chapter 3 for an introduction to the relevant models.

4 Topics in Chinese BL Fiction

4.1 Synchronic Analysis of Topics

To explore the topics within BL fiction and the associated cultural information, we applied the LDA topic model for unsupervised clustering analysis of story titles and introductions. Since the number of topics is a significant parameter for the model, we trained the model with an even number of topics, ranging from 6 to 50. After a comprehensive evaluation of each topic's connotation and extension, the differentiation degree between topics, and the study purpose, we selected a 10-topic model for subsequent analysis, which grouped all words under ten topics. Since words under the same topics are highly related, we summarized their features and named them.

Table 1 highlights the ten topics and words with the highest values for each topic, as analyzed by the LDA topic model. The more value a word has, the more frequently it appears and the more relevant it is to the topic. Furthermore, we eliminated words without substantive semantics, such as hehe (an onomatopoeia of laughter) and liangzhi (two). Since the introduction contains both the blurb and the synopsis, the ten topics are not entirely about plots. Among them, topic 10 contains story tags and is a functional topic through which authors mark their works and categorize them into various types to allow readers to find them easily. Considering that our aim was to study the plot of BL fiction, we will not discuss Topic 10 in detail below.

Among topics related to plots, Topic 1 and 2 both focus on sweet love. Topic 1 is a campus topic. The words "xiaoyuan" (campus) and "laoshi" (teacher) clearly indicate that the campus is the setting of the BL stories. Other words highlight that the love experienced on campus is pure and dreamy, such as "zhuma" (childhood sweetheart) and "wenrou" (tender). Similar features apply to Topic 2. It is named "fairy tale" since it has words such as "wangzi" (prince), which appear as the Westerner's appellation, as well as "meigui" (rose) and "baise" (white) that describe love

Table 1 LDA Topic Analysis of BL Fiction

Topic 1 Campus		*Topic 2 Fairy Tale*		*Topic 3 Chinese myths*		*Topic 4 Ancient China*		*Topic 5 Daily Happiness*	
Hanzi (pinyin, English)	*Value*	*Hanzi (pinyin, English)*	*Value*	*Hanzi (pinyin, English)*	*Value*	*Hanzi (pinyin, English)*	*Value*	*Hanzi (pinyin, English)*	*Value*
暗恋 (anlian, secret love)	0.018	王子 (wangzi, prince)	0.012	前世 (qianshi, previous life)	0.014	将军 (jiangjun, general)	0.014	爱情 (aiqing, love)	0.020
哥哥 (gege, elder brother)	0.010	少年 (shaonian, young boy)	0.011	轮回 (lunhui, reincarnation)	0.013	江湖 (jianghu, all corners)	0.014	幸福 (xingfu, happiness)	0.009
竹马 (zhuma, childhood sweetheart)	0.008	眼睛 (yanjing, eye)	0.010	今生 (jinsheng, present life)	0.012	公子 (gongzi, childe)	0.012	永远 (yongyuan, forever)	0.006
校园 (xiaoyuan, campus)	0.007	声音 (shengyin, voice)	0.008	相守 (xiangshou, to be together)	0.009	皇帝 (huangdi, emperor)	0.011	一生 (yisheng, all one's life)	0.006
老师 (laoshi, teacher)	0.007	男人 (nanren, man)	0.007	一世 (yishi, all one's life)	0.008	狐狸 (huli, fox)	0.010	人生 (rensheng, life)	0.005
恋爱 (lianai, love)	0.006	主人 (zhuren, master)	0.006	千年 (qiannian, one thousand years)	0.007	桃花 (taohua, peach blossom)	0.010	感情 (ganqing, sentiment)	0.005
弟弟 (didi, younger brother)	0.006	微笑 (weixiao, smile)	0.005	师兄 (shixiong, senior)	0.007	天下 (tianxia, the whole country)	0.009	相遇 (xiangyu, to meet)	0.005

(continued)

Table 1 (continued)

Topic 1 Campus		Topic 2 Fairy Tale		Topic 3 Chinese myths		Topic 4 Ancient China		Topic 5 Daily Happiness	
Hanzi (pinyin, English)	*Value*	*Hanzi (pinyin, English)*	*Value*	*Hanzi (pinyin, English)*	*Value*	*Hanzi (pinyin, English)*	*Value*	*Hanzi (pinyin, English)*	*Value*
温柔 (wenrou, tender)	0.006	玫瑰 (meigui, rose)	0.005	相知 (xiangzhi, to know each other)	0.007	相思 (xiangsi, lovesickness)	0.009	等待 (dengdai, to wait)	0.004
少年 (shaonian, young boy)	0.006	离别 (libie, separation)	0.005	师父 (shifu, master)	0.006	王爷 (wangye, princes)	0.007	生活 (shenghuo, to live)	0.004
兄弟 (xiongdi, brother)	0.005	白色 (baise, white)	0.004	故人 (guren, old friend)	0.006	书生 (shusheng, scholar)	0.007	简单 (jiandan, simple)	0.004
大学 (daxue, university)	0.005	思念 (sinian, to miss)	0.004	教主 (jiaozhu, hierophant)	0.004	戏子 (xizi, actor)	0.006	相信 (xiangxin, to believe)	0.004
告白 (gaobai, confession)	0.005	天空 (tiankong, sky)	0.004	反派 (fanpai, villain)	0.004	江山 (jiangshan, state power)	0.005	现实 (xianshi, reality)	0.003

Topic 6 Dramatic love		Topic 7 Entertainment		Topic 8 Game		Topic 9 Fantasy		Topic 10 Story tag	
Hanzi (pinyin, English)	*Value*	*Hanzi (pinyin, English)*	*Value*	*Hanzi (pinyin, English)*	*Value*	*Hanzi (pinyin, English)*	*Value*	*Hanzi (pinyin, English)*	*Value*
狗血 (gouxue, dramatic)	0.020	先生 (xiansheng, sir)	0.024	游戏 (youxi, game)	0.021	生活 (shenghuo, to live)	0.017	BL (boys' love)	0.018

Topic 6 Dramatic love		*Topic 7 Entertainment*		*Topic 8 Game*		*Topic 9 Fantasy*		*Topic 10 Story tag*	
Hanzi (pinyin, English)	*Value*	*Hanzi (pinyin, English)*	*Value*	*Hanzi (pinyin, English)*	*Value*	*Hanzi (pinyin, English)*	*Value*	*Hanzi (pinyin, English)*	*Value*
小受 (xiaoshou, uke)	0.019	老板 (laoban, boss)	0.015	拟人 (niren, personification)	0.012	人类 (renlei, human)	0.015	重生 (chongsheng, rebirth)	0.009
男人 (nanren, man)	0.016	烟花 (yanhua, firework)	0.011	恶魔 (emo, demon)	0.012	穿越 (chuanyue, through)	0.011	温馨 (wenxi, warm and sweet)	0.007
小攻 (xiaogong, seme)	0.013	娱乐圈 (yulequan, entertainment)	0.011	夏日 (xiari, summer day)	0.010	未来 (weilai, future)	0.007	杀手 (shashou, murderer)	0.007
总裁 (zongcai, CEO)	0.011	结婚 (jiehun, to get married)	0.010	大神 (dashen, great person)	0.010	传说 (chuanshuo, legend)	0.007	悲剧 (beiju, tragedy)	0.007
女人 (nvren, woman)	0.010	明星 (mingxing, celebrity)	0.009	网游 (wangyou, online game)	0.009	普通 (putong, ordinary)	0.006	无聊 (wuliao, boring)	0.007
耽美 (danmei, tanbi)	0.008	单恋 (danlian, one-sided love)	0.008	魔王 (mowang, dark lord)	0.008	少年 (shaonian, young boy)	0.005	轻松 (qingsong, relaxed)	0.006
爱上 (aishang, to fall in love)	0.008	电影 (dianying, film)	0.007	死亡 (siwang, death)	0.008	地球 (diqiu, the earth)	0.004	YY (to imagine)	0.006
分手 (fenshou, to break up)	0.008	公司 (gongsi, company)	0.007	天使 (tianshi, angel)	0.007	精灵 (jingling, elf)	0.004	怀念 (huainian, to memorize)	0.005
渣攻 (zhagong, unfaithful seme)	0.007	粉丝 (fensi, fans)	0.006	恐怖 (kongbu, terror)	0.006	战争 (zhanzheng, war)	0.004	耽美 (danmei, Tanbi)	0.005
替身 (tishen, substitute)	0.006	新闻 (xinwen, news)	0.005	电脑 (diannao, computer)	0.005	妖怪 (yaoguai, monster)	0.003	原创 (yuanchuang, originality)	0.005
逻辑 (luoji, logic)	0.006	演员 (yanyuan, actor)	0.005	任务 (renwu, task)	0.005	机器人 (jiqiren, robot)	0.003	结尾 (jiewei, ending)	0.004

in the Western cultural background. These two topics construct imagined romance based on realistic scenarios.

Topic 3 is about the one and only love in Chinese myths, which further puts imagined romances in the heterosexuality-like pattern. According to Radway's (1991) research, a successful heterosexual story should only focus on the love between two single protagonists. Similarly, Mizoguchi (2015) considered that the BL protagonists would only love each other and foils could never really intervene in their relationship, which was different from the ordinary gay couples in reality. In this case, it is hard to argue that BL authors have completely broken the heterosexual norms. Moreover, Chinese legends can add to the fatalism of the BL relationship, such as reincarnation, a Buddhist concept representing the repetition of birth, life, and death. The reincarnation words "qianshi" (previous life), "jinsheng" (present life), and "qiannian" (one thousand years) indicate that the protagonist's soul incarnates into another person, who will fall in love with his former gay lover again, thereby achieving an eternal "love myth." While still within a similar framework to heterosexuality, Buddhist karma adds new excitement to the love story. Also, the ability to "become a god" in Taoism, a Chinese indigenous religion, helps form a unique aesthetic rooted in Chinese religious culture.

The BL fiction involving Chinese myths predominantly contains ancient scenes, similar to Topic 4, which is based on the Chinese feudal dynasties, narrating the fight for the throne and the defense of the frontier. Words such as "jiangjun" (general), "huangdi" (emperor), and "jiangshan" (state power) highlight the struggle for the throne and the defense of the frontier, revealing a strong sense of nationalism. Compared with "god" related Topic 3, Topic 4 reveals more about Confucianism, advocating the realistic ideal of the "human" world, but not directly describing contemporary China, thus avoiding possible political innuendo. Besides the influence of China's long history, it appears that women authors' preference for this topic is rooted in their desire to participate in male-dominated fields, such as war and leadership. Women authors expect power beyond romance here, which embodies the close relationship between sexual pleasure and power pointed out by Foucault (1979:48). One possible explanation for why authors do not directly tell women's participation in power is that it was proven unrealistic in patriarchal history. A queen, for example, rarely occurred in China's actual history, so women chose to describe power in the relatively equal love between men. In this case, the existing gender division of labor remains unbroken. By projecting their power ideal onto men, women authors harvest both career and love at a minimal cost.

Topic 5 also includes the idea of love, and to some extent is a variation of the fantastic Chinese myths topic in reality. This topic portrays happiness within reach in daily life; therefore, it is named "daily happiness." Words under this topic, such as "rensheng" (life), "shenghuo" (to live), and "xianshi" (reality) refer to reality; "xingfu" (happiness), "yongyuan" (forever), and "yisheng" (all one's life) represent the authors' view on happiness, which is having love and the only lover forever.

Topics 6 and 7 continue to tell stories in reality. Topic 6 includes words on dramatic love, such as "gouxue" (dramatic), "zhagong" (unfaithful seme), and "tishen" (substitute). The money disputes that involve CEOs, the messy relationships between both sexes, and the disloyalty related to unfaithful seme, all result in conflicts and thus form dramatic stories. Topic 7 is relevant to the entertainment industry. "Laoban" (boss), "mingxing" (celebrity), "dianying" (film), and "yanyuan" (actor) present romantic stories among stars, highlighting women authors' preference for celebrity. Money, beauty, and fame entangled with sensory stimulations are the fundamental concepts in this topic, which allow authors to break through mediocre heterosexual norms and pursue an extraordinary life.

Topic 8 is about games, involving words such as "youxi" (game), "wangyou" (online game), "mowang" (dark lord), and "siwang" (death), where the protagonists must survive in killing games. Topic 9 describes a fantastical otherworld. Words such as "weilai" (future), "diqiu" (the earth), and "jiqiren" (robot) belong to science fiction; "Jingling" (elf) and "yaoguai" (monster) depict mysterious creatures. As Ni (2020) said, although the Chinese government's censorship cleared the pornographic contents, authors shifted their interests to construct scientific discourses and achieved great commercial success. This topic reveals that Chinese BL writers have acquired a revolutionary consciousness, enabling them to engage in dialogue with the wider social world and its future. Besides, the otherworld they create is a utopia of gender since it makes where the same-sex relationships can be more reasonable and the equal love between protagonists would naturally emerge as they fought together.

5 Diachronic Analysis of Topics

After analyzing each topic, we studied the proportions of BL fiction under specific topics in the total number from 2003 to 2019, as shown in Fig. 2. As we planned to analyze how the plots changed over time, the story tag topic was excluded from this analysis.

Fairy tales, daily happiness, and fantasy topics had a downward trend. The daily happiness topic accounted for about 45% of the topics in 2003, though decreased, it still accounted for nearly 18% of all topics in 2019. Its decline was relative to the rise of other topics. Compared with daily happiness, the fairy tale topic accounted for just 11% in 2003. After a decline of over 2%, its proportion was under 9% in 2019. In addition, the fantasy topic slightly declined from approximately 12% to 8%. Since the fairy tale topic is traditionally Western, and the fantasy topic also contains certain Western elements, the decline in their popularity suggested that authors' preference for Western settings was also declining.

In contrast, campus, Chinese myths, dramatic love, entertainment, and game topics increased. Among them, the campus topic had the largest proportion, increasing from 10% to nearly 20%. This suggests that youth love has increasingly become a favored topic for BL authors. Besides, the

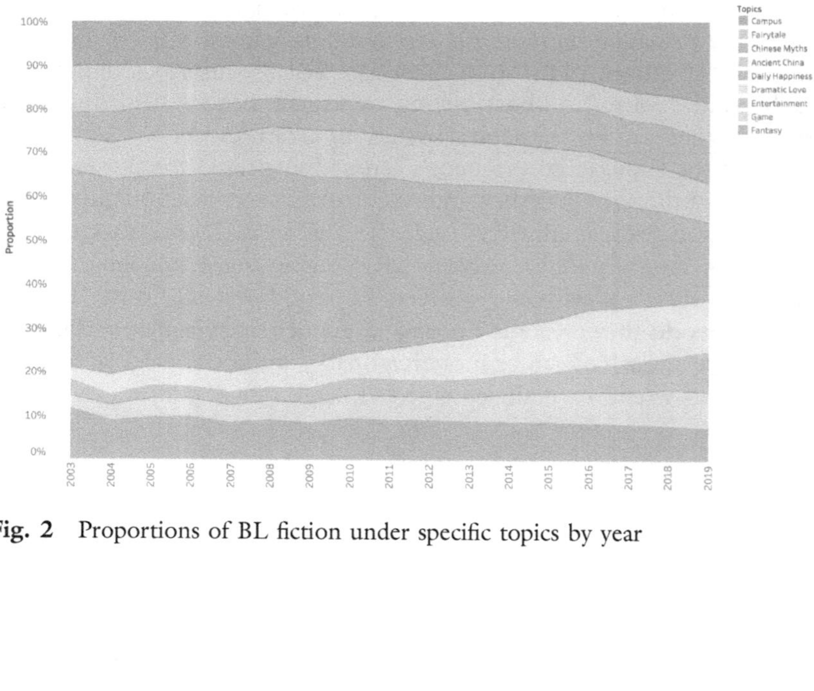

Fig. 2 Proportions of BL fiction under specific topics by year

share of game, dramatic love, Chinese myths, and entertainment topics all increased from approximately 2% to 10%. Lastly, the ancient China topic had retained a proportion of over 8% between 2005 and 2019. Its share, along with the rise of the Chinese myths topic, proved the ongoing popularity of China's native stories.

The above topic analysis formed the panorama of Chinese BL fiction. Chinese women authors prefer surreal BL stories, including reincarnation, ancient China, game, and fantasy topics. Even seemingly realistic topics, such as campus and entertainment, still involve dramatic turns and a dream-like atmosphere. Furthermore, the fantasy world in the past or future eliminates the obstacles, creating a paradise of love and freedom for gay men.

This fantasy world is almost departed from the influence of Japanese BL fiction. First, Chinese authors are free from the dependence on Western settings. Although Western elements still exist in Chinese BL stories, diachronic analysis reveals that their proportion is decreasing, while topics such as reincarnation and ancient China remain popular. Through local legends and religious thoughts, Chinese BL fiction has remained rooted in traditional Chinese culture. Besides, unlike the necessary tragedy in early Japanese BL fiction, Chinese authors also prefer relaxed stories. For instance, "wenxin" (warm and sweet) ranks high in the synchronic analysis of the story tag topic, and daily happiness even becomes one of the ten topics. Therefore, currently, Chinese authors have changed both features of Japanese BL fiction.

The above topic analysis formed the panorama of Chinese BL fiction. With the disappearance of Western elements in the most popular quarter of BL fiction, the Chinese BL world has departed from Japanese works. Unlike the necessary tragedy in early Japanese BL fiction, Chinese authors prefer relaxed stories. For instance, "wenxin" (warm and sweet) and "HE" (happy ending) both rank high in the synchronic analysis of the story tag topic. Therefore, Chinese BL novels have gained a strong cultural subjectivity.

Chinese women authors prefer surreal BL stories because the fantasy world in the past or the future eliminates obstacles, creating a paradise of love and freedom for gay men and for themselves. However, while gaining freedom in fantasy, Chinese women are bound by the "love myth." The formation of a myth indicates the separation of Chinese women BL authors from reality. They choose to describe the fictional relationship between men as similar to heterosexuality rather than their real heterosexual identity, which is an escape from their gender role. In addition, although conveying the desire for power, they only tend to project such ideals onto the male roles, not daring to overturn the existing patriarchy. To further examine those ideas, we will analyze women authors' perceptions of gender in the next section.

6 Gender-Related Contexts in Chinese BL Fiction

6.1 Synchronic Analysis of Contexts

Following the analysis of Chinese BL fiction topics, we proceeded to examine contexts related to gender and same-sex relationships through word vector technology, totaling 39,619 discrete words, which reflect how related concepts are discussed. We removed words that lack semantic significance and character names, like zhende (really) and jiju (very), listing hanzi (Chinese characters), pinyin (Roman spellings of Chinese characters), and English translations.

The words directly related to gender are women and men. In Chinese, two pairs of words could represent women and men; these words are "nvren" (the common term for women) and "nanren" (the common term for men), as well as "nvxing" (the biological term or the term used in written language for women) and "nanxing" (the biological term or the term used in written language for men). We analyzed the two pairs of Chinese gender names, respectively.

Table 2 presents words related to women. In the entry of "nvren" (woman), "tongqi" (homowife) ranks first. This term represents gay men's heterosexual wives, whose role is to reproduce and allow gay men to be accepted by Chinese society (Bie & Tang, 2016). However, their husbands deprive the marriage of love, exposing them to intimate partner violence. According to the raw data, homowives predominantly appear as shadowy presences in the story background. Instead of empathizing with their suffering, authors apply them as a tool for gay men to realize their sexual orientation ("he realized that he was gay after marrying a woman so his wife became a homowife") or as a child-bearer ("even though he married a woman and had a child, he could not forget the man he loved most"). Authors sacrifice homowives to reduce Chinese gay men's moral pressure, social stress, and the pressure to continue the clan.

Table 2 Distance of words to two keywords related to woman

Keywords 女人 *(nvren Woman)* *Words: hanzi (pinyin, English)*	*Value*	*Keyword:* 女性 *(nvxing, woman)* *Words: hanzi (pinyin, English)*	*Value*
同妻 (tongqi, homowife)	0.629206	男性 (nanxing, man)	0.749118
男人 (nanren, man)	0.616670	群体 (qunti, group)	0.703536
打光棍 (daguanggun, to stay single)	0.580685	异端 (yiduan, heresy)	0.702420
会爱上 (huiaishang, to fall in love)	0.572841	人种 (renzhong, race)	0.693559
扮作 (banzuo, to dress up as)	0.521901	失衡 (shiheng, imbalance)	0.687081
母爱 (muai, mother love)	0.511057	性向 (xingxiang, sexual orientation)	0.681993
女性 (nvxing, woman)	0.510529	特征 (tezheng, feature)	0.678382
共患难 (gonghuannan, through thick and thin)	0.508597	歧视 (qishi, discrimination)	0.677591
好人家 (haorenjia, good family)	0.505144	不分性别 (bufen xingbie, gender-neutral)	0.676506
初夜 (chuye, the night that loses virginity)	0.500894	局限 (juxian, limitation)	0.674164
待嫁 (daijia, to wait to get married)	0.500739	阐述 (chanshu, to explain)	0.672842
不孝子 (buxiaozi, unfilial son)	0.500367	地域 (diyu, territory)	0.669894
传宗接代 (chuanzongjiedai, continuity of a clan)	0.498150	人物形象 (renwu xingxiang, character image)	0.669158
母子 (muzi, mother and son)	0.495652	雌雄 (cixiong, male and female)	0.663825
壮实 (zhuangshi, strong)	0.494951	基础 (jichu, basis)	0.663206
男子汉 (nanzihan, true man)	0.494809	男同 (nantong, gay)	0.661649
生小孩 (shengxiaohai, to give birth to a child)	0.492920	生育 (shengyu, reproduction)	0.659755
嫁了人 (jialeren, already being married to someone)	0.492801	构造 (gouzao, to construct)	0.659078
善变 (shanbian, capricious)	0.492221	普遍 (pubian, common)	0.658011
外遇 (waiyu, affair)	0.488464	真实性 (zhenshixing, authenticity)	0.654076

The majority of the following words are similar to "tongqi," associating women with marriage and reproduction. "Muai" (mother love) and "muzi" (mother and son) bound women to the role of mother. Furthermore, "haorenjia" (good family) indicates the expectation for women to marry into a worthy family and have a successful marriage; "chuye" (the night that loses virginity) reflects the importance of chastity to women; "chuanzongjiedai" (continuity of a clan) and "shengxiaohai" (to give birth to a child) highlight women's instrumental reproductive function in BL fiction. Although the word "waiyu" (affair) reveals the desire of Chinese women to escape from the patriarchal marriage system, this plot in BL fiction is to provide gay men's love with a reasonable excuse, such as cheating by wife/girlfriend causes the protagonist to seek a male partner. In further exploration, we found that when the above words appeared in the original texts, few criticisms existed. Marriage and reproduction have already become women's roles' stereotypes in BL novels.

Compared to "nvren," words close to "nvxing" (woman) reflect the coexistence of negative and positive attitudes. According to the raw data, the relationship between "yiduan" (heresy) and women is that "not marrying a woman is a heresy," revealing the rejection of same-sex relationships in mainstream Chinese society. In contrast, "qishi" (discrimination) was predominantly used in sentences like "do not discriminate against women," representing kindness to women.

The woman-related contexts reveal Chinese BL authors' strong demand for heterosexual marriage. Although they describe unconventional gay men, they still regard marriage as the most standard and accepted criterion for them, and the same-sex relationship in the story has nothing to do with their own lives. This craze for marriage is a reflection of the thousand years of patriarchy, indicating that the women authors are still spokespersons of Chinese traditional ethics and moral discourse.

Among the words close to "nanren" (man) in Table 3, some have occurred in the entry of "nvren" (women), such as "tongqi" (homowife), "daguanggun" (stay single), and "muzi" (mother and son). This finding suggests a strong correlation between women and men. Along with the newly appearing term "hunsha" (wedding dress), these words prove again that marriage is the primary task even for roles in BL fiction.

In the entry of "nanxing" (man), an interesting phenomenon occurs: "nanxing," the biological concept of men, is associated with traditionally feminine words, such as "shengyu" (reproduction), "shenyu nengli" (reproductive ability), and "shouyun" (to get pregnant). Although women have "shengxiaohai" (to give birth to a child) and "shengyu" in their entry, "shengyu nengli" and "shouyun" appear for the first time. In addition, the word "shouyun" refers to the development of a fetus inside a woman's uterus, but a review of the raw data indicates that the term is used in BL fiction to refer to men, allowing males to have an intersex body. To make the seemingly impossible intersex pregnancy feasible, authors display bold imagination with words like "luansheng"

Table 3 Distance of words to two keywords related to man

Keyword: 男人 *(nanren, man)*		*Keyword:* 男性 *(nanxing, man)*	
Words: hanzi (pinyin, English)	*Value*	*Words: hanzi (pinyin, English)*	*Value*
女人 (nvren, woman)	0.616670	女性 (nvxing, woman)	0.749118
会爱上 (huiaishang, to fall in love)	0.472603	特征 (tezheng, feature)	0.707147
同妻 (tongqi, homowife)	0.446218	生育 (shengyu, reproduction)	0.701941
共患难 (gonghuannan, through thick and thin)	0.419871	生育能力 (shengyu nengli, reproductive ability)	0.700869
非你不可 (feini buke, it had to be you)	0.408004	受孕 (shouyun, to get pregnant)	0.692719
彩色 (caise, color)	0.397862	人种 (renzhong, race)	0.668976
薰衣草 (xunyicao, lavender)	0.394756	异端 (yiduan, heresy)	0.666218
局外人 (juwairen, outsider)	0.389660	雌雄 (cixiong, male and female)	0.662157
善变 (shanbian, capricious)	0.389231	卵生 (luansheng, oviparity)	0.658489
分清 (fenqing, to distinguish between)	0.383154	越强 (yueqiang, stronger)	0.656741
说出 (shuochu, to say)	0.382717	不分性别 (bufen xingbie, gender-neutral)	0.650829
看不清楚 (kanbu qingchu, cannot see clearly)	0.381484	药物 (yaowu, drug)	0.648868
如此而已 (ruci eryi, no more than that)	0.380990	百分百 (baifenbai, one hundred percent)	0.648514
难以想象 (nanyi xiangxiang, hard to imagine)	0.379918	吸引力 (xiyinli, attraction)	0.645707
打光棍 (daguanggun, to stay single)	0.379474	构造 (gouzao, to construct)	0.644502
傻傻的 (shashade, foolish)	0.377256	雄性 (xiongxing, male)	0.643349
婚纱 (hunsha, wedding dress)	0.374707	双性人 (shuangxingren, intersex)	0.639059
男生 (nansheng, boy)	0.372593	失衡 (shiheng, imbalance)	0.638778
知礼 (zhili, to know the etiquette)	0.370187	群体 (qunti, group)	0.637344
母子 (muzi, mother and son)	0.370144	特异 (teyi, peculiar)	0.636055

(oviparity) and "yaowu" (drug). Intersex people have the physiological features of women, while they have the gender role of men in society. Pregnancy provides almost all elements of heterosexuality to the male-male relationship, including unequal power.

The clan concept rooted within Chinese traditional culture mainly explains Chinese women authors' intentions. Reproduction has always been essential in maintaining the prosperity of the clan, as well as a vital means of maintaining filial piety; having no descendants is the gravest offense against filial piety (Luo, 2008). Therefore, motherhood is considered a major role for women, so the clan concept is closely entangled with patriarchy, and men can never be certain of their masculinity until they become fathers (Webb and Judith, 1999). The patriarchal values of "must-have offspring" explain why Chinese BL authors are interested in marriage and reproduction issues, although gay men cannot conceive children naturally. Considering same-sex marriage and surrogacy are illegal in China, BL authors either let women become homowives to bear children, which sustains the imprisonment of women's gender roles in the patriarchy, or empower gay men with the ability to conceive. When the clan continued, male-male love became socially acceptable in China.

Paradoxically, pregnant gay men's stories also result in feminist awareness. These authors could have written heterosexual love stories, but only a very heterosexual-like pattern of same-sex relationship, where women do not exist, would free them from patriarchal constraints. When women endow their physiological features to men, they can reexamine the ability to get pregnant and other features (without being oppressed by the patriarchy) and escape objectification through the male identity. This can be the first step toward feminism, as Kaja Silverman (1992: 389) put it, "for a female subject to re-encounter femininity from within a male body is clearly to experience it under different terms—to live it no longer as disenfranchisement and subordination, but rather as phallic divestiture, as a way of saying 'no' to power." However, although transferring women's characteristics to men frees women, it results in their absence. Women become more dispensable after the reproductive function is no longer exclusive to them. This phenomenon reflects the passive resistance by women in a patriarchal society: avoiding discussing the root of their oppression, which is their physiological capacity to get pregnant.

Since BL fiction involves a romance between gay men, we chose the Chinese expression of same-sex relationships, "tongxinglian," to analyze whether women authors' descriptions of this group were linked with reality or were all fantasies (see Table 4). Table 4 includes many words related to marriage, such as "jieguohun" (have ever been married), "hunyin shenghuo" (married life), and "hunyin guanxi" (marital relations). Although same-sex marriage is illegal in China, it has always been an important issue, and the debate about legalization is long-standing. Therefore, related legal terms also occur in this entry, involving "hefahua" (legalization), "fading" (legal), and "hunyinfa" (marriage law).

"Xinghun" (marriage of convenience) is a concept of marriage through which a gay man can obtain a legal but sexless marriage with a woman. Compared to homowives' marriages, the prenuptial agreement in the marriage of convenience guarantees more respect for women partners, but the essence of this marriage is still filial piety since gay men must satisfy their parents. "Daiyun" (surrogacy) also reflects a social phenomenon. Surrogacy is illegal in China, and most Chinese women believe that it objectifies women.[4] However, in BL fiction stories, the content related to surrogacy is primarily the intersex man assuming the role of the surrogate

Table 4 Distance of words to one keyword related to same-sex relationship

Keyword: 同性恋 *(tongxinglian, same-sex relationship)*	
Words: hanzi (pinyin, English)	*Value*
异性 (yixing, of the opposite sex)	0.746590
异性恋 (yixinglian, heterosexuality)	0.736952
形婚 (xinghun, marriage of convenience)	0.669822
合法化 (hefahua, legalization)	0.667510
GAY	0.651777
结过婚 (jieguohun, have ever been married)	0.650285
同性 (tongxing, of the same sex)	0.643919
性伴侣 (xingbanlv, sex partner)	0.640871
不分性别 (bufen xingbie, gender-neutral)	0.637963
歧视 (qishi, discrimination)	0.636857
性向 (xingxiang, sexual orientation)	0.636480
男同 (nantong, gay)	0.632264
同妻 (tongqi, homowife)	0.628283
代孕 (daiyun, surrogacy)	0.625376
法定 (fading, legal)	0.623512
婚姻生活 (hunyin shenghuo, married life)	0.620774
包办婚姻 (baoban hunyin, arranged marriage)	0.620051
实质性 (shizhixing, substantive)	0.617735
婚姻关系 (hunyin guanxi, marital relations)	0.614083
婚姻法 (hunyinfa, marriage law)	0.613692

[4] About the surrogacy controversy in China, see https://edition.cnn.com/2021/01/22/china/china-celebrity-surrogacy-scandal-dst-intl-hnk/index.html.

mother. However, when transferring surrogacy to a man, its exploitative nature is reduced, and women authors can shed this moral burden.

The "tongxinglian" (same-sex relationship) entry indicates that social reality still influences women authors' BL fiction creation, although they have fantasies about gay men. However, their imagination has feminist elements. For example, intersex surrogacy avoids the exploitation of women; therefore, their abandonment of the physiological features is not entirely negative. Besides, the aforementioned words remain closely related to marriage and reproduction, again demonstrating the influence of the Chinese tradition of "continuity of a clan" on BL fiction.

7 Diachronic analysis of contexts

After analyzing the overall entry for each keyword, we selected six words in Tables 2, 3, and 4 to track frequencies from 2003 to 2019. We focused on the diachronic changes in words that reflected the influence of traditional Chinese culture and society. Reflecting the dilemma of gay men's marriage in reality and the effect of filial piety on gay men, the word "Tongqi" (homowife) connecting women and the gay community merits close inspection. Similarly, "chuye" (the night one lost virginity) and "chuanzongjiedai" (continuity of a clan) relate to fertility, reflecting the shackles of traditional ethics on women in China. As for men, "shuangxingren" (intersex) is an important finding, which transfers women's physiological features to men. Also, "Shengyu nengli" (reproductive ability) can describe men's ability to get pregnant. These two words both reveal the emphasis on reproduction in Chinese culture. In terms of same-sex relationships, "hefahua" (legalization) means that the identity and marriage of gay people are legally recognized, highlighting BL authors' attention to reality.

In addition, we divided the word frequency of one term in a certain year by the total word frequency of the year to achieve a specific value, as shown in Fig. 3.

The top half of Fig. 3 reveals the frequencies of three words, namely, "tongqi" (homowife), "chuye" (the night that loses virginity), and "chuanzongjiedai" (continuity of a clan), all linked to the keyword "nvren" (woman). "Tongqi" only occurred after 2010, meaning that BL authors have increased their attention to homowives, a vulnerable group in reality. However, the word frequencies of "chuye" and "chuanzongjiedai" declined, indicating that the stereotypical ideas of women

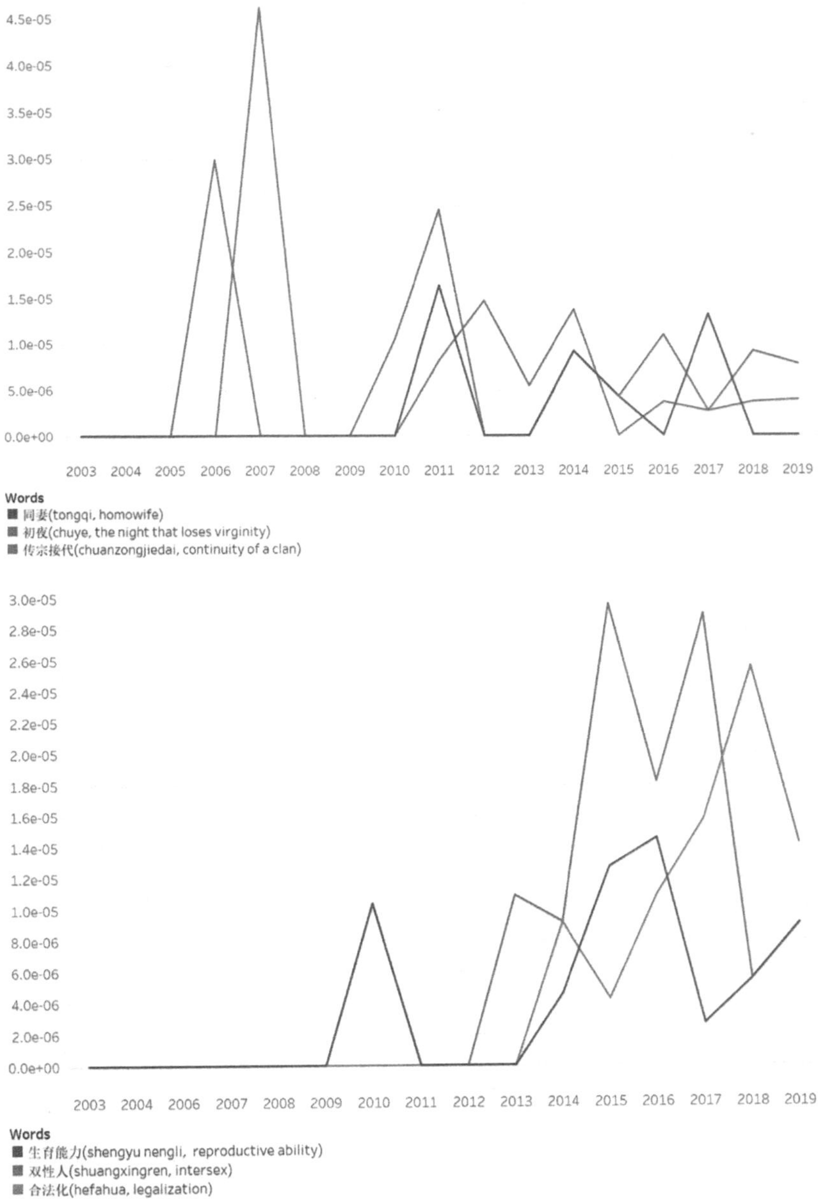

Fig. 3 Word frequencies by year

were less prevalent. Although women authors once emphasized virginity and their childbearing function, the traditional moral constraints on Chinese women have been reduced as Chinese women's education level, social status, and awareness of gender equality have improved.

The lower section of Fig. 3 indicates the frequencies of "shengyu nengli" (reproductive ability), "shuangxingren" (intersex), and "hefahua" (legalization). "Shengyu nengli" appeared in 2009 and increased rapidly after 2013. The trend of "shuangxingren," another word for men, was very similar to "shengyu nengli" from 2012 to 2018, implying that men's ability to reproduce in BL stories did relate to intersex people, especially their physiological feature that allows them to fall pregnant. Furthermore, "hefahua" refers to same-sex relationships, whose curve rose after 2013. After the Taiwan judiciary proclaimed that the current civil law did not make gay marriage unconstitutional in 2017, the discussion on legalizing same-sex marriage reached its peak, representing the reality of BL fiction.

This chapter illustrates the impact of Chinese culture, which both inspires BL fiction plots and influences the gender perspectives of women authors. They are contradictory when discussing gender issues. They allow gay men to fall pregnant, hoping to shatter the traditional gender ideologies, but patriarchal ethics make them deliberately ignore women's roles. Hence, Chinese women fail to break the shackles of the clan concept within BL fiction, and the extreme emphasis on reproduction brought by thousands of years of Chinese patriarchy still imprints on Chinese women's cultural creation.

8 Conclusion

In the previous two decades, the number of Chinese online BL fiction pieces has increased rapidly. Through the LDA topic model and word vector technology, we drew three main conclusions on the content of BL fiction. (1) Chinese women BL authors prefer surreal topics in the history and future, as well as the dreamy "love myth," which owns more heterosexual features than the real LGBTQ group. (2) Chinese traditional culture powerfully influences BL fiction, creating a distinct aesthetic style and strong nationalism. Besides the inspiration from Chinese history and myths, the patriarchal clan concept also makes BL authors focus on marriage and reproduction issues. (3) Chinese BL fiction reveals the paradoxical nature of women authors' gender perspectives. They want to feel power through the male protagonists' "equal love," and even transfer pregnancy to the intersex group. However, they avoid discussing their own gender, which means that they are still unable to escape the shackles of patriarchy.

Chinese online BL fiction remains in a state of contradiction. The authors created male-male romances but were distant from gays in reality; they expressed women's desire for love but lacked women characters. Eve Sedgwick (1985) pointed out that the male homosocial desire and homosexual desire both have a necessary relationship to misogyny, and we found that even within the fictional male-male romances written by women, misogyny remained. For instance, women who were closely associated with Chinese gay men, homowives, were ignored by early authors. As Toril Moi (2008: 268), who emphasized the significance of women's writing, stated, "to turn women into second-class citizens in the realm of literature is to say that women's experiences of existence and of the world are less important than men's." Though the stereotype of women in Chinese BL stories has been reduced, the awakening of Chinese women authors remains incomplete.

In addition, BL authors are also attempting to change the currently marginalized roles of women. For example, in *Heaven Official's Blessing* (2018), the most popular BL fiction on JLC, a powerful goddess character subverted the traditional image of the god of wisdom. In ancient China, only men were allowed to take the imperial competitive examination; hence, the god of wisdom in Taoism has always been depicted as male. This goddess of wisdom changed the patriarchal tradition and broke through the former gender roles of Chinese women as mothers and wives. Although such women characters cannot be protagonists in BL fiction, and the discussion on women is not the story's core, it still represents gratifying progress.

BL fiction is produced within a specific social and historical context. In today's Chinese society, with the market expansion of BL-adapted TV drama and animated works, Chinese BL fiction is developing. However, as BL forms a larger cultural industry, various questions will arise, such as the impact of pornographic elements on children and the hindrance of patriarchal culture to feminism. After thousands of years of sexual repression, Chinese women's desire has awakened, but the patriarchy remains an invisible net, limiting their transformative efforts. In this case, BL fiction becomes a woman's utopia. In the world of male-male romance, women can enjoy consuming men, albeit momentarily. Women return to reality;

they will only find that this incomplete awakening means deeper bondage since they have eliminated their own living space.

In the postmodern narrative, the boundary between fact and fiction is blurred (Brinkmann, 2009). BL fiction seems to remove women's existence, but even the most fantastic and bizarre plot cannot escape their life experiences. By discussing Chinese women BL authors' literary creations, this research has made two main contributions: (1) Theoretically, this chapter opens up a new perspective of Chinese traditional culture and ethics for the feminist study of BL fiction. The discovery of heterosexual relationship patterns and men's reproduction content both make the conclusion that BL women authors are still bound by patriarchy more convincing. (2) Methodologically, machine learning methods enable a comprehensive examination of JLC, helping to understand this cultural creation without thoroughly reading all the texts. It also avoids the omission of niche works. Since writing can provide the author with valuable experience, niche works also allow us to explore the perspectives and preferences of an audience with obscure tastes. Meanwhile, this chapter has certain limitations. We could not include full BL fiction texts in the model, so we hope to explore them and compare BL fiction to other related genres in future research.

References

Baruch, Elaine H. 1991. *Women, love, and power: Literary and psychoanalytic perspectives*. New York: New York University Press.

Bie, Bijie, and Lu. Tang. 2016. Chinese gay men's coming out narratives: Connecting social relationship to co-cultural theory. *Journal of International and Intercultural Communication* 9 (4): 351–367.

Brinkmann, Svend. 2009. Literature as qualitative inquiry. *Qualitative Inquiry* 15 (8): 1376–1394.

Burston, Paul, and Colin Richardson. 1995. *A queer romance: Lesbians, gay men, and popular culture*. London: Routledge.

Chang, Jiang, and Hao Tian. 2021. Girl power in boy love: Yaoi, online female counterculture, and digital feminism in China. *Feminist Media Studies* 21 (4): 604–620.

Chiang, Feichi. 2016. Counterpublic but obedient: A case of Taiwan's BL Fandom. *Inter-Asia Cultural Studies* 17 (2): 223–238.

Cui, Mingyu. 2018. Rerating the movie scores in douban through word embedding. *Journal of Physics: Conference Series* 1004 (1): 012030.

DiMaggio, Paul, Manish Nag, and D. Blei 2013. Exploiting Affinities between Topic Modeling and the Sociological Perspective on Culture: Application to Newspaper Coverage of U.S. Government Arts Funding. *Poetics* 41(6): 570–606.

Eads, Alicia, et al. 2020. Separating the wheat from the chaff: A topic and keyword-based procedure for identifying research-relevant text. *Poetics* 86: 101527.

Foucault, Michel 1979. *The history of sexuality / Vol.1, an introduction*. Trans. Hurley, R. London: Allen Lane.

Feng, Jin 2013. *Romancing the internet: Producing and consuming Chinese web romance*. Leiden: BRILL.

Genette, Gérard 1997. *Paratexts: Thresholds of interpretation*. Trans. Lewin, J. E. Cambridge: Cambridge University Press.

Grimmer, Justin, and Brandon M. Stewart. 2013. Text as data: The promise and pitfalls of automatic content analysis methods for political texts. *Political Analysis* 21 (3): 267–297.

Han, Xiao. 2020. Anti-feminist tendency in Chinese Tanbi novels. *Prose Hundred* 6: 58 (In Chinese).

Jenkins, Henry. 1992. *Textual Poachers: Television fans and participatory culture*. London: Routledge.

Jiang, Bo., and Wenbo Kuang. 2016. Research on profit model optimization strategy of online novels. *View on Publishing* 7: 28–31 (In Chinese).

Kurihara, Chiyo and Eiko Kakinuma 1993. *A guide to Tanbi and Gay Novels*. Tokyo: Byakuya-Shobo (In Japanese).

Martin, Fran. 2012. Girls who love boys' love: Japanese homoerotic manga as trans-national Taiwan culture. *Inter-Asia Cultural Studies* 12 (3): 365–383.

Meyer, Uli. 2013. Drawing from the Body - the self, the gaze and the other in Boys' Love Manga. *Journal of Graphic Novels & Comics* 4 (1): 64–81.

Mizoguchi, Akiko. 2015. *Theorizing BL as a transformative genre: Boys' love moves the world forward*. Tokyo: Ohta Books (In Japanese).

Moi, Toril. 2008. I am not a woman writer. *Feminist Theory* 9 (3): 259–271.

Nagaike, Kazumi, and Katsuhiko Suganuma. 2013. Transnational boys' love fan studies. *Transformative Works and Cultures* 12: 1–9.

Ng, Eve, and Xiaomeng Li. 2020. A queer "socialist brotherhood": The Guardian web series, boys' love fandom, and the Chinese state. *Feminist Media Studies* 20 (4): 479–495.

Ni, Zhange. 2020. Steampunk, zombie apocalypse, and homoerotic romance: rewriting revolution-plus-love in contemporary China. *Modern Chinese Literature and Culture* 32 (2): 179–229.

Luo, Chenglie. 2008. Mencius on Filial Piety and "having no descendant" is the gravest offence. *Confucius Studies* 2: 36–39 (In Chinese).

Luskey, Bridget. 2019. "The untamed": Chinese boy love drama we can't stop watching. *Film Daily*, 2 December. https://filmdaily.co/news/the-untamed/. Accessed 5 February 2022.

Pagliassotti, Dru. 2008. Reading BL in the West. *Participations* 5 (2): 1–19.

Radway, Janice. 1991. *Reading the romance: Women, patriarchy, and popular literature*. Chapel Hill, NC: University of North Carolina Press.

Silverman, Kajia. 1992. *Male subjectivity at the margins*. New York: Routledge.

Sedgwick, Eve 1985. *Between men: English literature and male homosocial desire*. New York; Chichester: Columbia University Press.

Takemiya, Keiko. 1993. Do women like gays? *Bungei Shunjū* 71 (6): 82–83 (In Japanese).

Tatlow, Didi. 2014. "Why many young Chinese women are writing gay male erotica." http://cn.nytimes.com/china/20140526/c26erotica/en-us/. Accessed 2 February 2021.

Tian, Xi. 2020a. Homosexualizing "boys love" in China: Reflexivity, genre transformation, and cultural interaction. *Prism: Theory and Modern Chinese Literature* 17(1): 104–126.

Tian, Xi. 2020b. More than conformity or resistance: Chinese "boys' love" fandom in the age of internet censorship. *Journal of the European Association for Chinese Studies* 1: 189–213.

Tian, Xiaoli, and Michael Adorjan. 2016. Fandom and coercive empowerment: the commissioned production of Chinese online literature. *Media, Culture & Society* 38 (6): 881–900.

Webb, Russell, and Judith Daniluk. 1999. The end of the line. *Men and Masculinities* 2 (1): 6–25.

Wei, John. 2014. Queer encounters between iron man and Chinese boys' love fandom. *Transformative Works and Cultures* 17 (17): 1–36.

Wong, Alvin K. 2020. Towards a queer affective economy of boys' love in contemporary Chinese media. *Continuum* 34 (4): 500–513.

Xu, Kaibin and Yan Tan 2021. The Chinese female spectatorship: a study of the network community of the "boys" love' movie "Call Me by Your Name" *Feminist Media Studies* 21(1): 35–50.

Xu, Yanrui, and Ling Yang. 2013. Forbidden love: Incest, generational conflict, and the erotics of power in Chinese BL fiction. *Journal of Graphic Novels & Comics* 4 (1): 30–43.

Yang, Ling, and Xu. Yanrui. 2017. The love that dare not speak its name': The fate of Chinese danmei communities in the 2014 anti-porn campaign. In *The end of cool Japan: Ethical, LEGAL, AND CULTURAL CHALLEnges to Japanese popular culture*, ed. Mark McLelland, 163–183. London and New York: Routledge.

Yi, Erika Junhui. 2013. Reflection on Chinese boys' love fans: An insider's view. *Transformative works and cultures* 12(1).

Zhang, Charlie Yi, and Adam K. Dedman. 2021. Hyperreal homoerotic love in a monarchized military conjuncture: a situated view of the Thai Boys' Love industry. *Feminist Media Studies* 21 (6): 1039–1043.

Zheng, Danan 2016. The construction of heterotopia and imagined community. *Youth Studies* (4): 76–84+96 (In Chinese).

Zhou, Yanyan, Bryant Paul, and Ryland Sherman. 2018. Still a hetero-gendered world: a content analysis of gender stereotypes and romantic ideals in Chinese boy love stories. *Sex Roles* 78 (1): 107–118.

Zsila, Ágnes., et al. 2018. Loving the love of boys, Motives for Consuming Yaoi Media. *PLoS ONE* 13 (6): e0198895.

CHAPTER 11

Modeling Ideology: A Distant Reading of *Marx/Engels Collected Works*

1 Introduction

Scholars in the relevant field have proposed introducing quantitative methods into the study of the history of Marx's thoughts to provide an empirical and scientific tool and a new dimension of thinking for the deepening analysis of classic texts (Zhang 2012). With the continuous digitalization and internet-based development of classic Marxist literature, a digital research path has been formed (Ji and Liu 2018). In recent years, the quantitative analysis of text, facilitated by computers and algorithms, has been integrated as a fundamental method into the research paradigms of text analysis, transforming traditional text analysis based on understanding and interpretation. With the maturity of machine learning techniques, especially natural language processing algorithms, quantitative text analysis is no longer limited to simple manual coding and word frequency counting. Various analysis techniques, such as topic analysis, semantic analysis, and network analysis, have led to breakthroughs and added value in the application of machine learning techniques. There have been some exploratory studies using the machine learning technique in sociology, political science, economics, psychology, and other areas of the social sciences (Grimmer and Stewart 2013; Klüver 2009; Pauwels 2011; Stubbs 2005), offering useful examples for understanding the reliability, validity, and application methods of this technique.

Y. Chen et al., *Machine Learning in Social Science*,
https://doi.org/10.1007/978-981-95-6465-1_11

Comparatively speaking, quantitative text analysis is more macroscopic, deductive, and objective, while qualitative methods are more interpretive, inductive, and exploratory. Marx and Engels wrote a vast number of works, but it is the grandness, richness, and complexity of their thoughts that make it difficult to acquire a micro-level and holistic understanding of their doctrines across space and time. As analyzed above, under an analysis framework dominated by segmented and interpretative methods, introducing machine learning methods into the analysis process of the works of Marx and Engels and re-reading these intellectual heritages of Marx and Engels "distantly" on the basis of full-text reading and large historical spans may bring a different perspective to the study of Marxism. Thus, this chapter is a new attempt to quantitatively analyze the texts of Marx and Engels using computational research methods.

2 Data and Methods

The *Marx/Engels Collected Works* (MECW), a collection of English translations of the works of Karl Marx and Friedrich Engels, was used in this study. It consists of 50 volumes and is compiled based on the second Russian edition of MECW published by the Institute of Marxism-Leninism of the Central Committee of the Communist Party of the Soviet Union (CPSU) and the German edition of MECW published by the Institute of Marxism-Leninism of the Central Committee of the Socialist Unity Party of Germany (SED), and printed by Lawrence & Wishart from 1975 to 2004. This compilation contains more than 5000 manuscripts written by Marx and Engels during 1835–1895, including: their works on philosophy, history, politics, economics, and other areas (vol. 1–27); Marx's *The Capital* and related manuscripts (vol. 28–37); and their letters (vol. 38–50). It is the most complete publication of the works of Marx/Engels in English. The main content and covered period of each volume are shown in Table 1.

The quantitative text analysis method based on machine learning was used in this study. It is a method for analyzing unstructured text data and extracting information from these texts in a quantitative way by capturing the relationships between words. When analyzing the holistic and historical properties of Marx and Engels' texts, the LDA topic model was employed. For the practical and communicative properties, a named entity recognition (NER) method based on the Stanford Named Entity Recognizer was used.

Table 1 Basic contents of vol. 1–50 of the MECW

Volumes	*Period*	*Contents*
1–3	1835–1844	Early writings of Marx and Engels
3–27	1844–1895	Classics and editorials of Marx and Engels
28–37	1857–1894	Works of Marxist economics, incl. economic manuscripts and the capital
38–50	1844–1895	Correspondence of Marx and Engels

Written material generally centers on specific topics/themes, which represent the elements that frequently appear in the text, including propositions, habitually used words, or contextual meaning. Topic analysis is the process of mining, describing, comparing, and reproducing these topics. The probabilistic topic modeling with LDA was used here, which can automatically identify the hidden topic information in a large text corpus through relational analysis of word meaning (that is, the co-occurrence of words). Moreover, NER is the algorithm of locating and categorizing important and proper nouns in a text, mainly including names of people, places, organizations, and time. In this study, the realistic attention to different countries in the texts of Marx and Engels was measured through recognizing the country names in the works or articles of Marx and Engels, and the social/relation network of Marx and Engels was also constructed by recognizing the people's names in their letters. See Chapter 3 for an introduction to the LDA topic model and NER algorithm.

3 Contents and Structure

The overall word frequency in volumes 1–50 of the MECW was first counted. To avoid situations where the same English word has different forms, all words were lemmatized. Figure 1 shows the top 100 high-frequency words after removing some meaningless function words. The larger the size of a word, the higher the frequency of its occurrence. Overall, *capital* (appearing 34,858 times) and *value* (appearing 32,625 times) are the two words that appear most frequently in the MECW, followed by *production* (appearing 18,384 times), *work* (appearing 17,785 times), and *money* (appearing 15,366 times). Many high-frequency words in the MECW are related to surplus value or labor, such as *commodity* (appearing 14,626 times), *surplus* (appearing 11,177 times), *profit* (appearing 10,795 times), *price* (appearing 10,304 times), *worker* (appearing 10,224 times), *exchange* (appearing 8646 times), and *wage* (appearing 7633 times). High-frequency words related to Marxist politics include *power* (appearing 9659 times), *class* (appearing 8797 times), *war* (appearing 8083 times), *government* (appearing 7487 times), *party* (appearing 6413 times), and *movement* (appearing 5055 times). *German* (appearing 11,733 times) and *French* (appearing 8896 times) are also frequently mentioned in the MECW.

For a more detailed quantitative analysis, the LDA topic model was trained using all the contents of vol. 1–37 of the MECW.[1] Without prior information, the model can use the co-occurrence of words to discover the probability distribution of different topics and words within each topic from a large number of documents. For the selection of topics, models with 8, 10, 12, and 16 topics were trained. After a comprehensive evaluation of the connotation and extension of each topic, the degree of

Fig. 1 Top 100 words appearing most frequently in the MECW

[1] Vol. 38–50 are letters and thereby not included in the topic analysis.

distinction between topics, and the research purpose, the model with 10 topics was selected for subsequent analysis.

Table 2 displays the 10 topics identified by LDA, along with the 25 words that have the highest probability or are most representative under each topic. For each work in the MECW, every word can be categorized as a topic, and the distribution of the content of the work over each topic can then be calculated. In some cases, there may be no words under a certain topic in the work, then the proportion of this topic is 0. Or, if there are many words in an article on a certain topic, then this article can be a representative work on this topic. An article can cover multiple topics or focus on a single topic. The name of each topic is summarized and extracted by considering all the keywords presented by the topic. In general, the topics revealed by the LDA topic model include: labor and surplus value, society and history, revolution and party, military and violence, trade and economic crises, class and rights, politics and editorials, international workers' organizations, nature and science, and "others" (which is difficult to summarize its specific meaning and thereby not analyzed in detail in this study).

Topics 2 and 9 both fall into the category of Marxist philosophy, with Topic 2 focusing more on the philosophical worldview of Marx and Engels, and Topic 9 more on the views of Marx and Engels on nature and science. Topic 2 relates to the basic views of Marx and Engels on the world and society and the laws of their development: terms such as *individual*, *society*, *form*, *history*, and *development* are directly related to the relationship between human and society and the historical development stage of human societies; terms such as *political*, *property*, *produce*, *principle*, *religion*, *law*, and *relation* refer to the elements of the socioeconomic base and superstructure, trying to reveal the general laws of social development; terms such as *right*, *spirit*, *freedom*, and *mass* correspond to the Marxist view of history on the roles of the mass and the realization of the kingdom of freedom; and terms such as *criticism*, *object*, and *contradiction* embody the methodological principles of the Marxist worldview. Topic 9 centers around the discussions of Marx and Engels on nature and science: terms such as *motion/move*, *form*, *process*, and *change* directly refer to Marx's opinion that matter is in constant motion; terms such as *nature/natural*, *atom*, *heat*, *energy*, *earth*, *animal*, *light*, *weight*, *quantity*, *physics*, *chemistry*, and *organic* reflect the attention of Marx and Engels to natural sciences including physics, chemistry, and biology and the influence of natural sciences on their view of nature; terms such as *force*, *product line*,

Table 2 The 10 topics of MECW

Topic 1		Topic 2		Topic 3		Topic 4		Topic 5	
Labor and surplus value		*Society and history*		*Revolution and party*		*Military and violence*		*Trade and economic crises*	
capital	0.042	world	0.009	revolution	0.012	army	0.024	trade	0.009
value	0.040	political	0.008	government	0.011	troop	0.011	factory	0.008
production	0.021	property	0.007	war	0.010	war	0.010	increase	0.008
commodity	0.018	individual	0.007	party	0.009	force	0.009	power	0.007
money	0.016	society	0.007	national	0.009	line	0.009	price	0.005
surplus	0.014	form	0.007	power	0.008	attack	0.008	bank	0.005
profit	0.013	nature	0.006	class	0.006	battalion	0.007	manufacture	0.005
product	0.012	philosophy	0.006	constitution	0.005	cavalry	0.006	class	0.005
price	0.011	law	0.006	political	0.005	corp	0.006	wage	0.005
capitalist	0.010	relation	0.005	revolutionary	0.005	military	0.006	child	0.005
exchange	0.010	right	0.005	bourgeoisie	0.005	battle	0.005	law	0.005
produce	0.008	history	0.005	republic	0.005	enemy	0.005	cotton	0.005
wage	0.008	power	0.005	army	0.004	infantry	0.005	amount	0.004
circulation	0.007	criticism	0.005	nation	0.004	form	0.005	market	0.004
rate	0.006	spirit	0.004	interest	0.004	artillery	0.005	industry	0.004
worker	0.006	freedom	0.004	movement	0.004	officer	0.005	machinery	0.004
rent	0.006	private	0.003	napoleon	0.004	division	0.005	capitalist	0.004
quantity	0.005	object	0.003	king	0.004	gun	0.004	manufacturer	0.004
productive	0.005	development	0.003	force	0.004	advance	0.004	export	0.003
material	0.005	free	0.003	struggle	0.003	regiment	0.004	employ	0.003
amount	0.005	principle	0.003	bourgeois	0.003	far	0.004	crisis	0.003
land	0.004	contradiction	0.003	empire	0.003	soldier	0.004	commercial	0.003
cost	0.004	religion	0.003	form	0.003	fire	0.004	capital	0.003
employ	0.003	mass	0.002	election	0.003	number	0.004	produce	0.003

Topic 6		Topic 7		Topic 8		Topic 9		Topic 10	
Class and rights		*Politics and editorials*		*International workers' organizations*		*Nature and science*		*Others*	
class	0.012	government	0.013	council	0.030	motion	0.019	imperial	0.009
worker	0.012	law	0.006	international	0.026	form	0.015	troop	0.004
bourgeoisie	0.009	treaty	0.005	congress	0.017	nature	0.013	god	0.004
peasant	0.009	war	0.005	association	0.016	atom	0.013	back	0.004
land	0.008	court	0.005	section	0.012	force	0.012	pest	0.004
social	0.007	minister	0.005	alliance	0.012	natural	0.007	heart	0.004
bourgeois	0.006	right	0.004	committee	0.010	heat	0.007	towards	0.003
society	0.006	police	0.004	federal	0.009	process	0.007	stand	0.003
condition	0.006	official	0.004	worker	0.009	weight	0.006	die	0.003

(continued)

Table 2 (continued)

Topic 6		*Topic 7*		*Topic 8*		*Topic 9*		*Topic 10*	
Class and rights		*Politics and editorials*		*International workers' organizations*		*Nature and science*		*Others*	
industry	0.006	newspaper	0.004	society	0.009	change	0.006	lead	0.003
property	0.005	ministry	0.004	rule	0.008	energy	0.006	battle	0.003
proletariat	0.005	cologne	0.004	central	0.006	system	0.006	lie	0.003
right	0.004	authority	0.004	resolution	0.006	mechanical	0.005	far	0.003
system	0.004	debate	0.003	Geneva	0.006	chemical	0.005	entire	0.003
small	0.004	cabinet	0.003	secret	0.006	dialectic	0.005	town	0.003
free	0.004	parliament	0.003	class	0.006	produce	0.004	fire	0.003
form	0.004	berlin	0.003	party	0.005	line	0.004	fight	0.003
interest	0.004	bill	0.003	delegate	0.005	earth	0.003	true	0.002
family	0.004	duty	0.003	federation	0.005	animal	0.003	eye	0.002
trade	0.004	tribune	0.003	league	0.005	light	0.003	look	0.002
town	0.004	power	0.003	political	0.005	action	0.003	love	0.002
law	0.004	noble	0.003	pamphlet	0.004	quantity	0.003	city	0.002
development	0.003	pay	0.003	meeting	0.004	physic	0.003	border	0.002
far	0.003	office	0.003	revolutionary	0.004	organic	0.003	early	0.002
force	0.003	statement	0.002	communist	0.004	move	0.003	along	0.002

mechanical, and *action* refer to the relationship between humans and nature; and the term *dialectic* directly presents the basic methodological principles of the Marxist view of nature.

Topics 1 and 5 relate to Marx's discussions on the capitalist system and the law of its development. Topic 1 mainly focuses on the theory of labor and surplus value. Its terms concern Marx's expositions of the core concepts of the capitalist mode of production and basic economic laws, such as *capital, money, circulation, commodity, market, value, price, production, exchange, surplus, value, profit, capitalist, worker, employ, wage, material, cost, rate,* and *productive.* The terms of Topic 5 are mostly related to trade and economic crisis, such as *trade, increase, price, wage, amount, market, machinery, export,* and so on, and refer to excess production capacity, insufficient consumption demand, and the contradiction between expanding production and weakening purchasing power of the people caused by the capitalist mode of production; terms such as *class, capitalist*, and *employ* refer to the manifestations of the basic contradictions of capitalism in class relations; and terms including *bank* and *crisis* concern the economic crisis resulting from this basic contradiction.

Topics 3, 6, and 8 are Marx's discussions on class, revolution, and the dictatorship of the proletariat, describing the nature, conditions, and laws of development of the struggle for the liberation of the proletariat. Topic 3 focuses on revolution and party, including both socialist and bourgeois revolutions. *Revolution* is the term that appears most frequently and is also the most important word in this topic. Terms such as *war, party, army, movement, force, struggle,* and *interest* show Marx's programmatic guidance for the proletariat to form parties, launch armed and violent revolutions, and fight for their own interests; and terms such as *constitution, bourgeoisie, republic, king, empire, election,* and *prince* relate to the anti-feudal capitalist revolutions fighting for democracy. Topic 6 is about Marx's theory of class and society. The first four most important words in this topic are *class, worker, bourgeoisie,* and *peasant. Proletariat* also appears in this topic. Terms such as *land* and *property* correspond to Marx's relevant discussion on the standards of class division; words such as *right, interest*, and *force* reflect the class struggle. Topic 8 discusses the establishment of international workers' unions in the works of Marx and Engels. Terms such as *council/committee, international, association/alliance/federation/league, worker, party,* and *communist* refer to Marx's basic view that the proletariat must unite internationally, establish international communist organizations, and use their international solidarity to fight the bourgeoisie; terms such as *rule, Geneva, delegate, pamphlets,* and *meetings* refer to the organizational principles, programmatic documents, and daily activities of the international federation of workers.

Topics 4 and 7 relate to the discussions of Marx and Engels on military and politics. The core vocabulary of Topic 4 is basically related to military and armed affairs, including terms such as *army/troop/battalion, war/battle, force, attack, enemy, infantry, artillery,* and *soldiers*. This topic explores the series of theoretical viewpoints developed by Marx and Engels on war, the army, violent revolution, and other issues, which were formed after reflecting on the wars of the nineteenth century and reflect the concerns of Marx and Engels regarding the realities of their time. Topic 7 mainly refers to politics. Terms such as *government, treaty, ministry, police, official, cabinet, parliament, power, law,* and *court* have obvious political and legal references; and terms such as *newspaper, debate,* and *tribune* indicate that this topic mainly relates to Marx's political editorials published in newspapers and periodicals that lashed out at the malpractices then.

With topics being detected, we further explored the proportion of each topic in the MECW. Since LDA can categorize each term in each document into a topic according to the optimal probability, the proportion of the terms assigned to each topic in the total words of the MECW was calculated. The results are shown in Fig. 2.

It can be seen that, in the MECW, expositions on the capitalist system and its law of development account for the largest proportion, up to 41%. The discussion on labor and surplus value accounts for 32% of the total content, and the discussion on trade and economic crisis accounts for 9%. The discussion at such great length can be directly attributed to the three economic manuscripts of Marx and the three volumes of *The Capital* compiled based on them. The discussions of Marx and Engels on class, revolution, and the dictatorship of the proletariat account for the second-largest proportion, approximately 23% of the total content. The discussions on class and revolution account for 9% and 10%, respectively, and the discussion on the formation of international workers' organizations accounts for 4%. The content related to Marxist philosophy accounts for about 14% of the MECW, including the discussion on society and

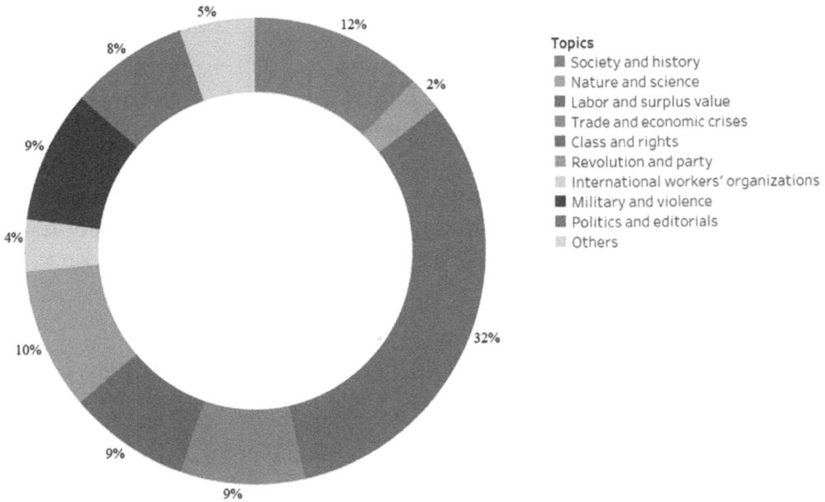

Fig. 2 The proportion of each topic in the MECW

history (12%) and the discussion on nature and science (2%). The discussion on military and violence accounts for 9% of the total content, and the topics of politics and editorials account for 8%.

In 1913, Vladimir Lenin outlined in his work "*The Three Sources and Three Component Parts of Marxism*" that Marxism could be divided into three components: Marxist philosophy, Marxist political economy, and scientific socialism. Through the quantitative analysis of the basic content of the main works of Marx and Engels, these three components do form a corresponding relationship with the topics of the classic texts of Marxism. The result of the topic analysis shows that, through textual counting, the overall exposition of the classic texts of Marx and Engels is an encyclopedia covering philosophy, politics, economics, military, law, society, etc.; the organic integration of the principles of the Marxist philosophy, political economy and scientific socialism; a multi-level theoretical system from abstract to the concrete level that includes worldview and methodology, the basic laws of human social development, and different stages of human social development; a comprehensive discussion from theoretical deduction to realistic criticism unifying theory and practice.

It is worth noting that our topic categorization of the MECW is not an artificial dismemberment of the overall writings, dividing Marx's thoughts into different branches or sub-categories. On the contrary, we intend to view all the focal points in the MECW generally from a macro perspective and understand the most comprehensive and complete theoretical implications from the original texts of Marx and Engels. From the perspective of analysis methods, the LDA topic model uses words as the analysis unit and categorizes words into different topics; therefore, each work may have multiple topics. Meanwhile, the words under each topic are not mutually exclusive, and the same word may be assigned to different topics due to different contexts. This can avoid an either-or division of the contents, and ensures an organic and holistic analysis of the classic texts of Marx and Engels.

4 Development of Marx and Engels' Thoughts

Marx and Engels are not only the founders of Marxism, but also its developers, while Marxism is constantly supplemented, enriched, and developed along with the changes in Marx and Engels' thoughts. A historical investigation of the development process of Marx and Engels' thoughts in the background of historical development, which implements the unity of theory and history, and theory and practice, can facilitate our re-understanding and summarization of the lessons and laws from the emergence and transformation of Marxism under specific conditions and understanding the internal logic of the development of Marx and Engels' thoughts.

Based on the above results, we further introduced the time dimension into the topic analysis. We divided and counted all the texts in the MECW year by year according to when they were written. For each year's texts, each word was assigned to a topic by the trained LDA topic model according to the context, and then the proportion of the words in each topic in the total text content of the year was calculated. A proportional distribution of each topic in the total text of the year was finally obtained to show the diachronic changes in the writing focuses of Marx and Engels. Figure 3 illustrates the topic changes in the texts written by Marx and Engels from 1835 to 1895, presented as a percentage stacked area chart.

Most works prior to 1847 fall into the philosophical category, focusing on philosophy, worldview, nature, and science. During this period, Marx focused on criticizing and transforming classical philosophy, discovering historical materialism, and founding Marxist philosophy. Marx's doctoral dissertation, *The Difference Between the Democritean and Epicurean Philosophy of Nature* (1841), *Critique of Hegel's Philosophy of Right*,

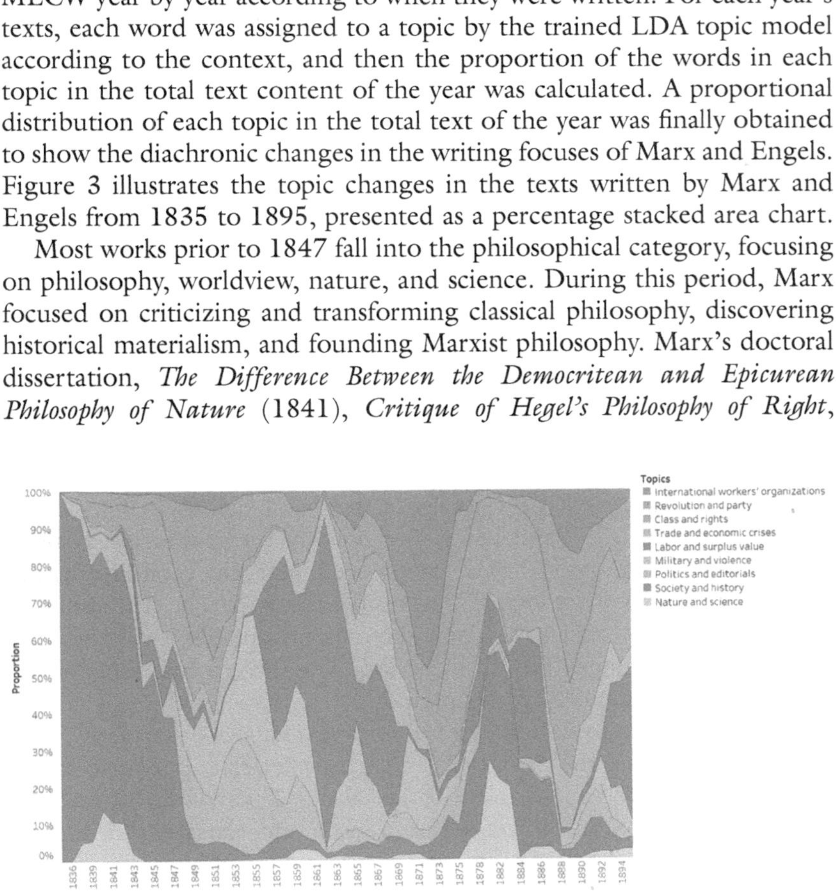

Fig. 3 The percentage stacked area chart of diachronic changes in the writing topics of Marx and Engels

Economic and Philosophic Manuscripts of 1844, *The Holy Family* (1844), *The German Ideology* (1845–1846), and *The Poverty of Philosophy* (1847) were all written during this period.

In the first half of the 1850s, under the influence of the revolutions in real life, Marx and Engels mainly focused on three topics: "revolution and political parties," "military and war," and "politics and law," and wrote a large number of editorial articles that pointed out the shortcomings of the times. Since the bourgeois revolutions broke out in Europe in 1848, the proportion of the treatises of Marx and Engels on revolution, military affairs, and politics has grown rapidly and reached a peak, reflecting the influence of the objective situation of revolutionary development on their thoughts. During this period, Marx and Engels not only conducted theoretical analysis and summarization of the lessons from the European revolutions in 1848, but also made real-time comments and analyses of the wars that occurred in reality. They wrote *The Class Struggles in France, 1848–1850* (1849–1850), *The Peasant War in Germany* (1850), *Revolution and Counter-Revolution in Germany* (1852), *The Eighteenth Brumaire of Louis Bonaparte* (1851–1852), *Revolutionary Spain* (1854), *The Armies of Europe* (1855), and other articles, mostly published in the *Neue Rheinische Zeitung*, *New York Daily Tribune*, and *Die Presse*.

In the second half of the 1850s, focusing on the two major themes, "labor and value theory" and "trade and economic crisis," Marx and Engels accumulated their systematic theoretical works on political economy that analyzed the capitalist system and the laws of its development. Between 1857 and 1868, as capitalism underwent steady post-revolutionary development and experienced periodic economic crises, Marx shifted his writing focus to economic research. The discussion on the theory of value and basic contradictions of capitalism was the main content of his writings during this period. The three manuscripts of *The Capital* were written during this period.

From the 1860s to the 1870s, the writing focus of Marx and Engels shifted to discussing the dictatorship of the proletariat, aiming to enrich and develop the theory of scientific socialism. Their works during this period centered on the three themes, "class and society," "revolution and political party," and "international workers' organization." Back to the historical background of this period, the 1860s, the proletariat's growth with the development of capitalism led to surging labor movements. There were labor strikes in the UK, France, and Germany. And from a global perspective, national liberation movements against colonial rule and democratic movements against feudal rule were surging, such as the national unification movements in Germany and Italy, the uprising in Poland, the Civil War in the U.S., and the Taiping Rebellion in China. When labor movements and national movements collaborated, Marx and Engels actively participated in analyzing and guiding revolutions in various countries. In 1863, they founded the International Workingmen's Association, endeavored to enhance the international unity of the proletariat, and published a large number of guiding opinions. In the 1870s, with the establishment and failure of the Paris Commune and the establishment of the German working-class political party, as the leaders and mentors of the international proletarian revolution, Marx and Engels, based on their experience in guiding labor movements and related reflections, wrote *The Civil War in France* (1871), and *Criticism of the Gotha Program* (1875), making scientific predictions on the development of communism and fighting against the opportunistic ideological trends such as Lassalleanism and Proudhonism in the labor movement.

In their later years, Marx and Engels returned to the study of history and natural philosophy, focusing on philosophical topics and summarizing and sublimating the thoughts of Marxism once again. It can be seen that the topics of philosophical worldview and natural sciences once again peaked in the works of Marx and Engels from 1875 to 1888. The ideas of the revolutionary mentors evolved from theory after decades of revolutionary practice. During this period, Marx conducted in-depth studies of the evolutionary laws of prehistoric society, especially the development of Indian society, and made notes on anthropology. At the same time, he extended his research on world history, especially European history, and made notes on history. Engels wrote *Dialectics of Nature* and *Ludwig Feuerbach and the End of Classical German Philosophy* to systematically explain the Marxist view of nature, worldview, and methodology. The works of this period further enrich and develop Marx's research on the relationship between humans and nature and the laws of development of human society.

From the historical development process of Marx and Engels' thoughts, the following characteristics were summarized.

First, the writing themes of Marx and Engels are clearly related to the time period in which they compiled their works. The distribution of the topics in the works of Marx and Engels is not evenly distributed over time. Marx and Engels focused on different themes in different periods.

In general, the early works of Marx and Engels are mainly philosophical; their works in the middle period mostly focus on the political economy of the bourgeois revolution and the nature of capitalism; and the works in the later period are devoted to the study of proletarian revolution, scientific socialism, and human history.

Second, the works of Marx and Engels contain an internal development logic that moves from practice to theory and then back to practice. After their initial discussion on historical materialism and dialectics in the early years, Marx and Engels revisited these topics following their practical experience in the real world for half a century. Meanwhile, the theory of surplus value came into being just after the failure of the European Revolution in 1848 and before the leadership of the Paris Commune, reflecting the theoretical and practical cycle of Marx and Engels from reflecting on reality to returning to reality.

Third, the themes of the works of Marx and Engels are the organic unity of concrete history. Although the works of each period have a clear topic emphasis, they are not disconnected from each other. Basically, the works of Marx and Engels in each period related to multiple themes. The historical materialism, theory of surplus value, and scientific socialism of Marx and Engels interact with each other and advance as a whole in the course of historical development.

5 Realistic Concerns of Marx and Engels

The works of Marx and Engels are not lofty theories confined to academic studies. Since their emergence, they have been deeply rooted in, serving, and developing in practice. Marx once said, "all social life is essentially practical…The philosophers have only interpreted the world, in various ways, the point, however, is to change it." Marxism was born under the waves of capitalist development and the workers' revolution. It has been tested, enriched, and developed during its attention to reality, and continuously applied in the social practice of guiding the social revolutions of the proletariat to realize its historical mission. When writing their classic texts, Marx and Engels drew on the development status and practical problems of various countries, reflecting distinct practicality and realistic concerns. Therefore, it will provide us with a better understanding of the formation process of Marxism arising from practice and returning to practice by exploring the realistic attention to countries in the classic texts of Marx and Engels.

The number of mentions of different countries by Marx and Engels in the writing process can directly reflect the scope and intensity of their realistic attention. The changes in such numbers of mentions on a yearly basis can intuitively reflect the shift in the attention of Marx and Engels to real society. Therefore, we have identified all the country names in the texts of Marx and Engels through the NER method and counted their frequency of appearance. Figure 4 shows a heat map to indicate the number of mentions of the countries/regions in the world across vol. 1–37 of the MECW. Moreover, five representative countries, England, Russia, America, India, and China, were selected to count the changes in their frequency of appearance. Data of two consecutive years were smoothed to draw the percentage stacking area chart for them (Fig. 5).

It can be observed that Marx and Engels primarily focused on the realities of most countries in Europe, Asia, and North America. The focus was on Britain, France, and Germany in Europe, Russia, and India in Asia, and the U.S. Attention was also paid to several countries in Latin America, Africa, and Oceania, indicating a very wide perspective. European countries were the most important ones. England received the most attention, being mentioned a total of 4648 times, followed by France and Germany. Italy, Turkey, Ireland, Switzerland, Poland, and

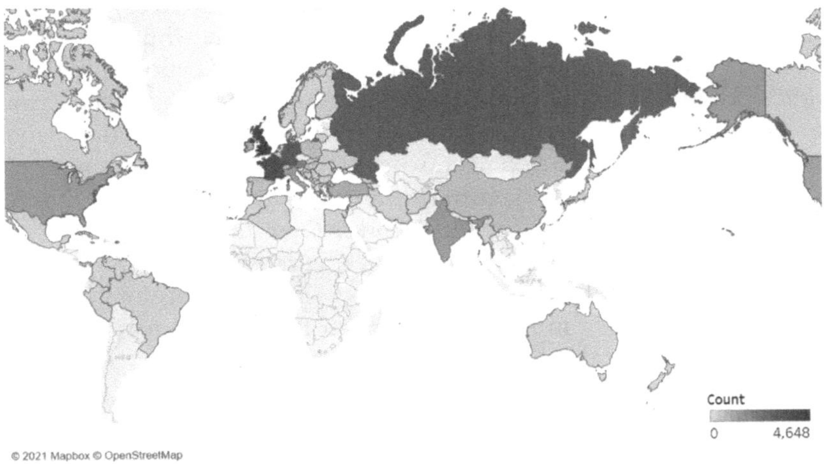

Fig. 4 Heat map for mention frequencies of different countries by Marx and Engels

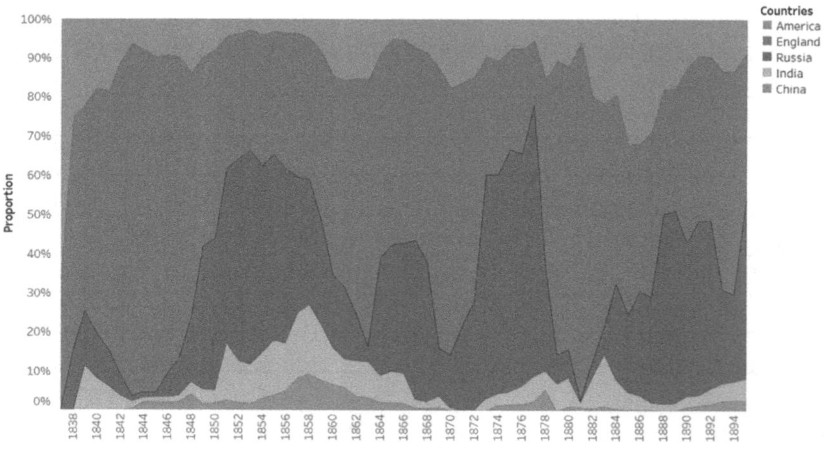

Fig. 5 Percentage stacked area chart for the mention frequencies of five countries

Spain were also the Western countries that received greater attention from Marx and Engels. Known from the diachronic data of England, a representative country in Europe, Marx and Engels paid great attention to this country during the country's Chartism (1842–1848), the later period of the European Revolution (1852–1856), the writing period of economic manuscripts (1861–1865) and the arms race period in the early 1890s (1890–1892). It indicated that Marx and Engels concerned themselves with real issues such as the European bourgeois revolution, labor movement, capitalist development, social status, and imperialist invasions.

Marx and Engels demonstrated a particular interest in Russia, mentioning it 3078 times in their works. Over time, there were four distinct peaks in the degree of attention, occurring around 1854, 1866, 1875, and 1889, respectively. The first two heated discussions coincide with the Crimean War in Russia and the anti-Russian national uprising in Poland, respectively. In the 1870s, Marx even taught himself Russian to give a very detailed discussion of the forms of land ownership in Russia. At that time, Marx and Engels no longer paid attention to Russia due to current affairs, but studied Russia's development path as a complete field, and explored the particularity of the Russian labor movement and socialist revolution. In fact, some of Marx and Engels' works were first published and disseminated in Russia. Marx and Engels paid great attention to issues such as the history of imperial colonial diplomacy in Russia, tsarist autocracy, serfdom, the village land system, and the revolutionary situation of the working class. Their ideas also had significant reverberations in Russia.

Marx and Engels paid attention to the U.S. mainly around 1862 and in the late 1880s. Around 1862, when the American Civil War broke out, Marx and Engels conducted a profound analysis of the reasons for the War, its tactical strategies, and the American slavery system situating distant America within their capitalist analysis framework. A series of reviews was written, such as *The Writings on the American Civil War*. The peaks of attention in the late 1880s were attracted for two reasons. The first peak corresponds to the strikes in Chicago. The labor movement in the U.S. reached its climax during this period and had a profound impact on socialist movements worldwide. Engels paid great attention to the working class in the U.S. He not only went to the U.S. in person, but also publicly set Labor Day to commemorate this movement in the U.S. at the founding meeting of the Second International. The second reason is the development of the American capitalist economy. After the Civil War, the U.S. capitalist economy experienced rapid development, marked by several trends and changes that foreshadowed its future growth, including credit accumulation, joint-stock companies, and trusts. To further improve his theory of political economy, Marx closely followed the new changes in the American economy, and even came up with the idea of revising *The Capital* and compiling his theory of credit using the U.S. as a model. Engels directly made new research on these phenomena, trying to provide a scientific basis for the proletariat to develop new struggle strategies.

Regarding Eastern countries, Marx and Engels mainly focused on India and China, mentioning 1152 times and 369 times, respectively. Over time, the focus on both China and India shifted in the 1850s, related to colonial aggression, the Second Opium War, and the waves of movements against Western colonialism in China and India during this period. On the one hand, Marx paid more attention to China and India out of his thinking on the historical destiny and future of the backward countries and eastern societies. On the other hand, the anti-feudal Taiping Rebellion and the Second Opium War broke out in China in 1851 and 1856. Meanwhile, India experienced a national uprising against British colonial rule in 1857. Marx and Engels analyzed the political and economic structures of the colonizers and colonies from a global and historical perspective, and began to explore the internal relationship between proletarian revolutions and movements, and national liberation movements in the oppressed regions.

According to our analysis of the realistic concerns of Marx and Engels, we can see that Marxism is not founded on the investigations or analysis of certain countries. Instead, Marx and Engels, with a very broad vision, investigated and analyzed countries with different geographical locations, social backgrounds, and political systems by taking into consideration the East and the West, the colonizer and colonized countries, the bourgeois revolution and national liberation movement, the labor movement and peasant uprising, the land, and economic systems and other aspects. As Marx and Engels repeatedly pointed out, their theories are not dogmas, but guides for action. Marxism is constantly being enriched and developed through the practice of various countries, and is constantly tested and realizing its own historical mission in this process. The basic principles of Marxism are not a one-sided generalization based on particularity, but a universal science sublimated on the basis of a comprehensive overview of the world. It is this practicality, which is closely integrated with the masses and the specific conditions of the times, that determines the scientific nature and vigorous vitality of Marxism.

6 Social Networks of Marx and Engels

A social network refers to a structure consisting of social relations. It reflects the social relations between actors. Marx and Engels' thoughts are not isolated, but came into being and spread in the collision and communication with other thinkers' thoughts. Vol. 38–50 of the MECW contains a total of 3957 personal letters of Marx and Engels. Compared to the treatises, the letters have a clear address. The correspondence reflects a person's social network to a certain extent. So, these letters can reflect the dissemination process of debate and influence among Marx, Engels, and other contemporary thinkers. In general, the letterhead and the closing part contain specific information about the writer and the recipient. If a third person is mentioned in the body of the letter, then this person is likely to have some kind of social relationship with both the writer and the recipient; or at least be someone that the writer or the recipient knows in real life, or a public figure that both of them pay close attention to.

Therefore, if two names appear at the same time in a letter, there must be some intersection of them in life, work, or thought, which can reflect the social networking and interaction of Marx and Engels. We automatically identified the person's names in each letter using the NER method as a node in the network analysis. If two person names appear at the same time in a letter, a set of co-occurrence relationships is recorded as edges in the network. Gephi, a network analysis software, is used to draw a global social network of Marx and Engels with figures appearing more than 20 times in their letters. As shown in Fig. 6, the size of a node reflects the frequency of appearance of a person's name in all letters; the connections between the nodes reflect the co-occurrence between the figures, and thicker lines indicate more co-occurrences between nodes and thereby closer social tiers. The obtained social network contains a total of 1079 nodes and 2973 edges. The diameter of the network is 3, the average path length is 1.968, and the average clustering coefficient is 0.859. To better present the information, we selected the persons' names that appeared over 160 times and the edges with two names that co-appear over 120 times to draw a local detailed social network of Marx and Engels (Fig. 7).

In the social network of Marx and Engels, there were many activists of the labor movement and followers of Marxism. As revolutionary mentors, Marx and Engels guided them in establishing the workers' parties and leading the workers' movement. August Bebel and William

Fig. 6 Social network in the letters of Marx and Engels (global)

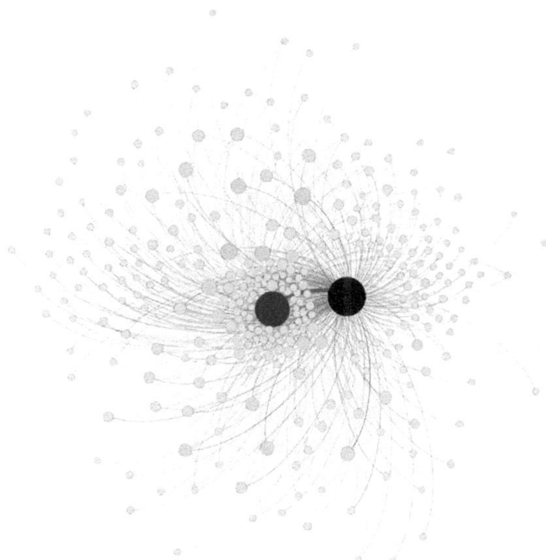

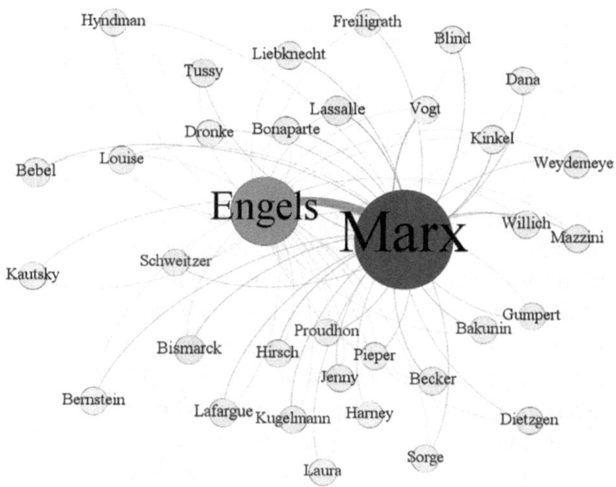

Fig. 7 Social network in the letters of Marx and Engels (detailed)

Liebknecht (the founders of the German Social Democratic Party), Paul Lafargue (the founder of the French Workers' Party), Friedrich Sorge (the founder of the Socialist Labor Party of America), Johann Philipp Becker, Karl Kautsky, Ludwig Kugelmann, and Joseph Dietzgen (German labor activists) were among these activists and followers. As close friends and comrades-in-arms of Marx and Engels, they jointly promoted the dissemination and development of Marxism, as well as the integration of Marxism with the specific revolutionary practices of various countries.

There were also many representatives of opportunism and revisionism in the social correspondence network of Marx and Engels: Ferdinand Lasalle and Jean Baptist von Schweitzer, the representatives of the Lassalleans; Mikhail Bakunin, a Bakuninist representative; Pierre Joseph Proudhon, a Proudhonist representative; Edward Bernstein, a revisionist representative; and some other representatives of petty bourgeoisie socialists, Gottfried Kinkel, Henry Mayers Hyndman, Giuseppe Mazzini, Julian Harney, August Willich, and Karl Blind. Most of these figures were activists in the international labor movement who had followed Marx in the early days or were close friends of Marx. However, their non-radical petty-bourgeois ideas on how to lead the working class diverged from those of Marx and Engels. They even severed relationships with Marx and Engels.

The families, doctors, and working partners of Marx and Engels also corresponded with them actively. Marx and Engels co-occurred most frequently, up to 23,238 times, reflecting their intimate revolutionary friendship. The frequency of Marx's co-occurrence with his eldest daughter Jenny Marx, his second daughter Laura Marx, his youngest daughter Eleanor Tussy Marx,[2] and his sister Louise Juta is 794 times, 686 times, 722 times, and 335 times, respectively. The social co-occurrence network also unveils that Engels' doctor and friend, Edward Gumpert, whose name co-appeared with Engels 418 times. In his letters to Engels, Marx often asked him to consult Gumpert for advice on illness treatments (Henderson 1976). At the same time, Marx and Engels had very good relationships with Joseph Weydemeyer and Ernst Dronke, the editors of the *Neue Rheinische Zeitung*, and Charlie Anderson Dana, the editor of the *New York Daily Tribune*.

7 Conclusion

This chapter undertakes a macro-level and distant reading of volumes 1 to 50 of the *Marx/Engels Collected Works* (MECW) quantitatively. Ten major topics were identified with their proportions determined in the works of Marx and Engels through the LDA topic model, making an objective and comprehensive statistical description of the basic content and writing focuses of the MECW from a macro perspective. Through a diachronic analysis of the changes in topic proportions, we viewed the research focus shift of Marx and Engels and the social background factors behind it in the grand spatiotemporal context, and understood and investigated Marx and Engels' thoughts by placing them within their historical background and its own development logic. Meanwhile, we examined the concerns of Marx and Engels regarding the fate of different countries and regions, and analyzed their realistic concerns in practice. Finally, by analyzing the social network within the letters of Marx and Engels, we revealed the social network of Marx and Engels, understood them in a three-dimensional manner, and tentatively explored the dissemination process of their thoughts. This chapter is an exploratory application of

[2] Tussy was the nickname given by Marx to his youngest daughter, Elena Marx.

machine learning methods in the textual research of the works of Marx and Engels. Compared with traditional textual criticism or hermeneutic textual research, this chapter provides a new perspective. It makes contributions in ensuring a macro-level, deductive, and objective analysis of the MECW and explaining the theoretical, historical, and practical logic within the thoughts of Marx and Engels.

This chapter also has several limitations. First, it mainly relies on computers to present quantitative and objective results of textual analysis, which may not be as in-depth and active as qualitative text analysis methods in terms of interpretation. Second, our analysis, which treats the word as a unit, can divide certain fixed phrases or important collocations during counting, and this can lead to simplification or misinterpretation of some words due to polysemy and the inability to restore the context. Third, due to space and time constraints, we provide a relatively rough distant reading and overview of the MECW from a single perspective, without focusing on a specific problem or providing more detailed analysis methods and angles. Fourth, the interpretation of the results of textual analysis is data-driven, deductive, and speculative. Further theoretical and practical evidence-based tests are needed to ensure the scientific and objective nature of the interpretation.

"*The weapon of criticism cannot, of course, replace criticism of the weapon, material force must be overthrown by material force, but theory also becomes a material force as soon as it has gripped the masses.*" The purpose of our study is not to summarize and interpret thoughts contained in the vast texts of Marx and Engels through one study. Instead, it intends to prove that the quantitative text methods introduced into the research on classical theoretical works is an approach that is parallel to the previous research and can facilitate the capture of the macroscopic context of a theory. Moreover, new sparks may fly out during the collision between computer algorithms and texts. We call for more in-depth and valuable quantitative text analyses to be on the agenda. For example, by quantifying text thoughts as variables, we can explore the relationship or causality between them and other social indicators; or, by calculating text similarity, we can explore the transformation process of Marx and Engels' thoughts in two periods, or its connections and differences with other thoughts; or, by further expanding the content and time span of the Marxist textual analysis data, we can explore the position of Marxism in the long historical process.

References

Grimmer, Justin, and Brandon M. Stewart. 2013. Text as data: The promise and pitfalls of automatic content analysis methods for political texts. *Political Analysis* 21 (3): 267–297.

Henderson, William O. 1976. *The life of Friedrich Engels*, vol. 01. London: Frank Cass and Company Limited.

Ji, Zhengju, and Sijin Liu. 2018. Research on the text of on marxist classical works in the past 40 years of reform and opening-up. *Studies on Marxist Theory* 4 (6): 49–61 (In Chinese).

Klüver, Heike. 2009. Measuring interest group influence using quantitative text analysis. *European Union Politics* 10 (4): 535–549.

Pauwels, Teun. 2011. Measuring populism: A quantitative text analysis of party literature in Belgium. *Journal of Elections, Public Opinion and Parties* 21 (1): 97–119.

Stubbs, Michael. 2005. Conrad in the computer: Examples of quantitative stylistic methods. *Language and Literature* 14 (1): 5–24.

Zhang, Yibin. 2012. Word frequency in academic text: A new perspective in the study of intellectual history within marxist philosophy—Beginning from the revision of the third edition of back to Marx. *Studies on Marxism* (9): 86–92+160 (In Chinese).

PART VI

Modeling Sentiments

CHAPTER 12

From Barbarism to Civilization: The Evolving Image of China in International Cinema

1 Introduction

Ever since Joseph Nye (1990) popularized the concept of "soft power," the approach to power through attraction, rather than coercion, has gained increasing acceptance among academics (Zhang and Wu 2019). As a kind of soft power, the national image could play a vital role in international politics. Jervis (1970: 3, 6) argued that a national image allows a country to exercise influence without incurring the high cost of changing its main policies, making the desired outcome more useful than a significant increase in military or economic power. A country is like a brand; its image and reputation are part of its strategic capital, which is why China considers its national image a new "battlefield" to develop its capability of international communication after decades of rapid economic development (Ding 2011).

More often than not, a country's self-image construction fails to achieve the desired effect, for the reason that the national image is not entirely determined by the subject of the image. Hegel (1975: 7) states that an image is the sensuous existence of a particular significance, including intuition, sensibility, and symbol. According to Boulding (1959) a country's national image is built on a combination of the country's self-cognition and other bodies' cognition of it within the international system. The image may even be distorted in other countries' depictions, especially through cultural and artistic works.

Y. Chen et al., *Machine Learning in Social Science*,
https://doi.org/10.1007/978-981-95-6465-1_12

For China, the most significant economic and political strategic issues in the country, such as the trade war with the U.S. and the Taiwan issue, all have a shared connection to the national image, so the perception of other nations and its underlying reality will influence the future of China's development and reform (Ramo 2007: 12). In this case, exploring the formation and change of China's national image becomes a top priority. Mainly, three directions lie in its research field. The first is the study of China's long-term national image changes, which helps to understand the historical facts behind the interactions between China and other countries (Xie and Page 2013; Zhu 2019). The second is the study of the Chinese government's construction of its national image, where most studies are based on specific events, such as the Beijing Olympic Games and the China-EU Cultural Festival (Brownell 2013; Maags 2014). The third category takes the perspective of other countries, examining the image of China in a variety of foreign and domestic media, like films and newspapers (Greene 2014; Birama and Röschenthaler 2017; Zhu and Ji 2018). The integration of these three directions points to China's position in world affairs.

Descriptive analysis of images helps to understand trends, policies, causes, and effects, making it the basis of all research. However, among all kinds of studies, few studies measure the change of image itself accurately, either due to the lack of data or the fact that no uniform and convincing results could be drawn. Most existing studies focus on individual and single-country surveys, which often lack a sufficient time span, geographical scope, and sample size (Page, Rabinovich, and Tully, 2008). To make up for these deficiencies, we began by choosing film as the medium to carry the image of China, for the reason that film can communicate more directly between the subject and the audience, better conveying the connotation contained in the image (Monaco and Lindroth 2000). Second, we obtained a huge sample size of 4,927 China-related films via the world's most popular and authoritative film source, the Internet Movie Database (IMDb), while machine learning methods process text analysis objectively and comprehensively. Lastly, to draw strong conclusions, Granger causality test was used to determine the potential relationship between the emotional changes of China's image and the macro-level socioeconomic factors. The above methods analyzed the image of China over the century and around the world from three aspects: content, sentiment, and determinants. The methods used fill the gaps of both quantitative and qualitative literature and lay a foundation for future mechanism analysis.

"Representations of films are interpretations (Malcolm 2004: 101)," The purpose of this article is to extract the representations through big data and machine learning methods and show the image of China as an interpretation. This "image" carries with it the filmmakers' real-time views of China, so to present it is to interpret its historical and political implications. On this basis, we can know the effect of various factors on the formation of this image, including comprehensive national strength and international relations. Its change is due to the accumulation of various historical factors, so the time of over a century is of great significance. One could glimpse the trend of China's soft power in the world and look to the future from the past.

2 Films and Image of China

Film was invented at the same time that China was forced to open to the outside world in the late nineteenth century. At that time, China had become a semi-colony and undergone exploitative practices related to colonialism. Coinciding with the rise of the film industry, the cinematic image of China seen across the globe, therefore, became closely related to the development of modern China and its diplomatic relations with other countries.

A significant amount of literature discusses China in global films. For example, Gina Marchetti and other scholars examine the depiction of China to judge China's status in global film culture and the connection between such cultural exchange and politics (Marchetti and Lu 2018). Since Hollywood nearly dominates global cinema markets, most literature studies the relationship between Hollywood and China. Literature on early films focuses on Hollywood's stereotypes of the "Orient," while articles on contemporary films explore how the rise, transition, and social context of China have affected the Hollywood film industry (Chung 2006; Gries et al. 2015; Su 2016). Their limitations are similar to those of the national image literature: the time range of these studies is limited, and they primarily conduct theoretical rather than empirical research.

Representations of China in Hollywood films have undergone several changes. For instance, films about China in the early twentieth century such as *Daughter of the Dragons* (1931) featured tenebrous and uncanny scenes, coupled with evil characters like Fu Manchu, and portrayed the

"Yellow Peril" and China's barbarism. During World War II, films like *The Good Earth* (1937) showed China's uncivilized status and garnered the sympathy of Western audiences (Meyer 2006). The 1960s witnessed the emergence of films with anti-Communist topics, and the 1970s saw the popularity of Kung Fu films starring Bruce Lee. By the twenty-first century, works such as *Kung Fu Panda* (2008) and *Wall Street: Money Never Sleeps* (2010), began to highlight China's cultural and economic power.

Postcolonialism and postmodernism are often used by scholars to interpret the image of China in world cinema (Marchetti and Lu 2018). Especially early films, produced in the West and later introduced to the East, bore colonialism's imprint. Gramsci (1992: 233–238) wrote of colonialism as the unapparent hegemony of one form of culture over another. Edward Said developed the above arguments for *Orientalism* (1978) and stated that the remote and strange Oriental World in Western artworks is artificially created to manifest the West's cultural superiority (Mamdani 2005; Said 1995). Moreover, Orientalism is an agent of "discourse" as defined by Michel Foucault, as it is highly social and "a political actuality of great and significant moment" (Said 1995: 247). This kind of cultural expression affects the East, even interfering with the way the East sees itself.

Chinese cinema is experiencing a kind of "re-Orientalism," which is evidenced in films like *Hero* (2002), which is remarkably close to the Hollywood aesthetic. Like many other Eastern artists, some Chinese filmmakers depict Chinese culture from Western perspectives, thereby submitting to Western cultural hegemony (Mendes and Lau 2015). Additionally, the editors of IMDb, the database used in this chapter for the quantitative research, have their preferences. Due to Western identity and ideology, they prefer films with Western perspectives. For these reasons and because the number of Chinese films within the sample size is relatively small (accounting for 15.4% of the 4,428 films examined), we can largely regard these representations of China as formulated according to an outsider's perspective, especially the West's.

It is worth noting that films inevitably use rhetorical devices to exaggerate reality. The international media system is shaped by idealism, so the art and culture it conveys always has an ideological shadow, which explains stereotypes of China that remain in Hollywood films (Said 1993: 309). With the help of big data research, we hope to suggest that film has become an integral player in the cultural interactions between countries and continues to shape China's national image in ways that are constantly evolving.

3 Data and Methods

A country's national image is an abstract cultural idea based on a group of general and ambiguous cognitive concepts spread through a social cognitive structure. Traditional methodologies, based on sampling and questionnaires, have difficulty accurately measuring such an amorphous concept. Recently, with the increased digitization of data, especially regarding the maturation of machine learning and its applications, as well as natural language processing technologies, text analysis has become a breakthrough for measuring cultural ideas.

In this study, we used the text data from IMDb's plot synopses of China-related films as the source for analysis. Founded in 1990, IMDb is an online film database that maintains a record of film plots, casts, lengths, production regions, release regions, and reviews. As of June 2020, IMDb had collected 6,534,894 works, involving 552,366 films, making it a high-quality source of data for academic research.[1] Currently, this database is being applied by scholars in literature, communication studies, sociology, and other related fields. Inquiries into this data have yielded an assessment of the relationship between film popularity and geopolitics, a comparative analysis of writing styles and metadata characteristics through film reviews, and an examination of the features of the most influential films in film history (Dodds 2006; Otterbacher 2013; Canet 2016). These studies have inspired further research projects, which can capitalize on this data to explore sociocultural issues.

There are other well-known film databases, such as Rotten Tomatoes, but its main feature is to review and evaluate films, rather than an archive or a search engine.[2] When it comes to older movies (especially before the 1950s), Rotten Tomatoes may not provide this study with accurate information about the movies, including film plots and regions of production and release. Hence, we chose IMDb as the primary data source.

[1] See https://www.imdb.com/pressroom/stats/?pf_rd_m=A2FGELUUNOQJNL&pf_rd_p=370e8fdc-d50b-4660-b053-1421f412efb7&pf_rd_r=SGX6KR6H4HQ0WNZ9RSH4&pf_rd_s=right-2&pf_rd_t=60601&pf_rd_i=pressroom&ref_=fea_pr_pr_lk7.

[2] See https://www.rottentomatoes.com/about.

To research how China is represented in these films, we set retrieval conditions, selecting films before 2020 with "China" and "Chinese" as keywords. Thus, the content of works retrieved under this condition is about the country China or the elements related to China. After removing duplicated data and missing values, a total of 4,428 China-related films from around the world are obtained, including 682 films made in China. According to the agenda-setting theory, Western perspectives might bias editors against China, affecting their choice of China-related films. In this case, audiences may be influenced to accept what the image of China "should" be rather than what it "actually" is McCombs (2005). This study wants to explore the "should" images produced in this mechanism.

We used web crawler technology to grab film titles and plots from IMDb. Such information directly reflects the basic plot-setting of each work, which has informed the content analysis of this study to gauge how China has been portrayed in global films. We also obtained information regarding the film's regions of production and release dates to further explore how these factors have impacted the international perception of China. Accurately measuring how China has been portrayed in these films depends on whether the plot descriptions of China can be effectively mined. Since film titles and plots are classified as unstructured text data, we mainly applied the text mining method based on machine learning in this study. To intuitively measure the main situation-setting of "China" and "Chinese people" in films from around the globe, we adopted word embedding technology to predict the contextual information of "Chinese" and "China." Then, we adopted the LDA topic model to explore how cinematic portrayals of China vary around the world, as the interpretation of images differs across different cultures. Finally, we applied sentiment analysis to calculate the general tone of relevant films in various global regions and measure audiences' overall attitude toward China. See Chapter 3 for an introduction to the relevant models mentioned above.

4 Contexts in Films Related to China

We first analyzed the trend of China-related films over time and found that China-related elements were incorporated into films beginning in the 1890s in Fig. 1. A small peak appeared around 1912 when the Republic of China (ROC) was founded, suggesting that the increase in films might be closely related to immense political events. In the early years of the People's Republic of China (PRC), the number of films involving China remained low, a likely product of the PRC's diplomatic isolation and one-sided foreign policy during this period. It was not until 1971 that the PRC returned to the United Nations and began to establish diplomatic relations with Japan (1972), the U.S. (1979), and European countries respectively. These events are probable causes of an increase in the number of films made about China in the 1970s. After the nation's leader Deng Xiaoping renewed the Open-Door Policy in 1978, the PRC began to welcome foreign involvement and investment in the country, deciding to go global. In 2001, the PRC joined the World Trade Organization, embracing the world on a broader scale. Since then, the PRC has played an increasingly important role in the international arena, and the number of China-related films has also shown exponential growth.

It is worth noting that the number of China-related films is also closely tied to the political histories of Hong Kong and Taiwan before 1997. These regions were more open to the world than the PRC at the time and thus served as important windows into China. As two of the "Four Asian Dragons" alongside South Korea and Singapore, Hong Kong and Taiwan experienced rapid economic growth and the commercialization of their film industries, which partly explains the increase in China-related films produced between the 1970s and the 1990s. Taken together, the international community's impressions of these regions and

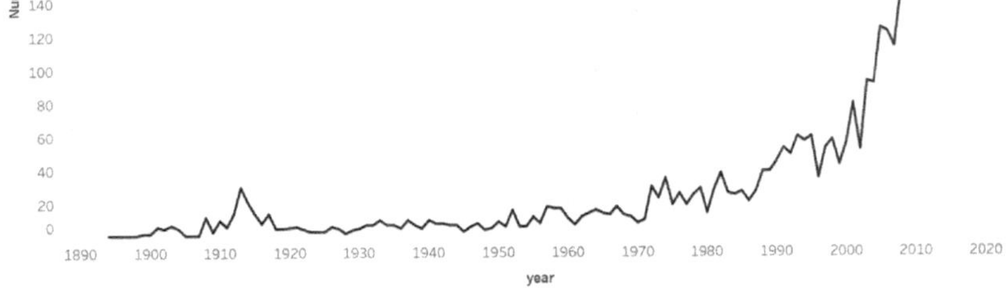

Fig. 1 Number of films related to China by year

Chinese mainland helped shape an overall image of "China" in the global cultural imagination.

To further explore the contexts related to China in the films, we adopted the Skip-gram algorithm in Word2vec to train a word vector model. Table 1 reveals the words with the shortest cosine distance to the center word "China" and "Chinese," that is, the words with the highest similarity to the center words.

According to the results, the words closely related to "China" and "Chinese" can be roughly divided into three categories—politics, society, and culture. First, political words include words related to international affairs, such as "Dalai," "refugee," "exile," "Europe," "India," and "African." These items touch on the Tibet issue, together with the PRC's relations with countries around the world, demonstrating the significance of its diplomacy in the international situation. Particularly, "Western" occupies a higher place in entries of both "China" and "Chinese," proving China's position as opposed to the West and suggesting the Western perspective of world cinema. In addition to foreign relations, "Chiang" (Chiang Kai-shek), "Taiwan," and "Mao" (Mao Zedong) also reflect the international audience's interest in China's perceived internal affairs.

Table 1 Distance of words to "China" and "Chinese"

Words close to "China"	*Value*	*Words close to "Chinese"*	*Value*
Shanghai	0.750	African	0.678
Tibet	0.718	Asian	0.673
Western	0.711	Chiang	0.665
Dalai	0.707	Western	0.664
Tibetan	0.705	Forbidden	0.659
Mao	0.703	Taiwan	0.654
Taiwan	0.701	Influence	0.650
Europe	0.688	Mao	0.650
1930s	0.688	Tibetan	0.643
Province	0.687	Taiwanese	0.641
Religion	0.685	Tea	0.637
Refugee	0.684	Activist	0.636
Revolution	0.682	Integrate	0.636
Exile	0.682	Religion	0.636
India	0.681	Islam	0.636

There are also many words about Chinese society, such as "Shanghai," "revolution," "activist," and "integrate." These subjects either occurred in Chinese history or are associated with broader social phenomena. Lastly, cultural issues involve words such as "Forbidden" (referring to the Forbidden City), "tea," "religion," and "Islam." Cultural phenomena like tea and the Forbidden City have gained significant influence worldwide, representing China. Meanwhile, these films pay close attention to the religious issues in China, especially the living conditions of Muslims.

Next, we predicted specific contexts by adding some keywords to the words "China" and "Chinese." These keywords, as listed in the table above, are worth studying, and we used the same word vector models to analyze them. We first ran an analysis of Chinese place names appearing in international films, and Table 2 reflects the predicted results.

According to Table 2, different regions have very different sets of films, while the same region has similar keywords when related to "China" and "Chinese." The setting related to Tibet primarily concerns refugees (may point to the Dalai Lama's decision to leave Tibet for India in 1959), and the sovereignty dispute between India and the PRC. In the case of Shanghai, many films focus on what it was like in the 1930s and 1940s. The words related to it, such as "travel," "rural," and "modern,"

Table 2 Words related to Chinese place names

China and Tibet	*Chinese and Tibet*	*China and Shanghai*	*Chinese and Shanghai*	*China and Taiwan*	*Chinese and Taiwan*
Tibet	Tibet	China	China	China	China
China	China	Mainland	City	Revolution	Film
Province	India	Province	Shanghai	Documentary	Documentary
Revolution	Tibetan	Revolution	Beijing	Beijing	Beijing
Refugee	Refugee	Beijing	Province	Mainland	Culture
Ancient	Province	Southern	1940s	Tibet	History
Documentary	Documentary	Ancient	Journey	Modern	Revolution
Republic	History	Tibet	Southern	Province	Modern
India	Capital	Modern	Mainland	Film	Story
Capital	Century	Travel	Travel	History	Explore
History	Revolution	Refugee	Rural	Culture	Tradition
Tibetan	Ancient	Republic	1930s	Ancient	Journey
Century	Thousand	1940s	South	Communist	Century
Communist	Invasion	Capital	Northern	Century	Generate
Invasion	Population	Journey	Modern	Explore	Mao

reflect Shanghai's position as a treaty port and a major prosperous city. Taiwan evokes various connotations, like "culture," "history," "revolution," "province," and "tradition," reflecting Taiwan's ups and downs in the past century and people's multiple perceptions toward it.

In this case, we extracted valuable information from the way historical figures or groups appear in the texts, as shown in Table 3. According to Table 1, "African," "Chiang," and "Mao" all rank high in the entry of "Chinese." Mao and Chiang are two of the most significant figures in Chinese history, while the relationship between Africans and the Chinese is also important.

Mao's textual associations involve dynasties, as evidenced by the appearance of "emperor," "communist," "Qing," "Han," and "Tang." China-related films mainly regard him as the head of state in the new period of Chinese history and compare him to the notable leaders of the Tang and Han dynasties. Words related to Chiang include "war," "invasion," and "1937," references to the Chinese Civil War and Resistance Against Japanese Aggression in which he served as commander-in-chief. Mao and Chiang, as leaders of the Communist Party of China and the Nationalist Party of China that confronted each other from the 1920s to

Table 3 Words related to figures and groups

China and Mao	*Chinese and Mao*	*China and Chiang*	*Chinese and Chiang*	*China and African*	*Chinese and African*
China	Dynasty	China	China	China	China
Mao	China	Communist	Mao	Revolution	American
Communist	Emperor	Tibet	Communist	Beijing	Culture
Revolution	Communist	Mainland	Dynasty	Province	Beijing
Dynasty	Li	Revolution	War	Mainland	Young
Mainland	Qing	Province	Documentary	Modern	Immigration
Ancient	Chi	Ancient	History	Culture	Documentary
Province	Yuan	Mao	Invasion	Documentary	Tradition
Tibet	Revolution	Documentary	Culture	Tibet	Chinese
1949	Han	1949	Tibetan	Ancient	African
Beijing	Beijing	Modern	1937	Republic	Country
Modern	Tang	History	Govern	History	Explore
Documentary documentary	Culture	Dynasty	Century	Southern	Journey
Republic	Ancient	Republic	Gong	Mao	Modern
Qing	Tradition	Beijing	Tibet	American	Community

1940s, are closely associated with each other. For example, "Mao" ranks second in Chiang's entry. As for "African," since its inception, the PRC has provided a huge amount of aid to African countries, which has made the connection between the two regions very close. Especially in the Mao era ("Mao" also appears in this entry), African nations were considered as brothers also from the Third World, and this closeness was born. In addition, the word "immigration" can imply that there are considerable African immigrants entering China, which is consistent with the reality that African immigrants in Guangzhou province have received academic attention (Liang 2014).

In the description of "China" and "Chinese," many political words appear. Even place and figure names also correspond to specific political events. Thus, the image of China in global films is highly politicized, and the ideological factors brought by the political agenda and trends may change the original neutral phenomena. As a cultural form, the way films convey political elements through different stories needs to be explained by film topics, which we will address later.

5 Topics of China-Related Films

To better delineate China's national image, we applied the LDA topic model to cluster all the plot summary texts. They also analyze the trend of variation in film topics over time. Since the number of topics is a crucial parameter, topic coherence, an indicator that measures the internal coherence of the topics in the model, is selected as a reference. The higher its value, the higher the polymerization degree of topics in the model. We chose a range of 5 to 50 topics and trained topic models every five steps for evaluation. Figure 2 shows the results. We finally used 10 topics to train the model.

Table 4 presents the 10 topics and the top 20 keywords that appear most frequently in relation to them. When naming the topics, we referred to the major keywords related to the topics. The top 10 topics are: daily life (23%), kinship and friendship (17%), crime (16.6%), culture (10.6%), suspense (8.7%), love (7.4%), war (6.6%), art (3.8%), business (3.7%), and food (2.6%).

Topics of daily life, kinship, and friendship account for the largest proportion of the data set, reaching 40%. Like the first two categories, love, though relatively small (7.4%), also relates to fundamental matters of human life. The most relevant words connected to the topic of

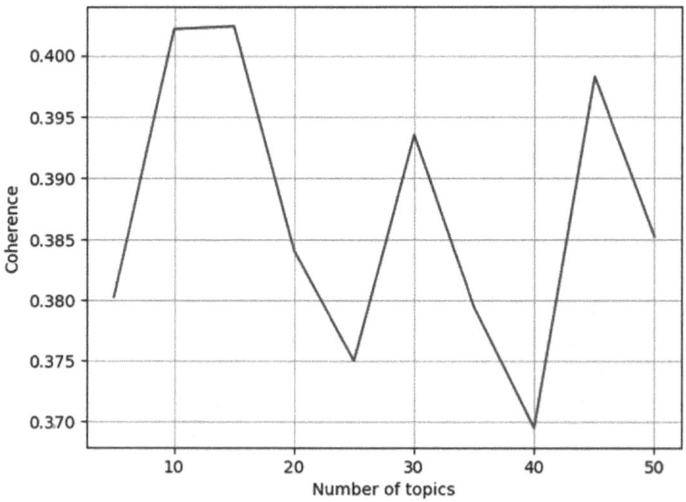

Fig. 2 Topic coherence values of the topic number models

daily life are "young," "family," "woman," "love," "father," "child," and words related to urban life such as "city" and "work." Words like "American" and "Hong Kong" also appear, indicating that with increased globalization, Chinese people's daily lives have become more internationalized.

Crime is the third most important topic in China-related films, accounting for 16.6% of the total. Most related words are derogatory or violent ("kill," "gun," "detective," "fight," "fire," "murder," and "drug"). Films involving this topic may tend to associate the image of China or Chinese people with violent situations and describe China as a country with a chaotic social order and high crime rate. Suspense, the fifth major focus of China-related films (comprising 8.7% of the data set), bears similar connotations. This topic mainly involves conspiratorial words like "escape," "secret," "CIA," and "James Bond" (the protagonist of the *007* series), which associate China with illegal behaviors like espionage, conspiracy, and smuggling.

Accounting for 10.6% of the total, culture is the fourth most concerning topic in international China-related films. The main descriptions in this topic include historical, geographical, and cultural items,

Table 4 LDA topic analysis of films

Topic 1 *Daily life* *23.0%*	*Topic2* *Kinship and friendship* *17.0%*	*Topic 3* *Crime* *16.6%*	*Topic 4* *Culture* *10.6%*	*Topic 5* *Suspense* *8.7%*
0.008 Young	0.007 Night	0.011 Police	0.022 Film	0.012 Team
0.007 Family	0.007 Home	0.006 Kill	0.014 World	0.010 Frank
0.007 Story	0.007 House	0.006 Crime	0.013 Story	0.009 Agent
0.007 Woman	0.006 Father	0.006 Gun	0.010 Documentary	0.009 Nick
0.005 City	0.006 Friend	0.005 Car	0.009 Series	0.007 Escape
0.005 Work	0.006 Room	0.005 Detective	0.007 Anonymous	0.006 Work
0.005 Anonymous	0.005 Jack	0.005 Fight	0.007 History	0.006 Ship
0.005 Home	0.005 Boy	0.005 Shoot	0.006 Culture	0.005 German
0.005 Kong	0.005 Girl	0.004 Fire	0.006 Journey	0.005 Captain
0.004 Love	0.004 Door	0.004 Murder	0.005 Traditional	0.005 Secret
0.004 Girl	0.004 Woman	0.004 Killed	0.005 Experience	0.005 Plan
0.004 Hong	0.004 Child	0.004 Case	0.005 Beijing	0.005 Crew
0.004 American	0.004 Leaf	0.004 Cop	0.004 Episode	0.005 Peter
0.004 Hong Kong	0.004 Mother	0.004 Officer	0.004 Cultural	0.004 Government
0.004 Dream	0.004 Son	0.004 Hand	0.004 Character	0.004 CIA
0.004 Father	0.004 Run	0.003 Drug	0.004 Different	0.004 Bobby
0.003 Local	0.004 Book	0.003 Building	0.004 Short	0.004 Mission
0.003 World	0.004 Walk	0.003 Dead	0.004 City	0.004 James
0.003 Wife	0.003 Stone	0.003 Eddie	0.004 American	0.004 Bond
0.003 Child	0.003 Martin	0.003 Pull	0.004 God	0.004 Group

Topic 6 *Love* *7.4%*	*Topic 7* *War* *6.6%*	*Topic 8* *Art* *3.8%*	*Topic 9* *Business* *3.7%*	*Topic 10* *Food* *2.6%*
0.028 Family	*0.02 War*	*0.023 Art*	*0.012 Tobacco*	*0.022 Food*
0.021 Love	0.012 Soldier	0.022 Master	0.009 Big	0.015 San
0.013 Mother	0.012 Army	0.019 Martial	0.008 Minute	0.014 Chef
0.012 Friend	0.009 World	0.017 Fu	0.007 Interview	0.013 Restaurant
0.012 Daughter	0.007 Lamp	0.016 Martial arts	0.006 Hotel	0.012 San Francisco
0.011 Father	0.006 Power	0.015 Gang	0.005 Agreement	0.012 Francisco
0.009 Son	0.006 Battle	0.014 Wang	0.005 State	0.011 Rogue
0.009 School	0.006 Prince	0.013 Kung	0.004 Party	0.011 Precious
0.007 Parent	0.006 Fight	0.012 Sing	0.004 News	0.011 Anonymous

(continued)

Table 4 (continued)

Topic 6 *Love* *7.4%*	*Topic 7* *War* *6.6%*	*Topic 8* *Art* *3.8%*	*Topic 9* *Business* *3.7%*	*Topic 10* *Food* *2.6%*
0.028 Family	*0.02 War*	*0.023 Art*	*0.012 Tobacco*	*0.022 Food*
0.007 Dick	0.006 Adventure	0.010 Kung fu	0.004 Story	0.011 Chinatown
0.006 Woman	0.006 Cave	0.009 Wu	0.003 CEO	0.010 Wei
0.006 House	0.006 King	0.009 Mei	0.003 Confidentiality	0.009 Chen
0.006 Wedding	0.005 Warrior	0.008 Fight	0.003 Producer	0.008 World
0.006 Child	0.005 Magic	0.006 Beast	0.003 Journal	0.008 Feng
0.005 Wife	0.005 General	0.006 Wong	0.003 Treachery	0.008 Unique
0.005 Young	0.005 Korean	0.006 Tiger	0.003 Lawsuit	0.007 Qi
0.005 Girl	0.005 Wish	0.006 Medicine	0.003 Truth	0.007 Adventure
0.005 Married	0.005 Princess	0.005 Brother	0.003 Contact	0.007 Gong
0.005 Relationship	0.005 Emperor	0.005 School	0.003 Manager	0.007 York
0.005 Anonymous	0.005 North	0.005 Japanese	0.003 Meeting	0.007 New York

reflecting the image of China with a long history, profound cultural traditions, and a varied natural landscape. Art is closely related to culture, which occupies 3.8% of the data. The associated keywords signal the interests of international China-related cinema, mainly "Kung fu" and "medicine." The word "master" also expresses these films' recognition of the Chinese people's superb skills in these aspects.

War ranks seventh, accounting for 6.6% of the total plot texts. It mainly involves military struggles ("soldier," "army," "battle," and "fight,") as well as royalty related key words ("power," "prince," "princess," and "emperor"). On the one hand, this topic reflects the international community's historical solicitude regarding wars in China (especially the China theater of World War II). On the other hand, it shows Westerners' great interest in the feudal royal power system of ancient China.

Finally, topics of business and food account for relatively small proportions of the sample set, about 3.7% and 2.6%. The business topic is associated with terms such as "CEO," "agreement," "producer," and "lawsuit," which refer to business practitioners and practices. The related keywords for food include "food," "chef," "restaurant," and "Chinatown," revealing the global influence of Chinese cuisine.

The results of the above topic clusters are static, meaning they do not account for how these data may have fluctuated over time. To explore topics concerning China from a more dynamic perspective, we further studied how these topics have changed proportionally since the invention of cinema. We defined the annual value of each topic as the average proportion of all the text data they retrieve from the plot synopses of films released in that year. We also incorporated values of the next three years for data smoothing and added the trend line, as shown in Fig. 3.

The topics of crime, war, and suspense represent the dark side of China's image to some extent. The top part of Fig. 3 shows that the proportions of all three topics have presented downward trends since the 1970s. This period coincides with the course of China's economic reform, which began with the renewal of the Open-Door Policy in 1978, together with the "peaceful development" policy in 2003. China has developed a prosperous domestic economy, improved social governance, and increased foreign exchanges. According to the Law Yearbook of China, since 1978, the crime rate in China has actually shown a rising trend. Therefore, world cinema has reduced the number of crime-related films, probably due to China's new image formed through foreign exchange and economic development.

The bottom part of Fig. 3 shows the trend fluctuations of four topics: daily life, kinship and friendship, love, and culture. By focusing

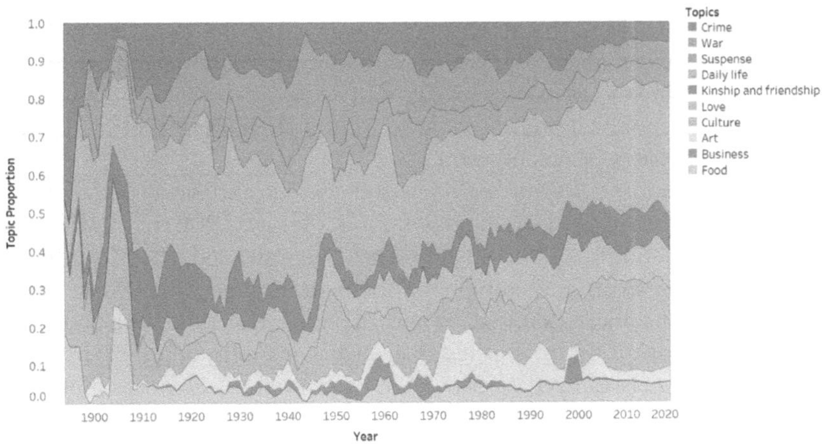

Fig. 3 Proportions of China-related films under specific topics by year

on these more universal subjects, China-related films could invite international audiences to connect with and appreciate everyday life in China. The frequency of these four topics appearing in China-related films has increased during the past 50 years, which stands in sharp contrast to the downward trends seen in the top part of the figure. In addition, the topics of art, business, and food fluctuated significantly in the early years, but their trend has been relatively stable recently. These results suggest that the image of China depicted by foreign films has changed from the violent and conspiratorial one to the tender and cultured one.

Many topics appear in China-related films, ranging from daily life, suspense, to history and culture. Despite the variety of topics, the audience has a preference for specific topics in different periods, such as crime films in the early twentieth century and love films in the twenty-first century. When combined with the historical background, it can be inferred that a country's image, if relatively negative in the world, will become a stage for suspense films. When its economy prospers and society becomes stable, stories about daily life will occur naturally.

6 Sentiment Analysis of China-Related Films

By conducting a sentiment analysis of these data sets, we were able to more directly investigate the evolving portrayals of China in international films. After calculating the average sentiment score of China-related films per year, we were able to chart how this score has changed since the inception of cinema, as shown in Fig. 4.

We applied political and diplomatic factors to analyze the fluctuation of sentiment scores in recent years.

First, the sentiment score before 1900 had an abnormal peak, which was due to the limited number of films. From 1900 to 1949 (the year of the founding of the PRC), China experienced chaotic internal affairs resulting in a fluctuating emotional tone. The valley from 1919 to 1926 was a typical example. When the government of the Republic of China was not long established, warlords constantly fought with each other and the masses lived on the edge of starvation. Hence, China was often depicted in Western films as a suffering and powerless nation. In contrast, the sentiment peaks of 1928–1930 and 1945–1948 were related to the end of tangled warfare among warlords and China's victory in the Resistance Against Japanese Aggression.

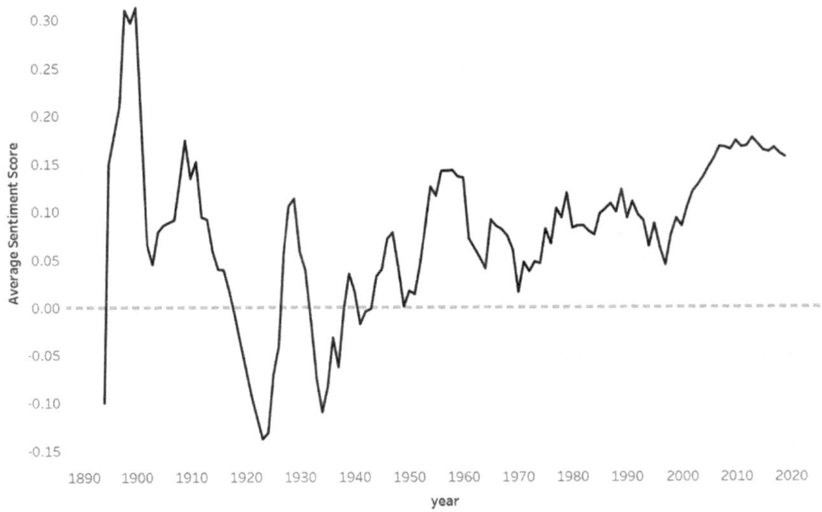

Fig. 4 Average sentiment score of films by year

However, the film is inevitably influenced by the subjectivities of the filmmakers, which can create disparities between cinema and the world it represents. This divide was especially stark during the early 1900s. In films like *Broken Blossoms* (1919), the Chinese were depicted as sickly and indecisive. Though its cause was related to China's waning national power in that period, prejudices against Chinese people were more likely due to the Western anti-Chinese feeling, which could be traced back to the Boxer Uprising and the U.S. implementation of the Chinese Exclusion Act in 1882.

Another typical case occurred during the Resistance Against Japanese Aggression from 1937 to 1945, when the sentiment score of international films was still on the rise in the face of constant domestic wars and poverty. This was because the outbreak of World War II caused the international community to become sympathetic toward China. The image of poor and hard-working peasants in *The Good Earth* (1937), for example, inspired the missionary spirit of salvation. Some scholars believe that the goodwill garnered by *The Good Earth* even won a more favorable Far Eastern policy for China from the U.S. government during World War II, showing interdependence between international media and global politics (Flynn and O'Neill 1993: 57).

After the founding of the PRC, stereotypes gradually became more complex ideological factors and continue to lead to emotional fluctuations. In the 1960s, the U.S. "Red Scare" against the Communist Party spread all over the world, making the PRC's image appear evil, which is also revealed in Fig. 4 (The Vatican 1965: 16). In the 1970s, the friendly interactions between the PRC and the rest of the world, such as the PRC representing China at the United Nations and the establishment of diplomatic relations between the PRC and Western countries, boosted the sentiment score of China-related films, which peaked in 1978.

Then, the Tiananmen Square incident in 1989 impacted the international views of the PRC. The valley in the 1990s was probably related to the incident, as well as the frequent diplomatic friction between the U.S. and the PRC, such as the U.S. linking the PRC's human rights performance to the most-favored-nation treatment in 1993 and bombing the Chinese Embassy in Belgrade in 1999. Due to these political factors, China's positive image of a rapidly growing economy and a prosperous society was not fully reflected in world cinema. It wasn't until 2001, when China acceded to the World Trade Organization, that the sentiment score soared again.

After 2010, the sentiment score declines again, which might be related to the positioning of China by the international community, especially the U.S. Since China overtook Japan to become the world's second-largest economy in 2010 and the Obama Administration began the "Pivot to Asia" strategy in 2012, the post-9/11 honeymoon between the two countries against terrorism was over. The U.S. tended to respond to China's growing national power with both engagement and deterrence (Harris and Trubowitz 2021). It suggests that ideologically driven action plays a crucial role in shaping the national image.

Considering the varying perceptions of China may differ across different political systems, relations with China, geographical locations, and cultural traditions in different countries, we further analyzed China-related films in the U.S., Russia, and Japan. Figures 5, 6, and 7 reflect trends in the number of films made and the sentiment score over time in these three countries. The U.S. has 2,165 films, accounting for 48.9 percent of the data set, while Russia has 23, and Japan has 125.

The three figures show that the U.S. started producing China-related films first and produces them most frequently, while far fewer films about

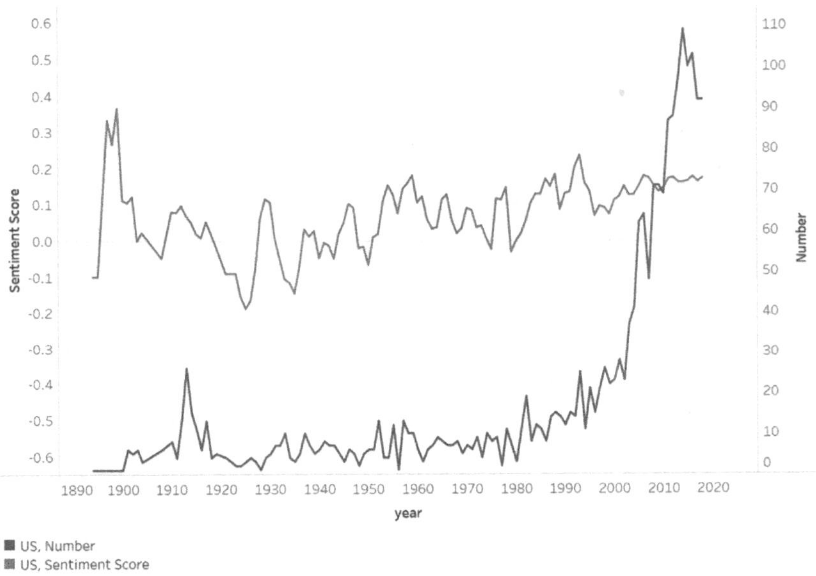

Fig. 5 Number and sentiment score of films by year in the U.S

China are produced in Russia and Japan. The U.S. trend in film sentiment scores and numbers is roughly the same as that of the whole world. Since global trends have been discussed above, they will not be repeated. The U.S. has always had the most influential China-related films, so we mainly discussed Western films, dominated by Hollywood, in the background part. The fact that U.S. films dominate and dictate global trends makes it even more crucial to examine the different sentiment scores in other countries. Thus, we conducted further research on the situations in Russia and Japan.

The sentiment scores of China-related films in the U.S. and Russia are generally the opposite. Around 1996, the sentiment score of U.S. films reached a low point and then continued to rise, showing a V-shaped trend. On the contrary, the Russian films' score peaked in 2000, then continued to decline, reflecting an A-shaped trend. The trends were tethered to the relationship between the U.S. and Russia. Also, they revealed the delicate balance between the PRC and the U.S., and between the PRC and Russia. In the early 1990s, Russia's pro-American diplomatic strategy

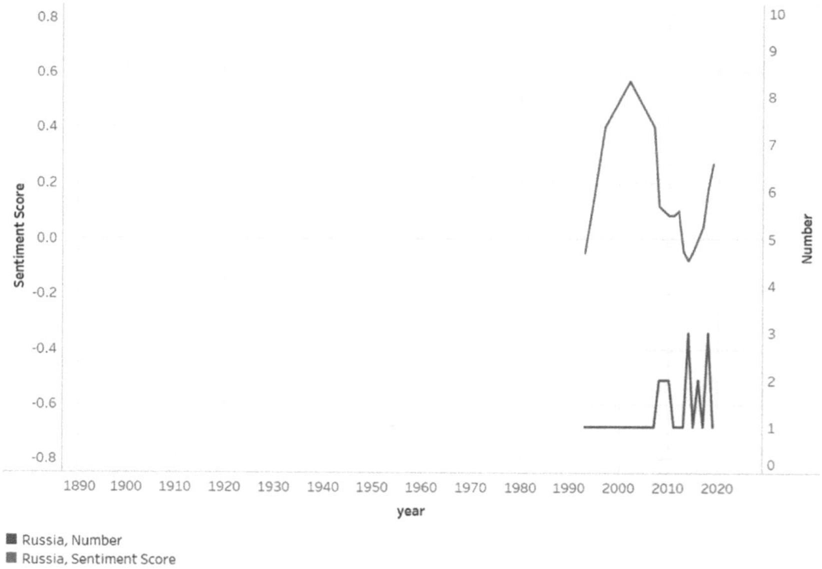

Fig. 6 Number and sentiment score of films by year in Russia

failed. From 1994 to 2000, with the North Atlantic Treaty Organization's eastward expansion and the outbreak of the Kosovo War, Russia's traditional influence in Eastern Europe was largely lost. As a counterbalance, Russia regarded the PRC as an essential diplomatic partner from 1995 to 2005, resulting in the positive attitudes expressed in China-related films produced in the country. The decline in Russia's sentiment score around 2010 may be linked to the global financial crisis of 2008 and the close trade relationship between the PRC and Russia.

Japan's attitude toward China is closely related to Japan's historical origins and the wars between the two countries. After World War II, from the 1950s to the early 1960s, Japanese films maintained a relatively positive emotional view of China. After that, the sentiment score dropped sharply and did not recover until the two countries established diplomatic relations in 1972. During this period, Japan feared the Sino-Soviet Treaty of Friendship and Alliance, the PRC's military strength, and the Communist Party's military threats (He 2009). The sentiment score peaked in the 1980s during the honeymoon period of Sino-Japanese relations and

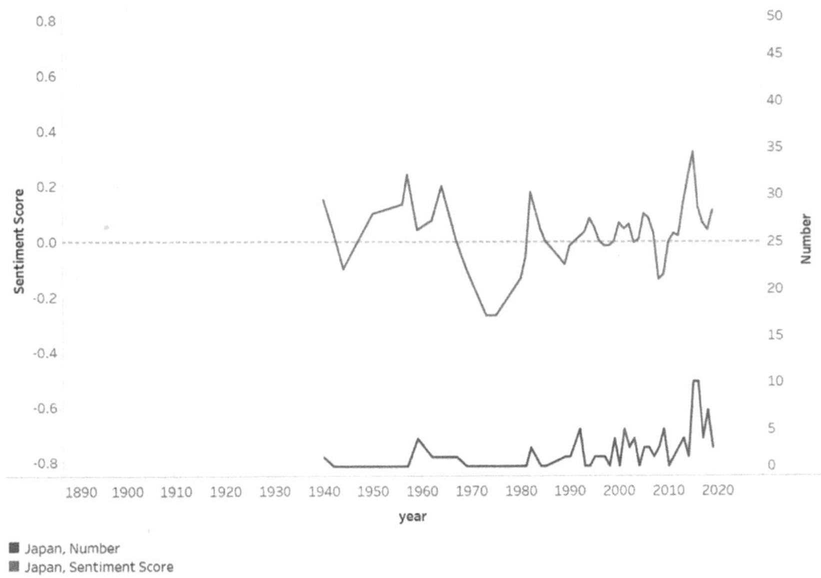

Fig. 7 Number and sentiment score of films by year in Japan

has fluctuated around 0 for the rest of the century. In the twenty-first century, the PRC's economy soared, while Japan's continued stagnation, combined with territorial disputes between the two countries, led to a decline in sentiment score. Since the PRC and Japan have maintained frequent economic and cultural exchanges, Japan's sentiment score has continued to rise since 2010, and the cinematic representations of China in Japan have become diversified as a result.

We further quantitatively examined the economic factors that could potentially influence the tone of films since 1950, as the data of economic variables in the first half of the twentieth century are not available. Based on previous literature (Xie and Page 2013), combined with existing data resources, this chapter proposes the following hypothesis:

Hypothesis 1: After 1950, China's domestic and international economic conditions have positive impacts on the emotional tone of the image in the films.

We applied China's gross domestic product (GDP) to represent China's economic power, and import and export value (IEV), foreign direct investment (FDI), and inbound tourism (IT) to represent international economic communications. All of these variables are collected from the China Statistical Yearbooks. We took the logarithms of GDP, IEV, and FDI, and calculated the three-year moving average of sentiment scores. Due to the difficulty in obtaining early data, the available years for each indicator vary. Starting from the earliest year of each indicator, we conducted a Granger causality test to verify if using the history of these time series could help to predict the emotional tone of China-related films.[3] The results are shown in Table 5.

Model 1 and Model 2 reveal the relationship between fd_lnGDP and fd_SS from 1954 to 2019. Model 1 is significant at a confidence level of 99%, so fd_lnGDP is considered to be the Granger cause of fd_SS. Model 2 is not statistically significant, so the null hypothesis cannot be rejected. The results indicate that China's economic growth is conducive to a positive portrayal of China in international cinema; however, there is not enough evidence to prove that the rise in sentiment score explains the economic growth. Therefore, there is a one-way association between China's economic power and the emotional tone of films.

According to Models 5 and 6, there is also a one-way connection between fd_lnFDI and fd_SS from 1986 to 2019, indicating that a significant increase in foreign direct investment can lead to a rise in the sentiment score at 95% confidence level, but the reverse relationship does not exist. Moreover, Model 3, Model 4, Model 7, and Model 8 show that there is no existence of Granger causality between fd_lnIEV and fd_SS, and also fd_IT and fd_SS. The emotional tone of China-related films is not significantly related to import and export value and inbound tourism.

So far, Hypothesis 1 has been partially verified. China's domestic economic strength positively influences the emotional tone of its image in the film. In terms of the international economic environment, only foreign investment has a positive impact on the tone. The possible reason is that foreign direct investment acts as a weather vane. Investors and

[3] Granger causality test is a statistical test that determines the association between the time series. We conduct the Dick-Fuller test for the unit root test. The related table is not reported here for the sake of space. The results show that the explanatory variables lnGDP, lnIEV, lnFDI (ln refers to natural logarithm) and IT are integrated of order 1, while the explained variable SS is stationary.

Table 5 Results of granger causality tests

Model	*Null hypothesis*	*Time range*	*Chi²*	*p-value*	*Lag length*
1	fd_lnGDP does not Granger cause fd_SS	1954–2019	6.897	0.009***	1
2	fd_SS does not Granger cause fd_lnGDP	1954–2019	0.013	0.909	1
3	fd_lnIEV does not Granger cause fd_SS	1952–2019	2.094	0.148	1
4	fd_SS does not Granger cause fd_lnIEV	1952–2019	0.093	0.760	1
5	fd_lnFDI does not Granger cause fd_SS	1986–2019	6.587	0.037**	2
6	fd_lnFDI does not Granger cause fd_SS	1986–2019	0.582	0.747	2
7	fd_IT does not Granger cause fd_SS	1980–2019	1.897	0.168	2
8	fd_IT does not Granger cause fd_SS	1980–2019	0.071	0.790	2

Note (i) fd_ refers to first difference;
(ii) The lag length is chosen according to final prediction error (FPE), Akaike's information criterion (AIC), Schwarz Bayesian information criterion (SBIC), and Hannan and Quinn information criterion (HQIC);
(iii) ***$p < 0.001$, **$p < 0.01$, *$p < 0.05$

ordinary people who benefit from economic returns would get a good impression of China naturally.

7 Conclusion

By processing word vector technology, LDA topic model, and sentiment analysis, this research has obtained the following conclusions. In general, China's image in world cinema is influenced by its overall national strength, including economic power and diplomatic ability. Meanwhile, Hollywood has been the foremost producer of China-related films and holds a vital role in setting cinematic narratives, topics, and perspectives. Therefore, the relationship between China and the U.S., who owns Hollywood, is particularly critical in all foreign relations. The opinions expressed in Chinese films about China differ according to the historical context within which they were made. Representations will vary depending on major sociopolitical events that bear a global impact.

The image of China in international films can be divided into five stages.

First, before World War II, few films were produced about China. Influenced by China's waning national power and the deep-rooted Orientalism, the Chinese were often imagined as sickly and barbaric in films during this time.

Second, during World War II, topics of war and love were on the rise. Filmmakers began to show the suffering of Easterners and the selflessness of Westerners. The attitudes toward the Chinese in these films turned to sympathy.

Third, due to the change of regimes, the image of China in international films fluctuated greatly between 1945 and 1975. Fears of the Communist Party and the Sino-Soviet alliance caused stereotypes to resurface, and the PRC was portrayed as a scheming entity that sought to rule the world.

Fourth, after 1975, with the thawing of relations between the PRC and other countries, a cinematic focus on daily life, kinship and friendship, and love in China increased. Since the PRC renewed the Open-Door Policy and the economic take-off of Hong Kong and Taiwan, the international community has turned the spotlight on the common Chinese people's lives.

Fifth, since the beginning of the twenty-first century, films related to China have witnessed sharp growth. This is not only because China's increasingly prominent position has attracted international films' attention, but also because China's cultural strength has improved. More films made in China have been exported abroad. In terms of subject matter, most films are related to Chinese culture, daily life, and love, resulting in a high sentiment score. This shift reveals that nowadays, the proportion of China's image influenced by politics is decreasing, and international films present a more approachable, open, inclusive, and positive image of China.

From the barbarian to the schemer to the civilized great power, China's image in international films conforms to these representational trends to an extent. However, it does not entirely accord with reality. As an art product, film does not simply convey reality. It can also distort it. Thus, in the development of China's image, it is evident that China's national strength and its relationship with the outside world significantly shape certain aspects of the image, while the filmmakers' ideology determines the remainder. This image is not the product of such a simple binary distinction but a complex and multi-layered system of influential factors, including national strength, interests, status, and diplomacy.

Besides drawing descriptive conclusions, quantitative analysis can also verify the propositions of cultural theory. Orientalist misapprehensions were especially evident before 1975, when the seemingly bizarre Oriental world portrayed in the film was exploited as the "other" that could best reveal the uniqueness of the West, and the sentiment score showed a relatively negative trend throughout this era. However, with the rise of the Chinese economy since 1978, Orientalism is declining but still hides in several recent films, like Disney's live-action film *Mulan* (2020). Its core concept of "being loyal, brave, and true" is separately picked out from Confucian classics and pieced together, while the Chinese seldom put these three words together. It is more like a constructed spirit by the West than the true belief of the Chinese. Such works will collide with nationalist films exported from China. Although the outcome is unknown, it is sure that Western filmmakers will not ignore Chinese audiences' views since China has grown to be the world's second-largest film market.[4]

According to Said, "culture is a sort of theater, where various political and ideological causes engage one another" (Said 1993: xvi). As a form of soft power, the cinematic image is produced when ideology interacts with social reality and holds great significance for a nation's self-identity. Due to the complexity of factors, it is difficult for us to analyze the mode and degree of this interaction comprehensively. This article mainly examines the impact of China's GDP and foreign direct investment on the tone of China's image, supplemented by the analysis of other factors. We hope to explore the formation mechanism of the national image in future research and provide data support and inspiration for scholars in sociology, international relations, communication studies, and other areas of the social sciences.

[4] See https://www.washingtonpost.com/business/2019/12/30/chinese-film-business-is-doing-unthinkable-thriving-without-hollywood/.

References

Birama, Diakon, and Ute Röschenthaler. 2017. The Chinese presence in the Malian mediascape. *Journal of African Cultural Studies* 29 (1): 96–113.

Boulding, Kenneth E. 1959. National images and international systems. *Journal of Conflict Resolution* 3 (2): 120–131.

Brownell, Susan. 2013. Brand China in the Olympic context: Communications challenges of China's soft power initiative. *Javnost* 20 (4): 65–82.

Canet, Fernando. 2016. Quantitative approaches for evaluating the influence of films using the IMDb database. *Communication & Society* 29 (2): 151–172.

Chung, Hye S. 2006. *Hollywood Asian Philip Ahn and the politics of cross-ethnic performance*. Philadelphia: Temple University Press.

Ding, Sheng. 2011. Branding a rising China: An analysis of Beijing's national image management in the age of China's rise. *Journal of Asian and African Studies* 46 (3): 293–306.

Dodds, Klaus. 2006. Popular geopolitics and audience dispositions: James Bond and the Internet Movie Database (IMDb). *Transactions of the Institute of British Geographers* 31 (2): 116–130.

Flynn, George Q., and William L. O'Neill. 1993. *A democracy at war: America's fight at home and abroad in World War II*. Cambridge: Harvard University Press.

Gramsci, Antonio. 1992. *Prison notebooks*, Trans. A. Joseph, Buttigieg and Antonio Callari. New York, Chichester: Columbia University Press.

Greene, Naomi. 2014. *From Fu Manchu to Kung Fu Panda*. Honolulu: University of Hawaii Press.

Gries, Peter, et al. 2015. Hollywood in China: How American popular culture shapes Chinese views of the "Beautiful Imperialist"—An experimental analysis. *The China Quarterly* 224: 1070–1082.

Harris, Peter, and Peter Trubowitz. 2021. The politics of power projection: The Pivot to Asia, its failure, and the future of American primacy. *The Chinese Journal of International Politics* 14 (2): 187–217.

He, Yinan. 2009. *The search for reconciliation: Sino-Japanese and German-Polish relations since World War II*. New York: Cambridge University Press.

Hegel, Georg W. F. 1975. *The philosophy of fine art*, Trans. F. P. B. Osmaston. New York: Hacker Art Books.

Jervis, Robert. 1970. *The logic of images in international relations*. Princeton, New Jersey: Princeton University Press.

Liang, Yucheng. 2014. The causal mechanism of migration behaviors of African immigrants in Guangzhou: From the perspective of cumulative causation theory. *The Journal of Chinese Sociology* 1 (1): 1–25.

Maags, Christina. 2014. Enhancing China's national image through culture festivals: A case study of China culture years in Europe. *Fudan Journal of the Humanities and Social Sciences* 7 (1): 33–55.

Malcolm, Grant. 2004. *Multidisciplinary approaches to visual representations and interpretations*, ed. Grant Malcolm. Amsterdam, London: Elsevier.

Mamdani, Mahmood. 2005. Good Muslim, Bad Muslim: America, the cold war and the origins of terror. *India International Centre Quarterly* 32 (1): 1–10.

Marchetti, Gina, and Sheldon S. Lu. 2018. *Citing China: Politics, postmodernism, and world cinema*. Honolulu: University of Hawaii Press.

McCombs, Maxwell. 2005. A look at agenda-setting: Past, present and future. *Journalism Studies (London, England)* 6 (4): 543–557.

Mendes, Anna C. and Lisa Lau. 2015. India through Re-Orientalist Lenses. *Interventions* 17 (5): 706–727.

Meyer, Mike. 2006. Pearl of the orient. *The New York Times Book Review*, 23-L.

Monaco, James, and David Lindroth. 2000. *How to read a film: The World of movies, media, and multimedia, language, history, theory.* New York, Oxford: Oxford University Press.

Nye, Joseph S. 1990. *Bound to lead: The changing nature of American power.* New York: Basic Books.

Otterbacher, Jahna. 2013. Gender, writing and ranking in review forums: A case study of the IMDb. *Knowledge and Information Systems* 35 (3): 645–664.

Page, Benjamin I., Julia Rabinovich, and David G. Tully. 2008. How Americans feel about Asian countries and why. *Journal of East Asian Studies* 8 (1): 29–59.

Ramo, Joshua C. 2007. *Brand China*. London: The Foreign Policy Centre.

Said, Edward W. 1993. *Culture and imperialism*. London: Chatto & Windus.

Said, Edward W. 1995. *Orientalism*. London: Penguin.

Su, Wendy. 2016. *China's encounter with global Hollywood: Cultural policy and the film industry, 1994–2013*. Lexington, Kentucky: The University Press of Kentucky.

The Vatican. 1965. *The Courier-Journal* 18 May.

Xie, Tao, and Benjamin I. Page. 2013. What affects China's national image? A cross-national study of public opinion. *Journal of Contemporary China* 22 (83): 850–867.

Zhang, Chang, and Ruiqin Wu. 2019. Battlefield of global ranking: How do power rivalries shape soft power index building. *Global Media and China* 4 (2): 179–202.

Zhu, Hailong. 2019. The change and construction of Chinese national image in 1949–2019. *English Language Teaching* 12 (11): 35.

Zhu, Wuhan, and Siyun Ji. 2018. The discursive construction of the Chinese national image in China Daily's reports on the G20 Summit. *English Language and Literature Studies* 8 (1): 126.

CHAPTER 13

A United Tale of Three Regions: A Century of China on Screen

1 Introduction

Films represent both the film industry and pieces of visual art. The film industry has thrived in mainland China, Hong Kong SAR, and Taiwan, Province of China since it was first introduced to China at the end of the nineteenth century (Lu 1997). The films from the above three regions have developed in different directions and, while they are mainly independent, each region exerts some influence on the others (Tan 2020). The differences and changes in the sociopolitical environments of the three regions have created complex contexts for the films they have produced. The history of film in China began with the Shanghai film industry, which experienced significant growth before 1949. After the founding of the People's Republic of China (PRC) in 1949, the Communist Party of China ruled Chinese mainland and the Nationalist Party of China occupied Taiwan, while until 1997 Hong Kong was a British colony, which explained the reason that the three regions and their films took very different paths. However, with the reforms and the opening up of Chinese mainland, collaboration between the three regions has increased since the 1990s. A golden age for the Chinese film industry is emerging.

The diverse histories and cultures of the three regions have given rise to distinct film styles. However, their films share the same cultural roots and show robust national features. Some scholars have argued that the Chinese have used the Western concept of the nation-state to participate in the international order and to resist the West (Berry and Farquhar

Y. Chen et al., *Machine Learning in Social Science*,
https://doi.org/10.1007/978-981-95-6465-1_13

2006: 2). Therefore, an analysis of China's image as evinced in the films from the three regions may elucidate the process of China's cultural connection with the Western world.

A national image is shaped by both objective and subjective factors. According to Kenneth Boulding (1959), a country's national image represents the amalgamation of its understanding of itself as well as outsiders' view of the nation. Thus, the subjective impression is pivotal to the interpretation of a national image. The cognitive subject belongs to a specific society, and individual impressions must bear the brand of the local culture, as is particularly evident in Hong Kong and Taiwan. As former colonies, Hong Kong and Taiwan were influenced by the states that dominated them. A separation between "self" and "the other" was thus bound to appear in their standpoints vis-à-vis China.

Films can integrate national images into specific plots and pictures, thus denoting one of the most vivid ways to express such cognitive representations. The audience effects model of agenda-setting theory states that media such as films influence audience perceptions; in turn, audience feedback modifies the focus of these media (Erbring et al. 1980; McCombs 2005). In reality, in the era of the Internet, editors of leading Western websites place selected films about/from China on their online platforms, and this selection governs Western audiences' initial view of China. The cinematic portrayals of China subsequently enable a second construction, the outsiders' view of China. The two processes reflect the media's influence on audience consciousness. Understanding the choice of film topics and the expression of ideas facilitates the study of the process through which the Western mind forms its impression of China.

This chapter conducted a comprehensive analysis of China's image in the Western world using big data. In doing so, it covered a century of films produced in the three regions mentioned, thus signifying a novel deconstruction of China's film history; it also represents a pioneering use of context analysis methodology. Traditional film studies have focused on case analysis (e.g., Lu 1997; Li 2016; Yeh 2018), but the conclusions deduced from specific instances cannot guarantee objectivity, generalizability, and comprehensiveness. In this study, the above issues were resolved using the Word2Vec toolkit, LDA topic model, and Google's sentiment analysis model to study the synopses of pre-2019 film plots on the Internet Movie Database (IMDb). A spatiotemporal analysis framework was constructed to explore changes in the conception of China in the content, topics, and sentiments of films from Chinese mainland, Hong Kong, and Taiwan.

2 Background

When describing Chinese films in the past, scholars usually constructed a linear historical narrative to explore a unified and coherent national boundary (Yoshimoto 1991). However, the grand conceptual construct of China actually comprises varied content types such as multiple spoken languages, former colonies, and religious affiliations (Berry and Farquhar 2006). The emergent notion of the Chinese-language film thus transcends the singular nation-state narrative, encompassing all types of local or global cinematic renditions related to the Chinese language (Sun 2016). However, some scholars have argued that viewing Chinese films through the lens of a Western cultural system could cause their "de-China-lization" (Li 2016), which means abandoning Chinese cultural connotation to cater to Western understanding. Chinese films face the challenge of balancing globalization and nationality as they attempt to establish a new subjectivity.

The confrontation between globalization and nationality is particularly evident in Chinese mainland. Since the founding of the PRC, filmmakers have made great efforts to resist foreign cultural invasion. Films have thus become a crucial political component of nationalism (Lu 1997) and a powerful instrument in promoting socialist ideology. Following the launch of reform and opening-up in the late 1970s, a new generation of directors, including Zhang Yimou, described a charming and barbaric East in films such as *Raise the Red Lantern* (1991). Although narratives that showed the eeriness of the East achieved massive success in the West, postcolonialists were highly critical of these renditions (Li and Wang 2009). The situation changed again as China entered the twenty-first century: the economy and the film industry in Chinese mainland soared together. Some films, such as *The Wandering Earth* (2019), combined a Hollywood narrative style and national confidence with mature film technology, expressing the ambition to dominate the international order and successfully constructing a China-centric subjectivity.

A former British colony, Hong Kong's early films followed British practices of live entertainment and included vaudevilles and cabarets (Yeh 2018: 6). The Hong Kong film industry was the first of the three regions to commercialize, producing many comedies and kung fu films in the

1970s, when films starring Bruce Lee became immensely popular worldwide. For instance, movies such as *Way of the Dragon* (1972) were set in a foreign country and represented "ethnic Chinese." They showcased a powerful national character by portraying the development of Chinese kung fu, and attained global fame as they defended Chinese identity. As an urban center representing ideological confrontations, Hong Kong has always avoided politics and prioritized entertainment, which helped the tide of consumerism sweep through its film industry. Nevertheless, consumerism could not dispel the identity-related dilemma of the colonized, and numerous films continued to discuss this issue after Hong Kong's return to the PRC. For example, *Port of Call* (2015) described the integration of Chinese mainland residents into Hong Kong society, showing that this region still sought its identity through the story of "the other."

The portrayal of China is more complicated in Taiwanese films than in films originating from Chinese mainland. As a former Japanese colony, Taiwan belongs to the Chinese mainland-Taiwan-Japan cultural triangle, and its colonial history and postcolonial context have caused an identity crisis (Li and Wang 2009). Homi Bhabha's (1994) postcolonial theory posits that the colonist's culture creates a continued pain in the colony, forming a hybrid culture. Taiwanese filmmakers have validated their identity through just such a cross-cultural construct. Directors such as Hsiao-Hsien Hou and Edward Yang contemplated Taiwan's turbulent history in the 1980s, exhibiting an intense nativeness and discovering a narrative path between Chinese and Western cultures. However, in establishing its nativeness, Taiwan emotionally and culturally distanced itself from the mainland. Films like *Cape No.7* (2008) manifested this de-China-lization and even evoked nostalgia for Japanese culture, revealing the lingering presence of the ghosts of the Japanese colonial period.

Chinese mainland, Hong Kong, and Taiwan share their origins but have taken different paths. Their cultural expressions of China have thus diverged under the joint influence of various factors, including the economy and politics: Chinese mainland has embarked on the socialist path, Hong Kong has an affinity with Great Britain and the U.S., and Taiwan leans toward Japan. Faced with the West, however, all three regions have been forced to demonstrate their distinctiveness as "the other." According to Bhabha (1990: 294; 1994: 34), the problematic boundaries of modernity are sketched out in these ambivalent temporalities of the nation-space. This ambivalence has evoked an irreversible inclination to construct cultural differences that can revise the history of critical theory. Therefore, the trend toward globalization drives the need to grasp the cultural distinctions within a nation. After a long cultural collision with the suzerain state, the former colony generates new power through mimicry and finally achieves cultural hybridity.

As a vital aspect of postcolonialism, numerous ideological and social forces have informed the impression of China expressed in the films of the past 70 years. It is challenging for theoretical studies to accurately compare the discrete features of the films from the three regions and to understand their changes over time. Therefore, using big data analysis and machine learning methods, we explored the transformations observed in the image of China in the films produced in Chinese mainland, Hong Kong, and Taiwan over the last century from a postcolonial theoretical perspective.

3 Data and Methods

Traditional methods using questionnaire surveys cannot accurately measure a country's image, which is diffused through an entire society and entails both subjectivity and universality. However, based on massive content, the current capabilities of unsupervised machine learning open the door to new methodologies. Natural language processing technologies enable the analysis of an extensive range of content and provide a more accurate measure of cultural concepts for social science disciplines.

As the data source, we selected the plot synopses of China-related films from Chinese mainland, Hong Kong, and Taiwan collected via IMDb. Founded in 1990, IMDb is a high-quality international online database of films, providing information including film plots, casts, regions of production and release, ratings, and reviews. As of June 2020, the IMDb collection consisted of 552,366 films. The database has been widely used in scholarly research. For example, researchers have applied statistical models to classify the sentiments expressed in film reviews (Tripathy et al. 2016) and to predict the popularity of future films (Abidi et al. 2020). Film reviews have also been used to study the attitudes of audiences toward elite values (Ridderstrøm 2018) or to explore the politicized role of humor (Ridanpää 2014). New quantitative and qualitative research breakthroughs have been reported using large datasets such as IMDb.

This study used the terms "China" and "Chinese" as keywords to screen pre-2019 film data from the three regions, aiming to determine the image of China. All of the selected films articulated an idea of China for international audiences. Some of the films involved multi-regional collaborations; thus, to avoid duplication, the first region where the film was made was considered the standard of judgment. After removing error values, 1047 relevant films were found: 682 from Chinese mainland, 261 from Hong Kong, and 104 from Taiwan.[1] For historical and political reasons, we mainly compared the films of the three regions between 1949 and 2018. We used web crawler technology to grab titles and plot synopses from IMDb, reflecting the plot and setting of each film. Furthermore, information about each film's region of production and release year was compiled to explore the process of transforming China's image, as well as the factors related to the films' social contexts.

The 1047 films selected from IMDb showed a multidimensional image of China. The quantitative analysis performed in this study endeavored to address three aspects of the main topics of the films from the three regions. We examined their mentions of China or the Chinese people; their specific propensities to treat particular topics; and their positive or negative attitudes in describing China. We used text mining in the analysis because film titles and plot synopses represent unstructured textual data.

First, for the contextual measurement, we used word embedding technology to predict the contexts associated with the term "China." Google's open-source toolkit, the Word2vec algorithm, can turn unstructured textual data into high-dimensional vector data. The similarity between words can be measured, and the context can be predicted by calculating the distance between the high-dimensional vectors.

Second, for topic analysis, films have changed according to the historical development of the different regions. The special relationship between Chinese mainland, Hong Kong, and Taiwan in the past has left the regions with closely related, yet very different, images of China. The films produced in the three regions often feature their preferred topics or events in their descriptions of China, and the LDA topic model can help tease these out.

[1] We also compared the results obtained from IMDb with those from Douban (a cloned version of IMDb and the most popular online movie review website in China) and found that the number of Douban-related films after screening was 1219 from Chinese mainland, 358 from Hong Kong, and 187 from Taiwan. This finding indirectly proves that there exists potential selection bias by IMDb editors and users worldwide.

Third, for sentiment analysis, we applied sentiment analysis to calculate the overall sentiment score of the relevant films from a more abstract perspective. Sentiment analysis entails the use of opinions or emotions (affective states) in the examination, cognition, and inference of subjective texts. The text hints at the varying feelings of different people. Researchers can use the trends that are discerned to analyze the public's views or evaluations on a specific issue using two methods of analysis: the sentiment dictionary can be used to assess the rule matching method and the sentiment classification task can be set up based on the sentiment dictionary and text features.

4 Contexts in China-Related Films

Figure 1 reflects the changes in the number of China-related films from Chinese mainland (navy), Hong Kong (orange), and Taiwan (red) from 1950 to 2020. It illustrates the number of China-related films originating annually from Chinese mainland, Hong Kong, and Taiwan. The number of films produced in Chinese mainland was relatively low for the three decades following the founding of the PRC, possibly due to the immaturity of film technology and the Cultural Revolution. Following China's reform and opening-up, the number of films increased explosively, given the context of a booming economy and the need to build national confidence.

China-related films peaked in Hong Kong and Taiwan in the 1970s and 1990s, respectively, likely due to the cognitive reconstruction of the concept of "China" by their citizens. These periods coincided with turning points in relations between the two regions and the mainland. In 1971, the PRC resumed its lawful seat in the United Nations, prompting people in Hong Kong and Taiwan to pay attention to China's position and build on China's legacy in their films. The Sino-British Joint Declaration that returned Hong Kong to the PRC in 1997 was announced in 1984. Hong Kong, which had been ruled by the UK since 1841, re-examined its relationship with the mainland. This reassessment was directly reflected in films made in Hong Kong, and the number of relevant films increased in the following decade (1985–1995).

To further explore the image of China constructed by films, the Skip-gram algorithm of Word2vec was used to train a 128-dimensional word vector model based on the film plot corpus using "China" as the central word to predict the principal context. Table 1 lists the words with the

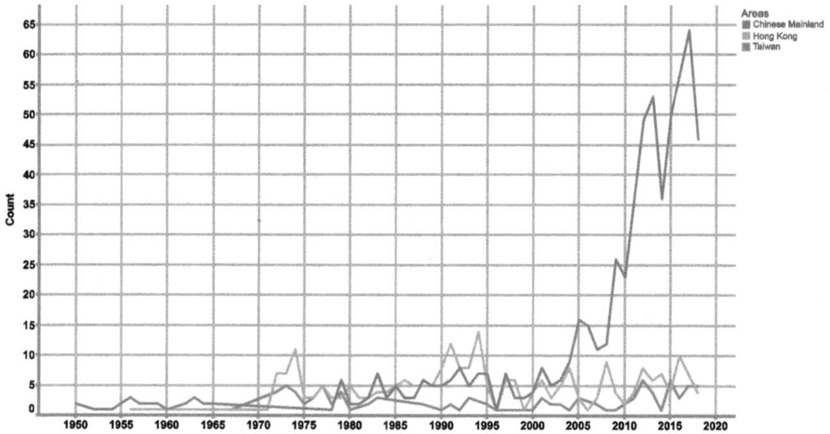

Fig. 1 Number of China-related films from Chinese mainland, Hong Kong, and Taiwan, by year

shortest cosine distance to the central word "China," which are also the words with the greatest similarity to the focal word.

The results of Word2vec reveal that "single" denotes the term closest in films made in Chinese mainland to the focal word. In terms of specific context, "single" is mostly combined with "child" and "mother," revealing the films' preference for family-related settings and their attention to the one-child policy and single mothers. In addition, the contextual terms around the word "China" primarily encompass three categories: first, *politics*, a classification involving mentions of the country's military and foreign policy or words such as "comrade"; second, the category of the *enemy*, referring to opponents of the nation and socialism; and third, the grouping of minorities, signifying issues pertaining to ethnic populations and their governance. The second category focuses on the provincial economy and livelihoods and typically includes words such as "resident," "province," "poverty," "market," and "economic." The third group discusses China's past and future, describing its historical memory and prospective development, and incorporates words like "overcome," "development," and "today."

The scenes of Hong Kong films are more relevant to the administrative status of the metropolitan area and include words like "revolve" and "canton," depicting its past status as a British colony and its current

Table 1 Distance of words to "China"

Chinese mainland		*Hong Kong*		*Taiwan*	
single	0.999557	revolve	0.999557	life	0.999683
cinema	0.999541	story	0.999504	Chinese	0.999647
overcome	0.999537	hit	0.999504	Taiwan	0.999584
resident	0.999527	conflict	0.999492	one	0.999573
province	0.999517	canton	0.999489	family	0.999562
development	0.999505	nothing	0.999489	world	0.999548
sound	0.999492	lead	0.999488	time	0.999538
poverty	0.999492	camp	0.999475	work	0.999534
comrade	0.999490	lonely	0.999468	film	0.999533
truth	0.999489	emerge	0.999467	Taiwanese	0.999521
stand	0.999489	journey	0.999465	Japanese	0.999520
enemy	0.999489	series	0.999465	young	0.999491
market	0.999488	little	0.999461	run	0.999485
minority	0.999485	worker	0.999460	sword	0.999485
freedom	0.999483	follow	0.999458	girl	0.999479
course	0.999482	search	0.999458	old	0.999471
secret	0.999481	lady	0.999458	village	0.999443
today	0.999481	sun	0.999457	war	0.999437
common	0.999479	fortune	0.999456	love	0.999437
economic	0.999475	hero	0.999454	martial	0.999434

standing as an SAR of the PRC. Furthermore, terms such as "hit," "conflict," and "hero" reveal Hong Kong's tradition of making films featuring kung fu, police actions, and bandits. Additionally, the words "worker" and "fortune" encompass the exchange of labor and capital between Hong Kong and the mainland.

The China-related context of Taiwanese films appears to be more oriented toward everyday life than the deliberate positive discourse on China in mainland films, using words such as "life," "family," "work," "girl," "love," and "village." Most of the relevant films focus on cross-strait exchanges, describing individual life experiences in Taiwan and Chinese mainland. The listed words "Chinese" and "Taiwanese" exhibit the distinction drawn between the identities of the people of Taiwan and "the other" character of mainland Chinese citizens. Meanwhile, the term "Japanese" reflects the complex Japanese context in Taiwanese films, and the words "war" and "martial" hint at the significance of military power in Taiwan.

The image of China constructed by these films spans the different perceptions held by the three regions and incorporates the attitudes of IMDb editors in summarizing the content of the films. The synopses of films produced in Chinese mainland include words such as "Comrade," "freedom," and "poverty," the outlines of Hong Kong movies contain terms such as "canton" and "fortune," and summaries of films originating in Taiwan use terms such as "world" and "war." These words to some extent reveal the subjective understanding of the international audience represented by IMDb editors. Influenced by their ideologies, the editors reveal certain sociopolitical tendencies, for instance by emphasizing liberal values and regional sovereignty.

5 Topics of China-Related Films

Although the films of the three regions influence each other to some degree, we postulated that the topics covered by the films would differ due to their respective social backgrounds and political environments. Bringing out these distinctions would facilitate understanding of the three regions' national identities. The LDA topic model was deployed to perform unsupervised cluster analysis based on the corpus of film synopses. After considering the overall length of the text and the model's actual effect,[2] the model with five topics was selected for the analysis.

Table 2 presents the top 20 words with the highest frequency corresponding to each topic after excluding words with no practical significance. Each word in each plot synopsis was assigned to a topic to calculate the distribution of synopses on each topic. Words pertaining to each topic were extracted, and the five topic names were summarized as "kung fu," "kinship and love," "rural and urban," "war," and "crime."

Most of the words in Topic 1 are related to kung fu, with "martial art," and "kung fu," as examples. Other terms include fighting verbs (e.g., "fight" and "win"), fighting objects (e.g., "master," "team," "gang," and "man"), and evaluations (e.g., "great" and "international"). Words such as "evil" and "dragon" are also commonly used in this topic, revealing the indomitable spirit of Chinese people in the face of evil as the "Chinese

[2] The number of topics is a vital parameter for training LDA topic models. In this study, models with 5, 8, 10, and 15 topics were tested. After a comprehensive evaluation of each topic's connotation, topic differentiation, and purposes, five topics were finally chosen to train the model.

Table 2 LDA topic analysis of China-related films

Topic 1		*Topic 2*		*Topic 3*		*Topic 4*		*Topic 5*	
Kung Fu		*Kinship & Love*		*Rural & Urban*		*War*		*Crime*	
art	0.058	life	0.029	village	0.105	Japanese	0.039	Hong	0.076
martial	0.047	love	0.024	modern	0.098	war	0.027	school	0.066
master	0.047	young	0.021	night	0.063	shanghai	0.026	Kong	0.066
fu	0.038	family	0.020	foreign	0.061	force	0.024	student	0.057
team	0.032	live	0.016	road	0.051	army	0.019	police	0.040
gang	0.031	woman	0.015	mission	0.048	help	0.019	order	0.037
great	0.026	city	0.013	say	0.047	work	0.019	kill	0.035
kung	0.025	old	0.012	shot	0.043	town	0.018	brother	0.032
fight	0.022	girl	0.011	hand	0.039	fight	0.018	government	0.023
money	0.022	man	0.009	question	0.039	group	0.018	short	0.022
result	0.019	home	0.008	deadly	0.037	back	0.018	head	0.022
yuan	0.018	series	0.008	body	0.037	leave	0.017	hero	0.021
rural	0.018	friend	0.008	outside	0.030	American	0.017	truth	0.020OK 0
power	0.017	Beijing	0.008	catch	0.029	learn	0.016	doctor	0.020
dragon	0.017	traditional	0.008	train	0.027	couple	0.016	leader	0.019
international	0.017	parent	0.008	local	0.019	return	0.015	murder	0.018
artist	0.017	movie	0.008	back	0.016	end	0.015	teacher	0.016
win	0.016	son	0.008	fail	0.003	red	0.014	officer	0.016

dragon's (i.e., *long*) offspring." Films belonging to this topic are primarily action-oriented, with thrilling stunts at their core to showcase traditional Chinese kung fu. They often involve scenes of fighting, destruction, and rescue. They call for social justice and strike the audience's senses. Representative movies include *Along Comes the Tiger* (1977) from Taiwan and *Kung Fu Quest* (2013) from Hong Kong.[3]

Topic 2, kinship and love, is generally exemplified by words of affection (e.g., "love," "young," "woman," "girl," and "man") and family associations (e.g., "family," "home," "friend," "parent," and "son"). The contexts of this topic relate to everyday life and often focus on the lives of ordinary people, resonating with audiences through emotional

[3] According to the LDA topic model, around 51.1% of the plot synopses of*Along Comes the Tiger* (1977) classify it to Topic 1, ranking first among 1047 films. Around 51.1% of the plot synopses of *Kung Fu Quest* (2010) categorize the film into this topic, suggesting that both movies are representative works of Topic 1.

expression. Typical works include *Rong and Her Mother in Law* (2012), *The Naughty boy Ma Xiaotiao* (2009), and *The Romance beside the Well* (2013).[4]

The representative words for Topic 3, rural and urban, include "village," "modern," "night," "foreign," "road," "outside," "local," "shot," and "catch." These words may reflect the collisions between the rural and the urban, the domestic and the international, and the local and the foreign, capturing their mutual integration and adaptation in the context of modernization. Terms such as "shot," "catch," and "deadly" reveal crime and violence as related to public security or guerrilla warfare. The two highest-rated films on this topic are *Chao Zhou Nu Ba Wang* (1974) and *Vampire VS Vampire* (1989). However, only 28.6% and 22.6% of the words in their plot synopses describe the topic, implying that the topic often appears as the background to the plot rather than as its primary content.

Topic 4 predominantly discusses war through words like "war," "force," "army," and "fight." Topic 4 is often anchored in significant historical military actions, describing scenes of battle, establishing the image of a hero, and reflecting on the disasters and trauma triggered by war. Words alluding to foreigners are also observed, for example, "Japanese" and "American," reflecting the fact that war in Chinese mainland, Hong Kong, and Taiwan often involved Japan and the U.S. Typical works are *Eternal Wave* (2017) and *Black Sun 731* (1988), in the context of the Anti-Japanese War (hereafter referred to as "AJW").[5]

Most words used for Topic 5 relate to police activities and crime, for instance, "police," "order," "kill," "hero," "murder," "officer," and "cop." This topic focuses on the antagonism between the police force and criminal elements, justice and evil, or law and wrongdoing, involving the detection of illegal acts and the fight against gang-related offenses. Meanwhile, "Hong Kong" is the core word of the topic, indicating that it is typically set in Hong Kong society. Films with the highest proportion of plot synopses classified in this topic are all produced in Hong Kong:

[4] According to the LDA topic model, the proportions of the three films belonging to this topic are 85.1%, 79.6%, and 78.6% respectively, and all denote representative works.

[5] According to the LDA topic model, the proportions of the two films belonging to this topic are 51% and 50%, respectively, meaning that both are representative works.

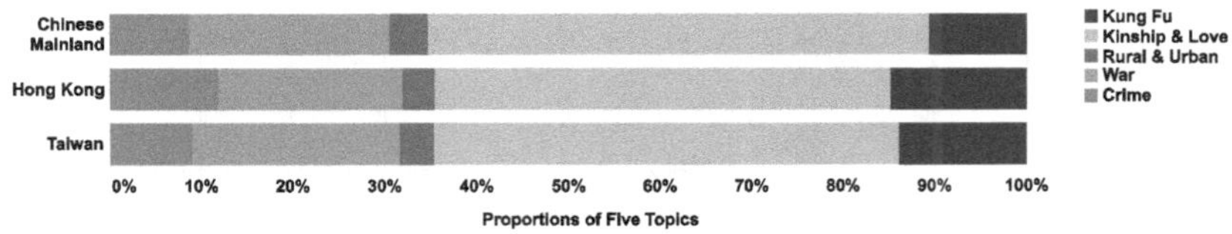

Fig. 2 Proportions of films on the five topics in the three regions

Long Arm of the Law: Part 2 (1987), *Fist of Fury II* (1992), and *Police Story III* (1992).[6]

The average proportion of each topic was calculated by region to further compare the differences between each region's films and the distribution of the five topics between the regions. Figure 2 illustrates that the three regions share elements of the distribution of topics. The topic of kinship and love is the most common context, accounting for more than 50% of the films and denoting the highest proportion of films. The topic of war accounts for nearly 20% of the films, while films on kung fu and crime represent around 10% of the total. The topic of rural and urban has the lowest share in all three regions at less than 5%.

Figure 2 compares the proportions of kung fu (navy), kinship and love (orange), rural and urban (red), war (blue), and crime (green) topics in Chinese mainland, Hong Kong, and Taiwan.

Meanwhile, the distribution of topics in the three regions also differs. To ensure the robustness of the results, we performed an analysis of variance (ANOVA) and least significant difference (LSD) tests on the proportion of film topics in the different regions. The detailed results are shown in Table 3.

First, the proportion of films about kinship and love in Chinese mainland is significantly higher than that in Hong Kong and Taiwan. Films from Chinese mainland on this topic account for 55% of the total, 4% and 5% higher than Hong Kong and Taiwan, respectively. Therefore, mainland Chinese films tend to focus on everyday contexts and depict the feelings, social relations, and destinies of characters at the micro level. There are also significantly more films about rural and urban issues in Chinese mainland and in Taiwan than in Hong Kong, which is more modern and

[6] According to the LDA topic model, the proportions of the three films belonging to this topic are 44.2%, 42.4%, and 37.9%, respectively, and they are all representative works.

Table 3 ANOVA and LSD tests on the proportion of film topics in the three regions

	CM	*HK*	*TW*	*ANOVA-F*	*CM vs HK*	*CM vs TW*	*HK vs TW*
Kung Fu	0.106	0.148	0.138	32.467***	−0.042***	−0.032***	0.010
Kinship & Love	0.547	0.497	0.507	21.658***	0.050***	0.040***	−0.010
Rural & Urban	0.041	0.035	0.038	2.756*	0.006**	0.003	−0.003
War	0.219	0.200	0.226	5.570***	0.018***	−0.007	−0.026***
Crime	0.087	0.119	0.090	26.686***	−0.032***	−0.003	0.029***

Note (i) CM represents the average proportion of relevant topics in Chinese mainland; HK represents the average proportion of relevant topics in Hong Kong; TW represents the average proportion of relevant topics in Taiwan; ANOVA-F represents the F value in the ANOVA test; CM vs HK represents the LSD test between CM and HK; CM vs TW represents the LSD test between CM and TW; and HK vs TW represents the LSD test between HK and TW
(ii) ***$p < 0.01$, **$p < 0.05$, *$p < 0.1$

internationalized. In addition, the long-standing household registration (Hukou) system that divides the mainland Chinese population into urban and rural residents with strikingly different living conditions and social welfare support schemes may have led to more films depicting both the conflicts and the connections between rural and urban areas.

Second, most Hong Kong films focus on kung fu and crime. Table 3 shows that the number of Hong Kong films about kung fu (15%) is significantly higher than that of mainland Chinese films (11%), while the proportion of crime films in Hong Kong (12%) is greater than that in the mainland (9%) and in Taiwan (9%). The film industry in Hong Kong showed increased commercialization and marketization characteristics in its early stages of development, resulting in the flourishing of high-drama action films. Thus, kung fu and crime films in Hong Kong were of high quality and well received both at home and abroad. In addition, as a former British colony and an international port city, the Hong Kong film industry learned from the crime films that were popular in Europe and America.

Third, Taiwan's proportion of war films is around 23%, slightly higher than the percentage of Chinese mainland (22%) and significantly higher than that of Hong Kong (20%). Taiwan has not been the main battlefield of any modern war, but it does show a preference for war stories in its films, especially the AJW. The Taiwanese share China's historical memory of wars as an aspect of their ethnicity. Thus, a group of patriotic filmmakers in Taiwan uphold the ethnic, kinship, and geographical relationships between Taiwan and the mainland through military films set in various modern wars (Chen 2008). However, Japan colonized Taiwan from 1895 to 1945, and many Japanese elements therefore persist in Taiwanese films, partly validating Homi Bhabha (1994)'s postcolonialism.

The above analysis primarily focused on the different proportions of major China-related topics in the cinema of the three regions, examining them at a static level. Films favor different topics at different times, depending on their social contexts, meaning that the topics prevalent at any given point may change. Thus, the topic of war is used as an example to introduce time, allowing for a dynamic comparative analysis.

Some war films are filled with nationalist emotions, stimulating anger toward aggressors, nostalgia for the homeland, and sympathy for the tragic destinies of victims. Some films about war raise crisis awareness, strengthen historical identity, and enhance social unity. Other war-related films construct fantastic images of heroes, showcasing their wise decisions. The three regions commonly give wars significance against the backdrop of historical efforts and the consciousness of these efforts to transform China into a modern nation-state. According to the Western ethos, only countries with such consciousness may claim their rights in the international arena (Duara 1995: 4). Hence, war is a topic suitable for discussion in all Chinese regions. War films are often based on historical facts and influenced by political, diplomatic, and other social characteristics. The distribution of this topic, as shown by the proportion of films dealing with it, was extracted by year. To smooth out extreme values, the moving average was calculated using the proportion values from the previous three years. Missing values and curves are plotted in Fig. 3.

Figure 3 reflects the changes in proportions of China-related films on the topic of war in Chinese mainland (orange), Hong Kong (navy), and Taiwan (red) from 1950 to 2020.

First, victories in war often lead to peaks in the number of war films in certain periods, such as in the 1950s in Chinese mainland. China was able to end its long history of war and establish a new nation after its victory in the AJW in 1945 and the Chinese Civil War (CCW) in 1949. Filled with joy, the people praised their war heroes and their new life, and this pride and happiness were reflected in the films of that era. The proportion of films on this topic rose significantly and peaked at 33% in 1954, right after the Korean Armistice Agreement was signed in the Korean War

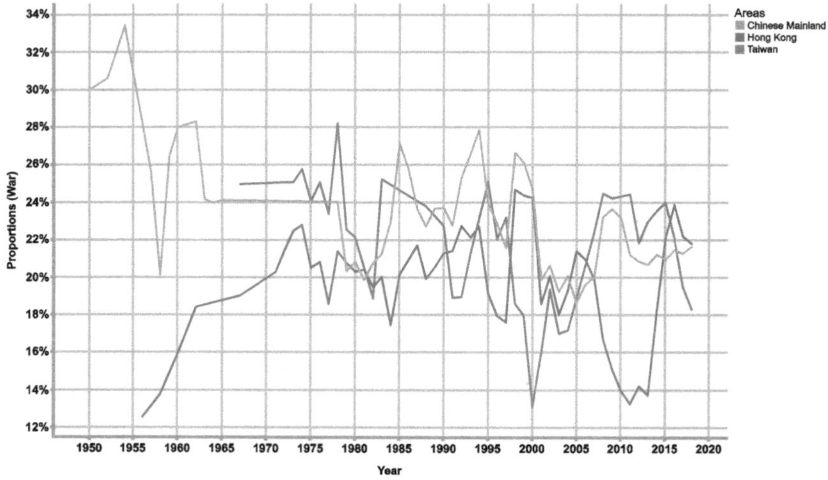

Fig. 3 Proportions of films on the topic of war by year in the three regions

(KW), which the PRC considered a victory. Similarly, the proportion of war films peaked in Chinese mainland around 1985 and 1995, the two years coinciding with the 40th and 50th anniversaries of the victory in the AJW. With the exception of a peak at nearly 24% in 2009, which met the 60th anniversary of the founding of the PRC, the proportion of war films in Chinese mainland has mostly remained below 22% since the beginning of the twenty-first century. During this period, the mainland's economy was growing rapidly, and its films' focus on peaceful development may have led to a reduction in the number of war films.

Second, international circumstances significantly influenced the extent to which this topic was highlighted in the films made in the three regions. War films often fulfill the political function of building nationalist feelings, which may explain the peak achieved by war films in the 1970s in Taiwan, when it confronted diplomatic turmoil. The United Nations ended Taiwan's membership in 1971. In 1972, Japan severed diplomatic relations with Taiwan, triggering a series of severances involving 27 countries. Japan then became the main object of resentment for Taiwan (Li 1997). War films reshaped historical memory at that time. The Taiwanese authorities hoped to relieve people's disappointment and anxiety and rebuild national confidence through such films. The proportion of Taiwanese war films reached its highest level, about 28%, in 1978. In contrast, war films declined to a low level (approximately 20%) in Chinese mainland during the late 1970s and early 1980s, a fact that could be associated with the establishment of diplomatic relations between the PRC, Japan, and the U.S. At that time, Chinese mainland needed to show an attitude of avoidance and restraint toward war.

Third, the war film curve of Taiwan reflects the change in its identity. Taiwan's attitude toward Japan and the AJW reflects these temporal shifts. Lee Teng-hui, who was strongly pro-Japanese and pro-American, was elected Chairman of the Kuomintang (KMT, or Chinese Nationalist Party) in 1990. He visited the U.S. in 1995 as the leader of Taiwan and broadcast his support for Taiwan's independence. From 1995 to 2000, the proportion of war films continued to decline, reaching a low of 13% in 2000. Taiwan's sense of identity with China weakened during his tenure, and the trauma of being colonized subsided. Instead, postcolonial nostalgia was evoked, and a new culture with a pro-Japanese color gained prominence. War films fell out of favor in Taiwan as a result. However, the proportion of war films was relatively high after the turn of the twenty-first century, especially under KMT rule between 2008 and 2016 when it rose to more than 22%. In contrast, the number of war films fell when the Democratic Progressive Party (DPP) came to power and advocated Taiwan's independence (e.g., 2000–2008, 2016–present), perhaps because of the attitude toward the PRC of the administration concerned. Currently, the KMT aspires to normalize relations with the PRC, whereas the DPP advocates for the opposite, calling for a distinctive national identity for Taiwan.

The people of Hong Kong demonstrate relatively little interest in war films compared to those in Chinese mainland and Taiwan, perhaps because Hong Kong films have long been marketized and are less subject to political influences. Few war films have recently been produced in Hong Kong. In 2011, for example, the proportion was only 13%. The reason is presumably that the region's war history is gradually receding, and therefore young audiences have no memory of war.

6 Sentiments of China-Related Films

The sentiment analysis of a text directly reflects the general positive and negative tones of films from the three regions. Figure 4 demonstrates that the general average sentiment scores of films made in the three regions are all greater than 0, implying that China is positively viewed in all three regions. Table 4 shows the results of the ANOVA and LSD tests on the sentiment scores in the three regions. No significant difference is found between the scores of Chinese mainland and Taiwan at 0.16 and 0.17, respectively. Hong Kong has the lowest score (0.03) with far fewer sentiment factors. We calculated the moving averages of the scores for the three regions by year and drew curves to accurately reflect the changes in the sentiments of the films produced in each region (Fig. 5).

Figure 4 compares the average film sentiment scores of China-related films in Chinese mainland (navy), Hong Kong (red), and Taiwan (orange).

Figure 5 reflects the changes in average film sentiment scores of China-related films in Chinese mainland (red), Hong Kong (navy), and Taiwan (orange) from 1950 to 2020.

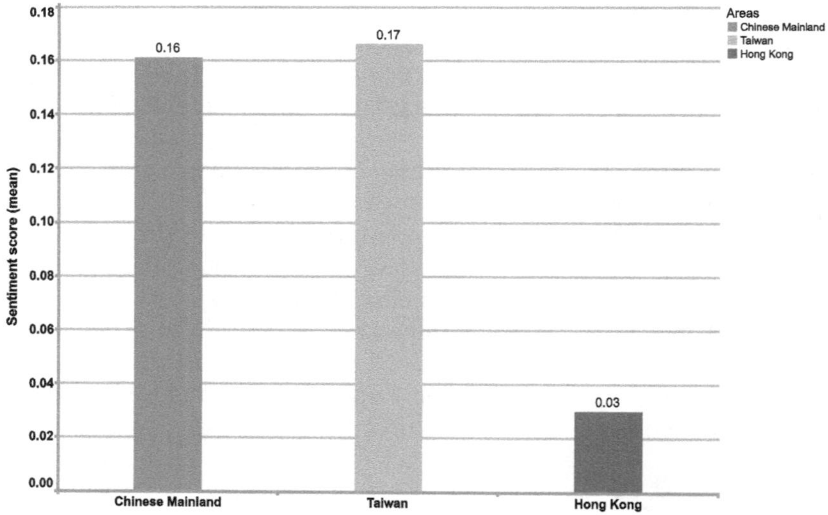

Fig. 4 Average film sentiment scores of the three regions

Table 4 ANOVA and LSD tests on sentiment scores in the three regions

	CM	*HK*	*TW*	*ANOVA-F*	*CM vs HK*	*CM vs TW*	*HK vs TW*
Sentiment score	0.161	0.030	0.166	14.474***	0.131***	−0.005	−0.136***

Note (i) CM represents the average sentiment score in Chinese mainland; HK represents the average sentiment score in Hong Kong; TW represents the average sentiment score in Taiwan; ANOVA-F represents the F value in the ANOVA test; CM vs HK represents the LSD test between CM and HK; CM vs TW represents the LSD test between CM and TW; and HK vs TW represents the LSD test between HK and TW
(ii) ***$p < 0.01$, **$p < 0.05$, *$p < 0.1$

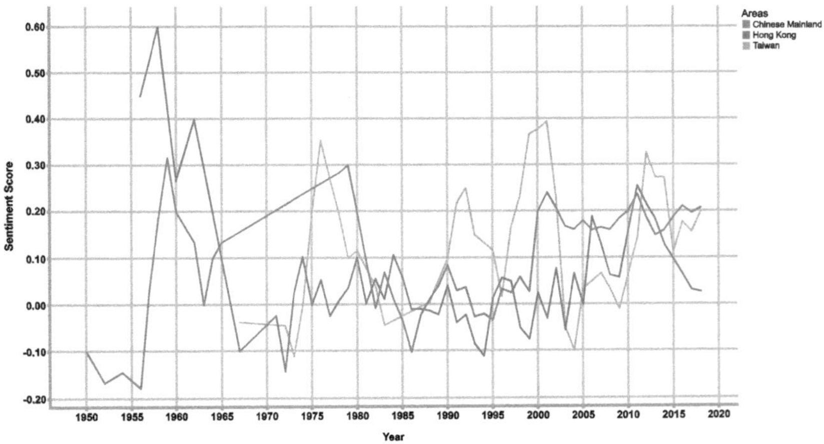

Fig. 5 Film sentiment scores of the three regions by year

The sentiment scores calculated for the films from the mainland are intricately related to China's political and economic circumstances. In the early days of the PRC, film sentiment in Chinese mainland was very low, ranging from −0.2 to −0.1. Subsequently, the political movements from 1958 to 1978 prompted particularly high positive sentiments in mainland films. For example, the films of 1959 reached the highest sentiment score of 0.32, a level almost 1.8 standard deviations above the average value

(0.10).[7] However, as political bubbles such as the Great Leap Forward and the Cultural Revolution burst by the 1980s, the moods depicted in the films also turned sour: the score was −0.01 in 1982 and −0.1 in 1986. Often dubbed "Scar culture," many of the films of this period focused on tragic destinies and traumas, reflecting the distortion of the national spirit and the deterioration of interpersonal relationships. Since the late 1990s, with the return of Hong Kong and Macao and the economic boom, the sentiment score of films produced in Chinese mainland has risen significantly, reaching 0.24, about 1 standard deviation above the mean, in 2001. This increase reveals the exploration of subjectivity by mainland films, which explains their optimistic and nationalist sentiments.

A complex and changeable cross-strait relationship has been forged between Taiwan and Chinese mainland due to their shared historical and political contexts. The early Minnan people who migrated to Taiwan, the Japanese colonial government, and the later Republic of China administration regarded Taiwan merely as a small island on the edge of their territories, deeming it far less critical than the mainland (Berry and Lu 2005: 4). Given the influence of different policies, such contrasts present diverse social and cultural states, as well as varying opinions and sentiments.

Taiwanese films produced during the period of martial law (1949–1987) were anti-Communist but not anti-China, exhibiting a "low-high-low" trend in their sentiment scores. In 1949, the KMT retreated to Taiwan and implemented a strict martial law policy. Films were used as ideological tools for political propaganda and were increasingly controlled by the KMT government. A substantial number of films made in Taiwan in the late 1960s portrayed hatred toward the mainland, and their corresponding sentiment scores were also very negative. For example, the scores from 1967 to 1974 were all lower than 0. In the mid-1970s, the focus of Taiwan-made films shifted from an anti-Communist to an anti-Japanese stance because of the diplomatic turmoil at the time. Resentment over the severance of diplomatic relations with Japan was expressed through the memory of the victory in the AJW, which created the growing sentiment toward China seen during this period, reaching 0.35 in 1976, approximately 1.5 standard deviations higher than Taiwan's annual average score. The sentiment scores declined in the late 1970s,

[7] The means and standard deviations here are calculated based on the smoothed time series, which differs from the means calculated based on films.

and their low values continued into the 1980s, reaching a low of −0.04 in 1983. Taiwan's film industry began to produce anti-Communist films such as *Message to Compatriots in Taiwan* (1979) as it constructed a cultural orthodoxy in the context of the mainland's Taiwan policy.

The KMT government announced the end of martial law in 1987. The same year, the isolation of the two sides of the strait ended. The sentiment scores rose rapidly immediately after the period of martial law (1987–1990), reaching a local peak of 0.25 in 1993, almost 1 standard deviation above the mean, reflecting both sides' desire to communicate. The Taiwanese could visit relatives on the mainland and see the thus-far imagined China. The higher sentiment scores of Taiwanese films in the late 1980s to the early 1990s may partly be attributable to this ability. After martial law ended, cinema no longer had the power to construct its version of China's reality; rather, it instinctively revealed Taiwanese feelings.

Since the 1990s, the emotional changes noted in Taiwanese films have been closely tied to the region's power politics. Cross-strait relations fell to a freezing point in 1995 following Lee Teng-hui's remarks on Taiwan's independence. The 1995–1996 Taiwan Strait Crisis made the situation even tenser, which explains that the sentiment scores of Taiwanese films related to China touched a nadir of only 0.02 in 1996. However, after the crisis, the sentiment score of Taiwanese films rose sharply, holding at about 0.38 from 1999 to 2001. In 2000, the DPP came to power for the first time, and Chen Shui-bian was elected Taiwan's leader. He reiterated Taiwan's independence, as well as carrying out several de-China-lization policies such as constitutional reform, corresponding to the downward trend of the sentiment scores in that period. The result is evident in the downward trend of film sentiment scores from 2001 to 2004, which reached a low of −0.1 in 2004. Then, in 2008 the KMT candidate, Ma Ying-jeou, was elected Taiwan's leader. At the same time as he promoted a peaceful exchange between Taiwan and the mainland based on the 1992 Consensus, from 2009 the sentiment score rose, peaking at 0.33 in 2012. Tsai Ing-Wen (member of the DPP) has been in power since 2016 and has stoked hostility between the two sides of the strait. Consequently, the moods of the films show a downward trend again, even as the overall sentiment remains positive.

Hong Kong and the mainland have made different journeys and developed distinct social environments, creating separate emotional cognitions and cultural expressions. This separation is reflected in Hong Kong films, in which sentiment sometimes moves in the opposite direction to that of the mainland. Hong Kong's economy was booming in the 1960s and 1970s, while the opposite was true of the political and fiscal environment on the mainland. Some Hong Kong leftists launched an armed uprising against the British colonial government in 1967, but this drive gave rise to Hong Kong's aversion to nationalist ideology. It may have contributed to the negative sentiments toward China from 1967 to 1974, with sentiment scores below 0. The PRC and the UK issued a joint declaration in 1984, agreeing to the return of Hong Kong's sovereignty to the PRC in 1997. The significant changes they were facing caused anxiety among Hong Kong people. In the words of author Leung Ping-kwan (2012: 243), "what most people worried about in the 1980s was losing their existing way of life and the obliteration of the existing culture." This assertion may explain the emotional low points registered in Hong Kong films from 1987 to 1995, most of whose values were negative, with a low of −0.11 in 1994. The increasingly frequent exchanges and growing cooperation with the mainland after the turn of the century led to progressively more positive feelings toward China in Hong Kong films. During this time the sentiment score rose, reaching 0.25 in 2011. However, the mood turned negative again because of political protests such as Occupy Central with Love and Peace, and in 2018 the sentiment score was just 0.03.

The above analysis, to some extent, showed that there are many factors influencing the China-related emotions articulated in the films of the three regions, although our aim was not to establish clear and robust causality. Among these factors, the relationship between the three regions is the most significant, followed by the economic and social environments. In this sense, the image of China is not merely a cultural concept; it is also greatly influenced by politics. Economic and social factors may also determine the sentiments expressed in films. The amplification of national strengths in periods of economic optimism and the resulting relaxed social environment represent ideal conditions for the proliferation of the arts, which shift from their reliance on the West to focus on indigenous expressions with a positive mindset.

7 Conclusion

This chapter presents a panoramic view of China (in the West) through a century of films from Chinese mainland, Hong Kong, and Taiwan from the perspective of postcolonialism. It did so by adopting machine learning methods (word embedding technology and LDA topic model) to explore the transformations observed in the image of China in films produced in the three regions over the last 100 years. The discrete historical contexts of the three regions have led to the construction of three distinct societies, even though all are rooted in Chinese culture. These social existences are articulated as divergent cultural characteristics in the films of the three regions, which convey different images of China to the international community. Their manifestations of China and Chinese culture have also transformed in tandem with the major historical events that the three regions have experienced over the last century.

The image of China is positive and realistic in films produced in Chinese mainland, and the number of such films is correlated with China's economic and political circumstances. For example, explosive growth may be observed in the number of films produced in China in periods of social stability and economic prosperity such as the twenty-first century. In addition, most contexts in which the word "China" appears in mainland films are related to the country's historical memory and future development. The sentiment scores of mainland films also correspond to the times. Greater optimism may be noted in films made during the Cultural Revolution, echoing political demands, and after the turn of the twenty-first century, as a natural expression of improved living standards and rising morale. Conversely, low moods were depicted in films made during the 1980s, a period of recovery from the traumas of the Cultural Revolution.

In Taiwan-made films, China's image is ambiguous and changeable, and the perspective is more individual than the standpoint of the mainland. The number of films produced in Taiwan fluctuates slightly, but remains relatively low compared to the number of films produced in mainland and Hong Kong. Taiwanese films primarily focus on personal topics, stories that reveal the changing times. In particular, Japanese and war elements proliferate in Taiwan-produced films, reflecting the persistent influence of Japanese colonization on Taiwanese society. In terms of sentiment, Taiwanese films are influenced by politics. Their sentiment scores related to China touched nadirs at important historical moments, such as the island losing its membership of the United Nations in 1972 and Lee Teng-hui's visit to the U.S. in 1995.

Hong Kong films showcase China through its traditions and international elements. Hong Kong was the first of the three regions to commercialize its films and achieve worldwide success. Consequently, the number of films produced in Hong Kong peaked between the 1970s and the 1990s. Subsequently, Hong Kong film production began to decline due to the boom in the mainland Chinese film industry and the rise in co-productions. Hong Kong-made films typically transcend reality, focusing on kung fu and crime, combining elements of traditional Chinese culture with Hollywood business models, and expressing the unyielding character of the Chinese people. Nevertheless, the sentiment scores of Hong Kong films are influenced by political events, revealing public confusion about the erstwhile colony's identity and future after its return to China. Sentiment scores increased after the beginning of the current century but have dropped again because of the political turmoil of recent years.

The results of our analysis of the content, topics, and sentiments in the films of the three regions reveal that political, economic, cultural, and ideological factors combine to influence China's image in the West. Cinema is a cultural product, and culture is both a practice and a system of symbols and meanings (Sewell 2005: 160–161). The reality is distorted by the consciousness of creators when films reflect society. In addition, truth and falsehood cannot be defined via simple binary distinctions: they are complex, multi-layered, and contextual systems influenced by national strengths and diplomacy. The vast increase in China's national strength has made filmmakers in the three regions increasingly eager to hone their image of China and spread local awareness of change in the West through their films.

The results of the quantitative analyses also validate some of the theories outlined in Sect. 2 of this chapter, particularly postcolonialism. In the 1980s, mainland films experienced a period of emotional depression because of the historical introspection of their directors, but they also offered the West an opportunity to understand Chinese mainland. Numerous Japanese elements persist in Taiwanese films, revealing the region's close relationship with its colonial history. Likewise, Hong Kong films demonstrate a cultural attachment to the suzerain state similar to that of Taiwanese films. To echo Bhabha's (1994) concepts, Hong Kong and Taiwan represent regions where multiple cultures congregate, allowing intercultural communications to occur in a third space and construct a new intersubjectivity.

However, some limitations merit attention. First, it is necessary to briefly acknowledge the status quo of the three regions' film industries. Films produced in Hong Kong and Taiwan have recently distanced themselves from those made on the mainland. For example, no Chinese-language films, whether local or mainland productions, achieved a top

10 box office ranking in either region in 2019. Conversely, 8 of the top 10 mainland films were locally made, reflecting the boom in the mainland Chinese film industry and the decline of Hong Kong and Taiwanese films. Some mainland films have succeeded locally but have failed to replicate their success in Taiwan, Hong Kong, and overseas markets, perhaps because of political factors or a lack of openness and inclusiveness. Second, classification-related difficulties prevented us from evaluating the features of co-productions.

Nevertheless, in spite of the drawbacks, this chapter makes several contributions to the literature. First, its methodology contributes to cultural research in the social sciences. It directs cultural studies away from the analysis of micro and individual cases to large-scale cultural data. The joint use of three quantitative methods means that the results are more comprehensive, and the features of the three regions' cultures are more objective and accurate than conclusions drawn from single cultural phenomena. Thus, this chapter better reflects social reality at the macro level. Second, the findings of this chapter increase understanding of the relationship between the three regions, a relationship that changed dramatically in the second half of the past century. Knowledge of the similarities and idiosyncrasies in the respective cultures of the three regions is not only useful for a deeper understanding of the distinctive development process of Chinese culture, but also helps to clarify the regions' ethnic, cultural, and emotional connections, which go beyond politics. Finally, the results of this chapter show that the image of China in the West as it is portrayed in movies is a combination of its self-portrayal and selection by IMDb editors and users worldwide who all have their own tastes and ideologies.

References

Abidi, Syed Muhammad Raza, et al. 2020. Popularity prediction of movies: From statistical modeling to machine learning techniques. *Multimedia Tools and Applications* 79 (47): 35583–35617.

Berry, Chris, and Feii Lu. 2005. *Island on the edge: Taiwan new cinema and after.* Hong Kong University Press.

Berry, Christopher J., and Mary Ann Farquhar. 2006. *China on screen: Cinema and nation.* Columbia University Press.

Bhabha, Homi K. 1990. *Nation and narration.* Routledge.

Bhabha, Homi K. 1994. *The location of culture.* Routledge.

Boulding, Kenneth E. 1959. National Images and International Systems. *Journal of Conflict Resolution* 3 (2): 120–131.
Chen, Feibao. 2008. History of Taiwanese Film. Beijing: China Film Press (In Chinese).
Duara, Prasenjit. 1995. *Rescuing history from the nation: Questioning narratives of modern China*. University of Chicago Press.
Erbring, Lutz, et al. 1980. Front-page news and real-world cues: A new look at agenda-setting by the media. *American Journal of Political Science* 24 (1): 16–49.
Leung, Ping-kwan. 2012. *Ten essays on Hong Kong culture*. Hangzhou: Zhejiang University Press (In Chinese).
Li, Daoxin. 2016. Subjectivity, integrity and concretization in the study of Chinese film history. *Literature & Art Studies* (8): 82–92 (In Chinese).
Li, Tianduo. 1997. *Taiwanese films, society, and history*. Taipei: Asiapac Books (In Chinese).
Li, Xiaoling, and Xiaomei Wang. 2009. Criticism of Chinese postcolonial film criticism. *Social Sciences in Yunnan* (2): 142–145 (In Chinese).
Lu, Sheldon H. 1997. *Transnational Chinese cinemas: Identity, nationhood, gender*. Honolulu: University of Hawaii Press.
McCombs, Maxwell. 2005. A look at agenda-setting: Past, present and future. *Journalism Studies (London, England)* 6 (4): 543–557.
Ridanpää, Juha. 2014. "Humour is serious" as a geopolitical speech act: IMDB film reviews of Sacha Baron Cohen's *The Dictator*. *Geopolitics* 19 (1): 140–160.
Ridderstrøm, Helge. 2018. Class concerns in a heritage setting: Viewers' responses to Downton Abbey on IMDb. *Series—International Journal of TV Serial Narratives* 4 (2): 91–101.
Sewell Jr, William H. 2005. *Logics of history: Social theory and social transformation*. Chicago; London: University of Chicago Press.
Sun, Shaoyi. 2016. Chinese-language film or Chinese cinema? review of an ongoing debate in the Chinese mainland. *Journal of Chinese Cinemas* 10 (1): 61–66.
Tan, Qiuwen. 2020. "Bifurcated history" and rewriting Chinese film history. *Film Art* (2): 149–154 (In Chinese).
Tripathy, Abinash, Ankit Agrawal, and Santanu Kumar Rath. 2016. Classification of sentiment reviews using n-gram machine learning approach. *Expert Systems with Applications* 57: 117–126.
Yeh, Emilie Yueh-yu. 2018. *Early film cultures in Taiwan, Hong Kong, and Republican China: Kaleidoscopic histories*. University of Michigan Press.
Yoshimoto, Mitsuhiro. 1991. The difficulty of being radical: The discipline of film studies and the postcolonial world order. *Boundary 2: An International Journal of Literature and Culture* 18 (3): 242–257.

Appendix: Code

This appendix contains basic Python code for the key analytical methods discussed in the book, organized into two parts.

The first part demonstrates regression and classification modeling using the California Housing and Iris datasets, including model training, evaluation, and SHAP-based interpretability analysis.

The second part focuses on text modeling with the Text8 corpus, demonstrating the implementation of Word2Vec for word embeddings and LDA for topic modeling.

Y. Chen et al., *Machine Learning in Social Science*,
https://doi.org/10.1007/978-981-95-6465-1

Regression and Classification Modeling

In [1]:

```
# Install necessary Python libraries using pip
# pip install scikit-learn pandas matplotlib numpy xgboost shap
```

In [2]:

```
# --- Core Libraries ---
import pandas as pd
import numpy as np
import matplotlib.pyplot as plt

# --- Scikit-learn Modules for Regression ---
from sklearn.model_selection import train_test_split
from sklearn.linear_model import LinearRegression, Ridge, Lasso, BayesianRidge
from sklearn.tree import DecisionTreeRegressor
from sklearn.ensemble import RandomForestRegressor, GradientBoostingRegressor
from sklearn.svm import SVR
from xgboost import XGBRegressor  # XGBoost regressor
from sklearn.metrics import mean_squared_error, r2_score
from sklearn.datasets import fetch_california_housing
from sklearn.preprocessing import StandardScaler

# --- Scikit-learn Modules for Classification ---
from sklearn.ensemble import RandomForestClassifier
from sklearn.tree import DecisionTreeClassifier
from sklearn.metrics import accuracy_score, precision_score, recall_score, f1_score
from sklearn.metrics import confusion_matrix
from sklearn.datasets import load_iris

# --- SHAP (SHapley Additive exPlanations) for Model Explainability ---
import shap
```

In [3]:

```
# --- 1. REGRESSION TASK: CALIFORNIA HOUSING PRICES ---

# Load the California Housing dataset
california = fetch_california_housing()
california_df = pd.DataFrame(data=california.data, columns=california.feature_names)
california_df['MedHouseVal'] = california.target
california_df.head(5)
```

Out[3]:

	MedInc	HouseAge	AveRooms	AveBedrms	Population	AveOccup	Latitude	Longitude	MedHouseVal
0	8.3252	41.0	6.984127	1.023810	322.0	2.555556	37.88	-122.23	4.526
1	8.3014	21.0	6.238137	0.971880	2401.0	2.109842	37.86	-122.22	3.585
2	7.2574	52.0	8.288136	1.073446	496.0	2.802260	37.85	-122.24	3.521
3	5.6431	52.0	5.817352	1.073059	558.0	2.547945	37.85	-122.25	3.413
4	3.8462	52.0	6.281853	1.081081	565.0	2.181467	37.85	-122.25	3.422

In [4]:
```python
# Prepare data for modeling
X = california.data
y = california.target
# Split the data into training (70%) and testing (30%) sets
X_train, X_test, y_train, y_test = train_test_split(X, y, test_size=0.3, random_state=42)
scaler = StandardScaler()
X_train = scaler.fit_transform(X_train)
X_test = scaler.transform(X_test)
# Define a dictionary of regression models to evaluate
models = {
    "Linear Regression": LinearRegression(),
    "Ridge Regression": Ridge(alpha=1.0),
    "Bayesian Ridge": BayesianRidge(),
    "Decision Tree": DecisionTreeRegressor(random_state=42),
    "Random Forest": RandomForestRegressor(n_estimators=100, random_state=42),
    "SVR": SVR(kernel='rbf', C=100, gamma=0.01, epsilon=0.2),
    "Gradient Boosting": GradientBoostingRegressor(n_estimators=100, random_state=42),
    "XGBoost": XGBRegressor(n_estimators=100, random_state=42)
}

# Create an empty list to store results
results = []
for name, model in models.items():
    print(f"Training {name}...")
    model.fit(X_train, y_train)
    y_pred = model.predict(X_test)
    mse = mean_squared_error(y_test, y_pred)
    r2 = r2_score(y_test, y_pred)

    results.append({
        'Model': name,
        'R²': round(r2, 4),
        'MSE': round(mse, 4)
    })
results_df = pd.DataFrame(results)

# Sort the DataFrame by R² in descending order
results_df = results_df.sort_values(by='R²', ascending=False)
results_df
```

```
Training Linear Regression...
Training Ridge Regression...
Training Bayesian Ridge...
Training Decision Tree...
Training Random Forest...
Training SVR...
Training Gradient Boosting...
Training XGBoost...
```

Out[4]:

	Model	R^2	MSE
7	XGBoost	0.8386	0.2118
4	Random Forest	0.8044	0.2567
6	Gradient Boosting	0.7803	0.2883
5	SVR	0.6587	0.4480
3	Decision Tree	0.5983	0.5273
0	Linear Regression	0.5958	0.5306
1	Ridge Regression	0.5958	0.5305
2	Bayesian Ridge	0.5958	0.5305

In [5]:
```
# --- Model Explainability with SHAP (for the best model: XGBoost) ---
shap.initjs()
best_model = models["XGBoost"]
explainer = shap.Explainer(best_model)
shap_values = explainer(X_test)

# Shows the mean absolute SHAP value for each feature
shap.summary_plot(shap_values, feature_names=california.feature_names, plot_type="bar")
# Shows the SHAP value for every sample (dot) for each feature
shap.summary_plot(shap_values, feature_names=california.feature_names)
```

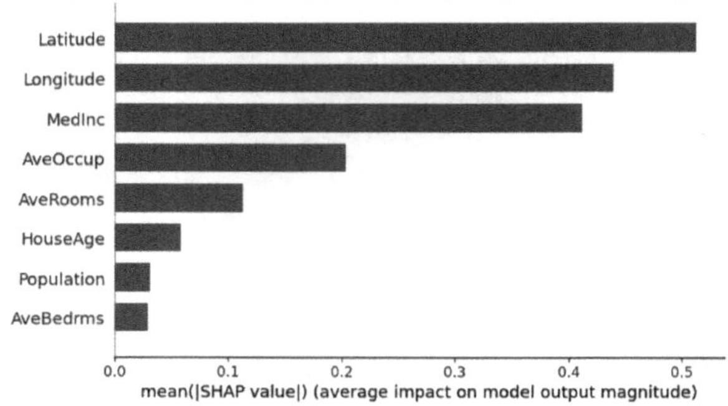

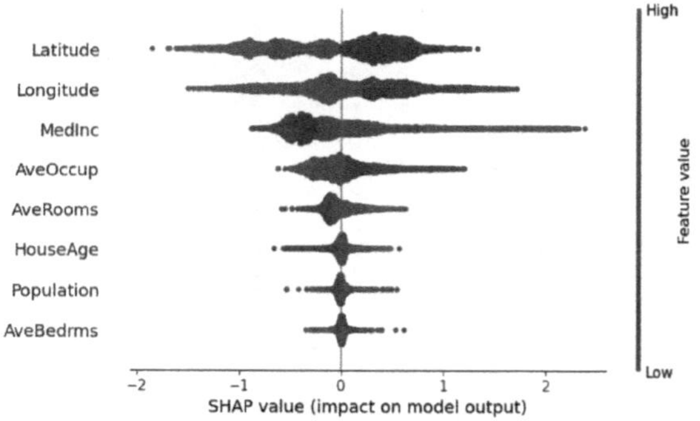

In [6]:
```
# --- 2. CLASSIFICATION TASK: IRIS DATASET ---
iris = load_iris()
iris_df = pd.DataFrame(data=iris.data, columns=iris.feature_names)
iris_df['target'] = iris.target
iris_df['species'] = iris_df['target'].map(lambda x: iris.target_names[x])
iris_df.head(5)
```

Out[6]:

	sepal length (cm)	sepal width (cm)	petal length (cm)	petal width (cm)	target	species
0	5.1	3.5	1.4	0.2	0	setosa
1	4.9	3.0	1.4	0.2	0	setosa
2	4.7	3.2	1.3	0.2	0	setosa
3	4.6	3.1	1.5	0.2	0	setosa
4	5.0	3.6	1.4	0.2	0	setosa

In [7]:
```
# Split the data (70% train, 30% test)
X = iris.data
y = iris.target
X_train, X_test, y_train, y_test = train_test_split(X, y, test_size=0.3, random_state=42)

# --- Model 1: Decision Tree Classifier ---
clf_DT = DecisionTreeClassifier(random_state=42, max_depth=3)
clf_DT.fit(X_train, y_train)

y_pred_DT = clf_DT.predict(X_test)
# Calculate metrics
accuracy_DT = accuracy_score(y_test, y_pred_DT)
precision_DT = precision_score(y_test, y_pred_DT, average='macro')
recall_DT = recall_score(y_test, y_pred_DT, average='macro')
f1_DT  = f1_score(y_test, y_pred_DT, average='macro')
cm_DT = confusion_matrix(y_test, y_pred_DT)
print('Decision Tree Classifier:')
print(f"Accuracy:{accuracy_DT:.4f}")
print(f"Precision:{precision_DT:.4f}")
print(f"Recall:{recall_DT:.4f}")
print(f"F1-score:{f1_DT:.4f}")
print(cm_DT)
print("\n")

# --- Model 2: Random Forest Classifier ---
clf_RF = RandomForestClassifier(n_estimators=10, random_state=42)
clf_RF.fit(X_train, y_train)

y_pred_RF = clf_RF.predict(X_test)
# Calculate metrics
accuracy_RF = accuracy_score(y_test, y_pred_RF)
precision_RF = precision_score(y_test, y_pred_RF, average='macro')  # 多分类用 macro
recall_RF = recall_score(y_test, y_pred_RF, average='macro')
f1_RF  = f1_score(y_test, y_pred_RF, average='macro')
cm_RF = confusion_matrix(y_test, y_pred_RF)
print('Random Forest Classifier:')
print(f"Accuracy:{accuracy_RF:.4f}")
print(f"Precision:{precision_RF:.4f}")
print(f"Recall:{recall_RF:.4f}")
print(f"F1-score:{f1_RF:.4f}")
print(cm_RF)
```

```
Decision Tree Classifier:
Accuracy:1.0000
Precision:1.0000
Recall:1.0000
F1-score:1.0000
[[19  0  0]
 [ 0 13  0]
 [ 0  0 13]]


Random Forest Classifier:
Accuracy:1.0000
Precision:1.0000
Recall:1.0000
F1-score:1.0000
[[19  0  0]
 [ 0 13  0]
 [ 0  0 13]]
```

In [8]:
```
# --- SHAP Explainability for Classification (Random Forest) ---
shap.initjs()
explainer = shap.Explainer(clf_RF)
shap_values = explainer(X_test)
shap.summary_plot(shap_values, feature_names=iris.feature_names,
    class_names=iris.target_names,plot_type="bar")
```

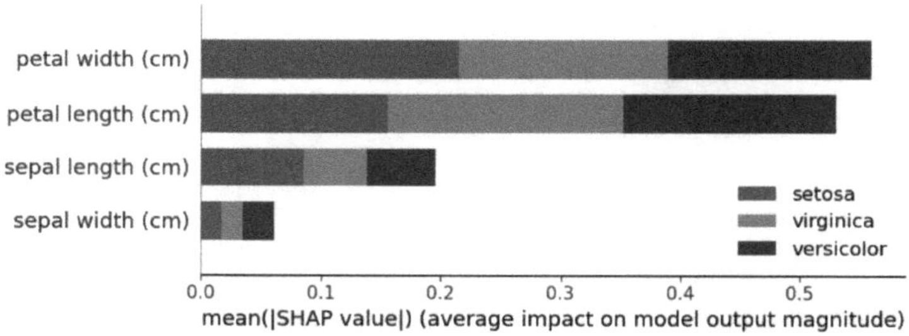

Text Modeling

In [1]:
```
# Install necessary Python libraries using pip
#pip install gensim nltk
```

In [2]:
```
import gensim
from gensim import corpora, models, downloader
from gensim.utils import simple_preprocess
from gensim.models import Word2Vec, LdaModel
from gensim.corpora import Dictionary
from gensim.models.coherencemodel import CoherenceModel

import nltk
from nltk.corpus import stopwords
import matplotlib.pyplot as plt
import pandas as pd

# --- Prepare Stopwords ---
# Download the 'stopwords' corpus from NLTK. This is a one-time download.
# nltk.download('stopwords')
```

In [3]:
```
# --- Load Dataset (Word2Vec & LDA) ---
# Download the 'text8' dataset: a cleaned text from Wikipedia.
print("Downloading 'text8' dataset (this may take a minute)...")
dataset = gensim.downloader.load('text8')
documents = list(dataset)
print(f"Loaded {len(documents)} sentences/documents from text8.")
# Show the first two sentences to see the data format
# use [:10] to get only the first 10 words
print(f"Doc 0: {documents[0][:10]}")
print(f"Doc 1: {documents[1][:10]}")
```

```
Downloading 'text8' dataset (this may take a minute)...
Loaded 1701 sentences/documents from text8.
Doc 0: ['anarchism', 'originated', 'as', 'a', 'term', 'of', 'abuse', 'first', 'used', 'against']
Doc 1: ['reciprocity', 'qualitative', 'impairments', 'in', 'communication', 'as', 'manifested', 'by',
'at', 'least']
```

In [4]:
```
# Keep the word if it's NOT in our stop_words set AND its length is greater than 1.
stop_words = set(stopwords.words('english'))
texts_for_analysis = [[word for word in doc if word not in stop_words and len(word) > 1]
                      for doc in documents]
# Show the same two sentences after preprocessing
print(f"Doc 0: {texts_for_analysis[0][:10]}")
print(f"Doc 1: {texts_for_analysis[1][:10]}")
```

```
Doc 0: ['anarchism', 'originated', 'term', 'abuse', 'first', 'used', 'early', 'working', 'class', 'radi
cals']
Doc 1: ['reciprocity', 'qualitative', 'impairments', 'communication', 'manifested', 'least', 'one', 'fo
llowing', 'delay', 'total']
```

In [5]:
```
# --- 1. Word2Vec Model Training ---
word2vec_model = Word2Vec(
    sentences=texts_for_analysis, # The preprocessed text data
    vector_size=300, # Dimensionality of the word vectors
    window=5, # Max distance between current and predicted word within a sentence
    min_count=5,  # Ignores all words with a total frequency lower than this
    sg=1,  # Training algorithm: 1 for Skip-Gram; 0 for CBOW
    seed=42, # Random seed for reproducibility
)
```

In [6]:
```
# --- Exploring Word2Vec Results ---
# Find words most similar to 'sociology'
similar_to_sociology = word2vec_model.wv.most_similar('sociology', topn=5)
print(f"Words most similar to 'sociology': {similar_to_sociology}")

# Calculate the cosine similarity between two words
sim_man_woman = word2vec_model.wv.similarity('man', 'woman')
print(f"Similarity between 'man' and 'woman': {sim_man_woman:.4f}")

# king is to man as [?] is to woman
# This is calculated as: (king - man + woman)
analogy_result = word2vec_model.wv.most_similar(
        positive=['king', 'woman'],
        negative=['man'],
        topn=1
    )
print(f"Result of 'king' - 'man' + 'woman': {analogy_result}")
```

```
Words most similar to 'sociology': [('behaviorism', 0.7562087774276733), ('ethology', 0.752770245075225
8), ('functionalism', 0.7510338425636292), ('bioethics', 0.7457544207572937), ('poststructuralism', 0.7
4189293384552)]
Similarity between 'man' and 'woman': 0.5215
Result of 'king' - 'man' + 'woman': [('queen', 0.49680382013320923)]
```

In [7]:
```
# --- 2. LDA (Latent Dirichlet Allocation) Topic Model ---
# Create a Dictionary
lda_dictionary = Dictionary(texts_for_analysis)
# Filter out words that are too rare or too common
lda_dictionary.filter_extremes(no_below=20, no_above=0.5)
lda_corpus = [lda_dictionary.doc2bow(doc) for doc in texts_for_analysis]
# Define the number of topics
num_topics = 10
lda_model = models.LdaModel(
    corpus=lda_corpus,      # The corpus
    id2word=lda_dictionary, # The dictionary to map IDs back to words
    num_topics=num_topics, # The number of topics to extract
    passes=20,         # Number of passes through the corpus during training
    random_state=42    # For reproducible results
)
```

In [8]:
```
# Print the top 10 words for each of the 10 topics
topics = lda_model.print_topics(num_topics=num_topics, num_words=5)
for topic_id, topic_words in topics:
    print(f"Topic {topic_id}: {topic_words}")

# Store topics in a more readable pandas DataFrame
topics_list_data = lda_model.show_topics(num_topics=num_topics, num_words=10, formatted=False)
topics_df_wide = pd.DataFrame({f"Topic {topic_id}": [word[0] for word in words]
                              for topic_id, words in topics_list_data})
topics_df_wide
```

```
Topic 0: 0.005*"college" + 0.003*"films" + 0.003*"emperor" + 0.002*"movie" + 0.002*"mary"
Topic 1: 0.003*"irish" + 0.003*"apollo" + 0.002*"alphabet" + 0.002*"moon" + 0.002*"chinese"
Topic 2: 0.006*"album" + 0.004*"band" + 0.003*"song" + 0.003*"rock" + 0.002*"songs"
Topic 3: 0.008*"actor" + 0.005*"writer" + 0.005*"player" + 0.005*"actress" + 0.005*"singer"
Topic 4: 0.009*"team" + 0.008*"league" + 0.006*"season" + 0.005*"players" + 0.004*"football"
Topic 5: 0.004*"software" + 0.003*"games" + 0.003*"bit" + 0.003*"code" + 0.002*"memory"
Topic 6: 0.003*"energy" + 0.002*"function" + 0.002*"aircraft" + 0.002*"cell" + 0.002*"frac"
Topic 7: 0.003*"jewish" + 0.002*"jesus" + 0.002*"dance" + 0.002*"hebrew" + 0.002*"bible"
Topic 8: 0.005*"km" + 0.004*"islands" + 0.004*"est" + 0.003*"economy" + 0.003*"minister"
Topic 9: 0.003*"soviet" + 0.002*"jews" + 0.002*"philosophy" + 0.002*"jewish" + 0.001*"laws"
```

Out[8]:

	Topic 0	Topic 1	Topic 2	Topic 3	Topic 4	Topic 5	Topic 6	Topic 7	Topic 8	Topic 9
0	college	irish	album	actor	team	software	energy	jewish	km	soviet
1	films	apollo	band	writer	league	games	function	jesus	islands	jews
2	emperor	alphabet	song	player	season	bit	aircraft	dance	est	philosophy
3	movie	moon	rock	actress	players	code	cell	hebrew	economy	jewish
4	mary	chinese	songs	singer	football	memory	frac	bible	minister	laws
5	henry	dialects	ford	prize	games	user	species	software	rate	communist
6	lincoln	letters	star	nobel	player	programming	chemical	bass	elections	alexander
7	comics	vowel	career	italian	israel	windows	cells	band	africa	religion
8	japanese	letter	australian	composer	baseball	apple	carbon	musical	parliament	bc
9	ball	spoken	love	musician	nfl	video	temperature	christ	independence	revolution

In [9]:
```
# --- Evaluate LDA Model with Coherence Score ---
coherence_model_lda = CoherenceModel(
    model=lda_model, # The trained LDA model
    texts=texts_for_analysis,  # The original tokenized text
    dictionary=lda_dictionary, # The dictionary mapping words to IDs
    coherence='c_v'    # The specific coherence measure to use
)
coherence_lda = coherence_model_lda.get_coherence()
# Higher scores are generally better
print(f"Model Coherence Score (C_v): {coherence_lda:.4f}")
```

```
Model Coherence Score (C_v): 0.5592
```

In [10]:
```
# --- Infer Topic Distribution for a Specific Document ---
doc_id = 1
doc_bow = lda_corpus[doc_id]
topic_distribution = lda_model.get_document_topics(doc_bow,minimum_probability=0.0)
print(f"Topic distribution for document {doc_id}:")
for topic_id, prob in topic_distribution:
    print(f"  Topic {topic_id}: {prob:.3f}")
```

```
Topic distribution for document 1:
  Topic 0: 0.244
  Topic 1: 0.215
  Topic 2: 0.000
  Topic 3: 0.000
  Topic 4: 0.000
  Topic 5: 0.014
  Topic 6: 0.345
  Topic 7: 0.000
  Topic 8: 0.168
  Topic 9: 0.015
```

Afterword

As Editor-in-Chief of *ACM Transactions on Social Computing* and former Editor-in-Chief of *Journal of Social Computing*, I have had the privilege of reviewing and publishing research at the intersection of machine learning and the social sciences. While **social computing** is often associated with the design of digital systems that support human interactions, its deeper purpose lies in fostering dialogue between social and computational domains—bringing social theory into conversation with computational theory, social models into dialogue with computational models, and social data into interaction with computational networks and interactions—all in service of understanding, creating, and computing social goods, flourishing, and innovation (Evans, Fu, & Luo, *Journal of Social Computing*, 2020). Professor Yunsong Chen's present book aligns with this vision: it demonstrates how machine learning can **bridge domains**—connecting theory, data, and models to advance both scientific insight and social value.

This book builds on research previously published in *Journal of Contemporary China*, *The Journal of Chinese Sociology*, and *Scientific Reports*. While the chapters present novel applications of machine learning to cultural texts and social dynamics, their deeper significance lies not in technical novelty, but in their methodological orientation—one that responds to a growing imperative in social computing: to move beyond isolated technical innovation and toward a more integrated, reflexive, and socially responsible practice.

Y. Chen et al., *Machine Learning in Social Science*,
https://doi.org/10.1007/978-981-95-6465-1

The work draws on the conceptual clarity of Hofman, Sharma, and Watts (*Science*, 2017), who first articulated the tension between prediction and explanation in social systems—a tension that remains central to the field. It also builds on Luo, Liu, Yang, and Fu (*Journal of Chinese Sociology*, 2019), whose triadic dialogue framework centers on the mutual shaping of theory, data, and models. This cyclical model resists data-first or model-first approaches, emphasizing theory-driven research. In this light, the book's focus on underrepresented communities and cultural phenomena is not incidental—it is methodologically intentional.

The chapters reflect this orientation: theoretical questions guide model design; model outputs prompt reflection on meaning; empirical findings feed back into theory. Yet the field—and this book—can go further. Future work must bridge prediction and explanation, using machine learning not just to uncover patterns, but to generate testable hypotheses—validated through statistical inference, causal modeling, and qualitative engagement.

This is not a call to abandon machine learning. It is a call to **reclaim** it—not as a substitute for social science, but as a tool for deepening it. The best models are not the most complex, but the most transparent, interpretable, and grounded in real-world context.

The book reflects a broader shift in science. For too long, social computing was seen as a Western export. But the work here—and the triadic dialogue—shows innovation is global. Scholars in China and beyond are not just applying methods—they are shaping them.

It responds to Lazer et al. (*Science*, 2020), who called for integration and responsibility across disciplines and cultures. This book reflects that vision—in its focus on cultural meaning, institutional context, and collective behavior.

This is not a summary of trends. It is a record of sustained, high-quality work—work that has influenced research, informed policy, and inspired better questions. It signals a shift: innovation in social computing comes from many places. Global diversity strengthens the science.

For those who study human behavior through data, this book offers more than methods. It offers a model: rigorous, thoughtful, and deeply attentive to the social world. It is a reminder that the best research does not just predict the future—it helps us understand the present, and think clearly about the kind of world we wish to build.

Xiaoming Fu, PhD, FIEEE, FIET, MAE, Member of acatech

Professor of Computer Science and Director of Sino-German Institute of Social Computing, University of Göttingen

Editor-in-Chief, ACM Transactions on Social Computing

References

Aas, Kjersti, Martin Jullum, and Anders Løland. 2021. Explaining individual predictions when features are dependent: More accurate approximations to Shapley values. *Artificial Intelligence* 298: 103502.

Abadie, Alberto, Alexis Diamond, and Jens Hainmueller. 2010. Synthetic control methods for comparative case studies: Estimating the effect of California's tobacco control program. *Journal of the American Statistical Association* 105 (490): 493–505.

Abbott, Andrew. 2007. Against narrative: A preface to lyrical sociology. *Sociological Theory* 25 (1): 67–99.

Abernethy, Jacob et al. 2016. Flint water crisis: Data-driven risk assessment via residential water testing. In *Bloomberg Data for Good Exchange Conference*, 25 September, New York City, NY, USA.

Abidi, Syed Muhammad Raza et al. 2020. Popularity prediction of movies: From statistical modeling to machine learning techniques. *Multimedia Tools and Applications* 79 (47): 35583–35617.

Adams, Adrienne E., et al. 2012. The impact of intimate partner violence on low-income women's economic well-being: The mediating role of job stability. *Violence Against Women* 18 (12): 1345–1367.

Alexander, Jeffrey C. 2003. *The meanings of social life*. Oxford: Oxford University Press.

Allison, Paul D. 2009. Missing data. In *The SAGE handbook of quantitative methods in psychology*, ed. Roger E. Millsap and Alberto Maydeu-Olivares, 72–89. London: Sage.

Anderson, Cameron, et al. 2012. The local-ladder effect: Social status and subjective well-being. *Psychological Science* 23 (7): 764–771.

Y. Chen et al., *Machine Learning in Social Science*,
https://doi.org/10.1007/978-981-95-6465-1

Angrist, Joshua D., and Jörn-Steffen Pischke 2014. *Mastering metrics: The path from cause to effect*. Princeton: Princeton University Press.

Athey, Susan, Julie Tibshirani, and Stefan Wager. 2019. Generalized random forests. *The Annals of Statistics* 47 (2): 1148–1178.

Athey, Susan 2015. Machine learning and causal inference for policy evaluation. In *Proceedings of the 21th ACM SIGKDD International Conference on Knowledge Discovery and Data Mining*, Sydney, NSW, Australia, 10–13 August.

Athey, Susan. 2018. The impact of machine learning on economics. In *The economics of artificial intelligence: An agenda*, ed. Agrawal, Ajay, Joshua Gans, and Avi Goldfarb, 507–547. University of Chicago Press.

Athey, Susan, and Guido Imbens. 2016. Recursive partitioning for heterogeneous causal effects. In *Proceedings of the National Academy of Sciences of the United States of America* 113 (27): 7353–7360.

Bai, Meijiadai. 2021. Regulation of pornography and criminalization of BL readers and authors in contemporary China (2010–2019). *Cultural Studies* 36 (2): 279–301.

Bailey, April H., Adina Williams, and Andrei Cimpian 2022. Based on billions of words on the internet, people= men. *Science Advances* 8 (13): eabm2463.

Barocas, Solon, and Andrew D. Selbst. 2016. Big data's disparate impact. *Calif. L. Rev.* 104: 671.

Baruch, Elaine H. 1991. *Women, love, and power: Literary and psychoanalytic perspectives*. New York: New York University Press.

Baumard, Nicolas, Huillery Elise, Hyafil Alexandre, and Safra Lou. 2022. The cultural evolution of love in literary history. *Nature Human Behaviour* 6 (4): 506–522.

Baumer, Eric P. S., et al. 2017. Comparing grounded theory and topic modeling: Extreme divergence or unlikely convergence? *Journal of the Association for Information Science and Technology* 68 (6): 1397–1410.

Becker, Howard S. 2008. *Tricks of the trade: How to think about your research while you're doing it*. Chicago: University of Chicago press.

Belloni, A., D. Chen, V. Chernozhukov, and C. Hansen. 2012. Sparse models and methods for optimal instruments with an application to eminent domain. *Econometrica* 80 (6): 2369–2429.

Berk, Richard. 2012. *Criminal justice forecasts of risk: A machine learning approach*, 27–41. New York: Springer.

Berry, Chris, and Feii Lu. 2005. *Island on the edge: Taiwan new cinema and after*. Hong Kong University Press.

Berry, Christopher J., and Mary Ann Farquhar. 2006. *China on screen: Cinema and nation*. Columbia University Press.

Bhabha, Homi K. 1990. *Nation and narration*. Routledge.

Bhabha, Homi K. 1994. *The location of culture*. Routledge.

Bie, Bijie, and Lu Tang. 2016. Chinese gay men's coming out narratives: Connecting social relationship to co-cultural theory. *Journal of international and intercultural communication* 9 (4): 351–367.

Birama, Diakon, and Ute Röschenthaler. 2017. The Chinese presence in the Malian mediascape. *Journal of African Cultural Studies* 29 (1): 96–113.

Blanchflower, David G., and Andrew J. Oswald. 2008. Is well-being U-shaped over the life cycle? *Social Science & Medicine* 66: 1733–1749.

Blei, David M., Andrew Y. Ng, and Michael I. Jordan. 2003. Latent Dirichlet allocation. *Journal of Machine Learning Research* 3: 993–1022.

Bodory, Hugo, Martin Huber, and Lukáš Lafférs. 2022. Evaluating (weighted) dynamic treatment effects by double machine learning. *The Econometrics Journal* 25 (3): 628–648.

Bonikowski, Bart, and Paul DiMaggio. 2016. Varieties of American popular nationalism. *American Sociological Review* 81 (5): 949–980.

Boulding, Kenneth E. 1959. National images and international systems. *Journal of Conflict Resolution* 3 (2): 120–131.

Bourdieu, Pierre. 1984. *Distinction: A social critique of the judgement of taste*, Trans. Richard Nice, London: Routledge & Kegan Paul.

Bourdieu, Pierre. 1993. *The field of cultural production: Essays on art and literature*, edited and introduced by Randal Johnson. New York: Columbia University Press.

Brand, Jennie E., and Yu Xie. 2007. Identification and estimation of causal effects with time-varying treatments and time-varying outcomes. *Sociological Methodology* 37 (1): 393–434.

Brand, Jennie E., Xiang Zhou, and Yu Xie. 2023. Recent developments in causal inference and machine learning. *Annual Review of Sociology* 49 (1): 81–110.

Breiman, Leo. 2001a. Random forests. *Machine Learning* 45: 5–32.

Breiman, Leo. 2001b. Statistical modeling: The two cultures (with comments and a rejoinder by the author). *Statistical Science* 16 (3): 199–231.

Brinkmann, Svend. 2009. Literature as qualitative inquiry. *Qualitative Inquiry* 15 (8): 1376–1394.

Brookman, Fiona, Edward R. Maguire, and Mike Maguire, eds. 2017. *The handbook of homicide*. Wiley.

Brownell, Susan. 2013. Brand China in the Olympic context: Communications challenges of China's soft power initiative. *Javnost* 20 (4): 65–82.

Burston, Paul, and Colin Richardson. 1995. *A Queer romance: Lesbians, gay men, and popular culture*. London: Routledge.

Cameron, Paul. 1975. Mood as an indicant of subjective well-being: Age, sex, social class, and situational differences. *Journal of Gerontology* 30 (2): 216–224.

Campbell, Angus. 1976. Subjective measures of well-being. *American Psychologist* 31 (2): 117–124.

Canet, Fernando. 2016. Quantitative approaches for evaluating the influence of films using the IMDb database. *Communication & Society* 29 (2): 151–172.

Cao, Jin, and Xinlei Lu. 2014. A Preliminary exploration of the gay movement in Mainland China: Legacy, transition, opportunity, and the new media. *Signs* 39 (4): 840–848.

Carrasco, Marine. 2012. A regularization approach to the many instruments problem. *Journal of Econometrics* 17 (2): 383–398.

Castle, Jennifer L., Xiaochuan Qin, and W. Robert Reed. 2009. How to pick the best regression equation: A review and comparison of model selection algorithms. Working Papers in Economics 09/13, University of Canterbury, Department of Economics and Finance.

Chandan, Joht Singh et al. 2020. COVID-19: A public health approach to manage domestic violence is needed. *The Lancet Public Health* 5 (6): e309.

Chang, Jiang, and Hao Tian. 2021. Girl power in boy love: Yaoi, online female counterculture, and digital feminism in China. *Feminist Media Studies* 21 (4): 604–620.

Chapman, Bruce, and Cahit Guven. 2016. Revisiting the relationship between marriage and wellbeing: Does marriage quality matter? *Journal of Subjective Well-Being Studies* 17 (2): 533–551.

Chen, Feibao. 2008. *History of Taiwanese film*. Beijing: China Film Press (In Chinese).

Chen, Tianqi, and Guestrin, Carlos. 2016. XGBoost: A scalable tree boosting system. In *Proceedings of the 22nd ACM SIGKDD International Conference on Knowledge Discovery and Data Mining*, 785–794. San Francisco, CA, USA, 13–17 August.

Chen, Yunsong, and Beate Volker. 2016. Social capital and homophily both matter for labor market outcomes-evidence from replication and extension. *Social Networks* 45: 18–31.

Chen, Yunsong, and Fei Yan. 2018. International visibility as determinants of foreign direct investment: An empirical study of Chinese provinces. *Social Science Research* 76: 23–39.

Chen, Yunsong, and Xiaoguang Fan. 2010. The endogeneity problem review in quantitative analysis: A review of estimating causal effects of social interaction. *Chinese Journal of Sociology* 30 (4): 91–117.

Chen, Yunsong, and Xu Qi. 2024. *Causal inference in social science*. Beijing: Peking University Press.

Chen, Yunsong, Fei Yan, Guangye He, and Wei Yan. 2020a. The Werther effect revisited: Do suicides in books predict actual suicides? *Poetics* 81: 101441.

Chen, Yunsong, Guangye He, and Fei Yan. 2021. *Understanding China through big data: Applications of theory-oriented quantitative approaches*. Abingdon, New York: Routledge.

Chen, Yunsong, Guangye He, and Guodong Ju. 2022. The hidden sexual minorities: Machine learning approaches to estimate the sexual minority orientation among Beijing college students. *Journal of Social Computing* 3 (2).

Chen, Yunsong, Xiaogang Wu, Anning Hu, Guangye He, and Guodong Ju. 2020. Social prediction: A new research paradigm based on machine learning. *Sociological Studies* 35 (3): 94–117 (In Chinese).

Chen, Yunsong, Xiaogang Wu, Anning Hu, Guangye He, and Guodong Ju. 2021. Social prediction: A new research paradigm based on machine learning. *The Journal of Chinese Sociology* 8: 1–21.

Chen, Yunsong. 2011. The causal effect of social capital in the labor market: Identification challenges and strategies. *Chinese Sociological Review* 44 (2): 76–100.

Chen, Yunsong. 2012a. Logic, imagination and interpretation: The application of instrumental variables for causal inference in the social sciences. *Sociological Studies* 6: 192–216+245–246 (In Chinese).

Chen, Yunsong. 2012b. Do networks pay off among internal migrants in China? An instrumental variable analysis. *Chinese Sociological Review* 45 (1): 28–54.

Chen, Yunsong. 2017. Out of Fei Xiaotong's paradox: The dispute of methodology in Sociology. Tsinghua *Sociological Review* 7.

Chen, Yunsong. 2022. *Causal effects of social capital: Labor markets and beyond.* London: Palgrave Macmillan.

Chen, Zhuo, and Yunsong Chen. 2024. Computing grounded theory: A quantitative method to develop theories. *The Journal of Chinese Sociology* 11 (1): 17.

Chernozhukov, Victor, et al. 2018. Double/debiased machine learning for treatment and structural parameters. *Econometrics Journal* 21: C1–C68.

Chiang, Feichi. 2016. Counterpublic but obedient: A case of Taiwan's BL Fandom. *Inter-Asia Cultural Studies* 17 (2): 223–238.

Chung, Hye S. 2006. *Hollywood Asian Philip Ahn and the politics of cross-ethnic performance.* Philadelphia: Temple University Press.

Clark, Andrew E., Paul Frijters, and Michael A. Shields. 2008. Relative income, subjective well-being, and utility: An explanation for the Easterlin paradox and other puzzles. *Journal of Economic Literature* 46 (1): 95–144.

Cui, Mingyu. 2018. Rerating the movie scores in Douban through word embedding. *Journal of Physics: Conference Series* 1004 (1): 012030.

Cui, Peng, and Susan Athey. 2022. Stable learning establishes some common ground between causal inference and machine learning. *Nature Machine Intelligence* 4 (2): 110–115.

Cui, Yi et al. 2012. A current situation survey and influential factors of domestic violence in seven provinces and cities of China. *Chinese Journal of Clinical Psychology* 20 (3): 360–362.

D'Amour, Alexander. 2021. Revisiting Rashomon: A comment on "The Two Cultures." *Observational Studies* 7 (1): 59–63.

De La Fuente, Eduardo. 2007. The "New Sociology of Art": Putting art back into social science approaches to the arts. *Cultural Sociology* 1 (3): 409–425.

Deng Zhiwei. 2009. *The dictionary of sociology* (In Chinese). Shanghai: Cishu Press: 513.

Diamond, Alexis, and Jasjeet S. Sekhon. 2013. Genetic matching for estimating causal effects: A general multivariate matching method for achieving balance in observational studies. *Review of Economics and Statistics* 95 (3): 932–945.

Diener, Ed. 2009. Subjective well-being. *The Science of Well-Being* 95 (3): 542–575.

Diener, Ed, et al. 1993. The relationship between income and subjective well-being: Relative or absolute? *Social Indicators Research* 28 (3): 195–223.

Diener, Ed, Shigehiro Oishi, and Louis Tay. 2018. Advances in subjective well-being research. *Nature Human Behaviour* 2 (4): 253–260.

DiMaggio, Paul, Manish Nag, and D. Blei. 2013. Exploiting affinities between topic modeling and the sociological perspective on culture: Application to newspaper coverage of U.S. Government arts funding. *Poetics* 41 (6): 570–606.

Ding, Sheng. 2011. Branding a rising China: An analysis of Beijing's national image management in the age of China's rise. *Journal of Asian and African Studies* 46 (3): 293–306.

Dodds, Klaus. 2006. Popular geopolitics and audience dispositions: James Bond and the Internet Movie Database (IMDb). *Transactions of the Institute of British Geographers* 31 (2): 116–130.

Domingos, Pedro. 1999. The role of Occam's razor in knowledge discovery. *Data Mining and Knowledge Discovery* 3 (4).

Donaldson, Dave, and Adam Storeygard. 2016. The view from above: Applications of satellite data in economics. *Journal of Economic Perspectives* 30 (4): 171–198.

Donoho, David. 2017. 50 years of data science. *Journal of Computational and Graphical Statistics* 26 (4): 745–766.

Doshi-Velez, Finale, and Been Kim. 2017. Towards a rigorous science of interpretable machine learning. *arXiv preprint arXiv:* 1702.08608.

Holt, Douglas B. 1997. Distinction in America? Recovering Bourdieu's theory of tastes from his critics. *Poetics* 25 (2): 3–120.

Downey, Douglas B., and Anastasia S. Vogt Yuan. 2005. Sex differences in school performance during high school: Puzzling patterns and possible explanations. *Sociological Quarterly* 46 (2): 299–321.

Draper, David. 1995. Assessment and propagation of model uncertainty. *Journal of the Royal Statistical Society Series B: Statistical Methodology* 57 (1): 45–70.

Duara, Prasenjit. 1995. *Rescuing history from the nation: Questioning narratives of modern China*. University of Chicago Press.

Dube, Arindrajit, et al. 2020. Monopsony in online labor markets. *American Economic Review: Insights* 2 (1): 33–46.

D'Amour, Alexander, et al. 2020. Underspecification presents challenges for credibility in modern machine learning. *Journal of Machine Learning Research* 23 (226): 1–61.

Eads, Alicia, et al. 2020. Separating the wheat from the chaff: A topic and keyword-based procedure for identifying research-relevant text. *Poetics* 86: 101527.

Easterlin, Richard A. 1973. Does money buy subjective well-being? *The Public Interest* 30: 3.

Easterlin, Richard A. 2003. Explaining happiness. *Proceedings of the National Academy of Sciences* 100 (19): 11176–11183.

Eberle, Thomas S. 2016. Qualitative cultural sociology. In *The Sage handbook of cultural sociology*, ed. David Inglis, et al., 237–254. London: Sage Publications.

Erbring, Lutz, et al. 1980. Front-page news and real-world cues: A new look at agenda-setting by the media. *American Journal of Political Science* 24 (1): 16–49.

Fafchamps, Marcel, and Julien Labonne. 2017. Using split samples to improve inference on causal effects. *Political Analysis* 25 (4): 465–482.

Farbmacher, Helmut, et al. 2022. Causal mediation analysis with double machine learning. *The Econometrics Journal* 25 (2): 277–300.

Farhangfar, Alireza, Lukasz Kurgan, and Jennifer Dy. 2008. Impact of imputation of missing values on classification error for discrete data. *Pattern Recognition* 41 (12): 3692–3705.

Felson, Richard B., et al. 2002. Reasons for reporting and not reporting domestic violence to the police. *Criminology* 40 (3): 617–648.

Feng, Jin. 2009. "Addicted to Beauty": Consuming and producing web-based Chinese "Danmei" fiction at Jinjiang. *Modern Chinese Literature and Culture* 21 (2): 1–41.

Feng, Jin. 2013. *Romancing the Internet: Producing and consuming Chinese web romance*. Leiden: BRILL.

Finkel, Jenny R., Trond Grenager, and Christopher Manning. 2005. Incorporating non-local information into information extraction systems by Gibbs sampling. In *Proceedings of the 43rd Annual Meeting of the Association for Computational Linguistics* (ACL'05), 363–370.

FitzRoy, Felix R., et al. 2014. Testing the tunnel effect: Comparison, age and subjective well-being in UK and German panels. *IZA Journal of European Labor Studies* 3 (1): 1–30.

Flynn, George Q., and William L. O'Neill. 1993. *A democracy at war: America's fight at home and abroad in World War II*. Cambridge: Harvard University Press.

Foucault, Michel. 1979. *The history of sexuality/Vol.1, an introduction*, trans. R. Hurley. London: Allen Lane.

Frey, Bruno S., and Alois Stutzer. 2010. *Happiness and economics: How the economy and institutions affect human well-being*. Princeton University Press.

Frijters, Paul, and Tony Beatton. 2012. The mystery of the U-shaped relationship between subjective well-being and age. *Journal of Economic Behavior & Organization* 82 (2–3): 525–542.

Fromm, Erich. 1971. *Marx's concept of man*. New York: Frederick Ungar.

Fu, Zhihui, Shukai Liu, Guodong Ju, Wen Ma, and Yunsong Chen. 2024. Instrumental Guanxi culture and inbound urban migration in China: A prefecture-level analysis using online search data. *The China Quarterly* 260: 1040–1058.

Fuhr, Jonathan, and Dominik Papies. 2024. Double machine learning meets panel data—Promises, pitfalls, and potential solutions. *arXiv preprint* arXiv: 2409.01266.

Claudia, Garcia-Moreno., et al. 2006. Prevalence of intimate partner violence: Findings from the WHO multi-country study on women's health and domestic violence. *The Lancet* 368 (9543): 1260–1269.

Garvey, Colin, and Chandler Maskal. 2020. Sentiment analysis of the news media on artificial intelligence does not support claims of negative bias against artificial intelligence. *Omics (Larchmont, N.Y.)*, 286–299.

Gates, Gary J. 2011. *How many people are lesbian, gay, bisexual and transgender?* Retrieved from UCLA School of Law: http://williamsinstitute.law.ucla.edu/wp-content/uploads/Gates-How-Many-People-LGBT-Apr-2011.pdf.

Geertz, Clifford. 1973. *The interpretation of cultures: Selected essays*. New York: Basic Books.

Genette, Gérard. 1997. *Paratexts: Thresholds of interpretation*. Trans. Lewin, J. E. Cambridge: Cambridge University Press.

Ghaziani, Amin, Verta Taylor, and Amy Stone. 2016. Cycles of sameness and difference in LGBT social movements. *Annual Review of Sociology* 42 (1): 165–183.

Ghosh, Shantanu, et al. 2021. Propensity score synthetic augmentation matching using generative adversarial networks (PSSAM-GAN). *Computer Methods and Programs in Biomedicine Update* 1: 100020.

Glaeser, Edward L., et al. 2016. Crowdsourcing city government: Using tournaments to improve inspection accuracy. *American Economic Review* 106 (5): 114–118.

Glaser, Barney G., and Anselm L. Strauss. 2017. *The discovery of grounded theory: Strategies for qualitative research*. New York: Aldine de Gruyter.

Glaser, Barney G. 2008. *Doing quantitative grounded theory*. Mill Valley: Sociology Press.

Glatzer, Wolfgang. 2000. Happiness: Classic theory in the light of current research. *Journal of Subjective well-being Studies* 1 (4): 501–511.

Goodfellow, Ian, Yoshua Bengio, and Aaron Courville. 2016. *Deep learning*. MIT press.

Goodman, Nelson. 1983. *Fact fiction and forecast*, 114–118. Cambridge: Harvard University Press.

Graham, Carol, and Julia Ruiz Pozuelo. 2017. Subjective well-being, stress, and age: How the U curve varies across people and places. *Journal of Population Economics* 30 (1): 225–264.

Gramsci, Antonio. 1992. *Prison notebooks*, Trans. A. Joseph, Buttigieg and Antonio Callari. New York, Chichester: Columbia University Press.

Green, Donald P., and Holger L. Kern. 2012. Modeling heterogeneous treatment effects in survey experiments with Bayesian additive regression trees. *Public Opinion Quarterly* 76 (3): 491–511.

Greene, Naomi. 2014. *From Fu Manchu to Kung Fu Panda*. Honolulu: University of Hawaii Press.

Gries, Peter, et al. 2015. Hollywood in China: How American popular culture shapes Chinese views of the "Beautiful Imperialist"—An experimental analysis. *The China Quarterly* 224: 1070–1082.

Grimmer, Justin, and Brandon M. Stewart. 2013. Text as data: The promise and pitfalls of automatic content analysis methods for political texts. *Political Analysis* 21 (3): 267–297.

Grimmer, Justin. 2015. We are all social scientists now: How big data, machine learning, and causal inference work together. *Political Science and Politics* 48 (1): 80–83.

Gross, Larry. 2012. *Up from invisibility: Lesbians, gay men, and the media in America*. Columbia University Press.

Gundelach, Peter, and Svend Kreiner. 2004. Happiness and life satisfaction in advanced European countries. *Cross-Cultural Research* 38 (4): 359–386.

Hainmueller, Jens, Jonathan Mummolo, and Yiqing Xu. 2019. How much should we trust estimates from multiplicative interaction models? Simple tools to improve empirical practice. *Political Analysis* 27 (2): 163–192.

Hamberger, L. Kevin., Sadie E. Larsen, and Amy Lehrner. 2017. Coercive control in intimate partner violence. *Aggression and Violent Behavior* 37: 1–11.

Han, Xiao. 2020. Anti-feminist tendency in Chinese Tanbi Novels. *Prose Hundred* 6: 58 (In Chinese).

Harris, Peter, and Peter Trubowitz. 2021. The politics of power projection: The Pivot to Asia, its failure, and the future of American primacy. *The Chinese Journal of International Politics* 14 (2): 187–217.

Hartford, Jason, Lewis Greg, Leyton-Brown Kevin, and Taddy Matt. 2017. Deep IV: A flexible approach for counterfactual prediction. In *International Conference on Machine Learning*, 1414–1423. PMLR.

Hartford, Jason et al. 2016. Counterfactual prediction with deep instrumental variables networks. *arXiv preprint arXiv: 1612.09596.*

Hartwig, Frederick, and Brian E. Dearing. 1979. *Exploratory data analysis*. USA: Sage.

Harvey, Penny. 2009. Between narrative and number: The case of ARUP's 3D digital city model. *Cultural Sociology* 3 (2): 257–276.

Hazlett, Chad. 2014. Kernel balancing (KBAL): A balancing method to equalize multivariate distance densities and reduce bias without a specification search. MIT Unpublished Manuscript.

He, Guangye, et al. 2018. Using the Baidu search index to predict the incidents of HIV/AIDS in China. *Scientific Reports* 8 (1): 9038.

He, Haibo, Yuan Cao, Yi Cao, and Jinyu Wen. 2013. Ensemble learning for wind profile prediction with missing values. *Neural Computing and Applications* 22 (2): 287–294.

He, Yinan. 2009. *The search for reconciliation: Sino-Japanese and German-Polish relations since World War II*. New York: Cambridge University Press.

Hedström, Peter. 2005. *Dissecting the social: On the principles of analytical sociology*. Cambridge: Cambridge University Press.

Hedström, Peter. 2008. Studying mechanisms to strengthen causal inferences in quantitative research. In *The Oxford Handbook of Political Methodology*, ed. J. M. Box-Steffensmeier, H. E. Brady, and D. Collier. New York: Oxford University Press.

Hegel, Georg W. F. 1975. *The philosophy of fine art*, Trans. F. P. B. Osmaston. New York: Hacker Art Books.

Hempel, Carl G., and Paul Oppenheim. 1948. Studies in the logic of explanation. *Philosophy of Science* 15 (2): 135–175.

Henderson, William O. 1976. *The life of Friedrich Engels*, vol. 01. London: Frank Cass and Company Limited.

Herlands, William et al. 2018. Automated local regression discontinuity design discovery. In *Proceedings of the 24th ACM SIGKDD International Conference on Knowledge Discovery & Data Mining*, 1512–1520.

Hervás, Gonzalo. 2009. Psicología Positiva: Una introducción. *Revista Interuniversitaria De Formación Del Profesorado* 66: 23–41.

Hill, Jennifer, and Yu-Sung Su. 2013. Assessing lack of common support in causal inference using Bayesian nonparametrics: Implications for evaluating the effect of breastfeeding on children's cognitive outcomes. *The Annals of Applied Statistics* 1386–1420.

Hirschman, Albert O., and Michael Rothschild. 1973. The changing tolerance for income inequality in the course of economic development: With a mathematical appendix. *The Quarterly Journal of Economics* 87 (4): 544–566.

Hoffmann, Sabine, et al. 2021. The multiplicity of analysis strategies jeopardizes replicability: Lessons learned across disciplines. *Royal Society Open Science* 8 (4): 201925.

Hofman, Jake M., Amit Sharma, and Duncan J. Watts. 2017. Prediction and explanation in social systems. *Science* 355 (6324): 486–488.

Hu, Anning, Xiaogang Wu, and Yunsong Chen. 2021. Analysis of heterogeneous treatment effect: New opportunities and challenges with machine learning techniques. *Sociological Studies* 36 (1): 91–114+228 (In Chinese).

Hu, Anning. 2012. Propensity score matching and causal inference: A methodological review. *Sociological Studies* 27(1): 221–242+246 (In Chinese).

Hu, Yang. 2016. Sex ideologies in China: Examining interprovince differences. *Journal of Sex Research* 53 (9): 1118–1130.

Huang, Ronggui. 2017. Network fields, cultural identities and labor rights communities: Big data analytics with topic model and community detection. *Society* 2: 26–50.

Imai, Kosuke, and Marc Ratkovic. 2013. Estimating treatment effect heterogeneity in randomized program evaluation. *Annals of Applied Statistics* 7 (1): 443–470.

Inglehart, Ronald, et al. 2008. Development, freedom and rising subjective well-being. A global perspective (1981–2007). *Perspectiveson Psychological Science* 3: 264–285.

Jacobs, Mark D., and Lyn Spillman. 2005. Cultural sociology at the crossroads of the discipline. *Poetics* 33 (1): 1–14.

Japkowicz, Nathalie, and Shaju Stephen. 2002. The class imbalance problem: A systematic study. *Intelligent Data Analysis* 6 (5): 429–449.

Jasny, Barbara R., and Richard Stone. 2017. Prediction and its limits. *Science* 355 (6324): 468–469.

Jenkins, Henry. 1992. *Textual poachers: Television fans and participatory culture*. London: Routledge.

Jervis, Robert. 1970. *The logic of images in international relations*. Princeton, New Jersey: Princeton University Press.

Ji, Zhengju, and Sijin Liu. 2018. Research on the text of on Marxist classical works in the past 40 Years of reform and opening-up. *Studies on Marxist Theory* 4 (6): 49–61 (In Chinese).

Jiang, Bo, and Wenbo Kuang. 2016. Research on profit model optimization strategy of online novels. *View on Publishing* 7: 28–31 (In Chinese).

Jo, Myoung-Ju. 2016. The factors related to subjective well-being among nursing students. *The Journal of Korean Academic Society of Nursing Education* 22 (2): 182–190.

Jockers, Matthew L. 2013. *Macroanalysis: Digital methods and literary history*. Baltimore: University of Illinois Press.

Jockers, Matthew L., and David Mimno. 2013. Significant themes in 19th-century literature. *Poetics* 41 (6): 750–769.

Jerez, José M., et al. 2010. Missing data imputation using statistical and machine learning methods in a real breast cancer problem. *Artificial Intelligence in Medicine* 50 (2): 105–115.

Kaplan, Oscar. 1940. Prediction in the social sciences. *Philosophy of Science* 7 (4): 492–498.

Khalilia, Mohammed, Sounak Chakraborty, and Mihail Popescu. 2011. Predicting disease risks from highly imbalanced data using Random Forest. *BMC Medical Informatics and Decision Making* 11 (1): 51.

Kleinberg, Jon, Annie Liang, and Sendhil Mullainathan. 2017. The theory is predictive, but is it complete? An application to human perception of randomness. In *Proceedings of the 2017 ACM Conference on Economics and Computation*, 125–126.

Kleinberg, Jon, et al. 2015. Prediction policy problems. *American Economic Review* 105 (5): 491–495.

Klüver, Heike. 2009. Measuring interest group influence using quantitative text analysis. *European Union Politics* 10 (4): 535–549.

Knies, Gundi, et al. 2008. Keeping up with the Schmidt's–an empirical test of relative deprivation theory in the neighbourhood context. *Journal of Contextual Economics-Schmollers Jahrbuch* 1: 75–108.

Kozma, Albert, and Michael J. Stones. 1983. Predictors of happiness. *Journal of Gerontology* 38 (5): 626–628.

Krug, Etienne G., et al. 2002. The world report on violence and health. *The Lancet* 360 (9339): 1083–1088.

Kuhn, Thomas S. 1962. *The structure of scientific revolutions*. Chicago: The University of Chicago Press.

Kuhn, Thomas S. 1977. *The essential tension*. Chicago: The University of Chicago Press.

Kurihara, Chiyo, and Eiko Kakinuma. 1993. *A guide to Tanbi and Gay Novels*. Tokyo: Byakuya-Shobo (In Japanese).

Kushlev, Kostadin, et al. 2020. Does subjective well-being improve health? Evidence from a randomized controlled trial. *Psychological Science* 31 (7): 807–821.

Lane, Jan-Erik. 2007. A new cultural cleavage in post-modern society. *Brazilian Journal of Political Economy* 27 (3): 375–393.

Lantz, Brett. 2015. *Machine learning with R*. Birmingham: Packt Publishing.

Larson, Reed. 1978. Thirty years of research on the subjective well-being of older Americans. *Journal of Gerontology* 33 (1): 109–125.

Lazer, David, et al. 2009. Social science. Computational social science. *Science* 323 (5915): 721–723.

Lazer, David, and Radford Jason. 2017. Data Ex machina: Introduction to big data. *Annual Review of Sociology* 43 (1): 19–39.

Lazer, David, Ryan Kennedy, Gary King, and Alessandro Vespignani. 2014. The parable of google flu: Traps in big data analysis. *Science* 343 (6176): 1203–1205.

Lee, Brian K., Justin Lessler, and Elizabeth A. Stuart. 2010. Improving propensity score weighting using machine learning. *Statistics in Medicine* 29 (3): 337–346.

Lee, Monica, and John Levi Martin. 2015. Coding, counting and cultural cartography. *American Journal of Cultural Sociology* 3 (1): 1–33.

Leung, Ping-kwan. 2012. *Ten essays on Hong Kong culture*. Hangzhou: Zhejiang University Press (In Chinese).

Lewis, Greg, and Vasilis Syrgkanis. 2020. Double/debiased machine learning for dynamic treatment effects via g-estimation. arXiv preprint arXiv:2002.07285.

Li, Daoxin. 2016. Subjectivity, integrity and concretization in the study of Chinese film history. *Literature & Art Studies* 8: 82–92 (In Chinese).

Li, Huang. 2012. *Statistical learning methods*. Beijing: Tsinghua University Press (In Chinese).

Li, Tianduo. 1997. *Taiwanese films, society, and history*. Taipei: Asiapac Books (In Chinese).

Li, Xiaoling, and Xiaomei Wang. 2009. Criticism of Chinese postcolonial film criticism. *Social Sciences in Yunnan* 2: 142–145 (In Chinese).

Liang, Yucheng. 2014. The causal mechanism of migration behaviors of African immigrants in Guangzhou: From the perspective of cumulative causation theory. *The Journal of Chinese Sociology* 1 (1): 1–25.

Linthicum, Kathryn P., Katherine Musacchio Schafer, and Jessica D. Ribeiro. 2019. Machine learning in suicide science: Applications and ethics. *Behavioral Sciences & the Law* 37 (3): 214–222.

Lu, Luo, and Yu Yi Lin. 1998. Family roles and subjective well-being in adulthood. *Personality and Individual Differences* 25 (2): 195–207.

Lu, Sheldon H. 1997. *Transnational Chinese cinemas: Identity, nationhood, gender*. Honolulu: University of Hawaii Press.

Luchesi, Bruna Moretti, et al. 2018. Factors associated with subjective well-being in the elderly persons living in the community. *Archives of Gerontology and Geriatrics* 74: 83–87.

Lundberg, Ian, Jennie E. Brand, and Nanum Jeon. 2022. Researcher reasoning meets computational capacity: Machine learning for social science. *Social Science Research* 108: 102807.

Lundberg, Scott M., and Su-In Lee. 2017. A unified approach to interpreting model predictions. In *Advances in neural information processing systems,* ed. I.

Guyon, U. V. Luxburg, S. Bengio, H. Wallach, R. Fergus, S. Vishwanathan, and R. Garnett, vol. 30, 4765–4774.
Lundberg, Scott M., et al. 2020. From local explanations to global understanding with explainable AI for trees. *Nature Machine Intelligence* 2 (1): 56–67.
Luo, Chenglie. 2008. Mencius on Filial Piety and "Having no Descendant" is the Gravest Offence. *Confucius Studies* 2: 36–39 (In Chinese).
Luo, Jiade, Jifan Liu, Kunhao Yang, and Xiaoming Fu. 2018. Reintroducing theory into the triangle dialogue of big data, theory and prediction model. *Sociological Studies* 5: 1–19.
Luskey, Bridget. 2019. "The Untamed": Chinese boy love drama we can't stop watching. *Film Daily*, 2 December, https://filmdaily.co/news/the-untamed/. Accessed on 5 February 2022.
Maags, Christina. 2014. Enhancing China's national image through culture festivals: A case study of China culture years in Europe. *Fudan Journal of the Humanities and Social Sciences* 7 (1): 33–55.
Majima, Shinobu, and Niamh Moore. 2009. Introduction: Rethinking qualitative and quantitative methods. *Cultural Sociology* 3 (2): 203–216.
Malcolm, Grant. 2004. *Multidisciplinary approaches to visual representations and interpretations*, ed. Grant Malcolm. Amsterdam, London: Elsevier.
Mamdani, Mahmood. 1995. *Good Muslim, bad Muslim: America, the cold war, and the roots of terror*. New York: Pantheon Books.
Manski, Charles F. 2007. Partial identification of counterfactual choice probabilities. *International Economic Review* 48 (4): 1393–1410.
Marchetti, Gina, and Sheldon S. Lu. 2018. *Citing China: Politics, postmodernism, and world cinema*. Honolulu: University of Hawaii Press.
Marshall, Emily A. 2013. Defining population problems: Using topic models for cross-national comparison of disciplinary development. *Poetics* 41 (6): 701–724.
Martin, Fran. 2012. Girls who love boys' love: Japanese homoerotic manga as trans-national Taiwan culture. *Inter-Asia Cultural Studies* 12 (3): 365–383.
Martin, Travis et al. 2016. Exploring limits to prediction in complex social systems. In *Proceedings of the 25th International Conference on World Wide Web*, 683–694.
Marx, Karl, and Frederick Engels. 1975–2004. *Marx & Engels Collected Works*, vol. 01-50. London: Lawrence & Wishart Publishers.
McBride, Michael. 2010. Money, subjective well-being, and aspirations: An experimental study. *Journal of Economic Behavior & Organization* 74 (3): 262–276.
McCaffrey, Daniel F., Greg Ridgeway, and Andrew R. Morral. 2004. Propensity score estimation with boosted regression for evaluating causal effects in observational studies. *Psychological Methods* 9 (4): 403–425.

McCombs, Maxwell. 2005. A look at agenda-setting: Past, present and future. *Journalism Studies (London, England)* 6 (4): 543–557.
McFarland, Daniel A. et al. 2013. Differentiating language usage through topic models. *Poetics* 41 (6SI): 1–19.
Menardi, Giovanna, and Nicola Torelli. 2014. Training and assessing classification rules with imbalanced data. *Data Mining and Knowledge Discovery* 28 (1): 92–122.
Mendes, Anna C., and Lisa Lau. 2015. India through re-orientalist lenses. *Interventions* 17 (5): 706–727.
Merton, Robert K., and Elinor Barber. 2011. *The travels and adventures of serendipity*. USA: Princeton University Press.
Merton, Robert K. 1968. *Social theory and social structure*. New York: Simon and Schuster.
Meyer, Mike. 2006. Pearl of the orient. *The New York Times Book Review*, 23-L.
Meyer, Uli. 2013. Drawing from the body—The self, the Gaze and the other in Boys' Love Manga. *Journal of Graphic Novels & Comics* 4 (1): 64–81.
Michalos, Alex C. 2017. Education, subjective well-being and wellbeing. In *Connecting the quality of life theory to health, well-being and education*, 277–299. Springer.
Mikolov, Tomas et al. 2013. Efficient estimation of word representations in vector space. arXiv preprint arXiv:1301.3781.
Mitchell, Tom. 1997. *Machine learning*. New York, London: McGraw-Hill.
Mizoguchi, Akiko. 2015. *Theorizing BL as a transformative genre: Boys' Love moves the world forward*. Tokyo: Ohta Books (In Japanese).
Mohr, John W., and Petko Bogdanov. 2013. Introduction-topic models: What they are and why they matter. *Poetics* 41 (6): 545–569.
Mohr, John W., Wagner-Pacici Robin, Breiger Ronald L., Bogdanov Petko. 2013. Graphing the grammar of motives in national security strategies: Cultural interpretation, automated text analysis and the drama of global politics. *Poetics* 41: 670–700.
Moi, Toril. 2008. I am not a woman writer. *Feminist Theory* 9 (3): 259–271.
Molina, Mario, and Filiz Garip. 2019. Machine learning for sociology. *Annual Review of Sociology* 45: 27–45.
Molnar, Christoph, Giuseppe Casalicchio, and Bernd Bischl. 2020. Interpretable machine learning-a brief history, state-of-the-art and challenges. *Joint European conference on machine learning and knowledge discovery in databases*. Cham: Springer.
Monaco, James, and David Lindroth. 2000. *How to read a film: The World of movies, media, and multimedia, language, history, theory*. New York, Oxford: Oxford University Press.
Mookerjee, Rajen, and Krista Beron. 2005. Gender, religion and subjective well-being. *The Journal of Socio-Economics* 34 (5): 674–685.

Morgan, Stephen L., and Christopher Winship. 2007. *Counterfactuals and causal inference: Methods and principles for social research*, 15–31. New York: Cambridge University Press.

Mozer, Reagan et al. Matching with text data: An experimental evaluation of methods for matching documents and of measuring match quality. *Political Analysis* 28 (4): 445–468.

Linda, Mshweshwe. 2020. Understanding domestic violence: Masculinity, culture, traditions. *Heliyon* 6 (10): e05334.

Mullainathan, Sendhil, and Jann Spiess. 2017. Machine learning: An applied econometric approach. *Journal of Economic Perspectives* 31 (2): 87–106.

Nagaike, Kazumi, and Katsuhiko Suganuma. 2013. Transnational boys' love fan studies. *Transformative Works and Cultures* 12: 1–9.

Nalisnick, Eric et al. 2016. Improving document ranking with dual word embeddings. In *Proceedings of the 25th International Conference Companion.*

Neyman, Jerzy. 1959. Optimal asymptotic tests of composite statistical hypotheses. In *Probability and statistics*, ed. U. Grenander. New York: Wiley.

Ng, Eve, and Xiaomeng Li. 2020. A queer "socialist brotherhood": The Guardian web series, boys' love fandom, and the Chinese state. *Feminist Media Studies* 20 (4): 479–495.

Ni, Zhange. 2020. Steampunk, Zombie apocalypse, and homoerotic romance: Rewriting revolution-plus-love in contemporary China. *Modern Chinese Literature and Culture* 32 (2): 179–229.

North, Rebecca J., Charles J. Holahan, Rudolf H. Moos, and Ruth C. Cronkite. 2008. Family support, family income, and subjective well-being: A 10-year perspective. *Journal of Family Psychology* 22 (3): 475.

Nye, Joseph S. 1990. *Bound to lead: The changing nature of American power.* New York: Basic Books.

O'Donohue, William, and Christine E. Caselles. 1993. Homophobia: Conceptual, definitional, and value issues. *Journal of Psychopathology and Behavioral Assessment* 15 (3): 177–195.

Olick, Jeffrey K. 2010. What is "the relative autonomy of culture"? In *Handbook of cultural sociology*, ed. John R. Hall, et al., 97–108. London: Routledge.

Otterbacher, Jahna. 2013. Gender, writing and ranking in review forums: A case study of the IMDb. *Knowledge and Information Systems* 35 (3): 645–664.

Page, Benjamin I., Julia Rabinovich, and David G. Tully. 2008. How Americans feel about Asian countries and why. *Journal of East Asian Studies* 8 (1): 29–59.

Pagliassotti, Dru. 2008. Reading BL in the West. *Participations* 5 (2): 1–19.

Palmer, David S., et al. 2007. Random Forest models to predict aqueous solubility. *Journal of Chemical Information and Modeling* 47 (1): 150–158.

Pantanowitz, Adam, and Marwala, Tshilidzi. 2009. Missing data imputation through the use of the Random Forest algorithm. In *Advances in computational intelligence*, 53–62. Berlin, Heidelberg: Springer.

Parish, William L., et al. 2004. Intimate partner violence in China: National prevalence, risk factors and associated health problems. *International Family Planning Perspectives* 30 (4): 174–181.

Pauwels, Teun. 2011. Measuring populism: A quantitative text analysis of party literature in Belgium. *Journal of Elections, Public Opinion and Parties* 21 (1): 97–119.

Pawson, Ray. 2000. Middle-range realism. *European Journal of Sociology* 41 (2): 283–325.

Pearl, Judea. 2000. *Causality: Models, reasoning, and inference*, 41–61. Cambridge: Cambridge University Press.

Perry, Chris. 2013. Machine learning and conflict prediction: A use case. *Stability: International Journal of Security and Development* 2 (3): 1–18.

Popper, Karl. 1962. *Conjectures and refutations: The growth of scientific knowledge*. New York: Basic Books.

Popper, Karl. 2005. *The logic of scientific discovery*. New York: Routledge.

Poster, Mark. 2010. The cultural turn: Language, globalization, and media. In *Handbook of cultural sociology*, ed. John R. Hall, et al., 45–46. London: Routledge.

Postsecondary National Policy Institute. 2018. *LGBTQ students in higher education*. Retrieved from Postsecondary National Policy Institute. https://pnpi.org/wp-content/uploads/2021/05/LGBTQStudentsinHigherEducation_PNPI_May2021.pdf.

Probst, Philipp, Anne-Laure. Boulesteix, and Bernd Bischl. 2019. Tunability: Importance of hyperparameters of machine learning algorithms. *Journal of Machine Learning Research* 20: 1–32.

Provost, Foster. 2000. Machine learning from imbalanced data sets 101. *AAAI Technical Report*. https://www.aaai.org/Papers/Workshops/2000/WS-00-05/WS00-05-001.pdf.

Quoidbach, Jordi, et al. 2010. Money giveth, money taketh away: The dual effect of wealth on subjective well-being. *Psychological Science* 21 (6): 759–763.

Radway, Janice. 1991. *Reading the romance: Women, patriarchy, and popular literature*. Chapel Hill, NC: University of North Carolina Press.

Ramo, Joshua C. 2007. *Brand China*. London: The Foreign Policy Centre.

Ribeiro, Marco Tulio, Sameer Singh, and Carlos Guestrin. 2016. Why should I trust you? Explaining the predictions of any classifier. In *Proceedings of the 22nd ACM SIGKDD International Conference on Knowledge Discovery and Data Mining*, 1135–1144.

Ridanpää, Juha. 2014. "Humour is serious" as a geopolitical speech act: IMDB film reviews of Sacha Baron Cohen's *The Dictator*. *Geopolitics* 19 (1): 140–160.

Ridderstrøm, Helge. 2018. Class concerns in a heritage setting: Viewers' responses to Downton abbey on IMDb. *Series—International Journal of TV Serial Narratives* 4 (2): 91–101.

Roberts, Carl W. 2000. A conceptual framework for quantitative text analysis: On joining probabilities and substantive inferences about texts. *Quality and Quantity* 34 (3): 259–274.

Roberts, Margaret E., Brandon M. Stewart, and Richard A. Nielsen. 2020. Adjusting for confounding with text matching. *American Journal of Political Science* 64 (4): 887–903.

Rogers, Stacy J., and Lynn K. White. 1998. Satisfaction with parenting: The role of marital subjective well-being, family structure, and parents' gender. *Journal of Marriage and the Family*, 293–308.

Rosenbaum, Paul R., and Donald B. Rubin. 1983. The central role of the propensity score in observational studies for causal effects. *Biometrika* 70 (1): 41–55.

Rubin, Donald B. 1974. Estimating causal effects of treatments in randomized and nonrandomized studies. *Journal of Educational Psychology* 66 (5): 688–701.

Said, Edward W. 1993. *Culture and imperialism*. London: Chatto & Windus.

Said, Edward W. 1995. *Orientalism*. London: Penguin.

Scott, John, and Gordon Marshall. 2009. *A dictionary of sociology*. USA: Oxford University Press.

Sedgwick, Eve. 1985. *Between men: English literature and male homosocial desire*. New York, Chichester: Columbia University Press.

Senik, Claudia. 2009. Direct evidence on income comparisons and their welfare effects. *Journal of Economic Behavior & Organization* 72 (1): 408–424.

Sewell William H., Jr. 2005. *Logics of history: Social theory and social transformation*. Chicago, London: University of Chicago Press.

Sherden, William A. 1998. *The fortune sellers: The big business of buying and selling predictions*. New York: Wiley.

Sherwood, Steven J. 1993. The British are coming...Again! The hidden agenda of "cultural studies". *Contemporary Sociology* 22 (3): 370–375.

Shu, Xiaoling, and Yiwan Ye. 2023. Knowledge discovery: Methods from data mining and machine learning. *Social Science Research* 110: 102817.

Silverman, Kajia. 1992. *Male subjectivity at the margins*. New York: Routledge.

Skurichina, Marina, and Robert P. W. Duin. 2002. Bagging, boosting and the random subspace method for linear classifiers. *Pattern Analysis & Applications* 5 (2): 121–135.

Sovilj, Dušan, et al. 2016. Extreme learning machine for missing data using multiple imputations. *Neurocomputing* 174: 220–231.

Stack, Steven, and J. Ross Eshleman. 1998. Marital status and subjective well-being: A 17-nation study. *Journal of Marriage and the Family* 527–536.

Steptoe, Andrew. 2019. Happiness and health. *Annual Review of Public Health* 40 (1): 339–359.

Sterzing, Paul R., Wendy F. Auslander, and Jeremy T. Goldbach. 2014. An exploratory study of bullying involvement for sexual minority youth: Bully-only, victim-only, and bully-victim roles. *Society for Social Work and Research* 5: 321–337.

Stevenson, Angus, eds. 2010. *Oxford dictionary of English*. Oxford University Press.

Stewart, Donna E., and Prabha S. Chandra. 2017. WPA international competency-based curriculum for mental health providers on intimate partner violence and sexual violence against women. *World Psychiatry* 16 (2): 223.

Strauss, Anselm L. 1987. *Qualitative analysis for social scientists*. England: Cambridge University Press.

Strauss, Anselm, and Juliet Corbin. 1994. *Grounded theory methodology: An overview. Handbook of qualitative research*. USA: Sage.

Stubbs, Michael. 2005. Conrad in the computer: Examples of quantitative stylistic methods. *Language and Literature* 14 (1): 5–24.

Su, Wendy. 2016. *China's encounter with global Hollywood: Cultural policy and the film industry, 1994–2013*. Lexington, Kentucky: The University Press of Kentucky.

Suel, Esra, et al. 2019. Measuring social, environmental and health inequalities using deep learning and street imagery. *Scientific Reports* 9 (1): 6229.

Suen, Yiu-tung, and Randolph Chun Ho Chan. 2020. A nationwide cross-sectional study of 15,611 lesbian, gay and bisexual people in China: Disclosure of sexual orientation and experiences of negative treatment in health care. *International Journal for Equity in Health* 19 (1): 46.

Sun, Shaoyi. 2016. Chinese-language film or Chinese cinema? Review of an ongoing debate in the Chinese mainland. *Journal of Chinese Cinemas* 10 (1): 61–66.

Swami, Viren, et al. 2009. Psychometric evaluation of the tagalog and German subjective subjective well-being scales and a cross-cultural comparison. *Social Indicator Research* 93: 393–406.

Swan, Suzanne C., et al. 2008. A review of research on women's use of violence with male intimate partners. *Violence and Victims* 23 (3): 301–314.

Takemiya, Keiko. 1993. Do women like gays? *Bungei Shunjū* 71 (6): 82–83 (In Japanese).

Taleb, Nassim Nicholas. 2010. *The black swan: The impact of the highly improbable*. New York: Random House.

Tan, Qiuwen. 2020. "Bifurcated history" and rewriting Chinese film history. *Film Art* 2: 149–154 (In Chinese).

Tang, Fei, and Hemant Ishwaran. 2017. Random Forest missing data algorithms. *Statistical Analysis and Data Mining* 10 (6): 363–377. https://doi.org/10.1002/sam.11348.

Tang, Guizhang. 2011. *Complete poetry collection of Tang Dynasty*. Beijing: Zhonghua Book Company (In Chinese).

Tatlow, Didi. 2014. Why many young Chinese women are writing Gay Male Erotica. http://cn.nytimes.com/china/20140526/c26erotica/en-us/. Accessed on 2 March 2021.

Tchetgen, Eric J. Tchetgen, and Ilya Shpitser. 2012. Semiparametric theory for causal mediation analysis: Efficiency bounds, multiple robustness, and sensitivity analysis.*Annals of Statistics* 40 (3): 1816.

The Vatican. 1965. *The Courier-Journal* 18 May.

Tian, Xi. 2020a. Homosexualizing "Boys love" in China: Reflexivity, genre transformation, and cultural interaction. *Prism: Theory and Modern Chinese Literature* 17 (1): 104–126.

Tian, Xi. 2020b. More than conformity or resistance: Chinese "Boys' Love" fandom in the age of internet censorship. *Journal of the European Association for Chinese Studies* 1: 189–213.

Tian, Xiaoli, and Michael Adorjan. 2016. Fandom and coercive empowerment: The commissioned production of Chinese online literature. *Media, Culture & Society* 38 (6): 881–900.

Tibshirani, Robert. 1996. Regression shrinkage and selection via the Lasso. *Journal of the Royal Statistical Society Series B-Methodological* 58 (1): 267–288.

Tripathy, Abinash, Ankit Agrawal, and Santanu Kumar Rath. 2016. Classification of sentiment reviews using n-gram machine learning approach. *Expert Systems with Applications* 57: 117–126.

UNDP. 2016. *Being LGBTI in China: A national survey on social attitudes towards sexual orientation, gender identity and gender expression*. https://www.asia-pacific.undp.org/content/rbap/en/home/library/democratic_governance/hiv_aids/being-lgbti-in-china-a-national-survey-on-social-attitudes-towa.html.

USAID. 2014. *Being LGBT in Asia: China country report*. https://www.usaid.gov/documents/1861/being-lgbt-asia-china-country-report.

Varian, Hal R. 2014. Big data: New tricks for econometrics. *Journal of Economic Perspectives* 28 (2): 3–28.

Varian, Hal R. 2016. Causal inference in economics and marketing. *Proceedings of the National Academy of Sciences* 113 (27): 7310–7315.

Veenhoven, Ruut. 1991. Is subjective well-being relative? *Social Indicators Research* 24 (1): 1–34.

Veenhoven, Ruut. 2015. Social conditions for human subjective well-being: A review of research. *International Journal of Psychology* 50 (5): 379–391.

Vera-Villarroel, Pablo, et al. 2012. Money, age and subjective well-being: Association of subjective wellbeing with socio-demographic variables. *Revista Latinoamericana De Psicología* 44 (2): 155.

Verme, Paolo. 2013. The relative income and relative deprivation hypotheses: A review of the empirical literature. *World Bank Policy Research Working Paper* (6606).

Wager, Stefan, and Susan Athey. 2018. Estimation and inference of heterogeneous treatment effects using Random Forests. *Journal of the American Statistical Association* 113 (523): 1228–1242.

Wallace, Walter L. 2017. *The logic of science in sociology*. Routledge.

Wang, Yuanyuan, et al. 2019. Discrimination against LGBT populations in China. *The Lancet Public Health* 4 (9): e440–e441.

Watts, Duncan J. 2011. *Everything is obvious: Once you know the answer.* Australia: Currency.

Watts, Duncan J. 2014. Common sense and sociological explanations. *American Journal of Sociology* 120 (2): 313–351.

Watts, Duncan J. 2017. Should social science be more solution-oriented? *Nature Human Behaviour* 1 (1): 0015.

Webb, Russell, and Judith Daniluk. 1999. The end of the line. *Men and Masculinities* 2 (1): 6–25.

Weber, Max. 1968[1921]. *Economy and society*, trans. and ed. G. Roth and C. Wittich. New York: Bedminster Press.

Wei, John. 2014. Queer encounters between iron man and Chinese Boys' love fandom. *Transformative Works and Cultures* 17 (17): 1–36.

Wells, Richard H., and J. Steven Picou. 1981. *American sociology: Theoretical and methodological structure*. USA: University Press of America.

Westreich, Daniel, Justin Lessler, and Michele Jonsson Funk. 2010. Propensity score estimation: Neural networks, support vector machines, decision trees (CART), and meta-classifiers as alternatives to Logistic Regression. *Journal of Clinical Epidemiology* 63 (8): 826–833.

Williams, Raymond. 1958. *Culture and society: 1780–1950.* New York: Columbia University Press.

Williams, Raymond. 1973. *The country and the city*. London: Chatto and Windus.

Willis, Paul E. 1977. *Learning to labour: How working class kids get working class jobs*. Farnborough, Hants: Saxon House.

Winter, Eyal. 2002. The shapley value. *Handbook of game theory with economic applications* 3: 2025–2054.

Witkin, Robert W. 1997. Constructing a sociology for an icon of aesthetic modernity: Olympia revisited. *Sociological Theory* 15 (2): 101–125.

Wong, Alvin K. 2020. Towards a queer affective economy of boys' love in contemporary Chinese media. *Continuum* 34 (4): 500–513.

Wong, Day. 2015. Sexual minorities in China. In *International encyclopedia of social and behavioral sciences*, 2nd ed., ed. James D. Wright, 734–739. Oxford: Elsevier.

World Health Organization. 2021. Violence against women prevalence estimates, 2018: global, regional and national prevalence estimates for intimate partner violence against women and global and regional prevalence estimates for non-partner sexual violence against women.

Xie, Tao, and Benjamin I. Page. 2013. What affects China's national image? A cross-national study of public opinion. *Journal of Contemporary China* 22 (83): 850–867.

Xie, Yu, and Xiaogang Wu. 2005. Reply to Jann: Market premium, social process, and statisticism. *American Sociological Review* 70 (5): 865–870.

Xie, Yu, Jennie E. Brand, and Ben Jann 2012. Estimating heterogeneous treatment effects with observational data. *Sociological Methodology* 42 (1): 314–347.

Xu, Kaibin and Yan Tan. 2021. The Chinese female spectatorship: A study of the network community of the "boys" love' movie "Call Me by Your Name". *Feminist Media Studies* 21 (1): 35–50.

Xu, Wenjian, et al. 2017. Internalized homophobia, mental health, sexual behaviors, and outness of gay/bisexual men from Southwest China. *International Journal for Equity in Health* 16 (1): 36.

Xu, Xiao, et al. 2005. Prevalence of and risk factors for intimate partner violence in China. *American Journal of Public Health* 95 (1): 78–85.

Xu, Yanrui, and Ling Yang. 2013. Forbidden love: Incest, generational conflict, and the Erotics of power in Chinese BL fiction. *Journal of Graphic Novels & Comics* 4 (1): 30–43.

Yamamoto, Yoko, and Susan D. Holloway. 2010. Parental expectations and children's academic performance in sociocultural context. *Educational Psychology Review* 22 (3): 189–214.

Yan, Yaojun. 1986. On social science and social prediction. In *Social science and contemporary society*, ed. Liu Zhongheng, 21–57. Shenyang: Liaoning People's publishing house.

Yan, Yaojun. 2005. *Basic principles of social prediction*, 15–33. Beijing: Social Science Academic Press.

Yang, Ling, and Yanrui Xu. 2017. The love that dare not speak its name': The fate of Chinese Danmei communities in the 2014 anti-porn campaign. In *The end of cool Japan: Ethical, legal, and cultural challenges to Japanese popular culture*, ed. Mark McLelland, 163–183. London and New York: Routledge.

Yao, Yao, et al. 2017. Sensing spatial distribution of urban land use by integrating points-of-interest and google Word2Vec model. *International Journal of Geographical Information Science* 31 (4): 825–848.

Yeh, Emilie Yueh-yu. 2018. *Early film cultures in Taiwan, Hong Kong, and Republican China: Kaleidoscopic histories*. University of Michigan Press.

Yi, Erika Junhui. 2013. Reflection on Chinese boys' love fans: An insider's view. *Transformative Works and Cultures* 12 (1).

Yoshimoto, Mitsuhiro. 1991. The difficulty of being radical: The discipline of film studies and the postcolonial world order. *Boundary 2: An International Journal of Literature and Culture* 18 (3): 242–257.

Zhang, Chang, and Ruiqin Wu. 2019. Battlefield of global ranking: How do power rivalries shape soft power index building. *Global Media and China* 4 (2): 179–202.

Zhang, Charlie Yi, and Adam K. Dedman. 2021. Hyperreal homoerotic love in a monarchized military conjuncture: A situated view of the Thai Boys' Love industry. *Feminist Media Studies* 21 (6): 1039–1043.

Zhang, Yibin. 2012. Word frequency in academic text: A new perspective in the study of intellectual history within Marxist philosophy—Beginning from the revision of the Third Edition of back to Marx. *Studies on Marxism* (9): 86–92+160 (In Chinese).

Zheng, Danan. 2016. The construction of heterotopia and imagined community. *Youth Studies* (4): 76–84+96 (In Chinese).

Zhou, Yanyan, Bryant Paul, and Ryland Sherman. 2018. Still a hetero-gendered world: A content analysis of gender stereotypes and romantic ideals in Chinese Boy love stories. *Sex Roles* 78 (1): 107–118.

Zhu, Hailong. 2019. The change and construction of Chinese national image in 1949–2019. *English Language Teaching* 12 (11): 35.

Zhu, Wuhan, and Siyun Ji. 2018. The discursive construction of the Chinese national image in China Daily's reports on the G20 Summit. *English Language and Literature Studies* 8 (1): 126.

Zsila, Ágnes., et al. 2018. Loving the love of boys, motives for consuming Yaoi media. *PLoS ONE* 13 (6): e0198895.

Index

Y. Chen et al., *Machine Learning in Social Science*,
https://doi.org/10.1007/978-981-95-6465-1

Kolibri 360 GmbH
Ferdinand-Jühlke-Straße 7
99095 Erfurt, Deutschland
produktsicherheit@kolibri360.de